BY THE SAME AUTHOR

The Rascal King

The World According to Peter Drucker

Colossus (editor)

Pols (editor)

Age of Betrayal

THE
LOST
HISTORY
OF 1914

Reconsidering the Year the Great War Began

JACK BEATTY

Walker & Company
New York

Published by Walker Publishing Company, Inc., New York
A division of Bloomsbury Publishing

All papers used by Walker & Company are natural, recyclable products made
from wood grown in well-managed forests. The manufacturing processes
conform to the environmental regulations of the country of origin.

LIBRARY OF CONGRESS CATALOGING-IN-PUBLICATION DATA

Beatty, Jack.
The lost history of 1914 : reconsidering the year the great war began /
Jack Beatty.—1st U.S. ed.
p. cm.
Includes bibliographical references and index.
ISBN 978-0-8027-7811-6
1. World War, 1914–1918—Causes. 2. World War, 1914–1918—Diplomatic
history. 3. Europe—History—1871–1918. 4. Europe—Politics and
government—1871–1918. 5. Mexico—History—Revolution, 1910–1920.
6. United States—Foreign relations—Mexico. 7. Mexico—Foreign relations—
United States. I. Title.

D511.B3263   2012
940.3—dc23
2011029285

Visit Walker & Company's Web site at www.walkerbooks.com

First U.S. edition 2012

1   3   5   7   9   10   8   6   4   2

Typeset by Westchester Book Group
Printed in the U.S.A. by Quad/Graphics, Fairfield, Pennsylvania

To the honored memory of John J. Beatty (1893–1982) and his fellow countrymen and women who served in World War I.

Born in the last year of World War II, I was raised on tales of World War I. My father conveyed affecting memories of London under bombardment by German dirigibles, of a pub brawl between American sailors and English soldiers ("You're four years late, Yank!"), of mustering the nerve to ask a posh Paris lady for a kiss, and of the thirty-six flag-draped coffins of his shipmates from the USS *Mount Vernon*, torpedoed by a German submarine in the Bay of Biscay on September 5, 1918, arrayed along a Brest dock and the captain weeping during the memorial service and the tears soaking his blouse.

After the torpedo. Sailors from the stricken U.S.S. *Mount Vernon*: The second kneeling sailor from the left is very likely John J. Beatty of South Boston. He banged his head when the torpedo hit, and for a time suffered nosebleeds. After the war he did not apply for disability compensation, for which the standard of injury was ridiculously low, because he could not cash in on an attack that killed so many of his shipmates. Sleeping in his car at WPA jobsites during the Great Depression, he cursed himself for a fool for passing up the money. His family venerated him for it.

CONTENTS

INTRODUCTION

Very few things happen at the right time, and
others do not happen at all.

—Herodotus

1914 might be remembered for a coup in Germany, a polar shift in foreign policy in Russia, a civil war in Britain, a leftist ministry in France pursuing détente with Germany. If any of these things had happened, 1914 would *not* be remembered as the year World War I as we know it began. If Franz Ferdinand, the heir apparent to the Austrian throne, had not been murdered at Sarajevo in June, the war might not have happened at all. Most books about 1914 map the path leading to war.* This one maps five paths that led away from it.

---

*Since the 1920s, successive generations of historians have produced stellar histories of the war's origins. I relied on the following: Winston S. Churchill, *The World Crisis*, vol. 1, 1911–1914 (London: Macmillan, 1923); Sidney Bradshaw Fay, *The Origins of the World War*, 2 vols. (New York: Macmillan, 1927); Luigi Albertini, *The Origins of the War of 1914*, 3 vols. (New York: Enigma Books, 2005; originally published in 1952); Fritz Fischer, *Germany's Aims in the First World War* (New York: Norton, 1967), *War of Illusions: German Policies from 1911 to 1914* (New York: Norton, 1975), and *From Kaiserreich to Third Reich: Elements of Continuity in German History, 1871–1945* (London: Allen & Unwin, 1986); Imanuel Geiss, ed., *July 1914: The Outbreak of the First World War* (New York: Scribners, 1967); Hew Strachan, *The First World War: Volume I: To Arms* (New York: Oxford University Press, 2001) and *The First World War* (New York: Penguin Books, 2003); Richard F. Hamilton and Holger H. Herwig, eds., *Decisions for War, 1914–1917* (New York: Cambridge University Press, 2003); and David Stevenson, *Cataclysm: The First World War as Political Tragedy* (New York: Basic Books, 2005).

I intend the subtitle in two senses. "Lost" as in forgotten, buried under the avalanche of the war. And "lost" as in "did not win." It is as if the events I relate were in a race with the war; and the war won . . . just.

My presentment of the war as contingent on Herodotus's chancy clock may be unexpected to readers who last encountered World War I in textbooks that depicted it as overdetermined to redundancy. One survey of Underlying Causes advanced by historians lists four Deep Causes, six under System Level, five under Organization and Bureaucracy, five under Leaders, four under Ideas, two under Domestic Politics, and one under State Structure. The subheads range from the Industrial Revolution to Social Darwinism to the Cult of the Offensive to Poor German Leadership after Bismarck, Poor Austrian Crisis Management, Poor Russian Crisis Management, and Poor British Crisis Management. With all these deep psychological ("war as escape from super ego constraints"), economic, political, cultural, and intellectual causes, how could war have been avoided? No wonder historians of the war sometimes stray from the trenches of empiricism into the metaphysical no-man's-land of historical inevitability. For example, here is F. H. Hinsley, a British scholar, voicing what has long been an unspoken assumption: "If the Sarajevo crisis had not precipitated a particular great war, some other crisis would have precipitated a great war at no distant date." Not surprisingly, some of the men most responsible for the war took a similar line. According to the Austrian chief of staff, Conrad von Hötzendorf, "the First World War came about inevitably and irresistibly as the result of the motive forces in the lives of states and peoples, like a thunderstorm which must by its nature discharge itself." Chroniclers of "the path to war" need not so explicitly embrace inevitability to convey the impression of it. Highlighting the milestones along the path with one eye fixed on its termination, they wind up, in R. H. Tawney's formulation, "dragging into prominence the forces which have triumphed and thrusting into the background those which they have swallowed up."

World War I historians of the Hinsley persuasion anchor their certainty in the fatalism, amounting to a "cult of inevitability," of contemporary decision makers. Armageddon happened because men believed it would happen. A twenty-first-century generation of historians demurs, finding that "the European population as a whole shared a common belief in the improbability of a Great War" with the civilian and military elite. Regarding war as improbable, Holger Afflerbach hypothesizes, leaders took risks that made it possible. Armageddon happened because men believed it could *not* happen. Other things seemed so much more probable than war, and some seemed to rule it out. They are my subject.

Exploiting the recent scholarship on World War I, *The Lost History of 1914* tells an old story new, depicting Franz Ferdinand's death, for example, not as the catalyst of a war that would have broken out over some other crisis "at no distant date" but rather as its all-but-unique precipitant.★

The German historian Annika Mombauer distinguishes three interpretive stances, or "topos," on the war's origins, "the topos of inevitable, avoidable, and improbable war." She identifies the weakness in the latter two: "War was still avoidable, but only if everyone had actually wanted to avoid it. This was not the case." To fit what was she suggests a fourth category, "the topos of desirable war," contending that "war broke out not because it was inevitable . . . but because certain key individuals [in Vienna and Berlin] felt the time was right for having it." The argument that the war was avoidable, therefore, if it rests on evidence of "the contingent . . . mistakes and misperceptions of a very small number of decision makers" during the July Crisis after Sarajevo, cannot address Mombauer's objection that by then, with war willed, even flawless crisis managing on all sides could not have stopped it. War would have had to be stopped earlier. And,

---

★ For the causes listed above and a cogent argument that Franz Ferdinand's assassination was a major cause of the war, see Richard Ned Lebow, "Franz Ferdinand Found Alive, World War I Unnecessary," in Philip E. Tetlock, Richard Ned Lebow, and Geoffrey Parker, eds., *Unmaking the West: "What-if" Scenarios That Rewrite World History* (Ann Arbor: University of Michigan Press, 2006). I draw on Lebow's paper in my account of Franz Ferdinand's assassination in chapter 5. For a new generation of historians, see William Mulligan, *The Origins of the First World War* (New York: Cambridge University Press, 2010), 1–22. Also see Holger Afflerbach and David Stevenson, eds., *An Improbable War? The Outbreak of World War I and European Political Culture before 1914* (New York: Berghahn Books, 2007) and Annika Mombauer, "Review Article: The First World War: Inevitable, Avoidable, Improbable, Desirable, Recent Interpretations on War Guilt and the War's Origins," *German History* 25, no. 1 (2007): 78–95.

when Germany relied on threats of war as an instrument of statecraft, Great Power diplomacy could not have stopped it. Only events *within* the powers could have. By exploring such events this book seeks to reconcile the "topos of improbable war" with the "topos of desirable war."[1]

The history I uncovered from beneath the war—the military overturning civil government in Germany, revolution stalking autocracy in Russia, political fanaticism threatening parliamentary democracy in England, incipient nationalism among its eleven peoples haunting the Austro-Hungarian Empire, imperialism in Morocco staining the honor of France and poisoning relations with Germany—challenges the received image of the Belle Époque as a "Golden Age of Security," as the Viennese author and playwright Stefan Zweig remembered it. Only for a sliver of Europeans was that true, and then only on holidays. At work men like Zweig's industrialist father worried about strikes (two thousand in Britain in 1912, four thousand in Russia in the first six months of 1914) shutting down their factories and Socialist parties winning power in Europe's parliaments. "Socialists! The word had a peculiar taste of blood and terror in the Germany and Austria of those days," Zweig recalled, "like 'Jacobin' before and 'Bolshevik' since." Fearful of being swept away by those below, the ruling classes of Europe mistook democratization for revolution, and brooded on "escaping forward" into war to head it off.[2]

Mexico, the subject of the one new world chapter, was ablaze with revolution. The European powers wanted it snuffed out before the contagion of example, the transformation of brown-skinned people from being the objects of history to its subjects, could spread. Also, the powers had interests at risk in Mexico. The Royal Navy, for example, was switching from coal to oil, and depended on supply from British-operated fields near Tampico. The Europeans expected the United States to back a military dictator in Mexico against the rebel peasant armies led by bandit generals like Francisco "Pancho" Villa.

The American president who took office in 1913, Woodrow Wilson, refused to recognize the dictator and armed the rebels. This was the only time in the twentieth century that the United States supported a poor people's revolution in Latin America. No one remembers Wilson for that. In Mexico they remember him instead for an

episode of "Yankee imperialism": sending in the marines to occupy
Veracruz in April. Imperialism was not the motive; stopping arms from
reaching the dictator was. Forgotten, too, is the historic consequence
of Wilson's decision: It cracked ajar the door through which, most improbably, the United States would enter the European war.[3]

Set in the months before the war, the first six chapters focus on in-
terpretively rich episodes in each belligerent country that light up
national character. Kaiser Wilhelm judged Russians by the only one
he knew, Tsar Nicholas II, a warning against representing wholes by
their most atypical parts. Still, the challenges faced by leaders often
implicate enduring strains in their nation's histories; such, at any rate,
is the perspective I brought to my portraits of the major figures of
1914. The familiar ones—Wilson, Nicholas, Rasputin, the kaiser,
Franz Ferdinand, the young first lord of the Admiralty Winston
Churchill, the aged emperor of Austria-Hungary Francis Joseph—
share the stage with unexpected characters like Villa and John Reed,
with once-famous politicians such as Joseph Caillaux, Herbert Asquith, and Sir Edward Carson, and with 1914's hero for unambiguous
good, Herbert Hoover.

Throughout, I treat personality—temperament, grandiosity, obsession, conviction—as event making, even history changing. That Kaiser
Wilhelm believed a "racial struggle" between "Teutons" and "Slavs"
was imminent was not without bearing on the war. That Nicholas II
got it into his addled head to launch a temperance crusade in besotted
Russia mattered; as it did that his consort, the Empress Alexandra,
was under the spell of the notorious Rasputin, a lecherous peasant
faith healer who swayed the royal couple to replace an able prime
minister opposed to war with a doddering nonentity. It mattered that
Conrad von Hötzendorf, the chief of staff of the Austro-Hungarian
army, believed that to break up the marriage of Gina von Reininghaus he must possess the irresistible charisma of victory in war. It
mattered that Woodrow Wilson was "ashamed as an American" of
the Mexican War of 1846–48, "a predatory enterprise" the United
States must never repeat. It immensely mattered that on the evening of March 16, 1914, the wife of France's minister of finance shot
dead the editor of *Le Figaro* for prosecuting a politically inspired
vendetta against her husband, Joseph Caillaux. If Madame Caillaux

had missed, her husband would have been premier in July 1914; his foreign minister would have been the Socialist Jean Jaurès, the titanic anti-war voice of the era. Their policy would have been détente with Germany. Because Madame Caillaux had defended her "woman's honor" by murder, Europe's greatest pacifist was not in power during Europe's greatest crisis. Historical inevitability is a doctrine for history without people.

The last three chapters, set in November and December, depict the war's transformation of war and of the societies seen earlier in peace. Extending the motif of lost history, they show how the beginnings of trench warfare in November, since regarded as the acme of mindless slaughter, represented a victory for life over death when placed in the forgotten context of the mass killing during the preceding months of fighting in the open. The "trenches," the defining battlescape of World War I, were war paralyzed; and the General Staffs feared that the live-and-let-live ethic between enemies dramatized in the Christmas Truce of 1914, when soldiers from the opposing armies met in no-man's-land to sing carols and exchange gifts, would end in war-suspended. Ahead of its hundredth anniversary, these chapters try to distill the essence of World War I—military, political, existential—on the western and home fronts. Toward that end, the text features work by famous artists like Otto Dix and Max Beckmann and now-obscure ones like C. R. W. Nevinson, the British war painter whose *Column on the March* from 1914 appears on the cover. The art may help readers feel the horror and sorrow of a war that George F. Kennan without fear of contradiction could call "*the* great seminal catastrophe" of the twentieth century.[4]

The last three chapters, set in November and December, depict the war's transformation of war and of the societies seen earlier in peace. Beginning with a reconsideration of the "cult of the offensive" that gripped the prewar military mind, chapter 7 breaks fresh ground, citing evidence that became available only after the fall of the Berlin Wall fatal to two shibboleths of World War I scholarship—the short-war illusion and the Schlieffen Plan.

When the kaiser promised the German people that the soldiers would be home before the leaves fell from the trees, he may have believed it but not his generals. For low bureaucratic-political reasons, they gave "lip-service" to the short-war scenario when talking to Germany's civilian leaders and politicians. Long thought to be fools, men like Helmuth von Moltke the younger, the army chief of staff, emerge from the new found history of 1914 as criminals.

Everybody knows that the German army followed the Schlieffen Plan in its August invasion of Belgium and France. Everybody read it in nearly every work of history published since the war. Everybody, it now appears, is wrong and every work. In August 1914 the document containing this alleged top-secret war plan was held by the elderly daughters of Alfred von Schlieffen, chief of the general staff from 1891 to 1905. The Schlieffen Plan was "invented" by the postwar general staff to reclaim the reputation of Prussian martial genius from the ruin of defeat. If von Moltke had not deviated from his predecessor's invincible strategy, the German army would have crushed the Allies in forty days and won the war. That was the legend. Everybody swallowed it. Chapter 7 will be the first place most readers encounter the real story as pieced together by a U.S. Army officer, who discovered it in the military archives of the former East Germany.

Extending the motif of lost history (and jostling another shibboleth), chapter 7 also shows how the trench warfare that began in November, since regarded as the acme of mindless slaughter, when placed in the forgotten context of the previous months of maneuver warfare represented a victory for life over death. The "trenches," the defining battlescape of World War I, were war-paralyzed; and the General Staffs feared that the live-and-let-live ethic between enemies dramatized in the "Christmas Truce" of 1914, when soldiers from the opposing armies met in No-Man's Land to sing carols and exchange gifts, would end in war-suspended.

Ahead of its one hundredth anniversary, the concluding chapters as a whole try to distill the essence of World War I—military, political, existential—on the western and home fronts. Toward that end, the text features work by famous artists like Otto Dix and Max Beckmann and now-obscure ones like C. R. W. Nevinson, the British war painter whose "Column on the March" from 1914 appears on the cover. The art may help readers feel the horror and sorrow of what George F. Kennan called "*the* great seminal catastrophe" of the twentieth century.[5]

1

GERMANY

SABER RULE

*Sometimes "incidents" occur in politics when the nature of a
certain order of things is revealed, as it were, suddenly, and
with extraordinary power and clarity in connection with
some relatively minor happening.*

—V. I. Lenin, writing in *Pravda*,
November 29, 1913

T HE AUSTRIAN CARTOON from 1870 shown opposite annihi-
lates libraries in communicating the essence of Imperial Germany.
Conceived in war in 1871, it died in war in 1918. Field marshals were
its founding fathers. Versailles, the conquered enemy's palace, was its
Independence Hall. Yet in the years after Germany's victory in the
Franco-Prussian War, the helmet did not smother political life—not
quite. The identity of the new Germany was contested from the start.
Its brief history saw a culture war between the "forces of order" sym-
bolized by the helmet and the "forces of change" that came to a crux
in late 1913. For a moment the forces of change gained the upper hand.
No one realized it at the time, but war hung in the balance. Everything depended on the forces of order overreacting to the threat of
change from below. The spiked helmet had to be slammed down hard,
plunging Germany into months of unrest. Militarists brooded on saber
rule, but in the end this is the story of a polity that to humanity's lasting regret escaped its caricature.

An icon is born: This Austrian cartoon tells the
story of Imperial Germany (1871–1918).

The cartoon captured what Allied statesmen and publics agreed
was the cause of World War I: Prussian militarism. Its first victims,
Woodrow Wilson argued, were the German people. The war was
ultimately about their "liberation" from the "military clique" in
Berlin. There were two Germanys. Once the Allies defeated the bad
one, the good one, liberal Germany—the Germany of the abortive
revolutions of 1848—would squeeze out from under the spiked
helmet.[1]

The bad Germany of the Prussian militarists was an accident of
history that history, acting through Allied arms, would correct. The
accident was a work of war, specifically, the three short successful
campaigns between 1864 and 1871 that forged Imperial Germany
(1871–1918) from four kingdoms, six grand duchies, seven princi-
palities, three free cities, and two imperial provinces. Only in Germany would the readers of an eminently respectable journal select, as
the nineteenth century's greatest *thinker*, Field Marshal Helmuth von
Moltke, the strategist credited with these nation-making victories.
Since the age of Frederick the Great (1712–1786) the army had ridden
high in Prussia, but von Moltke's triumphs lent it unrivaled prestige
across the new Germany and elevated the German officer into the
social empyrean.[2]

"An incident experienced by my father as a student visiting Berlin in 1913 aptly illustrates the militarization of German society," an Irish historian writes:

> He had come to Berlin to meet and bring the greetings of Irish colleagues to Kuno Meyer, the renowned professor of Gaelic, at the Humboldt University. Walking together along the Kurfürstendamm, they were approached by a young officer with a crimson stripe on his trousers, denoting membership of the General Staff. Meyer stepped down onto the roadway as he passed; my father, protected by his ignorance of the language and the history of the country, walked on . . . The young blood [was furious]. The professor had to explain . . . that my father was a foreigner and knew no better.[3]

Americans snicker at this parody of "militarism." Soldiers are respected, not worshipped, here. Yet on a comparative scale of militarization, defined as the degree of the state's organization for war, the United States—which "by some calculations, spends more on defense than all other nations in the world together" without a great rival power and with oceans between it and any future invader—today ranks as far more militarized than Imperial Germany, ringed by a hostile alliance rivers, not oceans, away.[4]

In 1888, when a colonial enthusiast lobbied Chancellor Otto von Bismarck (from 1862 to 1890, "master of Germany in all but name," in his own words) to enter the race for spoils in Africa, he replied with a lesson in strategic geography: "Your map of Africa is very nice. But there is France, and here is Russia, and we are in the middle, and that is my map of Africa." On the eve of war, France and Russia invested 10 percent of net national income in defense and fielded armies of 2.5 million compared to 7 percent (of a larger economy) and 1.2 million for Germany and its ally Austria-Hungary. Yet the map of Europe reveals that France and Russia were not surrounded by Germany and Austria. With sound reason George F. Kennan, the American diplomat and historian, traced the fuse of the war behind Prussian militarism to its geostrategic justification—the Franco-Russian military alliance of the early 1890s.[5]

"Our enemies are arming more vigorously than we, because we are strapped for cash," Helmuth von Moltke, the great thinker's nephew, and the army's chief of staff, complained in 1912. With a booming industrial economy based on applying science to production, Germany had the cash but spent it on the wrong priorities. In a country that could repel an invasion, or mount one, without so much as a dinghy, millions of marks were diverted from the army to the navy, a fatal enthusiasm of the German emperor.[6]

Whereas his ancestors had expanded the German Empire by conquests on land, Wilhelm II would take Germany out to sea. It would be a world power like Britain. Admiral Alfred von Tirpitz, the navy's salesman, knew his kaiser, catering to his whims in ship design—*his* ships had to have extra smokestacks to make them look more powerful. Tirpitz would have done as well consulting Germany's tailors, Wilhelm was an admiral of the fleet of the Royal Navy, as well as an admiral in the Imperial Russian, the Swedish, Danish, and Norwegian navies, and an honorary admiral of the Royal Greek Navy; and he sought out even remotely nautical occasions, like visiting Berlin's Zoo-Aquarium or attending a performance of Wagner's *The Flying Dutchman*, to dress up in their uniforms. So when Tirpitz told him, "Your Majesty can now be your own Admiral," that closed the sale on the Tirpitz Plan of 1897.[7]

The Tirpitz big-gun "battle fleet," the Social Democratic leader August Bebel predicted in 1900, would provoke a naval arms race with England, drive England to join France and Russia in an anti-German alliance, and drain resources from the army, which held Germany's life in its hands. Bebel was right about all of this, especially the last. In September 1914, after the army was forced to retreat from the River Marne east of Paris, General von Falkenhayn exploded at Tirpitz: "If we did not have the Navy, we would have had two more army corps and would not have lost the Marne battle!" He was undoubtedly right: Three battleships could have paid for five new army corps. In losing that battle, Falkenhayn told a Reichstag deputy, Germany had lost the war. Besides defeat, what did Germany get for the 855,890,000 marks it sunk into the navy? When the High Sea Fleet wasn't running from Britain's Grand Fleet (as it did even on May 31–June 1, 1916, at Jutland, the one fleet-against-fleet battle), it spent the war in port, rusting.[8]

The navy drained marks from the army, not men. Germany had

the men, just not enough of the right sort. Fearing contamination of its rural recruits, the army was loathe to conscript urban working-men, carriers of the socialist bacillus, leaving about half its eligible young men untouched by the draft.[9]

Politics, too, crimped the army's growth. While the kaiser answered only to a reliably teutonic God, Reichstag deputies faced a tax-averse electorate. Numerical superiority was vital to the army's victory over France in 1870. Yet the Reichstag rejected General Staff demands to grow the army to approximate the French and Russian numbers. In 1893, a coalition of parties rebelled against the one hundred-million-mark price tag of the 115,000 more men sought. In 1913, in an atmosphere of international crisis, the army wanted 300,000; it got 117,000. "Under the inexorable restraints of the tightness of funds," the kaiser acknowledged, "justified demands of the 'Front' had to be left unfulfilled."[10]

Germans liked the image of a strong army. They were unwilling to pay for the reality. Prussian conservatives championed a bigger army but would not tax their East Elbian estates to pay for it. Under Germany's federal constitution, income taxes were the prerogative of the states, which balked at revenue sharing with the central government. Fear of "adding grist to the mill of the Social Democrats," a War Ministry official noted in 1913, inhibited raising taxes on the working-man's beer and tobacco. Considering its security dilemma, Germany's martial bluster was an unfunded bluff.[11]

Bluster was the kaiser's department. The first "media monarch" specialized in frightening the world. In 1900, speaking in a moment of unguarded ferocity on a Bremerhaven dock, the kaiser adjured soldiers headed to China to lift the Boxer siege of Peking to conduct themselves "like the Huns under their king Attila a thousand years ago." That is, to give no pardon, take no prisoners—"Whoever falls into your hands will fall to your sword"—and by these barbarous acts make "the name of Germany . . . known to such effect that no Chinaman will ever again dare so much as look askance at a German."*[12]

---

*By the time these troops arrived in October, Peking was relieved and the war "virtually over." To force the Chinese to sign a degrading peace treaty, the Germans conducted scores of "punitive expeditions" against Chinese villages, executing

This French cartoon from 1900 accurately conveys the kaiser's
orders to his soldiers regarding the Chinese. From his Bremerhaven speech
dates the use of "Hun" for German soldiers in two world wars.

If the kaiser was the voice of German militarism, the Prussian lieutenant, "the unbearable prig of the Wilhelmine era," was its symbol. To the novelist Theodor Fontane he was Imperial Germany's

---

prisoners in batches of up to 175 and killing noncombatants who looked at them
"askance." See Isabel V. Hull, *Absolute Destruction: Military Culture and the Practice of
War* (Ithaca: Cornell University Press, 2005), 147–48. Hitler used the same word in
the same sense in instructing his troops on how to conduct themselves in Russia.
Eliciting his order was Stalin's July 1941 call for partisan warfare against the Nazi
invaders. "Hitler, who saw partisan warfare as a chance to destroy potential opposition, reacted energetically . . . Even before the invasion of the Soviet Union, Hitler
had already relieved his soldiers of legal responsibility for actions taken against civilians. Now he wanted soldiers and police to kill anyone who 'even looks at us
askance.'" Timothy Snyder, *Bloodlands: Europe Between Hitler and Stalin* (New York:
Basic Books, 2010), 234.

"Vitliptutzli"—"the warrior sun-god and idol of popular devotion." Even those bellicose professors classified by the Viennese satirist Karl Kraus as "a cross between a university chair and a submarine" resented his status. Socialists condemned his politics, cartoonists caricatured his monocle, writers satirized his fetish. In *The Sleepwalkers* (1932), Hermann Broch depicts a morally attractive nobleman transformed into a "military robot" by "his second and denser skin," his uniform, which he wears to bed on his wedding night: "She said softly, 'Joachim, we are not intimate enough yet . . .' Through his position his military coat had become disordered, the lapels falling apart left his black trousers visible, and when Joachim noticed this he hastily set things right again and covered the place." At the spectacle of her sleeping lieutenant, "Elizabeth could not help smiling."[13]

The smile, harbinger of the mystique-killing laugh, was the nemesis of the Prussian officer. The bluff of German militarism depended on Germany's enemies taking his aptitude for war seriously. He was the totem of contemporary "bellicism," Michael Howard's term for that "frank and even glad acceptance of war as a supreme experience of life" that along with the "unquestioning acceptance of war as an instrument of international politics" makes the world of 1914 so alien to us.* It weakened deterrence if foreigners found the Prussian officer funny.[14]

A 1906 incident illustrating the fetish of the uniform in Germany regaled newspaper readers the world over. To the socialist journalist Franz Mehring, the mockery brought down on the army by the "Captain from Köpenick" equaled a "second Jena," the 1806 battle in

---

* As an index of bloody mindedness (and of French militarism), consider *Le Matin*'s editorial response to Germany's unveiling of a statue commemorating the hundredth anniversary of the Battle of Leipzig in 1813: "We celebrate neither Jena, where 40,000 French crushed 70,000 Prussians and captured 200 standards; nor Austerstadt, when 25,000 men under Davout vanquished 66,000 of Brunswick, nor Lützen, nor Bauzen, where the Marie Louise Legion cut to pieces 15,000 of Blücher's veterans . . . We celebrate none of the 100 victories gained in Germany 100 years ago. Germans would do well to remember when celebrating the Battle of the Nations (so-called Leipzig) that only 157,000 French were, after a desperate struggle, finally thrown back by 350,000 of the allies." London *Times*, October 19, 1913.

which Napoleon defeated Prussia. The captain led the first of our four conspiracies to rule Germans by the saber. At stake in the third, a late 1913 plot against the Reichstag, was peace in 1914.[15]

Friedrich Wilhelm Voigt was an itinerant cobbler down and out in Berlin after completing a fifteen-year sentence for armed robbery. Exercising the power "to exclude released prisoners from certain localities" granted them by an 1842 law, the Berlin police ordered him to leave the city. Prevented from earning a living, in a flight of criminal anthropology, Voigt planned a sting conceivable only in Germany. Assembling pieces from uniforms and equipment found in used-clothing stores, the ex-soldier dressed as a captain in the First Foot Guards, "the premier regiment of the Prussian Army." In this character "in the name of the Emperor" he commandeered two armed

Wilhelm Voigt leaving prison in 1908. This photograph documents
the transformation required by the captain's overcoat to make
Voigt into a plausible Prussian officer.

detachments of enlisted men returning to barracks from guard duty, marched them to the nearby Putlizstrasse station, treated them to a beer, and boarded a train to Köpenick, a Berlin suburb.

At the Köpenick town hall, the mayor, a reserve officer, stood at attention and saluted the captain. On "all-highest command," the captain told him that he was under arrest. Dumbstruck, the mayor asked to see the captain's authorization. Voigt signaled two grenadiers, bayonets fixed, to step forward. "My authorization are these soldiers," he said, a plausible Prussian officer. "Anything more that you may want to see will be shown at the New Guard House in Berlin to which you are now to be conveyed." Locating the city treasurer, Voigt demanded that he hand over the contents of his safe and dispatched him under armed guard to the same place.

That afternoon the local *Landrath*, the agent of the Prussian central government, received an emergency telegram: "Town hall occupied by the military. We urgently desire information as to the reasons in order to reassure the excited citizenry." But Voigt had already seen to that, directing the police to preserve order in the town while the army overthrew its civil government.

Traveling by himself, Voigt took a fast train back to Berlin. He had a curtain to make. Stopping first at a clothing store in Friedrichstrasse, where he spent one thousand marks on a new suit and hat, he made his way to a café across from the New Guard House. He was in time to watch the mayor being delivered to the gate, the dumb show when his guards could not name the captain who had ordered the mayor's arrest under what charge they were at a loss to say, the unexpected arrival of a disaster-scenting General von Moltke, and the advent of a second carriage carrying the treasurer and a second dumb show.

Voigt was not alone in enjoying the travesty he had stage-managed. The Metropol Theater put on a lampoon of the crime mere days after its commission. Postcards depicting Voigt as cobbler and captain sold briskly. The popular press embraced this "robber's tale as adventurous and romantic as a novel," celebrating Voigt's "hero's deed" and his "unheard-of trickster's exploit." While in prison, Voigt had talked over his sting with his accomplice in the armed robbery, who betrayed him to the police. Ten days after Voigt left the Köpenick town hall carrying two sacks of cash, he was arrested. Halfway through his four-year sentence, Voigt was pardoned by the kaiser, said to have been amused at his stunt. Voigt wrote an autobiography, toured Germany, Britain, Canada, and the United States, retelling his story in nightclubs, restaurants, and state fairs. Madame Tussauds gallery in London celebrated him in wax. He bought a house in Luxembourg, where he stayed throughout the war. Ruined by the postwar inflation, he died broke in 1922, his saga having long since "established itself as one of the most beloved and enduring fables of modern Prussia."

Democratic and autocratic Germany submitted clashing interpretations of the fable. "Immeasurable laughter convulses Berlin and is spreading beyond the confines of our city, beyond the frontiers of Germany, beyond the ocean," commented the liberal *National-Zeitung*. "The boldest and most biting satirist could not make our vaulting militarism . . . stand comparison with this comic opera transferred from the boards into real life."

The conservative press found nothing to laugh at; rather, much to admire, spinning the credulity of the soldiers and officials as a sign of civic health. "[They] did not believe in the possibility of illegal action on the part of an officer," the *Kreuzzeitung* editorialized, because "our officers are regarded as absolutely trustworthy . . . If the Democratic Press and the enemies of Germany abroad interpret the success of the Köpenick hoax as an exposure of Prussian absolutism and militarism, they are making themselves ridiculous."[16]

The two Germanys had been arguing like this over the army's political and social displacement since Bismarck used victories against Denmark in 1864 and Austria in 1866 to silence agitation in the Prussian Diet for democratic control of the army. For liberals, arguing for change against this record of success proved an unequal struggle. Then, by conquering France in 1870–71, Bismarck overcame resistance among the South German states to unification in the German empire under the Prussian king. "The three wars were waged for internal political reasons," Jacob Burckhardt, the Swiss historian of the Renaissance, observed in 1871.[17]

Bismarck's cardinal goal was to solidify a feudal Hohenzollern dynasty shaken by the revolutionary surge of 1848. To that end, he sought to preserve the power and privileges of the "forces of order"—the

Junkers (the great landed barons of Prussia), the industrialists, the higher bureaucracy, and the army—propping up the monarchy against the "forces of change" represented by liberalism and socialism. War was Bismarck's answer to reform, his formula for state building, and his preventive for revolution. War worked, as did war scares. By playing up tensions with France or Russia, Bismarck won Reichstag majorities for regime-supporting parties. "Reactionary governments" always attempt "to divert the internal struggle to the foreign sphere," reflected the éminence grise of the Foreign Office, Friedrich von Holstein.[18]

War worked. In a prophetic 1871 appeal to the king of Prussia a liberal publicist saw that as an ominous message for Europe. Bismarck's victorious wars "had revived and magnified . . . the danger to this part of the world and the entire epoch from a social and political order one had believed was dying out. After five centuries of desiring, striving, and hoping to outgrow the military system of earlier times . . . a power based on the permanent use of war has emerged with a frightening superiority of which the military states of previous centuries, bent on conquest and expansion, could never remotely have conceived."[19]

In the memory of the German governing elite, Bismarck planted the idea of war as an "escape forwards" from domestic crisis. Historians still debate how much that memory influenced Germany's decision for war in July 1914. In the alarmed view of the American ambassador to Berlin, James W. Gerard, writing in 1917 at the height of the American propaganda campaign against Prussian militarism, the bad Germany provoked the war to escape from a political challenge to the status quo.[20]

In February 1914, a British observer predicated that war would flow from the same crisis singled out by Gerard, a national political showdown between the Reichstag and the monarchy, sparked by a military incident in a provincial backwater: "Possibly the two great forces of German public opinion which have clashed at Zabern will clash again and again, and Germany may go through a period similar to that through which England went in the time of Charles the First," J. Ellis Barker wrote in *The Nineteenth Century and After*. "It seems more likely that the powers of feudalism and absolutism, which, under the cloak of parliamentarianism at present govern the country, will try to avoid a domestic conflict by provoking a foreign one." In April, the Duke of Ratibor, close to the kaiser, remarked to the French ambassador that just as Bismarck's "wars of 64, 66, and 70 . . . had strengthened the position of the military" and the forces of order, so now, in 1914, war "would be necessary to put things back on the right track." In July, the German chancellor, Bethmann Hollweg, oppressed by a "deep sense of malaise over the domestic situation in Germany," "fatalistically decided to reverse [it] in one bold stroke" by handing Vienna a "blank check" to attack Serbia over its suspected role in the assassination of the Austrian archduke, Franz Ferdinand. An influential school of German historians cites evidence like this to highlight the long-overlooked domestic political causes of World War I. Strong enough to make the leaders of Germany want war, they were strong enough to deny them that deliverance.[21]

The crisis from which Ellis Barker feared Germany would escape in war was triggered by a real Köpenick with real soldiers mounting a real coup. It happened not in a Berlin suburb but in Zabern, a small town in Alsace, one of two French provinces Bismarck annexed in 1871 as the spoils of victory in the Franco-Prussian War, and because of its French connection the worst place in Germany for the army to run amok. In the "Zabern Affair" the two Germanys confronted each other over the basic "skirted decision" of the *Kaiserreich*—whether Germany was to be "a state with an army or an army with a state." The good Germany strode out from under the spiked helmet and, for the first time since 1871, found its voice before, divided by appeals to remember Germany's place on Bismarck's map of Africa, losing its nerve.[22]

To Léon Gambetta, the tribune of nineteenth-century French republicanism, the annexation of Alsace-Lorraine was "the death-germ of [Bismarck's] work." In a sensational book published early in 1914, Bernhard von Bülow, Germany's chancellor from 1900 to 1909, warned his countrymen that "France is given up to its ideal of *revanche* . . . We must take this into account, and consider that we ourselves should be the opponent against whom France would first turn if she thought she could carry out a victorious campaign against Germany." In the

1920s, the diplomatic historian C. P. Gooch ranked France's enmity toward Germany over Alsace-Lorraine the first of the "three antagonisms that produced the war of 1914," the others being Germany's challenge to Britain's naval supremacy and Russia's Balkan rivalry with Austria.[23]

In fact, by 1914 everywhere but on the extreme right the French had renounced going to war to recover the "lost provinces." Indicatively, "about half of all recruits, and quite a few junior officers, were unaware that France had lost territory to Germany in 1870." At the height of the Zabern affair, the German embassy in Paris held a dinner in honor of President Raymond Poincaré, a Lorrainer, the first French president to accept such an invitation.[24]

But assuming Gooch and Bülow were correct about French irredentism, Bismarck doubted they would have desired revanche any less if he had left the map of France intact. "What the French nation will never forgive us is their defeat as such," he maintained with his accustomed realism. "Even if we were now to depart France without any territorial concessions, without any indemnities, with no other advantage than the glory of our arms, the same hatred and vengefulness would persist among the French people . . . Any peace we may conclude, even without territory changing hands, will be but an armistice . . . We shall demand Alsace-Lorraine . . . merely to protect ourselves against the next attack." The annexed provinces would form a "glacis" between that future French attack and south Germany. Troops were garrisoned in Zabern, about thirty miles from the new French border, to implement Germany's forward defense strategy.[25]

Before its annexation by Louis XIV in 1679, Alsace had long been ruled by the House of Habsburg, and remained German speaking under the French. The lingua franca didn't concern Napoleon: "What matters that?—Though they speak in German, they saber in French!" In Alsace-Lorraine the French Revolution "had had a profound influence—the Marseillaise was composed in Strasburg—while the movement to unite Germany had passed them by untouched." Bismarck spoke of binding Alsace-Lorraine to Germany with "Teutonic patience and affection," but the latter—some would say oxymoron—proved weaker than the bonds of memory linking its people to France.

Under a policy of "Germanization," French language instruction was forbidden in most primary schools and French banned on street signs and on tombstones. Teutonic thoroughness turned "cafe" into "*Kaffee*," "concert" into "*Konzert*," the city of "Nancy" into "Nansig," and "Alsace-Lorraine" into "Elsass-Lothringen."[26]

The army also served as a school of Germanization; the draft swept deep among Alsace-Lorraine's young men. The army's treatment of its Alsatian conscripts may be guessed from the generic training methods documented by the left-wing socialists, Rosa Luxemburg and Karl Liebknecht. Beaten, bound to trees, and forced to eat their own excrement, recruits, the socialists charged, committed suicide at a rate fourteen times higher than the general population. That was how the army trained *Germans*. To Prussian officers and sergeants Alsace-Lorraine was still "the enemy's country."[27]

Jacob Burckhardt foresaw dire trouble for Germany in the annexation. Even "outside of war," he maintained, Alsace-Lorraine would "constantly provide at least the din of war," and this would make for "a quiet state of siege in Germany itself," putting at risk "constitutionalism and other such relics." Vindicating Burckhardt's prophecy, the Zabern Affair quickened rumblings of a right-wing putsch to declare a state of siege, suspend the constitution, and disband the parliament.[28]

German papers considered Zabern, the home since 1888 of the Ninety-ninth Prussian Infantry regiment, the "most German town in Alsace-Lorraine." The occasional brawl aside, soldiers and civilians got on tolerably well. But Zabern had never seen a soldier quite like Lieutenant Gunther Freiherr von Forstner before.

Just turned twenty, Baron von Forstner was notorious for being a bully on the training ground and a lout in the town. And that was *before* he insulted all six hundred thousand Alsatians. In late October 1913, a recruit with a police record started a scuffle on the rifle range. Forstner chastised the hothead, saying that if he wanted a fight he could easily find one in town, though, the lieutenant added, he ought to avoid fights. However, should "some *Wackes*" in town start something, the recruit should fight back, with bullets, if necessary. "And if that happens," the official report quotes him speaking within earshot of the whole squad, "and you happen to waste one of them, OK. For

every one of those dirty *Wackes* you bring me, you get 10 marks."
Wackes—vagabond, bum, coward—sounds anodyne to the American
ear, yet "in normal circumstances even Alsatians used it with care,
and non-Alsatians at their peril." The regiment had banned its use in
1903. That knowledge would have dissuaded prudent mortals from
using it, but Lieutenant Forstner was one of the "sun-Gods" of Wilhelmine Germany. In ordering at least one member of his squad to
repeat, "I am a *Wackes*, I am a *Wackes*" how could he sense the danger
to himself? The odds approach certainty that this Wackes was among
those who leaked the story to the local newspapers.[29]

Eight thousand people lived in Zabern; mobilized by the news,
a thousand of them, a few shouting "Vive la France!," gathered outside the army barracks to protest Lieutenant Forstner's presence among
them. Now began a campaign of harassment against Forstner. In restaurants and on the streets, hecklers dogged him, small boys, picking
up on the rumor that during a recent bender he had soiled his bed,
yelling "*Bettschisser!*"

Passions had cooled somewhat when, on November 14, Forstner
stepped in it again. Lecturing recruits against deserting to join the
French Foreign Legion, as more than a thousand Alsatians and

Making Zabern safe for Lieutenant von Forstner.

Lorrainers reportedly did in 1912, he remarked that for all he cared they could "shit on the French flag." A cartoon soon appeared in the window of a Paris ladies' shop showing him performing that act himself. In the music halls, songs rang with his shame:

> *Forstner said, "I'll lower my pants*
> *And go on the flag of France."*
> *But, my lad, to pull off that gag,*
> *You must first get your hands on that flag.*
> *And if I know where it's at,*
> *You'll go in your pants before that.*

Not all the French were so lighthearted. Acting on an impulse shared by many of his countrymen, Paul de Cassagnac, a Bonapartist journalist, challenged Forstner to a duel.

The Staathalter, or governor, of Alsace, Count Karl von Wedel, appealed to the kaiser to have Forstner transferred. Wedel had weight with the Supreme Warlord. He could not have climbed so high in office, it was said, except for his ability to "terrorize" the kaiser over "certain profligate actions" in Vienna. In the early 1880s, as a lowly military adjutant, he had covered up a messy ménage à trois between the newly married Prince Wilhelm and two Viennese women. But the kaiser brooked no civilian interference with his army, which, on succeeding his father as kaiser in 1887, he addressed in rapturous terms: "And so we belong together, I and the Army." He turned Wedel down. Forstner stayed, and Zabern was not spared the events that "made our town world famous," in the words of a rueful resident.[30]

For the next act in Zabern, Forstner passed the baton of calamity to Colonel von Reuter, his commanding officer. Reuter had lost his father in the fighting in Alsace in 1870 and treated Alsatians as if they were collectively responsible. Thus, for leaking the Forstner chronicles, Reuter arrested nine Alsatian privates along with an Alsatian sergeant major with relatives working in a nearby factory and transferred the remaining Alsatians in Forstner's company to other regiments. For printing the Bettschisser rumor, he had the offices of the *Zaberner Anzeiger* raided, and threatened to ban soldiers from patronizing any restaurant "where customers were even seen reading it." But he neglected to inform Zaberners that Forstner had been confined to his house for six days for Wackes. The apparent double standard—for all the locals knew, Forstner was free and clear—kept emotions on the boil.

So Zabern youngsters continued to heckle Forstner, again on the loose, and his bulldog-guarded companion, Lieutenant Kurt Schad. Reuter assigned an armed guard to escort the officers on their errands. When the raillery persisted, he issued an ultimatum to the local prefect: *Suppress disrespect for the army or I will.*

On the evening of November 30, he did. Sixty soldiers with fixed bayonets backed by two machine guns appeared at one end of the town square. Reuter sent half the force under Forstner to sweep one side, half under Schad the other. "The troops advanced; absurd scenes followed," the *Frankfurter Zeitung* dryly commented.

Groups of blue-collar workers were leaving their night school classes, single men were en route to their favorite haunts, shoppers were walking home with the makings of their suppers. Suddenly the drums rolled, the soldiers' hobnailed boots scraped the cobblestones, the civilians froze. Reuter expected them to cower before his bayonets. Instead they reacted like the audience at a light opera in which the goose-stepping soldiers were the extras. They laughed. One man was arrested for jeering, another for whistling, a third for standing in the way of the advancing skirmish line. Forstner was about to collar a fellow carrying sausage home, but on recognizing him thought better of it. "Lt. Forstner had had an affair with my wife's sister," he later testified, "who is only 14, and is currently in Paris."

On his side of the square, Lieutenant Schad encountered unexpected resistance. A bank teller returning home from work objected to Schad's accusation that he had laughed. Schad arrested him for his "smiling grimace." "I had every man I suspected of laughing at us arrested," Schad subsequently explained. "As they were too cowardly to laugh at our faces, we had to be guided by presumption." Judges emerging from the courthouse, struck dumb by the spectacle, were slow to obey Schad's command to keep moving—Reuter had ordered the arrest of "everybody who stood still even for a second"—so the lieutenant arrested them. They protested to Reuter. "This is where jurisprudence ends," he told them. "Mars rules the hour."

A district commissioner, representing the civil authority, pleaded with the colonel to withdraw his troops. He refused: "I am in command here now." People were just "standing about," the commissioner indicated to Reuter. What was wrong with that? "I intend to prevent this standing about at any cost," the colonel came back. And he did not "intend to let people laugh in this way. If it continues, I shall order the troops to shoot." Asked later if he would have shot people for laughing, he replied, "Certainly!" The "prestige and honor of the whole army" was at stake.

In a celebrated speech, Léon Gambetta had prophesied that "till [the Germans] have restored our ravished provinces . . . the peace of the world will remain at the mercy of an incident." A massacre in Zabern would have qualified.[31]

There was no massacre. Twenty-seven people were arrested, and jailed for the night in the barrack's coal cellar. The next day, a Sunday, order returned to Zabern, though that evening a young molder was arrested for singing. "The official report regrettably neglects to say what."[32]

It was awkward for the army that responsibility for the coup reached up the chain of command. "I . . . informed Col. Reuter personally that he was himself to arrest demonstrators," General Berthold von Deimling, Reuter's Strasburg-based superior, reported to Berlin, "and use armed force in case of resistance, should the jeering continue." Reuter also based his action on a cabinet order issued by the king of Prussia in 1820 that "permitted and obliged" the army to suppress riots when the "civil authorities are excessively hesitant to request military aid." No one had heard of this order; no officer before Reuter had invoked it. It was a military regulation, not a civil law, and even though the New York Times headline over its November 30 story read GERMAN BAYONETS STOP ALSATIAN RIOT, the Zaberners had not rioted, only stood about. Some had laughed.

The editorial voices of liberal Germany were beginning to unlimber on the army—the Hamburger Echo denouncing Reuter's action as "the dictatorship of the bayonet"—when the inexorable Lieutenant Forstner drew the only blood shed in the Zabern affair.[33]

Forty-eight hours after Zabern passed under the rule of Mars, on a dawn march through an outlying village, his company encountered a group of factory-bound shoe workers. Taunts were shouted and

Forstner ordered his men to pursue and arrest the quickly scattering taunters. One, Karl Blank, was not quick enough. Furiously protesting his innocence of the name-calling, Blank pronounced a curse on Forstner, who slashed Blank's skull with his saber, opening a deep cut. Forstner later testified that Blank was about to strike him, but the jury at his court-martial doubted this as Blank was restrained by five men.

Fear of insult, not injury, goaded Forstner. As the *New York Times* noted, "Lieutenant von Forstner said he acted [according to] the prevailing German assumption that an officer was irretrievably dishonored if he permitted himself to receive a blow." Forstner was the victim of a "military code . . . ill-adapted to the conditions and requirements of the modern world." Under that code, a blow from Blank would have required Forstner's "resignation from the army."[34]

It also would have required Forstner to strike at Blank, a person *unsatisfaktionsfahig*—so low socially as to be incapable of giving satisfaction in a duel—"with his entire energy and with the highest brutality of which he is capable," according to a manual of army etiquette. A cabinet order of the 1880s forbade the police from interfering in such moments of *Ehrennotwehr*—"the defense of honor in extreme emergencies through unusual measures."

Possibly as a result, the 1890s saw several notorious incidents. In 1892, on Berlin's Postdammerstrasse, a civilian menaced by a dog asked the lieutenant-owner to restrain his pet, at which the lieutenant drew his sword and inflicted "gruesome cuts" on the civilian's unoffending person. In 1895, jostled on a Hamburg street, an officer buried his sword in the jostler's scalp. In 1896, while the Reichstag was debating whether dueling among officers should be outlawed, a tipsy Baden plumber leaving a café brushed against a table occupied by Lieutenant Baron von Brusewitz, who followed the plumber out, demanded that he apologize, and, when he refused, stabbed him to death. Knowing the cut of a keen blade, the military court of appeals that reviewed Forstner's court-martial conviction primly noted that Forstner's sword "had not been specially ground; it was only the lieutenant's ordinary military sword." Blank should have counted his blessings.[35]

The code called for officers to bear the legal consequences of Ehrennotwehr, sacrificing their freedom, if necessary, to defend caste honor. But in practice, even brutes like Lieutenant von Brusewitz could usually count on a pardon from the kaiser. Pardon was rarely necessary for the protagonists in an officer duel. Dueling was expected, encouraged, even required; an officer who refused a challenge from a fellow officer could be drummed out of his regiment.[36]

The Social Democrats (SPD) advocated criminalizing dueling, collapsing it into the categories of assault and homicide. The duel's reactionary politics animated their campaign. "For us the duel is a purely political question," they announced ahead of the 1912 elections. "We perceive the duel not as a means of preserving Junker class honor but as a symbol of Junker class rule, and even more: a device for the maintenance of class rule." As dramatized in novels like Theodor Fontane's *Effi Briest* (1894), the German middle classes admired the aristocratic values epitomized by the duel. In social attitude and political outlook they were a heavily "feudalized bourgeoisie," according to an influential interpretation first advanced by the Weimar historian Eckart Kehr. In the obeisance shown the "cobbler-captain" by the citizens of Köpenick, the socialist Karl Liebknecht found "a compendium of that art of militaristic education and its results, the most sublime of which is the veritable canonization of the officer's coat by the whole of bourgeois society." Bought off by reserve officer commissions and hopes of ennoblement—by the lure of a "von"—the German bourgeoisie identified up, with the Junker-officer class, not down, with Germany's workers.* Unlike their French analogues, they refused history's

---

* "The society of the Empire was shaped by the aristocracy, the officer corps, and the civil service, with the aristocratic officer of the guard's regiments as the social model of all other classes. It was he whom the German bourgeoisie sought to emulate; its leaders—particularly the industrialists with newly-acquired wealth—copied the way of life of the aristocratic officer and frequently tried to join the ranks of the nobility." Fritz Fischer, *War of Illusions: German Policies from 1911 to 1914* (New York: Norton, 1975), 13. The counterview is argued at length by the British scholar David Blackbourn in an essay titled "The Discreet Charm of the Bourgeoisie," which includes these sentences: "If one looks at nineteenth-century Europe it is difficult to identify an unambiguous instance in which the bourgeoisie ruled as a class . . . It is even more difficult to find bourgeois revolutions of the supposedly classic type in any period." Blackbourn maintains that the bourgeoisie led a "silent revolution" in Germany, establishing their commercial values up and down the social scale. See David Blackbourn and Geoff Ely, *The Peculiarities of German History: Bourgeois Society and Politics in Nineteenth-Century Germany* (New York: Oxford University Press, 1984), 174.

"The Alsatian Bogeyman" (1913). Olaf Gulbransson's cartoon from *Simplicissimus* is an emblem of the culture war between the "two Germanys." Liberal Germany excoriated the army's conduct at Zabern while conservative Germany defended the army for restoring order.

assignment—to supplant the aristocrats and Junkers of the ancien régime as the ruling class. Marx drew the contrast memorably: "In France the bourgeoisie conquered so that it could humble the people; in Germany the bourgeoisie humbled itself so that the people should not conquer." As the Social Democrats discovered in the next act of the Zabern affair, in a crisis the middle-class parties shrank from challenging their feudal masters.[37]

*   *   *

Reuter attacked Zabern on Saturday night; Forstner struck Blank on Monday; Chancellor Theobold von Bethmann Hollweg answered for their conduct before an enraged Reichstag on Tuesday.

Crying "Militarism, military dictatorship, high treason!" a Social Democrat from Strasburg set the tone for what the *New York Times* called "one of the most tempestuous seatings in the history of the Reichstag." Giving the Zabern affair its signature headline, a deputy from Alsace denounced "sabre dictatorship." "Every thrust at the Army was applauded to the echo everywhere in the House save from the ultra-militarist back benches," the *Times* reported.[38]

In a sign of German militarism, Germany's highest civilian official sat below the generals and admirals at royal banquets and appeared in the legislative assembly dressed like a soldier. Wearing the uniform of a major, Bethmann Hollweg, appointed chancellor in 1909, rose "to stand in the fiery rain," as he described the ordeal to a friend. Initially he had criticized the army for having "transgressed its authority." However, cocooned by his military cabinet in a castle in distant Donaueschingen, the kaiser accepted the army's side of the story. Blaming the controversy on "journalist pigs," he refused to meet with Count Wedel to hear the civilian side. Privately, the Austrian ambassador reported to Vienna, "the Kaiser . . . accuses [Bethmann] of too much partiality for the civilians against the military." The kaiser expected his chancellor to defend his army. German citizens expected the government to defend their civil liberties. Alsatians required special attention. In 1911, Bethmann had persuaded the kaiser to grant a new constitution to the Reichsland (Alsace-Lorraine), providing for greater local self-government. Saber rule in Zabern, Bethmann knew, had jeopardized its objective—to knit the conquered provinces into the fabric of Germany.[39]

Bethmann Hollweg was cross-pressured, and it showed in his performance. Before he began speaking, his Social Democratic opponents lacked the votes to censure his government for failing to check militarism in Zabern. After he finished, the rout was on. Censure passed the next day by 5 to 1, with the Center, National Liberal, and Progressive parties merging with the Social Democratic tide.

Bethmann Hollweg. If Germany's chancellor, its highest
civilian official, wore his saber in the Reichstag, that would complete the
symbolism of "an army with a state."

Gesturing now to the army, now to public outrage at it, the chancellor, "his tall figure as melancholy as a leafless trunk," tried to
straddle a widening gulf. It was proper for Lieutenant Forstner to
instruct recruits to defend themselves if attacked, improper to put a
bounty on Alsatians. Wackes was perhaps improper—hisses from the
Alsatian deputies. Warning recruits against deserting to the Foreign
Legion was proper, insulting the flag of a country "we met in honorable battle forty years ago" decidedly improper. Regarding Reuter's
Saturday-night roundup, Bethmann observed, the military took one
view and the civilian authorities in Zabern another. Which "was absolutely in the right" was "impossible" for him to say. At this, from
all quarters of the House except the Right came cries of disapproval.
"I ask the gentlemen not to forget," Bethmann declared into the din,

"even in this serious and in many respects very sad case, that the military has the right to protect itself against direct attacks." The translation of the stenographic transcript continues:

(Shout from the Social Democrats: Children attacked!)
And it has not only the right; it also has the duty to do so.
(Commotion among the Social Democrats.)
Otherwise no army in the world can survive.
(Very true! from the Right.)
The uniform must be respected in all circumstances.

With that, amid the "angriest hisses ever heard in the Reichstag," the chancellor sat down.

The Prussian minister of war, General von Falkenhayn, his brindle-colored hair cut en brosse, spoke next. A stranger to ambiguity, he blamed "noisy agitators and newspaper campaigns" for the events in Zabern. He got no further. For five minutes the Social Democrats assailed him, shouting, among other things, the deadly accurate, "You are Forstner in the flesh!" Falkenhayn stood at attention throughout *his* fiery rain. When it subsided he counterattacked. Without the army, "there would not be a stone in its place in Germany today—including in this proud building!" It was no joy doing the job of the police in Zabern—why, a German soldier was safer in the "Congo"—but the German army was "a terrible instrument" and woe to any evening strollers standing in its awful way! In vain did the president of the Reichstag ring his bell for quiet.[40]

A Center Party member from Alsace replied to Falkenhayn at the next session. The army had built the Reichstag. It *had* conquered Alsace: "But I tell him today that it is also the German army that has lost Alsace-Lorraine to the German Empire."

That was only half the story. By treating Alsatians as if they were enemies, not Germans, the army caused what the *Times* called "a grave constitutional crisis." Alsace was *that* important to Germany. And many Alsatians were moved by the discovery. After sampling local opinion in the days following the censure vote, a correspondent identifying himself as "Old Alsatian Hand," wrote to Bethmann:

Erich von Falkenhayn. The War Minister (and general)
reminded the Reichstag what it owed to the
German army, which had forged Germany.

"Rarely has Alsace felt itself so German as when the Reichstag supported it with all its force."[41]

Several speakers in the Zabern debate had "plainly intimated" that absent immediate disciplinary action against Forstner and Reuter the army budget might not pass. That threat penetrated the kaiser's cocoon. Bowing to public opinion, the Supreme War Lord announced that Forstner and Reuter would soon face court-martials. Across Berlin, seventeen "huge" socialist meetings cheered that news. Zaberners greeted the kaiser's decision to move the Ninety-ninth infantry out of town with ambivalence; the economy depended on soldiers' spending. Over the subsequent announcement that Lieutenant Forstner would be transferred to a regiment on the Polish frontier, as far from Alsace as he could go and still be in Germany, their happiness was unalloyed.[42]

The papers speculated that the chancellor, "no longer taken seriously abroad since six-sevenths of the [Reichstag] disavowed him," would not survive the year. The politicians had bearded the army, forced the kaiser's hand, and discredited the chancellor. All in three days. "The Reichstag has risen to its full stature as the mouthpiece of the people," the *Times* exclaimed.[43]

Foreign observers wondered if the Reichstag would use the censure vote to oust Bethmann, a revolutionary step. Under Bismarck's constitution, the Reichstag could not change the government. If the Reichstag nevertheless successfully asserted such power by holding up the army bill until the kaiser removed the chancellor, de facto parliamentary government would have come to Germany, a political check, potentially, on the kaiser's power to make war. "We on the left favor parliamentary government," a Social Democrat declared. "The Reichstag cannot remain forever in its present state as [an] insignificant organ of control." The Saxon representative in Berlin predicted that "we are heading toward another domestic crisis and I fear that Bethmann will no longer be able to master it."[44]

With censure, however, the Reichstag had exhausted the available political courage. The Center Party and National Liberal press, while critical of Bethmann, deprecated any idea of provoking a "Chancellor crisis." Betraying reluctance within their ranks, the Social Democrats took a week to submit a resolution calling on Bethmann to resign "like a French or English prime minister." Meanwhile, the socialist press was framing Zabern in terms repugnant to the middle-class parties. "We will make clear to every member of the working class that every day this system of militarism continues to exist is an outrage and a danger," the *Düsseldorf Volkzeitung* editorialized. "However, this system can only be eliminated when the existing capitalist state with all its horrors is eliminated." Deputies who voted censure to defend civil liberties or from pique with Bethmann no doubt wondered what they were doing in *this* company.[45]

Bethmann could take satisfaction in the isolation of the Social Democrats. He had no intention of resigning, he declared to a Reichstag sobered by a week of second thoughts, adding, to applause, "The majority of the German people have no intention of subjecting the Imperial authority to the coercion of the Social Democrats." Neither did a majority of the Reichstag. Germany, Bethmann reminded the Socialists, was not England.[46]

But it was not a military dictatorship either, and hopes for an official repudiation of saber rule now focused on the trials of Lieutenant Forstner and Colonel Reuter. In late December, a military court sitting in Strasburg found Forstner guilty of assault on the shoe worker, Karl Blank, sentencing the lieutenant to forty-three days imprisonment, usually a prelude to discharge from the army. Forstner argued that he was carrying out the orders of Colonel Reuter, who had told his men to "bring down" threatening civilians. Forstner's secondary defense that a dangerous Blank was about to attack him collapsed when Blank walked across the courtroom, and it was seen that he dragged a clubfoot.[47]

In a vertiginous turn of events, on January 10, 1914, a military appeals court overturned Forstner's conviction. Sabering Blank was "putative self-defense." Seated in a Strasburg courtroom behind their spiked helmets lined up along a table separating them from the civilian public, a second panel of officers acquitted Reuter of the charges against him. The civilian authority having failed, Reuter had acted properly in restoring order in Zabern.[48]

The Berlin dailies broke this bombshell in special editions, which were "snatched from the hands of news dealers" as if they carried reports of "a great battle." There *had* been a great battle, and the good Germany had lost it: MILITARY MEN OPENLY EXULT, LIBERALS DENOUNCE THE OVERTHROW OF CIVIL LAW read a representative headline.

Outside the Strasburg courthouse, mounted gendarmes and hussars carrying sabers and carbines kept local citizens at bay while the verdicts were announced. The crowd displayed "sullen submission," a reporter noted, as if these Alsatians were afraid "the machine guns could be used on them." Still, fists were shaken at Forstner as he was hustled out of the building and into a waiting carriage.

Liberal editors greeted the Strasburg verdicts with resigned dismay, the *Frankfurt Zeitung* concluding that "militarism on the Bench" had pardoned "militarism in the dock." The *Berliner Tagenblatt* quoted a May 1912 threat of the kaiser's provoked by demonstrations surrounding his visit to Strasburg—"If this keeps up, I shall smash the constitution of Alsace-Lorraine to atoms"—and tartly added, "Today's events at Strasburg have saved the Supreme War Lord the trouble, as the work of years of reconciliation in the conquered provinces is now destroyed."

In France the socialist press urged Frenchmen not to let their anger at the Germany of the Strasburg verdicts eclipse their admiration for the Germany of the Reichstag censure vote. The semiofficial *Temps* jibbed at that: "French Radicals and Socialists find comfort in the reflection that there are 'two Germanies' . . . From the political and practical point of view, the Germany to which the French Socialists appeal in order to reassure us simply does not exist." Anticipating the anticlimax of the Zabern affair, the *London Daily News* observed, "If the Reichstag accepts this, we shall conclude that the sabre and not the law rules in Germany."[49]

The Reichstag did accept it, the leader of the Center Party agreeing with the chancellor that it was time to "heal not probe" the wound of Zabern. Progressive and Social Democratic bills calling for the army to obtain permission from the civil government before it went to Zabern and for prosecuting soldiers in civilian courts for offenses "other than military crimes" were referred to committee, where they disappeared. "The middle-class parties, which were composed of people who admired the military and imitated its values, could not be moved to more than momentary irritation over its faults, and a Reichstag that had voted the biggest peacetime military budget in history in October 1913 was not a body that was capable of disciplining the army three months later." Bethmann's tribute to the army as the guarantor of Germany's "place in the world" resonated: "We won't let them [the SPD] take that away from us, gentlemen, just because— well, gentlemen, because in one certain place in the great German Empire certain things happened that no one wants to see repeated."[50]

The deputies acted under the spell of the Staatsstreich—the coup— that had hung over the Reichstag, a democratic beachhead in an authoritarian state, since Bismarck's time. Germany enjoyed universal

male suffrage because Bismarck hoped the peasant vote would prove a
dependable support to the regime, a counterweight to liberalism. But
he had not reckoned with the rapidity of Germany's industrialization,
which powered the growth of an urban working class and the rise of
its political party, the Social Democrats, to near-majority status. Alive
to the danger of a socialist Reichstag, he waged domestic war on the
SPD, forcing the party underground.[51]

Bismarck throwing a tactical tantrum in the Reichstag. To keep the Social
Democrats from winning seats, he threatened saber rule. Along with "social
imperialism"—the playing up of international tensions to silence domestic
dissent—Bismarck bequeathed the Staatsstreich to the German future.

Yet with each election the SPD vote rose. In 1887, Bismarck contemplated a Staatsstreich if his war-scare campaign failed to produce a conservative majority. Two years later, in a letter to one of his ambassadors, he laid out the scenario that would trigger a coup: "With the eventuality of a hostile majority we must always reckon. You can dissolve [the Reichstag] three or four times but in the end you have to smash the crockery. These questions—like that of Social Democracy and that of the relationship between Parliament and the separate states—will not be solved without a blood-bath, just as the question of German unity was not."[52]

When, in 1890, the still-underground SPD won an "astonishing" 1,427,298 votes, Bismarck signaled the War Ministry to sharpen the sabers. A Bavarian political observer reported that the chancellor wanted to provoke the Reichstag "into a position in which it could be destroyed." But the new emperor, Wilhelm II, shied from beginning his reign with violence. "No one would ever forget that I did that, and all the expectations that have perhaps been placed on me would be converted into their opposite," he expostulated in a tense meeting with Bismarck. "Then we may have a conflict," Bismarck responded, and resigned under pressure.

So the door to the Reichstag stayed open, and every year more Social Democrats walked through it. After the impressive SPD success in the 1903 elections Bülow noted "the belief, now gaining ground all over Germany . . . that the Socialist movement [can] never be brought to a standstill, but must roll on ahead like some elemental force—like the sea or an avalanche."[53]

Stopping the avalanche became an urgent preoccupation of the military. As early as 1897, Alfred von Waldersee, the army chief of staff, advocated suspending civil rights for socialists, suppressing "undesirable" publications, and curtailing the suffrage for Reichstag elections. It was understood that the socialists would resist such measures. So in 1907 the General Staff's Second Section for Military Studies outlined a strategy for "fighting in insurgent towns," a template for civil war against "the Fatherland's enemy within." The SPD-led Reichstag censure vote over Zabern gave this scenario new life.[54]

As it piled up votes, the SPD trimmed its Marxist sails, becoming a

"revolutionary but not revolution-making party," content to organize the working class against the day when capitalism should collapse
of its own contradictions. This reformist positioning broadened the
SPD's appeal beyond the working class, and, in 1912, helped it win
nearly five million votes, one of every three cast and twice as many
as its nearest competitor, the Center Party.[55]

To achieve a Reichstag majority, the SPD helped the dying Progressives win seats. But Progressive voters rejected the SPD candidates they were supposed to support as part of the bargain, and after
the election the party changed front. Instead of consummating a
"shift to the left," the Progressives and Liberals joined with the Conservatives in a shift to the right, opposing the SPD on its central issue,
suffrage reform. In Prussia, a three–class property-weighted franchise
converted 418,000 Conservative votes into 214 seats, and 600,000
Socialist votes into an outrageous 7. This kept the Junkers on top in
Prussia, while in Germany as a whole, rural–skewed gerrymandering
saw "150 Reichstag representatives of the right . . . able to outvote
those on the left whose electors numbered almost twice as many." The
road to an SPD majority lay through fair elections. With that road
blocked, the SPD succumbed to frustration and factionalism.[56]

The growth rate of party membership declined from 49.7 percent
in 1911, the year of hope for reform through the ballot box, to 2.9
percent in 1913 and 0.4 percent in 1914. In Düsseldorf, the May
Day rallies of 1910 and 1911 drew more than ten thousand people;
in 1912, when barely five hundred turned out. While the union rank
and file despaired of politics, the SPD leaders split over tactics and
ideology.[57]

Bülow's "elemental force" was played out. However, the German
Right, fixated on its own political entropy with the Conservative share
of the vote plummeting from 43 percent in 1874 to 25 percent in
1912, saw the red tide rising, not receding, and brooded on a putsch.
Saber rule had triumphed in Köpenick and Zabern. Why not in
Berlin? When a Conservative deputy, Elard von Oldenburg-Januschau,
declared, "The King of Prussia and the German Emperor must always
be in a position to say to any lieutenant: 'Take ten men and shoot the
Reichstag!'" his fellow Conservatives in the Reichstag gave him a
standing ovation.[58]

Coup fever spread to the royal family through the person of Crown Prince Wilhelm. In November 1913, he forwarded to his father a memo urging an über-Zabern—the imposition of martial law, the shuttering of the Reichstag, the abolition of universal suffrage, a purge of the opposition press, and a "solution of the Jewish question," a cleansing to begin by banning Jews from teaching, the civil service, and the army and by stripping them of the right to vote. Drafted by a former cavalry general, this manifesto for saber rule echoed the views of Heinrich Class, chairman of the Pan-German League, which agitated for "living space" in the East and for a "national dictatorship." Writing in 1946, the historian Friedrich Meinecke characterized the League as a "curtain-raiser for the rise of Hitler," "a child of the Pan-German movement." The führer himself seems to be foreseen in this call by a Pan-German publicist for "the greatest possible expansion of the state or, to put it another way, the concentration of all the nation's energies for a united effort abroad to be carried out by a hero and master."[59]

To such extremists, the Reichstag censure vote represented a moment of peril. In lining up with the SPD, the middle-class parties enacted "the shift to the left" feared since the socialists' great victory in 1912. The feudalization of the German bourgeoisie—the confetti of "vons" falling on "any ass laden with money bags," the reserve officer commissions, the cult of dueling—had miscarried. In the face of Germany's deteriorating strategic position, with the French adopting a three-year conscription law to expand their army, the British signaling in the Morocco crisis of 1911 that they would stand with France in a war against Germany, and the Russians securing massive loans in Paris to build military railroads to the borders of East Prussia—in the face of these signs of danger the bourgeois politicians had sided with the socialists, enemies of the Reich who would paralyze Germany with a general strike while the Cossacks raped their way to Berlin. Seduction and fear failing to keep the bourgeois politicians from treasonous congress with the SPD, the men around the crown prince likely reasoned, it was time to "shoot the Reichstag."[60]

It's unclear how far fear of losing this beachhead of democracy motivated the middle-class parties to break with the SPD after the censure vote. The comment the crown prince's plotting drew in the Reichstag suggests that it was at least on the deputies' minds. "People see that if the Crown Prince lives in intimate friendship with men who despise the Constitution and preach the coup d'etat they must take their destinies into their own hands," Social Democrat Ludwig Frank, declared, warning plotters on the right that a coup would be met by extra-parliamentary action on the left.[61]

By Christmas 1913, however, the moment of peril for the right had passed, and with it a skein of lost history that might have anchored peace in strife. Shuttering the Reichstag would have plunged Germany into civil war. Socialist voters, an SPD deputy warned in 1913, "formed a fraction of the nation as large as all the southern states of the Reich put together," and saber rule would have radicalized many to protest and some to resist. As happened in 1905, foreign policy would be hostage to domestic crisis. In that year, citing a crippling miners' strike in the Ruhr, the kaiser rejected a "radical" plan for a preventive war against Russia, then torn by revolution, for a reason no less cogent in 1914: "Because of our Social Democrats we cannot send a single man out of the country without running the gravest risk to the life and property of the citizenry. First the socialists must be gunned down, decapitated and rendered harmless, in a blood-bath if necessary, and then war abroad!" Decapitating the SPD's elected leaders would have triggered a backlash at least as severe as a miners' walkout. In March 1919 to end a right-wing putsch the SPD called a country-wide general strike, an economic weapon that would have been equally potent in 1914. Franz Ferdinand would still have been assassinated in Sarajevo on June 28, 1914. The Austrians would still have asked Germany to support their war on Serbia. Pleading that he "couldn't send a single man out of the country without running the gravest risk," the kaiser could have refused without fear of jeopardizing Germany's alliance with Austria-Hungary, a brittle confection of peoples whose leaders would be the first to understand his dilemma. Unable to fight Serbia's ally Russia alone, chances are Vienna would have backed down.[62]

The kaiser often spouted Staatsstreich rhetoric, telegraphing Bethmann earlier in 1913: "The sooner such *Halunken* are blown to smithereens the better! The German parliamentarian and politician becomes daily more of a swine!" But late in the year, with the Reichstag rallying to Bethmann from fear of the Social Democrats, he chastised the crown prince for wanting to blow up the Halunken: "In Latin and Central America *Staatsstreiche* may belong to the instruments of the art of government. In Germany, thank God, they are not customary and must not become so, whether they come from above or below. People who dare to recommend such action are dangerous people, more dangerous for the monarchy than the wildest Social Democrat." This remonstrance was drafted by the head of the Civil Cabinet, a Bethmann ally, who under the kaiser's signature went on to label Pan-German fantasies to deny civil rights to Jews "down-right childish: they would cause Germany's departure from the ranks of civilized nations." That sentiment would not have flowed easily from the pen of the kaiser, a choleric anti-Semite who in 1919 wrote that Jews and mosquitoes were a "nuisance that humanity must get rid of in some way or other," adding, "I believe the best would be gas."[63]

Ostensibly for telegramming congratulations to Reuter ("Give it 'em!"), the thirty-one-year-old heir apparent was relieved of his command of the "Death's Head" hussars in Danzig and demoted to what the *Berliner Zeitung* with brutal candor characterized as "a wholly subordinate post on the General Staff" in Berlin. When it came out that in addition the crown prince was "ordered" to endure a nearly three-hour New Year's Eve duologue from his parents on the brilliance of the "Kaiser manoeuvres" during the 1913 war games, even Social Democrats must have felt that the young martinet had been punished enough.[64]

Tragically, the Staatsstreich happened not under the monarchy but in the closing days of the Weimar Republic. On the pretext that the legally elected Prussian State Government could not keep order— over a five-week period Nazi storm troopers had provoked five hundred brawls in which ninety-nine people were killed—the reactionary chancellor Franz von Papen deposed "the last bastion of republicanism and Social Democracy in Germany" and declared a state of siege in Berlin. These emergency powers belonged, under Article 48 of the Weimar constitution, to the president of the republic. In 1932 this was the aged field marshal, Paul von Hindenburg, who, with Elard von Oldenburg-Januschau—he of the "shoot the Reichstag" line— whispering in his good ear, authorized Papen's move. This coup, the

Lieutenant Gunther Freiherr von Forstner (1893–1915)

last in the series begun in comedy with the "Captain from Köpenick," was "a crucial step . . . along the road towards the total elimination of democracy in Germany" that "paved the way for Hitler," who came to power eight months later.* By this time Zabern was "Saverne," France having regained Alsace-Lorraine at Versailles in 1919. But the spirit of Zabern survived—and finally came to Berlin.[65]

The lame shoe worker Karl Blank had pronounced a "terrible curse" on Lieutenant Forstner; he retaliated by slashing Blank's skull with his

---

*June 1933 saw the "Köpenick blood-week." After a young Social Democrat shot and killed three Nazi storm troopers, "the brownshirts mobilized en masse and arrested more than five hundred local men, torturing them so brutally that ninety-one of them died." Richard J. Evans, *The Third Reich in Power* (New York: Penguin, 2005), 21.

saber, gifting headline writers with a metaphor for Zabern, one of those "relatively minor happening[s]," Lenin wrote at the time, that "sometimes occur in politics when the nature of a certain order of things is revealed." The future spoke through the shoe worker, for he said, "Young man, you will soon be slaughtered!" and in February 1915, months shy of his twenty-first birthday, while the lieutenant was engaged against Russian forces in the Carpathians, that prophecy came to pass.

2

RUSSIA

SEA OF TEARS

The revolution of 1905 grew directly out of the Russo-Japanese war, just as the revolution of 1917 was the direct outcome of the great imperialist slaughter.

—Leon Trotsky

SIX MONTHS BEFORE Russia entered World War I, Tsar Nicholas II received a clairvoyant prophecy of the war's final account with his three-hundred-year-old dynasty. Regarding a secretary as being incompatible with his purgatorial view of office, the Emperor and Autocrat of All the Russias opened and read his mail himself. But whether he ever saw the so-called Durnovo Memorandum submitted to him in February 1914, warning that war would make "social revolution in its most extreme form . . . inevitable," is unknown. He was an absolute ruler; he did what he liked with Russia. So if he had taken the warning to heart, Russia might not have gone to war; there might not have been a war. Russia might have been spared a revolution; Nicholas and his family might have been spared.[1]

The memorandum, written by the reactionary statesman Peter Durnovo, argued that war would bring revolution and Russia's membership in the Triple Entente war. Therefore Russia must break with its entente partners, France and Britain. Peace could be secured, revolution skirted, only by changing sides, renewing the nonaggression pact with Germany that had lapsed in the early nineties.

The dynamic factor in world politics, Durnovo wrote, was the "rivalry" between England and Germany. By building a great battle fleet Germany threatened England's lifeline to its colonies in Africa and Asia. Since "England cannot yield without a fight . . . between her and Germany a struggle for life or death is inevitable." England was a naval power, Germany a land power. England needed continental allies (like Russia) to fight the ground war for it. In fact, the documents reveal, the British believed only a "limited" commitment on land would be necessary—"because Russia would crush Germany from the east."

"The main burden of the war will undoubtedly fall on us," since

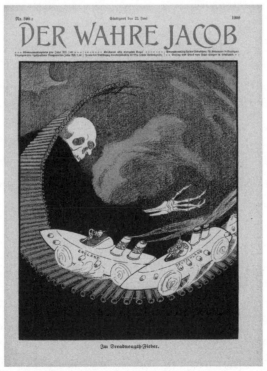

This 1909 cover of *Der Wahre Jacob* (The Real Jacob), a Socialist satirical journal with a circulation of nearly four hundred thousand, depicts the dynamic that Peter Durnovo viewed as driving the world to war. Historians demur: By 1914 Germany had given up the naval race, and as late as July 22, Lloyd George remarked the lack of "the snarling that we used to see" in Anglo-German relations.

France "poor in manpower, will probably adhere to strictly defensive
tactics . . . The part of a battering-ram, making a breach in the very
thick of the German defense, will be ours." Perhaps Russia could
fight a short war, Durnovo allowed, but not the coming war of attrition between industrialized states. "The insufficiency of war supplies" owing to the "embryonic condition of our industries" would
rapidly be exposed, and foreign sources of supply choked off.

Such a war would strain, perhaps crack, the social order. Nicholas's
rule might not survive victory, and defeat would loose an unstoppable
slide:

> The trouble will start with the blaming of the Government for all
> disasters. In the legislative institutions a bitter campaign against
> the Government will begin, followed by revolutionary agitations
> throughout the country, with Socialist slogans, capable of arous-
> ing and rallying the masses, beginning with the division of land
> and succeeded by a division of all valuables and property. The
> defeated army, having lost its most dependable men, and carried
> away by the tide of the primitive peasant desire for land, will find
> itself too demoralized to serve as a bulwark of law and order. The
> legislative institutions and intellectual opposition parties, lacking
> real authority in the eyes of the people, will be powerless to stem
> the popular tide, aroused by themselves, and Russia will be flung
> into a hopeless anarchy, the issue of which cannot be foreseen.[2]

Events vindicated that scenario in essence and detail.* Yet even as
Durnovo was circulating his views among Nicholas's ministers, his
alternative to war and revolution—détente with Germany—had
vanished like a forgotten dream. In March, the French chargé reported
"a veritable transformation in the feelings of official Russia with regard to Germany." Nicholas himself underscored the changed mood,

---

* "This document, discovered and published after the Revolution, so accurately
foretold the course of events that if its credentials were not impeccable one might
well suspect it to be a post-1917 forgery." Richard Pipes, *The Russian Revolution*
(New York: Alfred A. Knopf, 1991), 211.

telling the French ambassador that a recent German encroachment on the Turkish Straits had "made manifest the German threat to Russia's essential interests."[3]

Russia's metropolitan dailies exposed Germany's dark designs. In December 1913, *Novoe vremia*, an influential nationalist voice, editorialized that "the chief object of our foreign policy should from now on be to break that tightening Teutonic ring around us which threatens Russia and the whole of Slavdom with fatal consequences." To break the ring Russia needed to strengthen its ties to France "and convert into a firm alliance our existing indecisive agreement with England." Early in 1914 Russia began negotiating a naval convention with England. The foreign minister, Serge Sazonov, sought more—a "firm" military alliance like the one with France.[4]

In September 1913 Russian statesmen thought they saw signs that Germany wanted better relations. By February 1914 they were agreed that Germany meant Russia nothing but harm. To quote Alfred D. Chandler, the dean of business history in the United States, "History is the study of change over time." This celeritous reversal ranks as a momentous change, a precondition of World War I. In ninety days, Germany's actions, magnified by alarmed Russian perceptions, had rendered Germany's friends like Durnovo yesterday's men.[5]

The Durnovo Memorandum was the last in a series of warnings issued by the tsar's men in the crisis-charged years before 1914. From Russia's criminally unnecessary war with Japan in far-off Manchuria they drew the lesson of 1905: War would be the death of the dynasty.

The war with Japan originated in a mercenary lunge of Russian imperialism initiated by Nicholas's court favorites. To secure a timber concession in Korea, they employed a private army of Chinese bandits to extend Russia's reach down the peninsula—this in defiance of a prior Russian agreement with Japan to respect its sphere of influence there. Like nothing else since he ascended the throne in 1894, this crony-capitalist war exposed Nicholas's unfitness to rule. He knew it—"Peter Arkadevitch . . . I succeed in nothing I undertake," he once confessed to Prime Minister Peter Stolypin—but Russia's peasant millions, taught to revere him as "a being intermediate between

"Japan at Russia's Throat" from *London Illustrated Weekly.* The Russo-Japanese
War (1904–05) was a clash of rival imperialisms: Russia and Japan had
designs on the Korean peninsula. Japan was closer. It won. For Russia's
statesmen the lesson of 1905 was, No war . . . no revolution.

man and God," did not. For all but the most mystical royalists among
them, that awe died of a debacle in which Russia lost every battle on
land and sea.[6]

In a postwar memoir, a young army physician recorded the receding hopes of Russia's ill-equipped, ill-trained, badly led, haplessly
commanded, everywhere-battered army: "Earlier [soldiers] said that
the Japanese were born sailors and we would beat them on land; then
they began to say that the Japanese were used to the mountains and
we would beat them on the plain. Now they were saying that the
Japanese were used to summer and we would beat them in the winter. And everybody tried to have faith in the winter." Sergei Witte,
the prime minister who negotiated the Treaty of Portsmouth ending

the war, concluded that the army "was completely demoralized and revolutionized by defeats."[7]

Again and again in 1905, the war flowed into the revolution catalyzed that January by Bloody Sunday—the massacre, in the shadow of the Winter Palace, of striking St. Petersburg workers petitioning the tsar for "justice and protection" against their employers' abuses and his bureaucrats' indifference. The mobilization of reservists called up to fill the gaps in the ranks set off riots that fueled the revolution. The war drained the treasury of funds to cope with the revolution and deprived the government, which had dispatched Russia's one-million-man regular army to Manchuria, of the bayonets to end the storm of violence and criminality it unleashed. In September, desperate for those bayonets to picket his throne, Nicholas reached a peace settlement with Japan. The war had fed the revolution, and the revolution devoured the war.[8]

With St. Petersburg's two-thousand-man garrison too few, too weak, and too suspect to protect the government, by October 1905 the royal household was readying to flee abroad. With hope gone of riding out the maelstrom while keeping the family autocracy intact and with his uncle Nikolai drawing his revolver and threatening to shoot himself on the spot if he did not bend, Nicholas issued the October Manifesto. Along with granting civil liberties, a milestone in authoritarain Russia, it established a constitutional order, cabinet government, and Russia's first democratically elected legislature, the duma. "There was no other way out than to cross oneself and give what everyone was asking," he explained to his mother.[9]

In the vortex of war and revolution the tsarist regime had discovered the formula for its survival—"no war . . . no revolution." Following it too faithfully, however, risked undermining Russia's credibility as a Great Power. Russia's prime ministers, for whom restoring internal stability was paramount, repeatedly had to rein in her foreign and war ministers, charged with maintaining Russia's standing in the world.[10]

At an August 1907 meeting of the Council of Ministers, Prime Minister Stolypin spelled out the rationale of Russia's new domestically dictated diplomacy: "Our internal situation does not allow us to

"The Chamberpotless Tsar," from *Der Wahre Jacob* (The Real Jacob), May 1905.
Adjutant: "Majesty, they are asking for your head."
Nicholas: "Tell them I never had one."

conduct an aggressive foreign policy. The absence of fear from the point of view of international relations is extremely important for us since it will give us the opportunity to dedicate with full tranquility our strength to the repair of matters within the country." Russia's foreign policy had to buy time for the repairs to work. In a 1909 interview with a foreign journalist, Stolypin said, "Give the State twenty years of internal and external peace and you will not recognize Russia." To address the grievances that stoked the 1905 revolution, he proposed reforms ranging from granting property rights to peasants to ending discrimination against Jews. Only after this historic program and a parallel crackdown on revolutionary violence had "pacified" Russia, Stolypin insisted, could it "begin to speak its former language" in foreign affairs.[11]

Alexander Izvolski, Russia's first post–1905 foreign minister, backed

Stolypin's strategy of "being on good terms with everybody"—at first. During a Council of Ministers meeting in February 1907, he spoke against extending Russia's influence to the Persian Gulf: "The events of the last years have . . . shown the unattainability of this plan." In April he came out for abandoning Russia's forward policy in Afghanistan because it was "in insufficient accord with the real powers of the country." The minister of finance, Vladimir Kokovtsov, seconded that view: The "lessons of the past" required a "realistic" foreign policy. An early victory for realism was the Anglo-Russian entente of August 1907, which ended the so-called Great Game between the powers in Afghanistan and carved Persia into Russian and British spheres of influence.[12]

But no foreign minister could avert his eyes from the chessboard of Great Power politics for long, and in the British entente Izvolski saw an opening for a bold move. Anticipated "complications" in relations with Turkey, he declared at a January 1908 council meeting, raised anew Russia's "historical tasks in the Turkish East and the traditions of our past"—circumlocution for Russia's designs on the Turkish Straits. The foreign minister dangled the prospect of opening the straits to Russian warships—confined to the Black Sea by an international agreement of 1887, anti-Russian in origin, that had bottled up Russia's Black Sea fleet during the war with Japan. As Russia's new ally, Britain would support Russian diplomatic pressure to reopen the straits issue—perhaps even help Russia seize them by force. A border dispute between Turkey and Persia furnished the pretext for war. Unless Russia exploited this opportunity, Izvolski provocatively asserted, it would "no longer be a Great Power."

Stolypin and Kokovtsev were taken aback. The foreign minister had forgotten 1905. Stolypin, who felt "panicked terror" listening to Izvolski, italicized its lesson: "A new mobilization in Russia would lend strength to the revolution out of which we are just beginning to emerge . . . Any policy other than a purely defensive one would be at present the delirium of a Government which has lost its mind, and would bring with it danger for the Dynasty."[13]

Briefly humbled, Izvolski soon resumed his course toward the Straits. The Council of Ministers having rejected his approach to Britain, without informing the council he turned to Austria-Hungary.

In September 1908, at the Austrian foreign minister's castle in Buchlau, Izvolski and his host, Count Alois Aehrenthal, agreed on the outlines of a deal. Russia would look benignly on the annexation of Bosnia-Herzegovina by the Dual Monarchy, which under a Treaty of Berlin mandate had occupied and administered the still notionally Ottoman province since 1878. In return, Vienna would support Russia's attempt to seek a new international agreement opening the Straits to its warships. The one agreement would serve two imperialisms, Austria's over Bosnia, the first territorial acquisition made by the emperor Francis Joseph, and Russia's over the Turkish Straits.

No records were kept of the Buchlau meeting. Izvolski claimed he accepted the deal subject to the tsar's approval and the support of Paris and London. He thought he had the time to accomplish this.

"The Advance of Civilization." A Turkish caricature depicting
Austria-Hungary's 1908 Annexation of Bosnia-Herzegovina. Russia
was humiliated; Austria-Hungary cursed.

Two weeks after Buchlau he received the shock of his professional life. Aehrenthal wrote to him in Paris that in forty-eight hours Vienna would announce the annexation and counted on Russia to adopt a "friendly and benevolent attitude" toward it. A Vienna editor observed of Aehrenthal after the Buchlau meeting: "With almost rascally glee he related to me the trick he had played on Izvolsky to whom . . . he had formally announced the annexation without mentioning the moment chosen, which was imminent."[14]

Aehrenthal had played Izvolski for a fool. Stolypin threatened to resign if Nicholas, who awkwardly enough approved the overture to Austria, did not repudiate him *and* his deal. To bargain away "two Slavic provinces" to Catholic Austria to advance Russia's imperial interests—such jobbery must not stand. The Stolypin government refused to recognize the annexation and Serbia mobilized. A crisis gravid with war began that ended only in March 1909 when, lacking France's support and faced with an ultimatum from Austria's alliance partner, Germany, Russia formally recognized the annexation and at Berlin's dictate made Serbia follow suit. "The form and method of Germany's action—I mean toward us—has simply been brutal and we won't forget it," Nicholas confided to his mother.[15]

Invoking the 1905 battle in which Admiral Togo sunk a Russian fleet, the nationalist press assailed the government's capitulation as a "diplomatic Tsushima" and vociferated against the betrayal of Slavdom. "Be patient, Balkans, after Russia regains her strength she will take up her mission as protectress of the Slav world," counseled a St. Petersburg conference of Pan-Slav groups, which called on Serbia to free its fellow Slavs in Bosnia. Confident of Russian opinion, Serbia took up the challenge; a secret society of military officers targeted Bosnia with anti-Austrian propaganda and recruited Bosnian insurgents and assassins. In the words of a Serbian historian, "The crisis of 1908–9 contains all the elements that were to recur in 1914 and were the direct cause of the Great War."[16]

A second baleful legacy of the crisis was a promise by the chief of staff of the German army to his Austrian opposite number that if Austria attacked Serbia and Russia mobilized against it in response, Germany would mobilize against Russia. Bismarck thought he had ruled out that kind of commitment; the alliance he forged with Austria in 1879 was a defensive one—only an unprovoked attack on Austria, not an attack *by* it, could trigger German belligerence. Bismarck considered Austria to be on its own in the Balkans, which he assured Russia was not "worth the bones of a single Pomeranian grenadier." Fatefully renewed in July 1914, the promise of 1909 steeled Austria to confront Serbia over the assassination of Franz Ferdinand.[17]

In September 1910, Stolypin finally rid his government of Izvolski, consoled with the Paris embassy, where he schemed to revenge himself against the Central Powers. Taking no chances on another Izvolski, Stolypin secured the appointment of his brother-in-law, Serge Sazonov, Russia's ambassador to the Vatican, as the new foreign minister. "You know my views," Sazonov wrote Izvolski, miming Stolypin's. "We need peace, war during the next years, especially for reasons the people would not understand, would be fatal for Russia and for the dynasty." Because of illness, Sazonov had served with Stolypin for only a few months, when on August 31, 1911, the reforming prime minister, before Nicholas's eyes, was shot by a young man in evening dress at the Kiev Opera during an interval in Rimsky-Korsakov's *The Legend of Tsar Sultan.* "I am happy to die for the Tsar," Stolypin, sinking, avowed, and looking up at the royal box blessed Nicholas with the sign of the cross.[18]

In a system that selected for the toady, Stolypin's successor spoke his mind. Described by a former imperial official as "an intelligent man, scrupulously honest, slightly pedantic, conservative without excess, deeply patriotic and devoted to the service of the state," Vladimir Kokovtsov stood forth as the anti-Durnovo from his first decision as acting prime minister.[19]

Durnovo was minister of the interior—Russia's chief policeman—during the revolution of 1905 when his ministry subsidized pamphlets that blamed the revolution on Russia's Jews, inciting "loyal" Russians "to tear them to pieces and kill them." Encouraged to be beasts, vigilante gangs known as the Black Hundreds, carrying portraits of the tsar, mounted over three hundred pogroms (Russian for "devastation") against Jewish communities that killed more than three thousand people. No evidence links the government *directly* to the Black Hundreds, but history is not a court of law. An accessory after the fact, Nicholas granted clemency to seventeen hundred of them, many convicted of murder, and characterized the pogromists in general as "loyal people . . . outraged by the audacity and insolence of the revolutionaries and socialists, and since nine-tenths of them were Yids, then all the hostility was directed at them."[20]

Kiev was the scene of a gruesome 1905 pogrom, "an orgy of looting, rapine, and murder." Kiev would be the site of the medieval 1913 trial of Mendel Beilis, a Jewish clerk falsely accused of the ritual murder of a Christian boy in headlines like THE DRINKER OF CHRISTIAN BLOOD. Jews lived in dread in Kiev, the birthplace of Russian Christianity. With rumors spreading that Stolypin's assailant, D. G. Bogrov, a student revolutionary turned police informer turned terrorist, was a Jew, Kiev officials warned Kokovtsov that "the people . . . were preparing a tremendous Jewish pogrom" and that, since the local detachment of troops was away on maneuvers, nothing could stop it. Panic broke out in the Jewish neighborhoods. At first light whole families began to converge on the railroad station, anxiously watching the tracks for the first train. "Even as they waited, the terrified people heard the clatter of hoofs. An endless stream of Cossacks, their long lances dark against the dawn sky, rode past. On his own, Kokovtsov had ordered three full regiments of cossacks into the city to prevent violence." Calm returned, Kokovtsov recorded in his memoirs, "the exodus . . . stopped, and on the following day life resumed its normal course."[21]

At a mass held to pray for the gravely wounded Stolypin's recovery, a local member of the duma revulsed Kokovtsov by observing, "Well, Your High Excellency, by calling in the troops you have missed a fine chance to answer Bogrov's shot with a nice Jewish pogrom." Kokovtsov "could not conceal [his] indignation at such a remark," which awoke him to the necessity of doing more. "Directly after the mass, therefore, I sent an open telegram to all governors of this region demanding that they use every possible means—force if necessary—to prevent . . . pogroms." Rising above his prejudices ("An Englishman is a Yid!"), Nicholas gave Kokovtsov's order his "full approval,"

Vladimir Kokovtsov. Any system that produced
leaders of his character could not be *all* bad.

remarking, "What a nightmare to take revenge upon the guiltless
mass for the crime of one Jew."[22]*

From 1911 to early 1914, Kokovtsov pursued Stolypin's "peace at
almost any cost" policy against strengthening nationalist sentiment in
the duma, in the conservative press, and in a divided cabinet. A cabal
of ministers portrayed Kokovtsov's "policy of caution" to Nicholas
"as a proof of my personal cowardice and as the professional ruse of a
Minister of Finance to ensure at all costs the financial well-being of
his country."[23]

Kokovtsov's counsel of restraint in external policy had domestic
roots. "No one dreaded war for Russia as much as Kokovtsov," a
Russian diplomat wrote of him, "for he was aware both of our lack
of military preparation and of the revolutionary ferment which was
penetrating ever more deeply into the lower classes and daily gaining
ground."

---

* "Dull-witted and scared, an all-powerful nonentity, the prey of prejudices wor-
thy of an Eskimo, the royal blood in his veins poisoned by all the vices of many
generations, Nicholas Romanov, like many others of his profession, combined filthy
sensuality with apathetic cruelty." Leon Trotsky, *1905* (New York: Random House,
1971), 135.

As finance minister (he retained that portfolio after Nicholas named him prime minister), Kokovtsov monitored warily what the military did with the money he appropriated. In a 1913 meeting at his country house with the French chief of staff, Joseph Joffre, Kokovtsov showed Joffre figures documenting that the Ministry of War had yet to spend more than two hundred million gold rubles, or five hundred million gold francs, that Kokovtsov had earmarked for the military. "The amazement of the Frenchman at this knew no bounds," he recalled.

As chairman of a commission formed after Bloody Sunday to investigate the working conditions of industrial laborers, Kokovtsov learned firsthand why the revolution began in the factories. The petition carried by the Petersburg workers on Bloody Sunday protested hunger wages, punishing hours, no workers' compensation for injuries, no pensions for old age. The reforms proposed by the Kokovtsov Commission—from state-mandated accident and health insurance to paid maternity leave to pensions for all workers over fifty-five— would have vaulted Russia ahead of other industrialized countries in lifting the burden on those Theodore Roosevelt called "the crushable elements at the bottom of our industrial civilization." But familiar objections from industrialists—that a shortened working day would disadvantage Russia in international trade, for example—stalled progress until 1912, when the duma finally passed a watered-down version of the Stolypin-Kokovtsov program.[24]

In subordinating foreign to domestic policy, Kokovtsov had the support of his foreign minister but, mercurial in temperament, Sazonov needed steadying. Their "Izvolski" was the minister of war, General V. A. Sukhomlinov.

A rum character, Sukhomlinov captivated Nicholas by saucing his reports with jokes, anecdotes, and "surprise twists." One court watcher marveled at the way he held the tsar "in suspense right up to the last minute, even if his audience lasted a couple of hours." His colleagues, spared the raconteur, resisted his spell. In Sazonov's view, "It was very difficult to make him work, but to get him to speak the truth was well-nigh impossible."[25]

To the French ambassador, Sukhomlinov ("a small chubby man with a fat feline face") presented the spectacle of a sexually exhausted husband—his wife, described by an admirer as "a platinum blonde with wonderful blue eyes, a fascinating, intelligent, dangerous woman," being thirty years his junior. To maintain her hundred-thousand-ruble-a-year taste for exotic travel, sable furs, Paris gowns, and Fabergé objets d'art, as well as to pay European doctors to treat her kidney condition, Sukhomlinov accepted bribes from Vickers, the Anglo-American weapons manufacturer. Since Vickers' bid to produce light machine guns was 43 percent higher per weapon than that of Russia's Tula Armament Works, Russia would enter World War I with only four thousand machine guns to Germany's twenty-four thousand, owing in part to the exorbitant terms of the war minister's marriage.[26]

As war minister, Sukhomlinov reported above the prime minister to the tsar, a structural invitation to mischief that left Nicholas at the mercy of himself. A near-catastrophic incident in November 1912 that reverberated in the decision for war in 1914 dramatized the folly of that.

Fecklessly encouraged by Sazonov, in early 1912 Serbia and Bulgaria formed a Slavic league; then, joined by Montenegro and Greece, a Balkan League. Its purpose was to make war on Turkey. "Slavic banquets" were held in Petersburg to raise money for "our little Slavic brothers" in the Balkans, fighting to drive the Turk out of Europe for the first time in five hundred years, and to pressure the government not to leave them "in the lurch." Nicholas, who resented the idea of "public opinion," dismissed the Pan-Slav agitation, blaming it, risibly, on the usual suspects: "In Russia no decent person wants war for the sake of the Slavs; only the wretched Jewish newspapers . . . write that public opinion is stirred—it is a lie and calumny," he told his constant confidante.[27]

Pan-Slav opinion was exercised not only against Turkey but also against another power threatening Serbia over its reach for an Adriatic port from the territory—modern Albania—vacated by the retreating Turks. Speaking in the duma, a leader of the extreme right declared that "the hour has struck to settle accounts with our historic enemy, with that patchwork monarchy"—with Austria-Hungary.[28]

Such was the weave of events when, on the evening of November 22, 1912, Sukhomlinov telephoned Kokovtsov: The tsar wanted to see him and Sazonov the next morning. The minister of war had no idea why.

Before a map spread out on a table in his Tsarskoe Selo study, Nicholas informed his incredulous prime minister that to rectify an imbalance of forces developing vis-à-vis Austria, he had ordered the mobilization of the army divisions assigned to Russia's Austrian frontier, some 1.1 million men.[29]

The minister of war wanted to dispatch the orders "yesterday," but Nicholas thought it prudent first to sound out "those ministers who ought to be apprised of it"—Kokovtsov, Sazonov, and S. V. Rukhlov, the minister of communications.

"We three looked at each other with the greatest amazement," Kokovtsov recalled in his memoirs, "and only the presence of the Tsar restrained us from giving vent to the feelings which animated all of us . . . I spoke first and had to struggle to retain my composure."

The minister of war "apparently did not perceive" what European statesmen and generals had understood for a generation—that mobilization meant war with Austria and Germany. "The mobilization is the declaration of war," the chief of the French General Staff, General Charles Boisdeffre, had told Alexander III the day after France and Russia concluded their military alliance in July 1892. "To mobilize is to oblige one's neighbor to do the same," the general explained. "If your neighbor mobilizes a million men on your frontier and you do nothing you are like the man who, with a pistol in his pocket, should let a neighbor put a weapon to his forehead without drawing his own." Alexander agreed: "That is exactly the way I understand it."[30]

His son did not understand it at all. "I do not, just as yourself, Vladimir Nikolaevich, allow the thought of imminent war," he said. The mobilization was a "simple measure of precaution." The Germans, Kokovtsov came back, would not care what the tsar called mobilization. They would counter it with "actual war." Nicholas said he had no intention of mobilizing against Germany. Austria—which "is openly hostile and has taken a series of steps against us," including partially mobilizing against Serbia and showing signs of mobilization near the Russian border in Galicia—was the intended recipient of this warning signal. But, Kokovtsov pointed out, Germany and Austria were bound together: "These two countries could not be considered separately." Moreover, to mobilize against them without first consulting Russia's ally, France, would "permit France to repudiate her obligations to us." Russia would have to fight Germany and

Austria-Hungary alone, the nightmare to escape which Alexander, overcoming his political aversions, so far as to listen bareheaded to the Marseillaise at the Kronstadt Naval Base in 1891, had forged what George F. Kennan termed "the fateful alliance" with republican France—the doomsday machine of World War I.*[31]

Kokovtsov was righter than he knew about Germany. Days after the conference in the tsar's study, Kaiser Wilhelm, anticipating an aggressive Russian response to the Austrian troop buildup in Galicia, instructed his secretary of state: "Should Russian counter-measures or protests ensue which force the Emperor Francis Joseph to begin war, then he will have the right on his side and I am ready . . . to apply the *casus foederis* [the catalyst for the terms of an alliance to come into play] in the fullest measure and with all its consequences." He conveyed this message personally to the Austrian archduke, Franz Ferdinand, then visiting Berlin. "Emperor William says that as soon as our prestige demands it we should take energetic action in Serbia, and we can be certain of his support . . . More details Sunday verbally," he cabled Vienna. So the Russian mobilization against Austria would, it seems, have triggered war with Germany.[32]

But Kokovtsov was wrong about France, which, even without being consulted, might have joined in. Under their defensive military agreement, France was not obligated to aid Russia if Russia attacked Austria. But the French were in increasing doubt whether they could rely on a Russia frozen by fear of revolution to honor its side of the agreement and attack Germany if Germany attacked France. In the Morocco crises of 1905 and 1911, when as we will see Germany faced down France, the Russians signaled they were not ready for war; their internal condition would not permit it; they needed more time. Gen-

---

*In negotiating the Franco-Russian Military Convention and treaty of January 1894, "General Obruchev, Chief of the Russian General Staff, emphatically denied the possibility of a partial Russian mobilization against Austria [alone]" on technical grounds and because, as he explained to his French counterpart, "in making a partial mobilization we should expose ourselves to too great dangers with the menace of a rapid attack from Germany." The French wanted reassurance that Russia would not fight its own war against Austria-Hungary, leaving them to face Germany alone. L. C. F. Turner, "The Russian Mobilization in 1914," *Journal of Contemporary History* 3, no. 1 (January 1968): 66.

eral Joffre "questioned whether Russia could mobilize and implement her war plan without being paralyzed by internal disturbances." Earlier in 1912 the Russians confided to their ally that "even if Austria should attack Serbia, Russia will not fight," which could not have buoyed French confidence in Russia's will to fight for France. "[General Ferdinand Foch] says that he doesn't think Russia would actually interfere if Germany and France were to fight about Belgium," Sir Henry Wilson, British liaison to the French General Staff, noted. "In short, Foch is of opinion that, in the coming war in Belgium, France must trust to England and not to Russia."

French diplomats signaled a willingness to transform the Franco-Russian alliance from a defensive to an offensive one, if that was the only way to keep Russia in it. "Leading French military men," according to Wilson, went further; they wanted to get the big war with Germany over with now, when "in consequence of Balkan difficulties" they could count on "the whole-hearted support of Russia." On November 17, a week before the Tsarskoe Selo conference, then prime minister Raymond Poincaré crystallized France's new understanding of the Dual Alliance in a remark attributed to him (wrongly, he claimed after the war) by Izvolski: "If Russia goes to war, France too will go to war." In speaking so boldly to Russia, Poincaré may have hoped to cue the Russians to speak as boldly to France.[33]

Poincaré not only shifted the alliance's axis from defense toward offense, he also extended the alliance to Russia's Balkan ally, and that security guarantee, made without consulting the French people, enabled the war. In July 1914, after Austria showed unmistakenly that it intended to attack Serbia, the British ambassador cabled London with the Russian reaction: "Russia cannot allow Austria to crush Serbia and, secure of support of France, she will face all the risks of war." France had given her support because the implications of Russia's post-1905 formula—"no war . . . no revolution"—made her fear for her own security.

At the Tsarskoe Selo conference Kokovtsov ended his recital of the mysteries of mobilization with a plea to Nicholas to face "the sad actuality." Russia was "not ready for a war and our adversaries knew it well." The mobilization signal was a suicide note. He proposed that Russia send an alternative signal by extending the term of military service for Russian conscripts by six months; that would increase Russian manpower by one fourth, rectifying the perceived imbalance of forces that concerned Nicholas.

Quickly resigned to God's will when the Japanese sunk his fleet at Tsushima, Nicholas saved his anger for bad manners. Kokoktsov's "sharp thrusts at the Minister of War" had displeased him. Now he thanked the prime minister for suggesting a "splendid way out of our difficulties."

Nicholas then invited Sukhomlinov to speak.

"I agree with the views expressed by the Chairman of the Council and beg to be permitted to send telegrams to Generals Ivanov and Skalon that no mobilization should be undertaken," he said, and fell silent.

"Of course," Nicholas, ever emollient, responded.* How could he be angry with Sukhomlinov for dispatching the marching orders for continental war when they were *his* orders? Sukhomlinov habitually told Nicholas what he wanted to hear about the state of the Russian army—on one occasion, extolling as a success a failed horse mobilization in Kazan. Yet even after discovering that Sukhomlinov had lied about the Kazan exercise, after catching him in other trivial lies, Nicholas kept him on through the first year of the war. Later, in 1917, the Russian Provisional Government, in Russia's first "show trial," convicted Sukhomlinov of treasonable incompetence, corruption, and for having alleged Austrian spies as friends. Sentenced to life at hard

---

* "Although Kokovtsov's is the only detailed description of these events, other accounts testify that such a measure was under consideration . . . Diplomats in western Russia, and in the capital, reported rumors of a mobilization for the first two weeks of November. It was widely felt that 'military circles' were pressing for a strong stand against an anticipated Austrian aggression on Serbia." David MacLaren McDonald, *United Government and Foreign Policy in Russia 1900–1914* (Cambridge: Harvard University Press, 1992), 186. Interministerial conflict over resources also played a role in the mobilization. Sukhomlinov had exploited earlier war scares to pressure Kokovtsov to increase the military budget. Just a month earlier, Kokovtsov had refused his request for sixty-three million rubles to strengthen the defenses along the Austrian border. To get those rubles, he may have talked Nicholas into a mobilization, nearly topping his war scare with a war. See William C. Fuller Jr., *Civil-Military Conflict in Imperial Russia, 1881–1914* (Princeton: Princeton University Press, 1985), 223–24.

labor, he was spared only by his young wife's way with officials and
by the Bolshevik Revolution.[34]

"Russia is not ready for war" . . . "war would be a catastrophe" . . .
"war would bring revolution": Russia's would-be enemies overheard
Russia's leaders talking down Russian power and drew the conclusion reached by Wilhelm II. Russia "did not inspire him with any
worry," the kaiser told the Austrian foreign minister in 1913. "Haunted
by the specter of revolution," it could not make war for four or five
years. German strategists had settled on 1917 as the year of danger. By
then Russia's railways to Germany's frontier would be completed, the
Russian army would be bigger by half a million men, and Stolypin's
reforms and an expanding economy would have pared the risk of
revolution. Brooding on Russia's future, the German chancellor, Bethmann Hollweg, turned fatalistic, telling his son that planting new trees
on their estate near Berlin hardly made sense since "in a few years the
Russians would be here anyway." The perception of Russia as weak
now, stronger later, encouraged "now or never" arguments for "preventive" war and emboldened reckless diplomacy.[35]

In this climate, Germany precipitated "the last (and decisive) diplomatic crisis between [it] and Russia before the war." In December 1913,
the kaiser sent General Liman von Sanders to command a Turkish
army corps based in Constantinople on the Bosporus Strait. A. J. P.
Taylor put what that meant for Russia dramatically: "Previously
Germany had been estranged from Russia only indirectly because of
Austria-Hungary; now the two countries had a direct cause of conflict for the first time in their history."[36]

Nearly all of Russia's grain, "the most important item in the Russian economy, which guaranteed Russia a positive trade balance and
let the Russian state make regular interest payments on its foreign
loans," passed through the Bosporus. After the Balkan crisis Sazonov
resolved that Russia should never go to war for one of the Slav states
(a resolve he would break in July 1914 when Russia went to war for
Serbia) but "only for her vital interests." Asked by the French ambassador to identify one, he answered, "We shall not tolerate a change in
the status quo in the Straits. On the Bosphorus [sic] there can only be
either the Turks or ourselves."[37]

Persuaded by Russia's "peace at almost any price" foreign policy that Russia would stand for almost anything, Germany raised the price—and changed Russian minds irrevocably.

After the "Liman von Sanders affair," Peter Durnovo would be the last Russian statesman to argue that there were no territorial or strategic issues preventing "the conservative powers" from building an alliance around their ideological bond. "It was commonly supposed that there was nothing to keep Germany and Russia apart," the British ambassador reported Nicholas remarking in March 1914. "This was, however, not the case . . . From a secret source in Vienna he had reason to believe that Germany was aiming at acquiring such a position in Constantinople as would enable her to shut in Russia altogether in the Black Sea. Should she attempt to carry out this policy He would have to resist it with all His power, even should war be the only alternative." In substance that was Nicholas's rejoinder to the Durnovo Memorandum.[38]

The von Sanders appointment took flame only in November 1913, when the Russian Foreign Office first learned of it from a Turkish source and queried Berlin. General von Sanders and his retinue of officers would leave for Constantinople within the month, the Russians were told. His mission was a matter strictly between Germany and Turkey. It was a fait accompli—it would go ahead as planned.

The grand vizier of the Ottoman Empire had requested "a suitable Prussian officer" to organize the defenses of Constantinople. The city, on the European side of the Bosporus, was still vulnerable to attack by the forces of Bulgaria, one of the coalition of small states that in four months of war had pushed Turkey out of the Balkans.

A suitable Prussian officer was easily arranged: German officers had been instructing the Turkish army for decades (poorly, to judge from its rout by the Balkan states). But the German ambassador in Constantinople, Baron Hans von Wangenheim, saw imperialist possibilities in the new mission. Under the guise of "reforming" the Turkish army, he wrote in an April 26, 1913, cable to Berlin, Germany would transform Turkey into its protectorate as Britain had done with Egypt. "There is a large group of people here who would like to place Turkey completely under the direction of German instructors with the most extensive powers," Wangenheim reported, alluding to the young turks around Enver Pasha, the minister of war, and Talaat Pasha, minister of the interior.* From atop a "reformed" Turkish army a suitable Prussian officer could not only secure German territorial and economic interests in the Near East, like the Berlin-Baghdad railway, but also plan the strategy and operations of a "future war."[39]

Time would truncate the most grandiose features of von Wangenheim's scheme ("Many good intentions but much that is fantastic!" the kaiser wrote in the margin of the cable), but not this one.[40]

When, on August 2, 1914, Turkey and Germany concluded an offensive and defensive alliance against Russia, General von Sanders, on the ground since December, assumed effective command of the Turkish army. As Wangenheim had foreseen, for the next four years "Liman Pasha" directed the Turkish war effort, including the defense of the Dardanelles and the Gallipoli Peninsula, of sorrowful memory in Australia and New Zealand. Having prepared their gun emplacements beginning two months before Sarajevo, German artillerists closed the Straits against Russian shipping, severing the only all-season line of communications between Russia and its allies, stoppering its grain exports, and starving its army of supplies. Defeat, and revolution, followed. "In the perspective of history, Bolshevism may well appear as nothing more than the economic consequences of the closing of the Straits."[41]

From the first, the Russians treated the von Sanders mission like a reconnaissance for Wangenheim's "future war." They could hardly believe it: Germany was trying to seize "the keys and gates to the Russian house."

Kokovtsov was in Berlin when the von Sanders story broke. Returning home from Paris after weeks spent negotiating a 500-million-franc loan to build railroads, including those "strategic" lines to Russia's

---

*Wangenheim makes the Young Turks sound like fools. In fact, while acknowledging her imperial ambitions, they recognized that Germany and the Ottoman Empire shared a common strategic goal—containing an expanding "Slavdom." Theirs was an alliance of mutual convenience. See Mustafa Aksakal, "War as Savior? Hopes for War and Peace in Ottoman Politics Before 1914," in Holger Afflerbach and David Stevenson, eds., *An Improbable War? The Outbreak of World War I and European Political Culture before 1914* (New York: Berghahn Books, 2007), 296.

borders with Germany so worrying to Bethmann, he had stopped in Berlin to thank the kaiser for decorating him with the Order of the Black Eagle. His rarely cited memoirs, as those by no other statesman of the time, present extended scenes with both the tsar and the kaiser.

Sazonov telegraphed the details. The tsar tasked Kokovtsov with "requesting an explanation from the German government regarding its intentions concerning General Liman von Sanders and with announcing that we shall on no account agree to its plan."[42]

Carrying this peremptory demarche with him, Kokovtsov called on Bethmann Hollweg. The kaiser and his military cabinet had sent von Sanders; the chancellor had learned of it only at the same time as the Russians. German foreign policy was being made by the military clique that spurned government oversight in the Zabern Affair and with the same insouciance toward political complications. Now in the loop, Bethmann told Kokovtsov that he was at a loss to understand Russian protestations over von Sanders, since the tsar, in conversation with the kaiser, had approved the mission in May, when in Potsdam for the wedding of the kaiser's daughter, the Princess Louise.* If

---

*This marked the last occasion when the three royal cousins—Kaiser Wilhelm, Tsar Nicholas II, and King George V of Great Britain—were together. Every time he met privately with "Nicky" "Georgie" felt that "Willy's" ear was "glued to the keyhole." It's unlikely that Willy overheard anything significant. In an age of nationalism, family ties between rulers counted for little. Moreover, "monarchical government and, even more so, monarchical solidarity had ceased to be a trump card in international affairs." Willy was an obnoxious presence to Nicky and an object of detestation to his German wife, Alexandra. The "Willy-Nicky" correspondence, first released in 1917 by Russia's provisional government, shows Nicky acceding to Willy's importunities to make war on Japan or to sign a peace treaty with Germany without telling Nicky's ally, France—records Nicky saying yes to just about anything to shut Willy up. "The more one studies these telegrams the more one realizes how completely 'Nicky' was as clay in 'Willy's' hands," the American historian Sidney B. Fay wrote in 1918. Warmer relations might have weighed in the scales of peace in July 1914. Whether the strain between them, unacknowledged by Willy, made things worse is debatable. "The relationship between the three, their personal likes and dislikes, did indeed contribute to the outbreak of hostilities," Catrine Clay argues in *King, Kaiser, Tsar: Three Royal Cousins Who Led the World to War* (New York: Walker & Co., 2006). Robert A. Kann is less sure. "One would hesitate to say that the Tsar's dislike of the Kaiser had in itself a decisive influence on the tragic turn of events in 1914." He goes on: "After all, Russian policy was determined far less by relations with Germany than by relations

Nicholas had not seen fit to share the information with his own government, Bethmann implied, the German government could hardly be blamed.

"I sensed that war was becoming inevitable," Bethmann, speaking of this meeting, told a Berlin journalist in an off-the-record interview in 1915, and that it would start when Russia's rail lines through Poland were finished. Bethmann claimed that he "sensed from [Kokovtsov] that he himself feared this would set the war in motion."

The next day the emperor and empress received Kokovtsov at their Potsdam palace. Wilhelm wore the uniform of a colonel in a Russian regiment. As a private joke Nicholas had once given him the uniform of a "guard's regiment" that, unbeknownst to Wilhelm, had occupied Berlin during the Seven Years' War; perhaps this was the same one. Over lunch Kokovtsov voiced his "regret" that Germany had not informed Russia of the von Sanders mission "until this late date." But he *had* informed Nicholas, the kaiser insisted, and he found the tsar's "interference now that all the details had been arranged . . . inconsistent" and irritating.[43]

Kokovtsov sat on the kaiser's right at the luncheon table; a Russian colleague, L. F. Davydov, the director of the Special Credit Office, on his left. Wilhelm vented his irritation on this subordinate. The French loan to finance commercial railways in Russia, the kaiser complained, could also be used to construct "strategic railways," could it not? Next, he decried the "Germanophobia" in the French, British, and Russian papers. Then, the political unconscious punching through his vexation over a bad press, came a whiff of Armageddon: "The outbursts of your press . . . have become insufferable; they will lead inevitably to a catastrophe which I shall be powerless to avert." Nodding at Kokovtsov, the kaiser said, "Tell this to your chief."

Davydov began to explain about the "unruly . . . Russian press,"

---

with Austria-Hungary . . . German policy . . . was predetermined not by imperial likes and dislikes but by the alleged necessity to support the one reliable ally, Austria-Hungary, at any price." See Robert A. Kann, "Dynastic Relations and European Power Politics (1848–1918)" in *Journal of Modern History* 45, no. 3 (September 1973): 399–400. The quotation above about monarchical solidarity is from 406. For correspondence, see S. B. Fay, "The Kaiser's Secret Negotiations with the Tsar, 1904–1905" in *American Historical Review* 24, no. 1 (October 1918): 49.

pointing out how many papers were against the government and how little under Russian law it could do to censor what they published. "Can I help it if the situation is as you say?" the kaiser broke in. "Nevertheless I must tell you frankly that I fear there will be a clash between Slav and German, and I feel it my duty to apprise you of this fact." In a 1912 letter Wilhelm phrased this scenario more bluntly: "There is about to be a *racial struggle* between the Teutons and the Slavs who have become uppish."

Verbal violence was habitual with the kaiser. "He's raving mad!" Nicholas declared after suffering Wilhelm's feverish talk, punctuated by slaps on the back and pokes in the Romanov ribs, through an interminable 1902 weekend at Reval. Still, even discounting for his chronic vehemence, the kaiser's darkening mind licensed a dark Russian fear: Was the von Sanders mission the first move in a race war?[44]

Kokovtsov had not, after all, shown Sazonov's cable to Bethmann, forfeiting visual impact. Worse, on the eve of his departure from Berlin, he undercut the message Sazonov wanted conveyed ("we shall on no account agree to its plan") by remarks made in an interview with Theodor Wolff, editor of the *Berliner Tageblatt*, remarks that can only have reinforced the kaiser's belief that Russia's instability meant Russia was not ready for war. Wolff asked if the Russian prime minister "thought Russia's domestic peace could be preserved," given the impression in Germany that "the revolutionary movement" was deeply rooted. Kokovtsov replied that "revolutionary outbursts" being reported in the German press were confined to a few industrial centers. But, yes, "Russia needed peace more than any other country" to continue her rapid growth of the last seven years. Russia needed peace more than any other country . . . Germany counted on it.[45]

On December 14, 1913, General Liman von Sanders and the forty officers of his mission arrived in Constantinople, met at the terminal of the Hamburg-Baghdad railway, Sanders recalled, "by a company of a regiment . . . which I found later in the Dardanelles campaign to be an elite body of troops." Having vainly protested his going, the Russians now vainly protested his staying.[46]

They proposed a face-saving compromise: Sanders to stay but his

General Liman von Sanders. His presence in Constantinople was
historic. It gave Russia and Germany something they never
had before—a reason to fight.

command shifted to an army corps not based in Constantinople. The
Germans suggested an alternative, one their Major von Strempel, the
military attaché in Constantinople, had recommended in November
when the Russian storm broke, as a more advantageous arrangement for
Germany than the original Sanders mission: "If the German General
were Inspector-General . . . then he would have much more to say than
as a mere Chief of the Mission and Commanding General of a Corps."
Late in December 1913, Ambassador von Wangenheim cabled Berlin:
"We must try our best to offer Russia a sop." Sanders based in Constantinople as inspector general of the whole Turkish army was the sop.[47]

Russia's nationalist press was not fooled. Did Russia's diplomats
"really believe that by giving the German generals greater authority
over the Turkish forces than originally envisioned they had gained
a victory over anybody?" *Novoe vremia* asked. Nor was the Russian
military attaché in Constantinople, who warned St. Petersburg: "The
Germans weren't training the Turkish army for a war with Greece
but for a future European clash in which they counted on being able
to throw it on the scales on Germany's side."[48]

But the Russians had no choice. Their entente partners were unwilling to back their hard line; with an adviser attached to the Turkish

"The Opportunity of the Year 1914" by Alberto Martini. This Italian
postcard depicts the kaiser's courtship of Islam. The feathers allude to the sultan,
who kept peacocks at his court. Wilhelm holds a cup of blood. The hairy
figure on the left readying to ignite the globe is Death.

navy, Britain could not support Russia's call for the removal of a German adviser to the Turkish army. It was the sop or war. They chose the sop, making one condition—that to assuage Russian opinion the change of mission be announced at once. The Germans were sorry; they could not do that. Their public was aroused, too. As the German deputy foreign minister Arthur Zimmermann explained to Sazonov, the Reichstag debate over the army's conduct in Zabern had placed the government in a "very precarious position." It would be months before Germany could shift von Sanders to his new post, weeks before the deal could be publicly announced. Meanwhile, the Russians should trust in Germany's good intentions.[49]

Germany had *no* good intentions toward Russia. Nicholas and Sazonov had now to face the implications of that epiphany. International relations theorists use the Liman affair as a case study in threat perception. Lacking trustworthy communication between them, rival states govern their behavior toward each other by observing mutually understood rules of the game. The von Sanders mission broke the rules. "The sign from which an intention is inferred consists of stepping over a 'boundary' on a conceptual dimension," according to one theorist. "The boundary was created, whether tacitly or explicitly, as a mutually recognized and recognizable limitation of other actors' behavior. Beyond it there is unlikely . . . to be another stopping place . . . Since the boundary . . . marks the only agreed restraint on action, the victim will understand the infringement as a statement of intent by his opponent to proceed further," an action that he "would only have undertaken if he were prepared to risk conflict. Therefore, the victim will conclude, his action can only be interpreted as a challenge to the existing balance of relations as whole." To Sazonov, Germany was breaking the "gentleman's agreement" on equality of status among the Great Powers in Constantinople. Seeking a "privileged position," it threatened to upset the "balance of powers" in the Ottoman Empire, he told the French ambassador.[50]

In an emergency meeting on January 13, 1914, amid not-yet-confirmed reports that the Germans would shortly announce von Sanders's transfer to inspector general after all, the tsar's ministers met to decide what to do.[51]

In a long memorandum to Nicholas, Sazonov set the agenda, advocating coercing the Turks to expel von Sanders—perhaps by occupying a Turkish city on the Black Sea coast. Act forcefully over Germans at the Straits, Sazonov urged, or risk losing Russia's allies: "In France and England there would be strengthened the dangerous conviction that Russia will accept any conditions whatever for the preservation of peace" because of her internal condition "and each of them would endeavor to seek security . . . by making agreements with the powers of the opposite camp." France ally itself with Germany because Russia declined to attack *Turkey*? Offended that Bethmann had told him nothing about the von Sanders mission when they met in Berlin in October (Bethmann knew nothing about it then), Sazonov let his pique rule his judgment.

At the conference on the thirteenth, Kokovtsov, stipulating that "the potential for revolutionary unrest" remained strong, rallied his divided cabinet against Sazonov's daft proposal. Seizing a Turkish city "would inevitably be followed by war with Germany." Then he came up with an inspired framing: "Is war with Germany desirable and can Russia wage it?" There could be only one answer to that— how can any war be *desirable*?—and the cabinet gave it, unanimously. It was Kokovtsov's final service to Nicholas, who fired him two weeks later, "like a domestic," Nicholas's uncle remarked, sending him his notice by messenger.[52]

"Strange as it may seem," Vladimir Kokovtsov wrote in his 1935 memoirs, "the question of Rasputin" not only convulsed public life during his two years as prime minister, it entangled Kokovtsov and pulled him down.

Notorious still, Rasputin wandered into history as the *"starets* from Siberia," the type of self-anointed holy man venerated by simple folk like the "many thousands of Orthodox people" of Tsaritsyn who signed a petition attesting that Rasputin bore "the marks of divine vocation" and listing "thaumaturgy" among his "gifts of grace." Stopping bleeding, perhaps through hypnosis, was his signature gift. Beginning in 1905, it made him a fixture at the court of Nicholas and Alexandra, a power behind the throne, and a scandal to Russia's educated classes. He won royal favor by stopping the internal bleeding of the hemophiliac *tsarevich*, Alexis. Where doctors failed, Rasputin succeeded. Neither the testimony of their governess that he spied on the tsar's four daughters as they changed into their nightgowns, nor allegations by the Orthodox hierarchy that he belonged to a banned sect of flagellants "who preached that sinning reduced the quantity of sin in the world," nor dossiers of his misdeeds compiled by Stolypin could break the royal couple's attachment to the manipulative "Man of God," who, sensing a chill, reminded the empress: "If I am not

Grigori Rasputin (1869–1916). This Russian book cover from 1922 captures
the rogue's hypnotic stare. According to French president Raymond Poincaré,
who twice visited Russia, Rasputin "so completely dominated [the Empress] that
every evening in her presence, under pretext of exorcising the Grand Duchesses,
he slips his hands for some moments under their bedclothes."

there to protect you, you will lose your crown and your son within
six months."[53]*

Public comment on Rasputin was conducted in whispers and

---

*Richard Pipes regards it as doubtful whether Rasputin possessed the extraordi-
nary "sexual prowess" with which his legend endows him. A doctor who treated
Rasputin after a "jealous mistress" stabbed him in June 1914 found his "genitals
shriveled, like those of a very old man." The doctor "ascribed this to the effects of
alcohol and syphilis." Protected by the Tsarina, Rasputin "felt above the law." Pipes
offered this example: In March 1915, the chief of the Corps of Gendarmes, V. F.
Dzhunkovskii, had the courage to inform the tsar that his agents had overheard
Rasputin boast at a dinner party at Moscow's Praga Restaurant that he 'could do
anything he wanted with the Empress.' His reward was to be sacked and sent to the
front." Richard Pipes, *The Russian Revolution* (New York: Knopf, 1991), 259–60.

euphemisms. It took a sensational incident late in 1911 to surface the "Rasputin question." "This incident was discussed everywhere—in the newspapers, in high circles of society, in government offices, and in the lobbies of the Duma," according to Kokovtsov. On December 29, two disillusioned former allies of Rasputin, a monk and a bishop, aided by one Mitya Kolyaba, a deformed holy fool, lured Rasputin to the monk's room in Petersburg to grill him over accusations that he had raped a nun. With his good hand Mitya grabbed Rasputin by the penis and held it in his fanatic grip while the bishop, shouting, "Is this true? Is this true?" clubbed him with a heavy cross. Bludgeoned into a confession, Rasputin burst out. "It's true, it's true, it's all true!" It almost certainly was.[54]

With material like this to run with, the press taboo on Rasputin, enforced by fines, broke down. To quote a leading Moscow journal, that "cunning conspirator against our Holy Church, that fornicator of human souls and bodies—Gregory Rasputin" sold newspapers. The *Rasputinshchina* roiled politics. In the duma, voices called for the government to do something.[55]

In early February 1912, Kokovtsov "was amazed" to receive a note from Rasputin: "I am thinking of leaving forever and would like to see you so as to exchange some ideas; people talk much of me nowadays. Say when."

Rasputin sought the meeting at Alexandra's behest to "examine [the] soul" of the new prime minister. Hoping against probability to "show Rasputin that he was digging a grave for the Tsar," Kokovtsov sent for him.[56]

With his deep-set, small gray eyes, the bearded starets first turned his mesmeric stare on Kokovtsov; then tried his luck with the ceiling; then the floor. All without saying a word. At length Kokovtsov asked, "You wanted to tell me something?"

"Well, shall I go? Life has been hard for me here . . ."

"Indeed, you would do well to go away," Kokovtsov recalled saying. He spoke unguardedly: Rasputin's presence harmed the monarchy and Russia. "I do not insist on going to the royal palace—they summon me," Rasputin insisted. He would return to his village. "But mind, let them take care not to call me back." The next day, reporting on his conversation with Kokovtsov, he poisoned the well with Alexandra. Within hours word reached Kokovtsov that he was in trouble.[57]

To set things right he met with the tsar, who asked if he had threatened to deport Rasputin if he did not leave St. Petersburg voluntarily. Kokovtsov assured him he had said nothing of the kind. Relieved, Nicholas solicited his impressions of the "little peasant."

Kokovtsov "held nothing back," telling Nicholas what he testified to a committee set up after the February revolution to investigate Rasputin's influence on state policy. In the eleven years he served in the Central Prison Administration, he saw "many Rasputins among the Siberian vagrants . . . men who, while making the sign of the cross, could take you by the throat and strangle you with the same smile on their faces." Nicholas stared out the window as Kokovtsov ripped the one person on earth who could stop his son's bleeding and stay his wife's despair.[58]

Nicholas assured Alexandra that Kokovtsov intended no threat to Rasputin. If he left, it would be by his own wish. That failed to mollify her. She could not fathom why Kokovtsov permitted the press to attack her "Friend," and could only imagine that, in his words, he was "a tool of the enemies of the state and, as such, deserving dismissal." On Kokovtsov's next visit to the summer palace at Yalta, the empress spoke to officials of lesser rank to his left and right in the greeting line but ignored the prime minister. Kokovtsov owed his appointment partly to her advocacy; she had come to loathe Stolypin for ordering Rasputin to return to Siberia. Bogrov's bullet saved Stolypin from certain removal. Now Kokovtsov joined Stolypin in the Siberia of her affections.[59]

By the fall of 1913, having come to see the dual appointment of Kokovtsov as prime minister and finance minister as a mistake, Nicholas kept him on primarily to negotiate the French railroad loan. Subordinating the higher to the lower office, Kokovtsov reduced all issues to rubles. To hear him talk, Russia could not afford to be a Great Power. Kokovtsov's policies amounted to "the politics of financial aversion," a friendly member of the duma remarked. What finally girded the "pathologically polite" Nicholas to fire Kokovtsov was their clash of perspectives over a controversial social issue.

To commemorate the tercentenary of Romanov rule, in May 1913 Nicholas traced the route taken by the newly crowned tsar Mikhail Romanov from his home on the Volga to Moscow. Nicholas and his party traveled in the royal train, its bathroom equipped with a "special device to prevent His Imperial Majesty's bathwater from spilling when the train was moving." But to visit out-of-the way places, they had to rough it in caravans of thirty open-topped Renaults. Through the dust kicked up by the tires Nicholas saw enough signs of drunkenness in the villages to be disturbed. He resolved to ban drink in Russia. He was poised to become tsar of the worldwide temperance movement, and Vladimir Kokovtsov told him that Russia could not afford his zeal.[60]

Starting in 1894 the state held a monopoly on the vodka trade. By 1910, one third of its revenue (the equivalent of two trillion dollars in today's U.S. budget) derived from the sale of vodka at state liquor stores. The "drunken budget" lights up the parasitism of the tsarist order. The monarchy, the nobility, the intelligentsia, and the bureaucracy lived off the peasant sober *and* drunk.

Drink was the "Joy of the Rus," the opium of the Russian peasant, and a surer tool of "pacification" than Stolypin's gallows. In the villages, on the farms, the *"Pomoch"*—work for "hospitality," not pay— structured a way of life. "The work begins with vodka, it continues with vodka, it ends with vodka," a priest wrote of the harvest in his parish. Folk cures for "alcoholism," a word coined by a Kiev psychiatrist in 1892, testify to its tenacity: "The drunkard seeking to break his addiction gulped down his vodka with eels, mice, the sweat of a white horse, the placenta of a black pig, vomit, snakes, worms, grease, maggots, urine, and the water used to wash corpses." Foreign holders of Russia's debt banked on the drunkard's craving for vodka surviving the eels—and so did Kokovtsov. When calls arose in the duma to curb the state's vodka addiction, he dug in. Russia needed the revenue for military modernization; drunkenness would wane with economic development. Yet when even Rasputin plumped for temperance ("It's time to close the Tsar's saloon," he reportedly told Nicholas), change was at hand.[61]

To mitigate the human damage, the government had closed the saloons, but this forced drinkers onto the streets. From the late 1890s, drunken young idlers had terrorized St. Petersburg. To describe this crime wave, the Russians borrowed a word from the English, who had borrowed it from the Irish—"hooliganism." For the knife-wielding hooligan only an American word would do—"apache." Hooligan and apache crimes against persons—assaults, robberies, rapes, murders—climbed apace. A state commission found that "alcohol was not only the irreplaceable companion of hooliganism but practically its primary cause."[62]

The crime and premature death statistics, the "children, priests, women, and army officers" ruined by drink, *Novoe vremia* charged, were the "fruit" of Kokovtsov's policy of milking rubles from misery.

It was "with profoundest grief" that Nicholas, on his royal progress, glimpsed the besotted sources of his revenue stream. "We cannot make our fiscal prosperity dependent on the destruction of the spiritual and economic power of many of my subjects," he wrote in an imperial re-script to the new finance minister, Kokovtsov's replacement, in February 1914.[63]★

After the duma passed a law in July giving localities the option of going dry, Nicholas moved swiftly. Starting with the mobilization of the army in August, Russia banned the sale of liquor in all but first-class restaurants. The masses seethed over this exception and drank varnish, moonshine, and a Chinese-made concoction that killed hundreds—but the government received no revenue from these vodka substitutes. As it pained an American temperance activist ruefully to note, "The financial receipts of the monopoly collapsed like a pricked

---

★ Things are worse today. "Teenage Russians have less of a chance of living to the age of sixty than they had a hundred years ago . . . The latest gimmick to encourage drinking is the sale of talking vodka bottles: When you open the bottle, the cap starts talking. It starts with practical instructions like 'pour' and then, as the evening progresses, it produces an increasing drunken mixture of shrieks, giggles, and sound effects." From Patricia Herlihy, *The Alcoholic Empire: Vodka and Politics in Late Imperial Russia* (New York: Oxford, University Press 2002), 161. More recently, the *Lancet* reported, "The extraordinary consumption of alcohol, especially by men in the last several years, has been responsible for more than half of all deaths of [Russians] aged 15 to 54." Moscow Times.com, July 2, 2009.

bladder." Prohibition deprived the treasury of nine hundred million rubles to pay for the war, some 28 percent of the state's income, leaving Russia "with unarmed soldiers and unfed citizens," the latter because peasants, to supply the black market, diverted grain from bread to vodka. Thus Nicholas's crusade against drink helped bring on the "bread riots" in St. Petersburg in February 1917 that began the revolution that drove Nicholas from power. As he confided to Stolypin, "Peter Arkadevitch . . . I succeed in nothing I undertake."[63]

"It is not a feeling of displeasure but a long-standing and deep realization of a state need that now forces me to tell you that we have to part," Nicholas wrote Kokovtsov at the end of January. At a farewell meeting, the tsar remarked, by way of justifying Kokovtsov's dismissal, "I wanted a man fresh for the work." From that description few political-class Russians would have identified Ivan Goremykin, a seventy-five-year-old reactionary who had won Rasputin's favor, "the quickest way up the greasy pole." When briefly prime minister in 1906, Goremykin had nodded off in his ministerial seat during duma sessions. When he appeared before it for the first time in 1914, the deputies rioted in protest.[64]

If Durnovo is to be believed, Nicholas asked him to head the government before resuscitating Goremykin. Durnovo declined, telling Nicholas that his authoritarian "system" would take too long to achieve results—the rollback of the constitutional monarchy created after 1905 and a return to rule by ukase and the knout. In the meantime, Durnovo predicted, Russia would be in a "complete rumpus" with "dissolution of the Duma, assassinations, executions, perhaps armed uprisings . . . Your majesty . . . would not endure these years and will dismiss me." His refusal of the premiership belongs to the tormenting annals of what might have been. Durnovo's domestic repression might have provoked the revolution postponed by his foreign policy, a tragedy for Russia. But if, by following the path marked out by his memorandum (no war, no revolution) or by creating a "complete rumpus" in Russia with his "system," Durnovo had kept Russia from mobilizing, World War I would not have happened in August 1914 and perhaps not at all.[65]

What of Kokovtsov? Could *he* have slowed the rush to war long enough for events foreclosed by the mobilization to stop it? To Berlin he was a force for peace, his firing seen by Germany's ambassador in St. Petersburg as a triumph for the "anti-German party." To Baron Taube, a former legal council at the foreign ministry, Kokovtsov was "a convinced partisan of international peace, capable of casting his veto in a critical moment in the council of ministers." Without him, "there was no such restraining brake in the council." Bethmann Hollweg used the same word, regretting the removal of a "brake" on war. The American historian Sidney Bradshaw Fay, writing in 1928, argued that Kokovtsov's dismissal was "an incalculable misfortune for Russia and the world" . . . because without him no one in the Council of Ministers could "stand against M. Sazonov and the Russian Pan-Slavs and militarists" during the July crisis.

The humiliating settlement of the von Sanders crisis had embittered Sazonov toward the diplomats of the Central Powers. "From the psychological point of view this . . . is far from unimportant for the just appreciation of the crisis of July 1914," according to Taube, "Sazonov's state of mind in 1913–1914 contributed greatly to that over-agitated handling of the Serbo-Austrian crisis which precipitated the final catastrophe . . . A little more cool-headedness would perhaps have sufficed once more to keep the peace." At the July 24 meeting of the council of ministers convened to decide Russia's response to Austria's ultimatum to Serbia, Kokovtsov not only would have supplied "cool-headedness," but also in Sidney Fay's words "might have been able to prevent the over-hasty steps which helped cause the war."[66]

The fatal "over-hasty" step was to order partial mobilization of the southern military districts opposite Austria. Through this move, Sazonov intended to send an intimidating signal to Austria, not to attack her. Kokovtsov was not there to remind him of their joint position on partial mobilization against Austria in 1912—that it meant war with Germany. "Had Sazonov known [or been reminded] that for Germany any mobilization was equivalent to war there is no doubt he would have shaped his course differently," Luigi Albertini concluded in his exhaustive diplomatic history, *The Origins of the War of*

1914 (1953).★ As it was, Sazonov unknowingly set Russia's course toward war. For on discovering that a south-only mobilization against Austria would impede a northern mobilization against Germany, exposing Russian territory to a German attack, the Russians faced an "all-or-nothing choice": back down and destroy their credibility, or commit "the decisive act leading to war," the order for general mobilization that Nicholas issued on the evening of July 30.

That night, Alexandra and Count Vladimir Fredericks, minister of the Imperial House, confronted Nicholas in his study, where he was conferring with Sazonov, to plea for peace. The count told a member of his circle that Alexandra burst out: "Give the orders about demobilization, do it, Nicky, do it!" Nicky wavered. Then Sazonov, addressing Fredericks, cut in: "You . . . who ought to be watching His Majesty's interests, you are asking him to sign his death warrant; for Russia would never forgive him this humiliation." Did fear of a deadly Russian version of the Staatsstreich nerve Nicholas to side with his foreign minister over his wife? He did not cancel the mobilization order. Forty-eight hours later Germany answered it with a declaration of war.[67]

Kokovtsov would have challenged a second decision taken at the July 24 conference—that war would *not* bring revolution. "We live on a volcano," an archconservative paper noted in April, expressing a sense of impending social eruption shared across the political spectrum. *Novoe vremia*'s provincial correspondents reported a surge of brutal murders, of assaults by gangs extorting tribute from gentry and peasant alike, of estates torched, crops plundered, forests despoiled. In February, the director of police had told a conference of criminologists that "the countryside was gripped by terror and the cities are anxious." During the first six months of 1914 one million of Russia's industrial workers went on strike, more than in any year since 1905; the factory inspectorate classified nine hundred thousand

---

★ "Sazonov might have taken a different course; Kokovtsov might have successfully argued against war-triggering risks." But they might not have. "It is difficult to conceive of any Russian government that could have held back from action in support of Serbia in July 1914," David M. McDonald writes in *United Government and Foreign Policy in Russia, 1900–1914,* 218.

of these strikers as "political," animated by *buntarstvo*, a violent opposition to all authority. In March, fifty thousand men "downed
tools" in Petersburg to protest the regime's prosecution of the radical
press. Their temper, the British ambassador observed, "was distinctly
menacing, the demonstrators going so far as to assault and disarm the
police—a step which marks a distinct advance in the daring of the
Petersburg mob who have hitherto stood in wholesome awe of that
force."[68]

In July "a strike as massive and explosive as any that had erupted
among the workers in 1905 swept the outlying working-class districts
of Petersburg." Involving 130,000 workers, many from the massive
ironworks and steel mills in the Vyborg District, it quickly grew into
a general strike with political overtones. Strikers strung wires across
the streets to trip up the cossacks' horses. They axed down telegraph
and telephone poles, ripped up paving stones, and carted out armoires
to build street barricades. The striking workers were mostly former
peasants drawn into the city by Kokovtsov's remedy for Russia's
backwardness, rapid industrialization, and they acted on their own,
without the guidance of the vanguard of the proletariat. The Bolshevik Party's city committee (three of whose seven members were on
the payroll of the Okhrana, the tsarist secret police) wanted no part of
a political strike doomed by a "lack of weapons." On July 22 and 23,
police detachments, cossacks, and when they weren't enough, a cavalry
brigade, surged across the Neva to smash the barricades and disperse
the thousands of workers behind them. With rocks and clubs, joined by
women and children, they fought for each strongpoint. Order returned
only on the twenty-fifth, as soldiers with fixed bayonets patrolled the
shattered empty streets.[69]

In the midst of this convulsion, the French premier, René Viviani,
and President Raymond Poincaré arrived on a state visit, welcomed
by *Novoe vremia* with a special edition entirely in French. As they drove
through St. Petersburg, "at each corner, a group of poor devils shout
'hurrah' under the eyes of a policeman," the French ambassador observed. Sidney Fay highlighted the irony that "at the same moment
when the Russian military bands, in the [tsar's] camp at *Krasnoe Selo*,
had been welcoming Poincaré with the Marseillaise, the Cossacks in
the suburbs of St. Petersburg had been striking down working-men

for singing the same martial anthem." Yet, as Count Pourtalés, the German ambassador, cabled Berlin on July 25, he had it "from a trustworthy source" that "the majority of the ministers present" at the July 24 conference decided that the Petersburg street fighting and the nationwide strike wave "did not presage revolution, nor would war bring domestic upheaval."[70]

The attack by a mob of five thousand on the Neva bridges between the industrial district and the city center, the cries of men whipped by mounted cossacks, the gunfire, the red banners made from French flags torn from the lampposts—from their offices close to the Neva embankment it was as if the ministers had seen, heard, sensed none of this. Reviewing twenty-six international crises between 1898 and 1967, the political scientist Richard Ned Lebow concludes, "These case histories suggest the pessimistic hypothesis that those policy-makers with the greatest need to learn from external reality appear the least likely to do so." The "shadow of the future" was on the reality outside their windows, but the ministers could not see it there and act. So they argued away Russia's internal crisis.[71]

Though by Stolypin's 1909 reform timetable, Russia still needed fourteen more years of peace to achieve stability, some ministers maintained that Russia was already "pacified." Others conceded the current unrest, but held that war, if it came, would unite the nation against the common foe. At that moment in Berlin, the French ambassador, Paul Cambon, was hearing similar talk about the counterrevolutionary uses of war: "Some want war . . . for social reasons, i.e., to provide the external interests which alone can prevent or retard the rise to power of the socialist masses." Yet others inside the narrow circle of decision in Petersburg were less alarmed by the violence in the streets than impressed by its efficient suppression. The French ambassador to Russia, Nicholas Paléologue, pushed that line with Paris, arguing that General Joffre's apprehensions that internal disturbances would paralyze Russia's mobilization were misplaced. The regime could still "drown the revolutionary forces in blood."[72]

Policy makers' beliefs follow their necessities. The government felt it had to assert Russia's identity as a protector of the Slavs or cease its Great Power mummery. And Kokovtsov was not there to ask the ministers to weigh sentiment against survival; not there to stipulate that Russia still lacked the social cohesion "to speak in its former language" as a Great Power; not there to reiterate the lesson of 1905, seizing on the St. Petersburg workers' revolt to shake the ministers from the death spell of foreign policy abstraction and make them confront "the sad actuality" outside their windows.

Meeting with Nicholas days later, the ministers inverted the lesson of 1905. In a rendition of the coup threat he deployed to beat back Alexandra, Sazonov warned Nicholas that "unless he yielded to the popular demand and unsheathed the sword in Serbia's behalf, he would risk revolution and perhaps the loss of his throne"—a reversal of the maxim of Russian policy since 1905 that in Stolypin's words "a new mobilization in Russia would lend strength to the revolution . . . and would bring with it danger for the Dynasty." Sazonov insisted that "popular demand," "public opinion," demanded that Stolypin's maxim "no war . . . no revolution" be turned on its head.

But *which* public? The Pan-Slav banqueters, the center-right politicians in the duma, and that sliver of Russians swayable by the printed word, including the two hundred thousand readers of *Novoe vremia* (which could assume its subscribers' ease with French). In January, columnists and editorial writers of this persuasion had branded the von Sanders compromise "a diplomatic Mukden," after the worst land defeat suffered by Russia in the war with Japan. Throughout the spring they had complained that "we seem only to be retreating" and that "our opponents have misused our love of peace to deal us a series of blows which for long will reflect on our position in Europe," and conjured the specter of a Russia "encircled" by a "Teutonic ring."[73]

This public greeted war with something like gratitude, to judge by *Novoe vremia*: "Our enemies helped us to find ourselves: we did not know it and nor did they." In February 1915, a liberal review marveled at the way the polarization between "society" and the reactionary regime, widening month by month in 1914, had ended at the moment of war, "which like a magic knife divided the two halves of the year . . . bringing the nation to its senses." A member of a Center Party in the duma, speaking at a congress of city officials, celebrated the war as an agent of domestic renovation: "The war, by revealing all our internal strength, will give us the opportunity to defeat not only the external enemy, but will also open up joyful hopes for solving the problems of internal construction and reform." That deluded man would not have joined a revolution if deprived of his war. Nor would the other politicians, editors, lawyers, and liberal aristocrats in the official "opposition."[74]

Nicholas had nothing to fear from this chattering-class elite. Danger came from below, from the peasant masses dreaded by Durnovo. The "narod" only wanted to get on with their lives in peace. News of the war reached them more or less as it did the inhabitants of a village in the Aleshka district. "On 17 July, a policeman who had never been to our village before arrived and went door to door calling everyone to a meeting, and so I went," recalled Ivan Kuchernigo in an unpublished memoir written in 1915 as he convalesced from his wounds in a military hospital. The village elder called for quiet, then explained the war: "Here's what's afoot, boys! An enemy has turned up! He has attacked our Mother Russia, and our Father Tsar needs our help; our enemy for now is Germany." The young men should "show up at

"Russian Prisoner of War with Fur Hat" by Egon Schiele.
During the war Schiele (1890–1918) guarded Russian POWs,
and in work like this 1915 drawing honored
an enemy's humanity.

9 o'clock on the 18th in the office of the District Military Commander in Aleshka, and I advise you to bring with you two pairs of underwear." This largely illiterate public greeted the war with incredulity—*Germany?*—and grief.

"My God, how many tears were spilled when we had to go," Kuchernigo wrote. "My five-year-old daughter sat in my arms and, pressing against me, said, 'Daddy, why are you going? Why are you leaving us? Who's going to earn money and get bread for us?'" The revolution began with the asking of such questions about a war fought to show Russia's stuff as a Great Power that inflicted 10.7 million casualties (including 3 million deaths). As "the army gradually turned into one vast revolutionary mob," a cycle of anarchy and civil war followed that between 1918 and 1924, by battle, terror, and famine, brought death to 10 million more Russians. Writing to Alexandra, Rasputin foretold "a sea of tears immeasurable, and as to blood?"[75]

One evening in early July 1914 a young official in the Russian Foreign Office and his friend, the Austro-Hungarian military attaché in St. Petersburg, rode out in an automobile on the Finland road. "It was the time of the marvelous white nights of the northern summer," recalled Nicolas de Basily, the young Russian. "The sun had scarcely disappeared beneath the horizon only to rise again about an hour later. A faint, pale light illumined the landscape, sad and austere, and increased in us a certain state of anxiety inspired by the recent political news"—the murder of the archduke Francis Ferdinand in Sarajevo on June 28. As they talked, the impending consequences of that act flickered before them in the firefly light. Gripping Basily by the arm as if to convey the intensity of his conviction, Franz von Hohenlohe, his Austrian companion, echoed Durnovo and Kokovtsov: "Do you understand that you cannot go to war? If you do, you will expose yourself to revolution and to the ruin of your power." In the voice of official Russia, Basily replied that "public opinion was clamoring for an intervention in support of Serbia . . . add[ing] forcefully, 'You commit a serious error of calculation in supposing fear of revolution will prevent Russia from fulfilling its national duty now.'"

Russian statesmen had encouraged that error. They had believed it themselves. Then Liman von Sanders arrived in Constantinople and fear of revolution yielded to fear of "encirclement," of conquest, of a war of Teuton against Slav—a war that Russia would fight alone, *unless* she stood up to Austria to preserve credibility with her allies. Its rhetoric of weakness since 1905 compelled Russia to act tough in 1914 both to hold its friends and to deter its enemies, or so the tsar's men believed. Looking back on that white summer night in the black pine forest on the road to Finland, Basily asked himself, "Had Austria and Germany . . . allowed themselves to be swept into the European crisis in the beginning by the illusion that Russia would yield before their threats of war?" Did this "fatal illusion" set Europe on fire? If so, the price of "peace at almost any cost" was war.[76]

3

ENGLAND

ULSTER WILL FIGHT

*He remarked that it was providential that the one bright spot
in this hateful war was the settlement of Irish civil strife . . . and
he added, nearly breaking down, "Jack, God moves in a
mysterious way, his wonders to perform."*

—Prime Minister H. H. Asquith speaking to J. A. Pease,
Liberal Party Whip, August 3, 1914

ASQUITH WAS RELIEVED because world war, declared the
next day, had saved the United Kingdom from civil war. Better
kill the Hun than each other was a widespread sentiment among Britons. Not Germany with its seditious Right boiling to shoot the Reichstag, not Russia with its seething revolutionary underground, but
England, long-peaceful England, was the society nearest cracking in
1914. "The damnable question" of Ireland had brought it to what the
London *Times* called "one of the great crises in the history of the
British race." Up to the last days of July, the "Revolt in Ulster" received more coverage in 1914 than any other story in the world. England was the sun of the British Empire, and from India to Canada,
from Australia to South Africa, from Malta to Hong Kong, millions
followed the stages of its eclipse—the attempt by Asquith's Liberal
government to grant "Home Rule" to Ireland; the forming of a private army in the Protestant north of Ireland to resist "Rome Rule";
the mustering of "Volunteers" in the Catholic south to resist the

IRELAND
1914

Shetland Islands

Orkney Islands

Hebrides Islands

SCOTLAND

COUNTY
TYRONE

ULSTER

• Larne

• Belfast

COUNTY
DOWN

North
Sea

Boyne R.

• Dublin

Curragh •

IRELAND

Irish
Sea

WALES

ENGLAND

London
•

• Aldershot

Atlantic
Ocean

English Channel

FRANCE

0 Miles   50   100
0 Kilometers 100

© 2012 Jeffrey L. Ward

resisters; the landing of German guns up and down the Irish coast; a Tory party talking rebellion taunted by the young lion of the Liberal Cabinet, Winston Churchill, to bring it on. Millions followed this news sensing, fearing, hoping that, in Ireland, the Empire was on trial.

Unsettling across the English-speaking world, in two foreign capitals the trajectory of events raised a question of grand strategy: Would trouble in Ulster bar England from fighting a continental war? The crisis stirred hope in Berlin and dismay in Paris.[1]

The French needn't have worried. England was wired for war. Starting in early 1906 the foreign secretary, Sir Edward Grey, authorized secret "military conversations" with the French that bound the British Expeditionary Force (BEF) to the French army and, in a degree, Britain to France, tighter than anything contemplated by the Entente cordiale of 1904 between them—tighter even than the formal military alliances between France and Russia, Germany and Austria-Hungary. Through its spy in the Russian embassy in London, Berlin learned of these and subsequent security initiatives in Anglo-French and Anglo-Russian relations; Parliament and public remained in the dark.[2]

At the Foreign Office, Grey's aides competed in ripping the Teuton, certain he meant Grey rejected their more extreme advice, but years of it colored his conduct of foreign policy. A cabinet colleague, Charles Hobhouse, could plausibly name him "the author of our rupture with Germany." The king warned Grey of the "constitutional gravity" of the French military talks—talks that amounted to planning for a joint Anglo-French defense of France against a German attack, talks that were not approved by the cabinet or Parliament, talks whose import Grey reportedly kept from Asquith for three years. When they came partially to light in 1911 there was a blowup in the cabinet. Liberals in and out of Parliament scored Grey for his "severe economy of truth." With E. D. Morel in the *Nineteenth Century*, they wanted to know "where this entente with France is leading us" and whether "the nation has lost all control of its foreign policy."[3]

Two years later Britain effectively surrendered control over its foreign policy to France. To close a feared battleship gap with the German navy without asking Parliament to pay for new dreadnaughts, the Royal Navy transferred battle squadrons based in the Mediterranean to home waters. To replace these British warships, the French navy moved its fleet to the Mediterranean, leaving France's Atlantic coast unguarded. Churchill, as first lord of the Admiralty, championed the agreement, arguing that it did not obligate Britain in advance of any future war. At the same time he identified the potential dagger in the deal, the *implicit* quid pro quo: "How tremendous would be the weapon which France would possess to compel our intervention, if she could say, 'On the advice of and by arrangement with your naval authorities we have left our Northern coasts defenseless. We cannot possibly come back in time [to repel a German naval attack].'" And so France would look to England to protect its Atlantic coast from German attack. That argument, Churchill shrewdly surmised, "would probably be decisive whatever is written down now." So it proved when in the last days of peace Britons discovered that what the *Manchester Guardian* termed "a little knot of men working by evasion and equivocation" had signed them up for war. Only dodging the worst in Ulster cushioned the shock.[4]

In the first half of 1914 civil war over Ulster was in a race with continental war over Serbia. The Austrian chief of staff, Conrad von Hötzendorf, urged the foreign minister, Count Berchtold, to postpone Austria's ultimatum to Serbia until mid-August. If he had got his way, civil war in Ireland likely would have won, and Britain, not Germany, would have confronted the hydra of rebellion *and* war. In that event, even if the government had declared war on Germany for invading Belgium, it could not have spared troops from Ulster to ship to France in the war's decisive opening weeks.[5]

On July 4, 1914, the Military Members of the Army Council warned the British cabinet that there were two hundred thousand armed men in Ireland, and that if civil war broke out the entire Expeditionary Force, the Special Reserve, and the Territorial Army would be required to restore order. "If the whole of our Expeditionary Force were used in Ireland," the Army Council concluded, "we should be quite incapable of meeting our obligations abroad." Stipulate that the BEF, committed in Ulster, could not be sent to France. "If the BEF had never been sent, there is no question that the Germans would have won the war," Niall Ferguson asserts with startling certainty.[6]

Whether through the BEF's contribution in the opening weeks, when the "ocular presence" of British soldiers buoyed French morale, or the Royal Navy's blockade of Germany for the duration, or the addition of Britain's industrial, financial, and technological strength to the Allied cause, Britain's entry into the world war was the necessary condition of Germany's defeat.*

Yet, a century on, can *that* be how one wishes the thing had come out? "It is hard to imagine the conflict that began in Europe in 1939 without the legacy of the Great War," Ian F. W. Beckett concludes in *The Great War 1914–1918*. Put plainer, it is hard to imagine World War II without Germany's *defeat* in World War I. If Germany had won in 1914, as Ferguson believes it would have done if the British army were tied down in Ulster, then "Hitler could have lived out his life as a failed artist and a fulfilled soldier in a German-dominated Central Europe about which he could have found little to complain." Starker yet, Richard Ned Lebow writes: "If Germany had won, there almost certainly would have been no Hitler and no Holocaust."[†]

---

*This claim is borne out by statistics. In 1913 the Central Powers, Germany and Austria-Hungary, accounted for 19.2 percent of the world's manufacturing production and 20.2 percent of steel production; France and Russia for 14.3 and 9.4. Add Britain to their column and the percentages jump to 27.9 of world manufacturing and 17.1 of steel, an edge in the former and a near tie in the latter. The sufficient condition of Germany's defeat, the numbers suggest, was the U.S. entry into the war, which increased the Allied—U.S., UK, and France—number to 51.7 for manufacturing and 44.1, more than twice the percentage of the Central Powers, for steel. See Paul M. Kennedy, "The First World War and the International Power System," *International Security* 9, no. 1 (Summer 1984): tables on 19 and 25.

[†] "The conventional wisdom holds that the allied victory in World War I was a good thing; it prevented an expansionist continental power from achieving hegemony in continental Europe. This assessment represents the view of the world from the corporate boardrooms and corridors of power in London, New York, and Washington. From the perspective of say, Polish Jewry, the outcome was a disaster." Richard Ned Lebow, "Counterfactual Thought Experiments: A Necessary Teaching Tool." *History Teacher* 40, no. 2, accessed at www.historycooperative.org/journals/ht/40.2/lebow.html. Ferguson's picture of Hitler as a victorious and fulfilled soldier living out his days in a German-dominated Central Europe needs this corrective: Hitler would probably have had to keep fighting and killing to fasten German rule on vast alien populations. "If the official war aims of the First World War had been achieved, it would have resulted, estimated very roughly, in an empire of 400 to 500 million inhabitants, with a ruling group of 60 million Germans." Norbert Elias, *The Germans: Power Struggles and the Development of Habitus in the Nineteenth and Twentieth Centuries* (New York: Columbia University Press, 1996), 367.

That vertiginous perspective lends the events in Ireland in the spring of 1914, buried beneath the war, a significance beyond themselves.[7]

Today Northern Ireland (comprising most of the historic province of Ulster) is part of the United Kingdom. So was the whole of Ireland in 1914. Today Northern Ireland elects members of Parliament who serve in the House of Commons in London. So did the whole of Ireland in 1914. In addition, today Northern Ireland has a regional assembly. It meets in Belfast, and deals with domestic issues. That is "Home Rule"; Ireland lacked Home Rule in 1914.

Meeting of the Asquith cabinet. Having foxed the House of Lords into a general election over its power to veto legislation, the Liberals are gleeful. Lloyd George is hugging Churchill. Asquith is standing. But the future hovers over the semi-recumbent Augustine Birrell, the Irish Secretary. The election would make the Liberals beholden to Irish Nationalist MPs and their goal, that smile-stopper, home rule.

Home rule, a "demand that captivated the majority of the Irish people for almost a half a century," was the Irish norm. Since 1264, Ireland had had a parliament of some kind, losing it only after 1798, when the Irish—few and doomed—with French troops fighting beside them rose up against their English overlords. To prevent Napoleon's meddling in their backyard again, Britain annexed Ireland in the Act of Union. Home rule was the one way the Irish could work out to live in dignity under the "English system in Ireland . . . founded on the bayonets of 30,000 soldiers, encamped permanently in a hostile country," as defined by the Liberal Joseph Chamberlain. The Union sustained by those bayonets was felt as an affront, a punishment for bad behavior. Ireland had grown "intensely disloyal and intensely disaffected" under the Union, the great Anglo-Irish leader of the 1870s and 1880s, Charles Stewart Parnell (1846–1891), argued in the House of Commons. Though Parnell could offer no guarantees about the future, for "no man can fix the boundary to the march of a nation," he promised the English that home rule would calm the passion to "break the connection with England" animating Irish nationalism through seven centuries of alien rule.[8]

In the 1880s, Parnell pledged the MPs of his parliamentary or Nationalist Party to whichever English party came out for home rule. Under Prime Minister William E. Gladstone the Liberals took this deal, and twice tried to deliver on the promise of what Parnell called their "Union of Hearts" with the Nationalists. The first time, in 1886, the Liberals lost in the House of Commons, their party splitting, and the rebels, led by Chamberlain, defecting to the Conservative opposition, relabeled the Unionist Party to receive them. The second Home Rule Bill passed the Commons in 1893 but was vetoed by the House of Lords.[9]

When the Liberals regained power in 1906, their majority was large enough that they did not need Nationalist votes and so could delay the fated appointment with Irish home rule. That changed in 1909, when the House of Lords vetoed Lloyd George's so-called People's Budget for taxing its members' estates, and the Liberal prime minister, Herbert Henry Asquith, called for a general election to be fought over the issue of stripping the veto from the unelected House of Lords. That election, and a second eleven months later, left the Liberals and Unionists tied, with 272 seats each. But the latter had received three hundred thousand more votes, one source of Unionist bitterness.

Another was the "corrupt bargain" to remain in power that the Liberals struck with forty-two Labour and eighty-four Nationalist MPs, the latter regarded by Unionists as a "purely sectional interest [with] no right to impose their views on the kingdom as a whole." The corrupt bargain was a myth to fire up the Unionist base. The Liberals could govern without Nationalists; there were enough Labour MPs to assure their majority, but Asquith & Co. were chary of depending on a party they competed with in England.

As his price the Nationalist leader, John Redmond, obliged the Liberals to drain the cup. "I believe the current members of the Liberal Party are sincere," he told a Limerick audience. "Whether they are or not we will make them . . . toe the line." By the newly enacted Parliament Act, a bill that passed in three sessions of the House became law. Home rule passed in 1912; it passed again in 1913; and, as soon as the government submitted it, it would pass a final time by summer 1914.[10]

The bill envisioned a parliament with the powers of a "glorified County Council." It would, Redmond assured an English audience, "be solely to deal with those plain, common, hum-drum, every-day Irish affairs which you cannot understand as the people themselves do." This modest assembly was to meet in Dublin.[11]

The "Protestant people of Ulster" would sooner be governed from Berlin. They would not submit to the Catholic majority in the south of Ireland. "Ordinary people [in Ulster] had wildly exaggerated ideas of Papal influence in Ireland, and thought of the Pope as a personal and inveterate enemy, who spent all his time scheming to get his hands on the Belfast shipyards . . . Religion was the dynamic in Ulster, not merely a cloak for other motives." In "Ulster 1912" Rudyard Kipling expressed the regnant prejudice:

> *We know the wars prepared*
> *On every peaceful home,*

We know the hells declared
For such as serve not Rome.[12]

Some of the reasons Ulster's Protestants gave for their bigotry soften judgment on it. They touch on family: the Catholic Church's decree of 1908, for example, voiding mixed marriages between Catholics and Protestants unless performed by a priest. In one incident, a Belfast man, supposedly egged on by a priest, had abandoned his Protestant wife and absconded with their children. The Government of Ireland Act (home rule) forbade the state from establishing any religion, whether Catholicism or Protestantism, but frightened people could not be expected to credit politicians' promises over fear-inflated facts. And as to the worth of those promises, the reported words of Joseph Devlin, Nationalist MP for Belfast, known to be close to the Catholic hierarchy, were not reassuring: "He did not believe that artificial guarantees in an Act of Parliament were any real protection."[13]

To save them from their fears, Ulstermen looked to a fanatic, the member of Parliament from Trinity College Dublin, Sir Edward Carson, drafted in 1910 to lead the Ulster Unionist Party in the surety that compromise was foreign to his nature. "I like being chairman of the Ulster Unionists," he confided to Lady Londonderry. "I feel boiling with rage & I hope there will be violence."[14]

Carson, a barrister, won fame as Oscar Wilde's inquisitor in the famous 1895 libel trial. At first things seemed to be going Wilde's way. Treating the dour Carson, his Trinity College classmate, like a straight man in one of his comedies, Wilde elicited guffaws from the courtroom. Carson quoted a line from *The Picture of Dorian Gray* spoken by one man to another—"I quite admit that I adored you madly"—and then asked Wilde, "Have you ever felt that feeling of adoring madly a beautiful male person many years younger than yourself?" Wilde replied, to loud laughter, "I have never given adoration to anybody except myself."

But, catching Wilde in petty lies and inconsistencies, Carson wove an inexorable web. Wilde had sued for libel the Marquess of Queensbury, his lover's father, after Queensbury inscribed "To Oscar Wilde, posing as a somdomite [sic]" on his calling card and left it at Wilde's

Sir Edward Carson. The lawyer crusading for truth in Terence Rattigan's 1946
play *The Winslow Boy* is based on Carson. Robert Donat stars in the 1948 film;
Jeremy Northam plays the Carson figure in David Mamet's 1999 version. That
was the good side of Carson. Ulster brought out the other side.

club. But truth is a defense against libel, and armed with evidence
gathered by Queensbury's detectives of Wilde's dalliances with young
working-class men Carson was ready to show that there was no "posing" to it, when Wilde's counsel called a halt.[15]

Gaunt, haunted-looking, frequently impaired by acidic emotions,
Carson had the look of a man gnawed at by his convictions. His
speeches were seditious. But lest riots erupt over the prosecution of
Ulster's hero-savior★ before whom women knelt and kissed his hands,
the Liberal Cabinet left him free to declaim sentiments like, "We

---

★ "Protestant Ulster's devotion to 'King Carson' . . . became so unanimous and
intense that the Ulster Unionist Council's standing committee might have served
as a model of Mussolini's Fascist Grand Council." Thomas C. Kennedy, "War,

must be prepared, the morning Home Rule passes, ourselves to become responsible for the government of the Protestant Province of
Ulster." For Carson, "there could be no permanent resting place between complete union and total separation." Given the Catholic
predominance in the whole of Ireland, home rule was the entering
wedge. Begin there and Ireland would end as an independent republic, "a foreign, probably hostile, neighbor along Britain's western
coast." As the Liberals prepared their Home Rule Bill, he confided in
Lady Londonderry, "I never felt more savage."[16]

The Conservative Party backed Carson with giddy relish. Indulging in what Asquith labeled "reckless rodomontade . . . furnishing
for the future a complete grammar of Anarchy," the Tory leader
Andrew Bonar Law pledged to a crowd of angry Unionists in September 1912: "I can imagine no length of resistance to which Ulster
can go in which I should not be prepared to support them . . . They
would be justified in resisting . . . by all means in their power, including force."[17]

That "monster demonstration" was held on the grounds of Blenheim
Palace in Oxfordshire. Built as a gift for the Duke of Marlborough in
the early eighteenth century and named for his great victory in the
War of the Spanish Succession, Blenheim was selected as the first English site for an anti–home rule rally partly to twig Marlborough's de-
scendant Winston Churchill, who was born there in 1874. In January
1912, escorted by five battalions of infantry and a detachment of
cavalry, Churchill had braved showers of "Belfast confetti" (steel riv-
ets) to deliver a home rule speech in Belfast that incensed all Unionism
against him.[18]

Churchill's swoop into Belfast stirred local memories of his father's.
In 1886, Lord Randolph Churchill, an ambitious Tory politician, at-
tacked home rule there in a speech that fanned intolerance against
Belfast Catholics. In a public letter to a Belfast paper Lord Randolph
distilled his message in the notorious line "Ulster will fight and
Ulster will be right."[19]

In his 1905 biography of Lord Randolph, Winston published a letter

---

Patriotism, and the Ulster Unionist Council, 1914–18," *Éire-Ireland* 40, nos. 3 and 4
(Fall/Winter 2005): 192.

that impeached the sincerity of his father's indignation: "I decided some time ago that if the G.O.M. [Grand Old Man, Gladstone's sobriquet] went for Home Rule, the Orange card would be the one to play. Please God it may turn out to be the ace of trumps and not the two." "Orange," shorthand for "Orangemen," referred to Ulster's Scots Presbyterians. They took their color from King William of Orange, "who saved us from Popery, slavery, knavery, brass money, and wooden shoes," to quote an Orange Order toast—saved them in 1689 when his forces arrived in time to lift the hundred-day siege of Derry by Catholic troops under King James before every Protestant within the city walls had died of hunger with the Ulster anthem "No Surrender!" on his lips.[20]

Liberal commentators compared Lord Randolph's expedient playing of the "Orange card" with Bonar Law's. Tories detested Winston as a turncoat for "crossing the floor" to join the Liberals in 1904. To that partisan animus, Law, who had Ulster roots, added personal rancor over Churchill's belaboring him with his ancestral shorthand for cynical politics.

"When you are dealing with Orange Ulster, you are dealing with the real passions and real anxieties of real people," Churchill sallied in a House speech. "No such excuse applies to Mr. Bonar Law . . . You can always detect the rasp of the Tory party manager" in his die-hard Ulster rhetoric. And then Churchill, voicing Law's thoughts, surfaced Law's hidden demagogue: "*Ulster is our best card; it is our only card . . . our chance to smash the Parliament Act, to restore the veto of the House of Lords, and to carry a protective tariff unto the statute books.*"[21]

In *The World Crisis*, written in the 1920s, Churchill rendered in still-resonant terms the "excesses of partisanship which on both sides disgraced the year 1914":

No one who has not been involved in such contentions can understand the intensity of the pressures to which public men are subjected . . . The vehemence with which great masses of men yield themselves to partisanship and follow the struggle as if it were a prize fight, their ardent enthusiasm, their glistening eyes, their swift anger . . . the sense of wrongs mutually interchanged, the extortion and enforcement of pledges, the infectious loyalties,

Prime Minister Herbert Asquith. His calm verged on inanition. He
could not fathom Protestant Ulster's rebellion over home rule—
the Pope did not frighten *him*.

the praise that waits on violence; the chilling disdain, the honest
disappointment, the cries of "treachery" with which every proposal of compromise is hailed; the desire to keep good faith with
those who follow, the sense of right being on one's side, the harsh
unreasonable actions of opponents—all these acting and reacting
reciprocally upon one another tend toward the perilous climax . . .
At a certain stage it is hardly possible to keep that contention
within the limits of words or laws. Force, that final arbiter that last
soberer, may break upon the scene.[22]

We will follow the last act of the Ulster crisis through Churchill's
eyes, picking up the story in March 1914, when Churchill, so the
Times charged, sprung THE PLOT AGAINST ULSTER.

★   ★   ★

Asquith woke to the extremity of the Ulster danger only in late 1913. His man in Ireland, Chief Secretary Augustine Birrell, tended to see the North through the "green glasses" of Nationalist politicians who mocked fears of rebellion as so much "Ulsteria." Birrell's emollient counsel allowed Asquith to do something he found congenial—nothing. Sixty-two in 1914, Asquith had reached the top in politics on the confidence inspired by his level temperament. "I was never able to find any fault with Asquith as a human being except that he was always very much the same," Birrell said of him. Less kindly, Lord Lovat regarded Asquith as "incapable of doing anything except drift," because of "drink, bridge, and holding girls' hands." Asquith, a Latin scholar at Oxford, styled himself a "cunctator" who preferred to out-wait events. In Ireland they had got ahead of him, and would not wait for him to catch up.[23]

Asquith thought to put off compromise with his Irish opponents until circumstances had shown the necessity of it to his Irish friends. Baffled by Ulster's adamancy—"No Surrender!" did not stir his blood—he hoped that the Unionists would propound a plan of their own, lifting the burden of accommodation from him and sparing the Liberals accusations of betrayal from the Nationalists. Knowing Asquith's ways, the Unionists sat tight, drilling their army in Ulster and winning support in England, where prominences like Kipling and Sir Edward Elgar contributed thousands of pounds to their gun fund and, with two million other Englishmen, signed the British Covenant, pledging to "resist a government dominated by men disloyal to the empire . . . to whom our faith and tradition are hateful."[24]

A letter received in January 1914 from a spy in the Liberal camp left Carson in doubt whether Asquithian dithering or Machiavellian strategy lay behind the cabinet's delay in seeking a compromise:

> I am a private secretary to the wife of one of the Under-Secretaries; members of the government meet at his house socially and informally at all hours and discuss matters with considerable freedom. Less than a week ago Mr. Asquith, Mr. McKenna [the home secretary] and Mr. Pease [the House whip] were there about the same time. The plan is to procrastinate until the patience of the hooli-

gan element in Belfast is exhausted and they begin to riot. That is
the moment when the troops will step in and crush the riot . . .
They have agents in Belfast . . . who . . . are to say when it is the
right moment to stir up a riot.

Needing to keep the flame high under his movement to deter the
government from imposing home rule, Carson was gambling that
"the hooligan element" would not act on his indictment of the government as brigands in hock to the papist enemies of the Union south
of the Boyne and their Ulster coreligionists—the 690,000 Roman
Catholics sharing a province smaller than Delaware with 880,000
Protestants. Pogroms against Belfast's Catholic shipyard workers had
disfigured the resistance to Gladstone's home rule bills. Any repetition, Carson knew, would give the government the pretext to send
the army to protect the Catholic people of Ulster.[25]

The climactic third passage of the Home Rule Bill was set for May
1914. Before then, Asquith must strike a deal with Carson or "the
morning Home Rule passes" a Provisional Government, backed by a
lightly armed but strongly motivated people's army, would seize power
in Belfast.

On March 9, Asquith announced the government's idea of a compromise. Any of the six Ulster counties could vote themselves out of
the home rule scheme for a period of six years—long enough for two
general elections "so that the electorate in both countries would have
ample experience of the working of the Irish executive"—then "au-
tomatically" be included. During that interval the competence of the
Dublin government would silence charges that home rule, to quote a
prevalent Unionist sentiment, would release a wave of "corruption
and graft, and probably the country would be inundated with un-
scrupulous Irish-American low class politicians." Good government
in Dublin, Asquith assumed, would motivate the counties opting out
of home rule to opt in. (But, Unionists sensibly asked, why force them
in with automatic inclusion if they'll come in willingly?) Redmond
pronounced the six-year opt-out "the extremist limit of concession."
Carson rejected the whole scheme: "We do not want sentence of
death with a stay of execution for six years."[26]

The government had some hard thinking to do. With no deal in prospect, why should Carson wait until May? Why not act sooner? Why not declare himself uncrowned king of Ulster now? Struggling with such questions, the government could not flinch from one more. What will *we* do when they act? Nothing? Fight? But whom? And with what? The prime minister would not have long to wait for events to settle the last question.

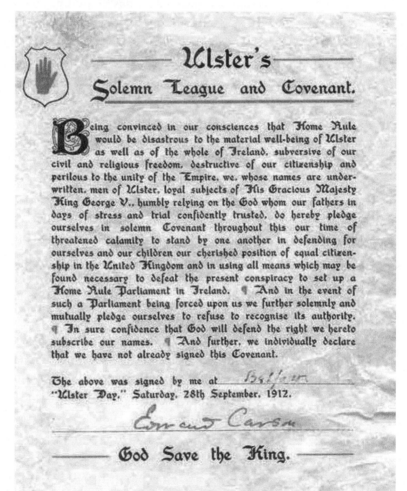

Ulster would be right. A few ultras signed the Covenant in blood. The British Empire was on trial in Ulster. If Nationalist Ireland got its way, what was to stop Nationalist India from trying? No wonder Kipling signed.

In early March the government received troubling reports from the Ulster security services. County Down police had discovered a "confidential circular" requesting information from the Ulster Volunteer Force (UVF), a sectarian militia mustered to defy home rule, about the strength of the government forces defending police barracks, coast guard stations, and the like. County Tyrone police found a UVF typescript outlining the seizure of "all arms at military barracks . . . and it is said that wax impressions of keys of military stores and magazines are in possession of the Volunteers." More ominously, "the number of soldiers at each military depot willing to assist the Volunteers are given."[27]

A UVF document titled "The Coup" called for a "sudden, complete, and paralyzing blow" to be struck at the "right moment."

Simultaneously:
1) Cut rail lines so that no police or Army could be sent to Ulster.
2) Cut telegraph and cable lines.
3) Seize all depots containing arms, ammunition, etc.
4) All avenues of approach by road for troops or police into Ulster should be closed by isolated detachments.
5) Guns of field artillery [caliber] should be captured either by direct attack—or else by previous arrangement with the gunners.
6) All depots for supply of troops or police should be captured.

"The Coup" displayed tactical acumen; possibly it was the work of a staff officer who had resigned his commission in 1910 to train Ulstermen to resist home rule. Retired officers had gone over to Carson by the handful. Serving officers would follow at his call: "We have pledges and promises from some of the greatest generals in the army that when the time comes and if necessary they will come over to help us keep the old flag flying and so defy those who dare to invade our liberties."[28]

Asquith appointed a five-man committee to think through the government's response to imminent rebellion. The three key members of

the Army Council were Attorney General John Simon, Secretary of War John Seely, and Churchill. But, as Lord Esher noted, "Winston is running the whole show!"[29]

What did Winston do and when did he do it? To Unionists, the answer was clear. Churchill, one wrote, was "the author of [a] 'Plot' or 'Pogrom'" against Ulster. At a Unionist rally in Hyde Park, Carson branded him "Lord Randolph's renegade son who wanted to be handed down to posterity as the Belfast butcher who threatened to shoot down those who took his father's advice." Churchill's scheme was to provoke violence in Ulster and then, under cover of restoring order there, to crush the UVF. Churchill called that "a hellish insinuation." The "plot" charge, which appealed to those motivated to see contingency planning as conspiracy, damaged Churchill's reputation.[30]

"Most historians," Patricia Jalland notes in her invaluable *The Liberals and Ireland*, believe Churchill "planned a large-scale military and naval

coup against Ulster." He devised "an operation . . . for the coercion
of Ulster," asserts one of these historians; the operation was "designed
for the sudden and complete paralyzing of the Ulster Volunteer Force,"
states another.[31]

Was Churchill eager to play the Belfast butcher? He was undoubtedly "a war man," in the words of Admiral Sir John Fisher, who
served with him turbulently at the Admiralty. At thirty-nine, a veteran of campaigns against the Dervish in the Sudan, the Pathans
in Afghanistan, and the Boers in South Africa, Churchill was full of
fight. When, under Tory pressure, Asquith removed him as first lord
of the Admiralty in May 1915, Clementine Churchill protested, defending her husband's belligerent spirit in prophetic terms: "Winston
may in your eyes & in those with whom he has to work have faults
but he has the supreme quality which I venture to say very few of
your present or future Cabinet possess, the imagination, the deadli-
ness to fight Germany."[32]

Concluding that democratic governance was about to be overturned in Ulster, Churchill ordered eight battleships based in Gi-
braltar and eight destroyers of the Fourth Flotilla in England to sail
to the waters between Scotland and Ulster, "where they would be in
proximity to the coasts of Ireland in case of serious disorders occur-
ring." In addition, he dispatched HMS *Pathfinder* and HMS *Attentive*
to Belfast Louch with orders to defend "by every means" the eighty-
five tons of ammunition at Carrickfergus Castle, held by only twenty
soldiers. Indulging his penchant for verbal melodrama, Churchill told
Sir John French, chief of the General Staff, that "if there were opposition to the movement of the troops, he would pour enough shot and
shell into Belfast to reduce it to ruins in 24 hours." That is evidence
for the "Churchill pogrom" thesis; it is also how he talked when his
blood was up.[33]

It was thumping in his ears on March 14 when he journeyed to
Bradford in Yorkshire to loose an oratorical pogrom. Lloyd George
put him up to it, making the argument from fame. "This is your
opportunity," George said, according to the diary of Lord Riddell.
"Providence has arranged it for you. You can make a speech that will
ring down the corridors of history . . . You are known to be in favor
of conciliation for Ulster. Now you will have to say that having

secured a compromise Ulstermen will have to accept it or take the consequences."[34]

Churchill arrived at Bradford station that afternoon "accompanied by two oxygen cylinders, as well as no doubt by a suitable retinue, the task of one member of which was to pump the oxygen into him before the meeting so as to secure an adequate level of exuberance."[35]

Churchill required every ounce of breath to shout out, so the three to four thousand Liberals in the audience could hear it, his final sentence:

> If Ulstermen extend the hand of friendship, it will be clasped by Liberals and by their Nationalist countrymen in all good faith and in all good will; but if there is no wish for peace; if every concession that is made is spurned and exploited; if every effort to meet their views is only to be used as a means of breaking down Home Rule and of barring the way to the rest of Ireland; if the Government and Parliament of this great country and greater Empire are to be exposed to menace and brutality; if all the loose, wanton, and reckless chatter we have been forced to listen to these many months is in the end to disclose a sinister and revolutionary purpose; then I can only say to you, "Let us go forward together and put these grave matters to the proof."[36]

In his memoirs, Asquith hailed this un-Liberal call to arms "as proof that the Twentieth Century can hold its own in an oratorical competition." At the time he approved it in advance, though telling Lloyd George (as if one could not have guessed), "My game is more the olive-branch." Asquith must especially have liked this shameless bit: "Those who think that these events can be adjusted by the use of threats of violence against the Government do not know British democracy. They do not know England. They do not know Yorkshire and they do not know Asquith."[37]

Churchill delivered his speech on Saturday, March 14; by Saturday, March 21, everything had changed. Besides the second week of May 1940, when Hitler invaded France, Neville Chamberlain stepped down as prime minister, and Churchill realized his destiny, few weeks in modern British political history have been as decisive as the one that began on the Monday after Bradford, when, to "tumultuous cheers" from the Liberals, Churchill strode into the House of Commons and took his seat near Asquith on the Treasury Bench.

Asquith had raised the frailest hope of a settlement by introducing a new principle—temporary Ulster exclusion from home rule. On Thursday the opposition would respond.

Thursday afternoon in the House, Bonar Law asked Asquith whether the government would agree to hold a referendum on home rule. If home rule passed, Asquith retorted, would the Unionists agree that the government "would be justified in coercing Ulster"? Law nodded his agreement. Asquith stared across the dispatch box at Sir Edward Carson and asked if Ulster would agree. Carson replied, "Let the Prime Minister give me a fair offer and then I will answer him." But the government, Asquith indicated, had made its final offer—Ulster exclusion for six years.

Declaring that Churchill's Bradford threat made him "feel I ought not to be here but in Belfast," Carson dramatically announced that he was leaving the House to catch the night boat to Belfast, there to lead his forces against Churchill's battleships, at which a heckler shouted, "With your sword drawn?" Slamming the brass-bound boxes in front of him, Carson echoed Churchill's menacing last line: "Let the Government come and try conclusions with them in Ulster." When he exited the chamber, the opposition rose and cheered.

Introducing a motion to censure the government for coercing Ulster, Law, too, focused on Bradford, saying that he had hoped that "a catastrophe" could still be avoided: "I *had* that hope, but in view of the speech given at a critical time by the First Lord of the Admiralty—a speech the spirit of which was understood quite as clearly [in Ulster] as it was by the hon. gentlemen on the benches opposite when he came into the House on Monday . . . I really believe that the situation today is far more dangerous than it has ever been; and if a way of escape is to be found it will come from some cause which I am quite unable to foresee."

In fact Law had arranged an escape. He had planned to instruct his fellow Tories in the House of Lords to attach an amendment to the Army Annual Act forbidding the army from being used to suppress resistance in Ulster (shades of the Social Democrats in Germany). But intelligence from his spy in the War Office, the director of Military Operations, Sir Henry Wilson, persuaded Law that taking such a politically risky step at a time of rising international tensions was unnecessary. "If [the army] were ordered to coerce Ulster there would be wholesale defections," Wilson assured Law.

This was in Law's mind as he asked Asquith how the government meant to impose its will on Ulster: "What about the Army? If it is only a question of dealing with civil disorder, the Army, I'm sure, will obey you. But if it is really a question of civil war, soldiers are citizens like the rest of us. The Army will be divided and you will have destroyed the force . . . upon which we depend for the defense of this country."

Asquith was having none of that: "Who is to judge whether a particular contest in which the armed forces of the Crown are called upon to intervene does or does not fall into the category of civil war?" To leave it to the judgment of individual officers would be "to make the Government subject to the Army."[38]

Forty-eight hours later that occurred. For the first time in over two hundred years, high army officers would dictate to the government in what has come to be known as the Curragh Mutiny.*

To stop the UVF from seizing government stores as contemplated in "The Coup," on Monday, March 16, Seely sent the commander of

---

*The invaluable source on the Curragh, which includes the relevant documents as well as eyewitness accounts, is Ian F. W. Beckett, ed., *The Army and the Curragh Incident 1914* (London: Bodley Head, 1986). The standard narrative remains A. P. Ryan, *Mutiny at the Curragh* (London: Macmillan, 1956). More recent academic treatments can be found in Elizabeth A. Muenger, *The British Military Dilemma in Ireland: Occupation Politics, 1886–1914* (Omaha: University of Nebraska Press, 1991) and Stephen Mark Duffy, *"No Question of Fighting": The Army, the Government and the Curragh Incident, 1914* (Ph.D. diss., Texas A&M University, 1993). For service gossip on the officers involved see *The Marquess of Anglesey: A History of the British Cavalry 1816–1919*, vol. 7, *The Curragh Incident and the Western Front, 1914* (London: Leo Cooper, 1996). For an in-depth analysis of the politics of the Curragh, see the relevant chapter in Patricia Jalland, *The Liberals and Ireland: The Ulster Question in British Politics to 1914* (New York: St. Martin's Press, 1980). Also see the

the British army in Dublin a list of four depots needing enhanced protection. When the commander refused to move troops to those places because it would "create intense excitement in Ulster," the Army Council—Seely and Churchill—summoned him to the War Office for a stiff bracing.

The commander was Sir Arthur Paget, sixty-two, of whom his 1928 *Times* obituary observed, "Had he only devoted to military study a fraction of the time which he gave up to the observation of trees and shrubs, he might have ranked as a learned soldier." The two ministers later maintained that they instructed Sir Arthur to move only two battalions of infantry to secure undermanned depots across Ulster. But they also committed to dispatch "large reinforcements" from England if, as seemed unlikely to them, Paget's troops should encounter resistance. "You can have as many more men as are necessary . . . even to the last man," Seely averred. At this, picturing himself at the head of a massive host, Paget remarked, "I shall lead my army to the Boyne." "Don't be a bloody fool!" Sir John French cut in.[39]

Returned to Dublin, Paget convened a meeting of his senior officers on Friday morning. As discussed with the Army Council, he informed those with homes in Ulster that they could "quietly disappear." He gave the others an ultimatum: Obey orders or resign their commissions. They had two hours to make up their minds. The troop must be moved that night.

Presenting that option to the officers was Paget's inspiration. His civilian chiefs had not authorized giving them the choice to do their duty. They had stipulated, according to Churchill, that in "grave emergencies" officers refusing to obey orders should be dismissed from the army discreetly, not put as "a test or trial to the whole body of officers in the Irish command." That nuance eluded Paget. Nor, Churchill

---

excellent brief account in A. T. Q. Stewart, *The Ulster Crisis: Resistance to Home Rule, 1912–1914* (London: Faber & Faber, 1967). Also see Charles Townsend, "Military Force and Civil Authority in the United Kingdom, 1914–1921," *Journal of British Studies* 28, no. 3 (July 1989): 262–69; Donald Lammers, "Arno Mayer and the British Decision for War: 1914," *Journal of British Studies* 12, no. 2 (May 1973): 137–65; Ian F. Beckett and Keith Jeffrey, "The Royal Navy and the Curragh Incident," *Historical Research* 62 (February 1989): 54–69. Indispensable is the *Times* for March and April 1914.

later claimed, did the Army Council say anything warranting Paget to tell the startled officers that "the whole place would be ablaze by tomorrow." The officers left the Dublin meeting shaken, believing that large-scale "active operations" in Ulster were beginning. Many had relatives there; nearly all were sympathetic to Carson and the Ulster "Loyalists," as they styled themselves to emphasize that they asked only to be allowed to remain loyal citizens of the United Kingdom. The officers recoiled from the prospect of being ordered to fire on people who marched under the same flag.[40]

On Friday afternoon, Seely received a telegram from Paget: "Regret to report Brigadier and fifty-seven officers, 3rd Cavalry Brigade, prefer to accept dismissal if ordered north." The officers were stationed just outside Dublin at the Curragh military camp, the main British base in Ireland. The brigadier who chose to resign rather than go north was Herbert Gough, a contumacious cavalry commander who disobeyed orders during the war in South Africa and would do so again in August during the BEF's retreat from Mons.* Brigadier Gough contacted his brother, a highly decorated colonel stationed at Aldershot. Soon the news spread through the military grapevine, with officers taking sides in the controversy—some affirming their duty to follow lawful orders, more standing with Gough. "There are two

---

* "Gough embodied to the core [the cavalry's] ethos of lax discipline and independent decision making. Edward Bennington, who served under him before and during the First World War, related a prewar incident in his memoirs which exemplifies Gough's attitude:

It so happened that I was in command of "A" Squadron one day and brought it on to parade five minutes before time. Goughy appeared at 9.00 am and had his trumpeter sound "Squadron Leader." We all galloped up and saluted, and he addressed us as follows. "Good morning Gentlemen. I noticed 1 squadron on parade this morning five minutes early. Please remember that it is better to be late rather than early. The former shows a sense of sturdy independence and no undue respect for higher authority, the latter merely shows womanish excitement and nervousness. Go back to your squadrons."

See Nikolas Gardner, "Command and Control in the 'Great Retreat' of 1914: The Disintegration of the British Cavalry Division," *Journal of Military History* 63, no. 1 (January 1999): 38.

camps in the army both very bitter against each other," reported a naval officer with friends in each.

The virus of "mutinous disaffection" spread to Churchill's navy in which a "significant number" of high officers had strong Ulster connections. They included the commanders in chief of the Home Fleet and the Second Battle Squadron, who both threatened to resign if "ordered to go against Ulster." The wife of a commodore testified that "the feeling is universal in the Navy of sympathy with the Army . . . and especially with the younger officers with whom Gough is a hero." The captain of HMS *Pathfinder*, so confidently dispatched to Belfast Lough by Churchill, informed the admiral in charge of his division that "I have no intention of going against Ulster should the occasion arise." Ordered to guard Carrickfergus Castle from a UVF assault, he met socially with the UVF commander and allowed his sailors to be "entertained" by Sir Edward Carson. When Churchill heard of this he was furious. "We might have had something like a general mutiny," Sir Spencer Ewart, the adjutant general at the War Office, noted in his diary.[41]

Asquith learned of the Curragh, a Jena for his government, only on Saturday. King George V wrote to him that he was "grieved beyond words at this disastrous and irreparable catastrophe which has befallen my Army."

Brigadier Gough was called to the War Office forthwith to explain himself. There had been a "misunderstanding," so Asquith couched it in a letter he dashed off that Saturday to the twenty-seven-year-old Venetia Stanley, the "girl" with whom he was then holding hands. ("There is nothing (as you know) that I would not shew you: so great and deep is my trust," he had written her in February.) Paget had misspoken. The officers got the wrong idea about the mission. No large-scale operations against the UVF were planned. "There was no plot," Lloyd George commented, "but no doubt Winston and Seely talked to Paget about hypothetical situations, and led him to think active operations were intended."[42]

The government requested General Gough and the other officers to withdraw their resignations. Negotiating the terms of his return to service with the War Office, Gough, counseled by Sir Henry Wilson, rightly regarded as a "tireless intrigue" by Asquith, laid down conditions. The government agreed to these, using talking points prepared by the ambidextrous Wilson. Gough demanded more concessions. Seely on his own agreed. ("If he had a little more brains," a War Office wit remarked, "he'd be half-witted.") Gough left London with a letter promising that the army would not be used to "enforce the present Home Rule Bill on Ulster." Waiting for his train at Euston Station, Gough told the military correspondent for the *Morning Post*, "I have got the assurances I asked for . . . I dictated the terms, and wrote them in my own hand."[43]

Probably tipped off by Wilson, the press broke the Curragh story on Saturday the twenty-first. Finding Seely at his desk at the War Office "long after midnight," a *Times* reporter confirmed the "rumors emanating from the Curragh." He witnessed "Mr. Churchill pay[ing] a visit to Col. Seely at a very early hour this morning." The First Lord of the Admiralty and the Secretary of State for War had a lot to talk about. Someone had blundered.[44]

Seely would be fired within a week. The Tories clamored for the archplotter against Ulster to follow him. "From the beginning to end of this sorry business," the MP Leo Amery charged in the *Times*, "the Secretary of State for War has been a mere tool in the hands of his masterful and sinister colleague of the Admiralty." But, Bradford having made him a Liberal hero, and Asquith valuing him as a lightning rod, Churchill rode out the storm.[45]

Sounding like the *Berliner Tagenblatt* and *Frankfurter Zeitung* on saber rule in Zabern, the Liberal press arraigned the army for intervening in politics. "For the first time in modern British history a military cabal seeks to dictate to Government the Bills it should carry or not carry into law," the *Daily Chronicle* editorialized. "We are confronted with a desperate rally of reactionaries to defeat the democratic movement and repeal the Parliament Act. This move by a few aristocratic officers is the last throw in the game." The *Daily Express* captured the significance of the Curragh Mutiny in a headline: THE HOME RULE BILL IS DEAD.[46]

Churchill agreed: "The Army have done what the Opposition failed to do." That conclusion was ineluctable. Home rule could be put on the statute books; it could not be enforced in Ulster without shattering the army. As in America's Civil War, some officers would throw in

Asquith submitting home rule bill to General French. Carson and Law are
whispering sedition to the general. After the Curragh Mutiny, the army
could not be counted on to suppress rebellion in Ulster.

with Ulster, others with the government. "Ulster," a letter to the *Times*
proclaimed, "is free."[47]

A third party now entered the conflict: The majority Catholic population in the south of Ireland. Home rule was their reconciling dream.
Before Parnell placed it at heart of party politics, Ireland, under "regular law" for only five years during the nineteenth century, had been
wracked by rural terrorism—including the "houghing" of livestock
with scythes and the "carding" of humans with nail-studded boards.
"Physical force is physical farce," the Nationalist Party politicians ad-
monished the gunmen of the secret republican societies. With home
rule Ireland could live in peace and dignity under the British crown.
The politics of patience calmed Ireland for more than two decades.
But Ulster's defiance of the rule of law lent new life to the secret societies and stirred new faith in their dream of a free Ireland and their
tools to get it—the gun and the bomb.

   An article published in *An Claidheamh Soluis*, a Gaelic League paper,
in November 1913, "The North Began," hailed the reemergence of

physical force in Ulster as a model for the rest of Ireland. In the newspaper of Sinn Féin, an organization dedicated "to the re-establishment of Irish independence," Patrick Pearse, a young Gaelic poet and schoolteacher, professed himself "glad that the North has 'begun' . . . glad that the Orangemen have armed for it was a goodly thing to see arms in Irish hands." Guns would deliver Ireland: "A thing that stands demonstrable is nationhood is not achieved otherwise than in arms . . . We must accustom ourselves to the thought of arms. We may make mistakes in the beginning and shoot the wrong people; but bloodshed is a cleansing and sanctifying thing . . . There are many things more horrible than bloodshed; and slavery is one of them." That exalted blood talk motivated much shooting of the wrong people, and not just in the beginning. Pearse himself was shot by a British firing squad for his leading role in the 1916 Easter Rising in Dublin. His martyrdom proved his prophecy that "from the graves of patriot men and women spring living nations."[48]

The North had begun; the South would follow. Of the post-Curragh mood in the North, a reporter wrote: "They will not even discuss concessions. They have lost interest in the parliamentary cause. They are not talking politics; they are talking rifles." After a sensational April landing of German rifles at Larne in Ulster (to which the commander of the destroyers Churchill ordered to blockade such shipments later said he had "turned a blind eye"), the *Roscommon Herald*, in the South, struck the same note of tribal belligerence: "If nationalist Ireland means to hold its own, it must cease talking and dreaming; it must get down to real practical work, and that work is *to get in the guns* and get the men to use them."[49]

A late 1913 government embargo on the importation of arms to Ireland stimulated ingenuity to get in the guns. Getting the men was easy, especially after the Curragh took lawful force against Ulster off the table.

Addressing Carson in the House, Churchill referenced a cartoon of a British soldier asking an Irish Nationalist, "Do you think I am going to fight for you?" That, Churchill said, was "a favorite point with the right hon. Gentleman, but what is the answer which the Nationalist is bound to make? It is a very simple one. 'Will you let me fight

for myself?'" Spurred by the government's diffidence about prosecuting the UVF leaders behind the Larne gunrunning, thousands of
such men (seventy-five thousand by May), deciding to fight for themselves, joined the Irish Volunteers, the South's answer to the UVF,
and pending guns drilled with broomsticks.[50]

The civil war scenario now shifted from the UVF versus the army
to the UVF versus the Volunteers, which, with units in the North, had
the longer reach. A Nationalist MP stated succinctly the insoluble turn
the crisis had taken: "It was now abundantly clear that if passing Home
Rule meant civil war, so also would abandonment of Home Rule."
Writing to the king, Asquith made the same point: "If the ship, after
so many stormy voyages, were now to be wrecked in sight of port, it
is difficult to overrate the shock, or its consequences . . . It is not too
much to say that Ireland would become ungovernable."

Ireland in 1914 was hastening toward a guerrilla war between
Protestant and Catholic paramilitaries—some fighting for home rule,
others against, yet others for Irish independence—with the British
army in the middle. Think of a bloodier version of The Troubles that
erupted in the late 1960s and ground on until the Good Friday Agreement of 1998, which brought the political wing of the Irish Republican Army, Sinn Féin, into a power-sharing government in Belfast
with the Ulster Unionist party. Home Rule at last!

Unwilling to punish rebellion in the North, the government fostered
it in the South. To the Nationalist in the cartoon who wanted to fight
for himself, the government, Churchill said, must say, " 'No, you shall
be obliged to confine yourself to constitutional action,' and we are
bound to make sure that constitutional action is not frustrated by law-
less violence." But they had not made sure.[51]

"If the Government are not going to enforce the law in one part of
Ireland they have no right to it in another," Bonar Law had the cheek
to declare. "There is anarchy in Ireland." That verdict on the Liberals
and Ireland left out the blocking roles of Law and his Tories, Carson
and the Protestant People of Ulster, the Redmond veto, and the army
strike. "Between these difficulties," Churchill wrote, "Mr. Asquith's
Government sought to thread their way."[52]

★　★　★

"Complete disaster is now but a few weeks—it may be only a few days—away," the *Times* asserted on June 29, in the same edition carrying the news of the assassination in Sarajevo of the Austrian archduke Franz Ferdinand. The editorial got the time right—"a few weeks"—but the disaster wrong.

Writing in 1923, Churchill remarked on "the strange calm" glazing the surface of European affairs in the years nearest the war. In July

Churchill and Kaiser Wilhelm at the German army maneuvers
in 1909. In May 1940, with Hitler poised to invade Holland, where
the kaiser went into exile in November 1918,
Prime Minister Churchill offered him asylum in Britain.

1914 this yielded to a manipulated calm. After Sarajevo, Austria-Hungary launched a judicial inquest into the Serbian government's alleged participation in the assassination. European capitals were reassured: Vienna was proceeding carefully. Led by the kaiser, who, instead of sailing up the Norwegian coast on his summer cruise, departed and anchored off Bergen for two weeks, high military and government figures left Vienna and Berlin on holiday. Bethmann Hollweg orchestrated this ruse to lull the Entente and convey the appearance of German nescience regarding any pending conflict between Austria-Hungary and Serbia, while at the same time secretly handing Vienna a "blank check"—cashable in war—to "square accounts" with Serbia.

Britain had worked strenuously to prevent the Balkan War of 1913 between Serbia and Bulgaria from touching off a European conflagration. If Bethmann had not "deliberately deceive[d] him," while Austrian soldiers on "harvest leave" used the time to complete their work in the fields before quietly returning to the colors, Sir Edward Grey might have repeated this performance after Sarajevo.

Instead, and perhaps to focus public attention away from the impending cliff of Ulster, the government sounded eupeptic on Europe. Ten days after Sarajevo, Lloyd George assured his auditors at London's Guildhall that "in the matter of external affairs, the sky has never been more perfectly blue." As late as July 22, describing the recent course of Anglo-German relations, the chancellor said, "There is none of the snarling which we used to see." Until the last days of July the headlines—MACHINE GUNS FOR ULSTER, 30,000 RIFLES AND 10,000 ROUNDS LAND IN BELFAST, 3000 TRAINED NURSES FOR ULSTER—heralded civil war.[53]

With Parliament paralyzed by the onrushing fatality, on July 21 the king convened an emergency peace conference at "my house," Buckingham Palace. Led by Asquith and Bonar Law, the politicians filed silently by the press waiting at the gates. Left to themselves, the two English parties might have struck a deal, but they were hostage to their Irish wings, and though after the first day of the conference Redmond told associates that "as an Irishman you could not help being proud to see how [Sir Edward Carson] towered above the others" and the two leaders shook hands warmly yet, a Redmond ally wrote, "there was a point beyond which neither of them could take their followers, and these points could not be brought to meet." When they were reached on the third day, the conference broke up.[54]

The *Times* blamed the Nationalists: "The British Empire numbers over 400 million human beings . . . The whole of this vast structure is to be imperiled, and for what reason? Because Mr. Redmond wants to get control of two counties in the North of Ireland with a total population of 204,000, and the Government dares not say him nay." Asquith had persuaded Redmond to accept the time-limit scheme for excluding Ulster from home rule, but Redmond dug in his heels over the counties to be excluded. He wanted the majority Catholic ones under home rule from the start.[55]

Churchill wrapped the stalemate over these counties in a memorable flourish:

> And so, turning this way and that in search of an exit from the deadlock, the Cabinet toiled around the muddy by-ways of Fermanagh and Tyrone. One had hoped that the events . . . at the Curragh and in Belfast would have shocked British public opinion, and formed a unity sufficient to force a settlement on the Irish factions. Apparently they had been insufficient . . . The discussion had reached its inclusive end, and the Cabinet was about to separate, when the quiet grave tones of Sir Edward Grey's voice was heard reading a document which had just been brought to him from the Foreign Office. It was the Austrian note to Serbia . . . It was an ultimatum such as had never been penned in modern times . . . No State in the world could accept it [nor fail to see] that any acceptance, however abject, would satisfy the aggressor. The parishes of Fermanagh and Tyrone faded back into the mists and squalls of Ireland, and a strange light began immediately, but by perceptible gradations, to fall and grow upon the map of Europe.[56]

But days later, the mists parted and Fermanagh and Tyrone were still there, daubed with blood. The *Times* for July 28, which announced Austria's declaration of war on Serbia, led with the headline

SHOOTING IN BACHELOR'S WALK above a bulletin of the worst news yet from Ireland.[57]

A landing of 1,500 Mauser rifles for the Irish Volunteers in Howth Harbor outside Dublin had ended in mayhem, when soldiers from the King's Own Scottish Borderers shot into a crowd of stone-throwing Dubliners, killing three and wounding thirty-six. Addressing the House of Commons, mild John Redmond sounded militant: "Four-fifths of the Irish people will not submit any longer to be bullied, or punished, or penalized, or shot, for conduct which is permitted to go scot-free in the open light of day in every county of Ulster by other sections of their countrymen."[58]

The "Bachelor's Walk Massacre" fueled rage across the South. In Roscommon a speaker arraigned the "dirty hacks of the English government" as cowards and murderers. Stokestown showed a "grim determination of revenge." In Sligo three hundred Volunteers heard a speaker bewail the Irish blood shed by "the cursed dogs of England" and their "cursed Scottish hounds" and threaten the UVF: "We will not stand any nonsense in the future . . . if a shot is fired at our people in the North we are prepared to meet them . . . I say here publicly, in the presence of the press, that Ireland is out for blood and murder." Ireland, North *and* South, was out for blood and murder. "One spark," the *Times* judged, "may serve to set off the long-dreaded conflagration."[59]

With civil war a spark away, the *Times* caught the moment when war irrevocably overtook Ulster in the race of disasters. It came on July 27 in the House. The Tories had been blistering the government over Ulster when "suddenly the atmosphere changed as Mr. Bonar Law advanced to the table and asked the Foreign Secretary for information about the situation between Austria and Serbia."[60]

Edward Grey rose; the House fell still. "It must be obvious to any person who reflects upon the situation," Grey said, "that the moment the dispute ceases to be one between Austria-Hungary and Serbia and becomes one in which another Great Power [Russia] is involved, it can but end in the greatest catastrophe that has ever befallen the continent of Europe."

Amid news of Serb engineers blowing up a bridge across the Danube, of pink paper notices announcing the mobilization of four million

men going up on hoardings in St. Petersburg, of Kaiser Wilhelm pro-
claiming, "The sword has been forced into our hands!" from the bal-
cony of the Royal Palace in Berlin, of German troops seizing French
locomotives in Alsace, the *Times* voiced the thought of Britain: "Civil
war in these islands seems unthinkable at such a time." It even seemed
unthinkable in Ulster. "Over the last forty-eight hours [there] has been
a sudden and complete change in the Irish attitude," the *Times* correspondent reported from Belfast. "On Wednesday night Ulstermen and
Nationalists were . . . going on deliberately with their preparations for
combat. Then came the grave words . . . in the House of Commons on
Thursday . . . Now Irishmen of all complexions have suddenly become
Britons."[61]

It remained for the politicians to register the change. After the
Buckingham Palace Conference impasse, Asquith finally dared to say
Redmond nay. He prepared an Amending Bill permitting any Ulster
county to vote itself permanently out of the home rule scheme. This
about-face carried political risk. Appeasement of Carson's Unionists
might roil Redmond's Nationalists to vote against the government,
bringing it down. But Redmond, recognizing that replacing the Liberals with the Unionists would only doom his cause, had "reluctantly
agreed" to accept exclusion when the Bachelor's Walk Massacre
made that politically impossible.[62]

Austrian and Serbian forces had already engaged in a firefight along
the Sava River when the House met to take up the Amending Bill on
July 31. "At this moment unparalleled in the experience of any one of
us," the prime minister told the House, it was necessary "to present a
united front and to be able to speak and act with the authority of an
undivided nation." In that spirit, he postponed the Amending Bill
indefinitely. There would be no civil war. Only one barrier to British
intervention in the European war remained: the Liberalism of the
Liberal Party.[63]

On August 2, as the *Times* went to press, it received word from the
French ambassador that GERMANY HAS INVADED FRANCE WITHOUT DEC-
LARATION OF WAR. In this desperate hour, the editors were "stupefied to
learn that a section of Mr. Asquith's Cabinet is in favour of leaving
France in the lurch . . . France crushed means Britain degraded." In-
deed, as Asquith confided to Ms. Stanley, "a good ¾ of our own party

in the House of Commons are for absolute non-interference at any price." Churchill judged that the same percentage of the cabinet, invoking the Liberal tradition of keeping clear of Europe's wars, would vote to remain neutral. Asquith had two incompatible goals: to take the country, and his party, into war. Ulster helped him merge them in an unexpected way.[64]

In the decisive cabinet meeting of August 2, Asquith, speaking as a politician to fellow politicians, wrapped the war in party loyalty, party preservation, and repugnance toward the opposition party. "The P. M. is anxious we should see this thing through as a Party," one minister reported to his wife. Another recalled Asquith arguing that "if a block were to leave the Government at this juncture, their action would necessitate a Coalition Government which would be the grave of Liberalism." Since the coalition with the hawkish Unionists would be a war government, quitting the cabinet might salve the Liberal conscience but would not keep Britain out of the war. And, Asquith said, looking around the cabinet table at colleagues who had stood in the arena together through many battles for many years, men from "the other party" would fill their places, men whose conduct over Ulster had exposed their unfitness to govern. Principle retreating before party spirit and partisan animus, Asquith secured a cabinet majority. In the end only two of twenty ministers resigned. Germany's invasion of Belgium, meanwhile, swung the Liberal backbenchers behind war.[65]

Asquith did not make his strongest argument: He knew that loyalty to *him* would work powerfully on his colleagues. Asquith's intellect and eloquence commanded respect, but his readiness to praise inspired affection. His notes to his colleagues display an appreciation not merely of what they did but of who they were. For example, when, to allay public doubts raised by the "shells crisis" that rocked the government in May 1915, Lloyd George stepped down as chancellor of the exchequer to fill the newly created post of minister of munitions, Asquith wrote him:

My dear Lloyd George,
    I cannot let this troubled & tumultuous chapter in our history close without trying to let you know what an incalculable help &

support I have found in you all through. I shall never forget your devotion, your unselfishness, your powers of resource, what is (after all) the best of all things your self-forgetfulness.

These are rare things that make the drudgery and squalor of politics, with its constant revelation of the large part played by petty & personal motives, endurable, and give to its drabness a lightning streak of nobility.*

I thank you with all my heart.

Always yours affectionately

H. H. Asquith

Over his six years as prime minister Asquith had won the heart of every man in the cabinet with exquisitely tailored testaments like that. Leading by generosity helped him keep his party together in August 1914, when Britain entered the Great War as an undivided country behind an undivided government.[66]

On August 4, Britain gave Germany twelve hours to withdraw its forces from Belgium or face war. "Cheered from every quarter of the House," Asquith read this ultimatum aloud to the House. Churchill, listening, cried.[67]

It had been a near-run thing. Austrian shells were falling on the Grand Hotel in Belgrade when Captain Craig, the UVF commander in Belfast, wired Carson in London that "you may take it that immediately you signify by the pre-arranged code that we are to go ahead, everything prepared will be carried out to the letter . . . All difficulties have been overcome and we are in a very strong position." Anticipating that Churchill would order a blockade of Ulster as soon as the Ulster Provisional Government was proclaimed, Craig was arranging the delivery of mass quantities of flour, tea, and other staples from Glasgow to stockpile against scarcity when Churchill was mov-

*Asquith used "lightning" in describing Churchill to Venetia Stanley. "He is a wonderful creature with a curious dash of school boy simplicity (quite unlike Edward Grey's) and what someone said of genius—'a zigzag of lightning in the brain.'" Seen in Roy Jenkins, *Churchill: A Biography* (New York: Farrar, Straus and Giroux, 2001), 230.

"War Declared" by Max Beckmann

ing to mobilize the Royal Navy for war against Germany. Russia *had* mobilized against Austria when Lord Milner, a Unionist ultra, was still at work designing the currency of the Provisional government. Berlin was about to implement its Period Preparatory to War measures when Asquith was in the cabinet room poring over maps of Ulster, preparing his speech for the last reading of the bill amending home rule. He was interrupted, he wrote to Ms. Stanley, by "a telephone message from (of all people in the world) Bonar Law, to ask me to come & see him and Carson at his Kensington abode . . . He had sent his motor car, which I boarded, and in due time arrived at my destination . . . It was quite an adventure, for I might easily have been kidnapped by a section of Ulster Volunteers." Law proposed that "in the interest of the international situation" the home rule controversy be suspended. From that moment— the last moment!—the Ulster crisis began receding into the mists of history. Carson received Captain Craig's telegram a few hours before this meeting. If he had wired back "Go ahead," Ulster 1914 might be remembered still.[68]

As it was, the Ulster crisis ranks as a cause of the world war rather than as a barricade to Britain's participation in it. Impending civil war in Ireland signaled Berlin that "Britain was so deeply mired . . . that the danger of [its] becoming involved in a continental war was . . .

negligible," according to John C. G. Röhl, the kaiser's biographer, who adds that "this grave miscalculation more than any other neutralized the deterrent effect till then implicit in the Triple Entente."[69]

"I don't think there's any point in being Irish if you don't know that the world will break your heart eventually," Daniel Patrick Moynihan remarked after the death of John F. Kennedy. Ulster is an Irish story, and so it is fitting to end with heartbreak.

For the first time since Gladstone introduced his second home rule bill chairs were set out on the House floor on Tuesday, August 3, to accommodate the overflow crowd come to hear Sir Edward Grey make the government's case for war on grounds of interest, honor, and the maintenance of the balance of power against German hegemony in Europe. Toward the end, after Grey called Ireland "the one bright spot in the very dreadful situation," and declared that "the position in Ireland—and I should like this to be clearly understood abroad—is not a consideration among the things we have to take account of now," John Redmond was seen conferring with members of his Irish party. "I am going to tell them," he said, "that they can take all their troops out of Ireland, and we will defend the country ourselves."

With memorial masses for the Bachelor's Walk victims held across Ireland on the Sunday, two days past, with ten thousand rifles for the Irish Volunteers just landed on the Wicklow Coast, with feelings still running high on the Nationalist back benches, Redmond, swept beyond his base by patriotic emotion, addressed the House. "I say to the Government that . . . Ireland will be defended by her armed sons from invasion, and for that purpose the armed Catholics in the South will only be too glad to join arms with the armed Protestant Ulster men," he daringly pledged. He had a dream of Ireland united in England's war: "Is it too much to hope that out of this situation a result may spring which will be good, not merely for the Empire, but for the future welfare and integrity of the Irish nation?" He finished to "deafening applause" even from the Unionists. Redmond not only lent political support to the British war effort; his son also enlisted and won a Distinguished Service Order for gallantry. Unlike one of Asquith's sons, one of Grey's, and two of Bonar Law's, William Redmond survived the war.[70]

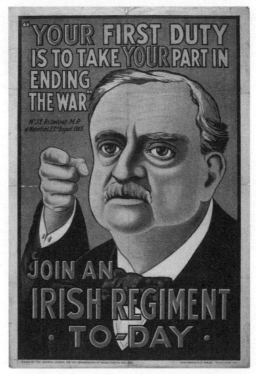

John Redmond: England's Irish patriot

Initially Redmond wanted the Irish Volunteers to serve only in Ireland. But on September 20, addressing a body of East Wicklow Volunteers in the Vale of Avoca, he once more got carried away. It would, he said, "be a reproach to her manhood . . . if young Ireland confined their efforts to staying at home" to defend against "an unlikely" invasion. "I say to you, therefore, your duty is twofold": to go on "drilling and make yourselves efficient for the work, and then account for yourselves as men, not only in Ireland itself, but wherever the firing-line extends." Whether this, as F. S. L. Lyons writes, was a "reaction of gratitude for Home Rule's having at last been entered on the statute books" (with its operation suspended until after the war) or "a gesture of competition with the Ulster Volunteers whom Carson had already urged to fight overseas," it was a political debacle. It split the Volunteers, with eleven thousand rejecting any idea of fighting *for* England and lining up behind leaders like Patrick Pearse, who

John Redmond (as seen by Sinn Féin): England's Irish traitor

soon operated a "revolutionary cell" within the Volunteers, source of the foot soldiers of the Easter Rising.

From the Wicklow speech also dates the fall of the Nationalist Party, with their candidates losing key by-elections in 1917 to Sinn Féiners, including the lone survivor among the leaders of the rising, Éamon de Valera. "Dev," free Ireland's first president, ran on the Proclamation of the Irish Republic that Pearse read out to puzzled passersby in front of the Dublin General Post Office on Easter Monday 1916, which began: "IRISHMEN AND IRISH WOMEN: In the name of God and of the dead generations from which she receives her tradition of nationhood, Ireland, through us, summons her children to her flag and strikes for her freedom." Next to Irish freedom, home rule under Britain quickly lost its grip on Irish hopes, and Sinn Féin's definition of the home rule politicians as "a body of green-liveried servants of the British connection" took hold.[71]

To Irish Republicans Redmond's English patriotism was perfidy. An editorial voice of Ireland's "exiled children in America," as the Proclamation called them, was virulent. In 1912, when the House voted for the third home rule bill and the cause looked won at last, New York's *Irish World* saluted Redmond as "the idol of the race." Three and a half years later, after British firing squads had anointed the Republican cause with the martyrs' blood of the rising, Redmond was reviled by the *World*: "We can almost pity the fallen leader and his followers, but what has Ireland done that she should be cursed with such a canting, cringing, cowardly crew? Ireland has had traitors before but none quite so despicable."[72]

John Redmond died in March 1918 knowing that his "lifelong struggle to reconcile nationalist with Unionist and Ireland with England had ended in unrelieved failure."[73]

A month later, needing men to check the Ludendorff offensive tearing holes in the British lines in France, an "order in council" from London extended conscription to Ireland. That inspired an Irish toast: "May the shadow of John Redmond never fall upon your sons."[74]

4

THE UNITED STATES AND MEXICO

THE PRESIDENT AND THE BANDIT

*He said his Mexican policy was based upon two of the most deeply
seated convictions of his life. First, his shame as an American over
the first Mexican war, and his resolution that there should never be
another such predatory enterprise. Second, upon his belief . . .
that a people has the right "to do what they damn please with
their own affairs." (He used the word "damn.")*

—From notes made by the journalist
Ray Stannard Baker on a May 11, 1917,
conversation with Woodrow Wilson

BEFORE AUGUST, THE world's killing ground in 1914 was
Mexico, where a violent revolution had been raging since 1910.
Mexico was a portent of social upheaval for Europe's possessing classes
and of anti-imperialist revolt for Europe's foreign offices. For European and American mining and oil companies with property there,
fortunes were at risk in Mexico. The new American president who
took office in March 1913 shared none of these fears. For Woodrow
Wilson Mexico was a moral proving ground. On it he would show
that U.S. hemispheric imperialism was a thing of the past. For the best
of reasons, he wanted to stay out of the Mexican Revolution; for the
best of reasons, he got pulled in. When Wilson intervened in Mexico,
in April 1914, no one could have guessed that he was plunging the
United States into a stream of events that, in April 1917, would sweep

it onto the stage of world history. No other Great Power would follow so improbable a path to belligerency. The United States would enter the European war through Mexico.

Throughout the twentieth century and with ideologically charged vigor during the Cold War, the United States acted as a counterrevolutionary power in Latin America, intervening either directly or by proxy against Marxist-Leninist revolutions (Cuba, Nicaragua), leftist guerrilla movements (El Salvador), and democratically elected socialist governments (Guatemala, Chile). Brazilian generals, Panamanian, Paraguayan, and Chilean strongmen found friends in Washington. The apocryphal quip attributed to Franklin D. Roosevelt, that Nicaraguan strongman Anastasio Somoza was an SOB but *"our* SOB," captured the cynical maxim guiding the conduct of a succession of American presidents toward right-wing dictators who plundered their people but protected U.S. economic interests.

Woodrow Wilson, too, intervened in the hemisphere, sending marines to protect U.S. businesses in Haiti in 1914, occupying Santo Domingo in 1916, and, in aid of American bankers, concluding a treaty with Nicaragua that according to Senator George W. Norris made the "dollar diplomacy" of Wilson's predecessor in the White House, William Howard Taft, "look like the proverbial 30 cents."[1]

However, in Mexico Wilson allowed arms to flow to a peasant revolution against a military dictator. More through understanding its genesis in "the great and crying wrongs the people have endured," he accepted that the overthrow of the existing unjust order must precede the American nostrum of free elections. The president even defended the revolutionary violence perpetrated by the rebel general and sometime bandit Francisco "Pancho" Villa.[2]

Historical empathy moved Wilson to reach out his hand to Villa. The bandit made himself acceptable to the president by protecting American businesses in areas he controlled, deporting union organizers from the Industrial Workers of the World (IWW), for example, at the request of the Guggenheims' American Smelting and Refining Company. In addition, Villa buffed his image with a propaganda campaign focused on Hollywood and progressive journalists. By late 1913, the susceptible organs of the American press had transformed the bandit into a robin hood, the butcher into a brilliant commander,

"In the Interest of Peace." Sykes in the Philadelphia *Public Ledger*.
Well might Uncle Sam look puzzled. What was an American president
doing arming Mexican revolutionaries?

the subliterate muleteer into a plausible statesman. Regarding Villa as "the greatest Mexican of his generation," Woodrow Wilson briefly saw in him the lineaments of Mexico's next president.

Villa cast himself as an American progressive in a hurry. When he told an El Paso newspaper that he wanted Mexico to be like the United States "where all men are equal before the law and where any man who is willing to work can make such a living for himself and his family as only the wealthy in Mexico [now] can enjoy," he might have been Wilson speaking in the 1912 campaign about America under "The New Freedom," the slogan for his program of progressive reform.[3]

In early 1914, Wilson tilted decisively toward Villa and the rebels by lifting the arms embargo imposed in March 1912 by President Taft. Smuggling had poked holes in the embargo, the revolutionary armies paying Mexican men, women, and children three cents for every cartridge smuggled across the border, the women carrying hundreds in belts under skirts that hung nearly to their knees. But Wilson's decision opened the tap. Muscled up with a shipment of fifteen million rounds of ammunition, fourteen thousand rifles, and four machine guns long waiting in New Orleans, in late March, General Villa's Division of the North attacked Torreón, a key rail junction in northern Mexico. Villa entered the city on April 3. Meanwhile, to prevent a shipment of arms from reaching the dictator General Victoriano Huerta in Mexico City, on April 21 Wilson ordered American bluejackets and marines to occupy the port city of Veracruz. These two military actions finished Huerta, who fled Mexico in July.[4]

Few, though, would have predicted that outcome on April 22, for not only did soldiers of Huerta's federal army resist the landing of the Americans; Mexican civilians, too, defended their city, their country. The streets of Veracruz were strewn with the bodies of at least 126 Mexican soldiers and civilians killed by U.S. sailors and marines, who themselves lost seventeen dead and sixty-three wounded in house-to-house fighting. Huerta used Veracruz to rally nationalist anger around him, even appealing to the rebels to join in a war against the Yankee invader, whose troops, the Huerta-controlled Mexico City papers falsely reported, were pouring across the Rio Grande. Wilson swore that Huerta was his target, that by seizing their leading seaport and killing scores of them he intended no harm to the Mexican people; but in all Mexico, it seemed, only Pancho Villa swallowed that farrago. Risking a forfeit of the nationalist card to Huerta, Villa told a U.S. consul in northern Mexico that "as far as he was concerned we could keep Veracruz and hold it so tight that not even water would get in to Huerta."[5]

The seizure of Veracruz sped the exit of the dictator and the victory of the revolution. But south of the border it went down as an imperialist grab, La Nación of Buenos Aires accurately predicting that "the memory of this conflict will live in the history of the relations between the U.S. and Latin America."

Wilson took office with an exalted view of his mandate (informing the chairman of his party the day after the election, "Remember that God *ordained that I should be the next president of the United States*") and

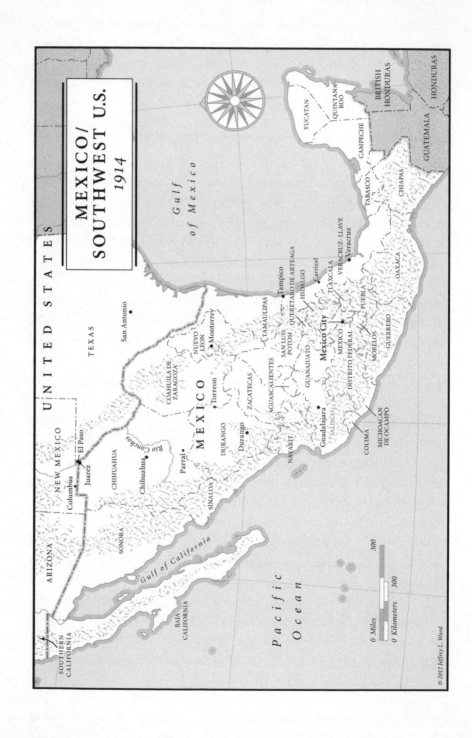

MEXICO/
SOUTHWEST U.S.
1914

UNITED STATES

Gulf
of Mexico

BRITISH
HONDURAS

HONDURAS

GUATEMALA

QUINTANA
ROO

YUCATAN

CAMPECHE

TABASCO

CHIAPAS

OAXACA

VERACRUZ- LLAVE
Veracruz

Carrizal

HIDALGO

QUERETARO DE ARTEAGA

TLAXCALA

PUEBLA

GUERRERO

MEXICO

MORELOS

DISTRITO FEDERAL

Mexico City

Tampico

SAN LUIS
POTOSI

GUANAJUATO

MICHOACAN
DE OCAMPO

COLIMA

JALISCO

Guadalajara

TAMAULIPAS

ZACATECAS

AGUASCALIENTES

NAYARIT

TEXAS

San Antonio

NUEVO
LEON

Monterrey

COAHUILA DE
ZARAGOZA

Torreon

DURANGO

Durango

Rio Conchos

El Paso

CHIHUAHUA

Chihuahua

Parral

SINALOA

NEW MEXICO

Juarez

Columbus

ARIZONA

SOUTHERN
CALIFORNIA

BAJA
CALIFORNIA

Gulf of California

*Pacific
Ocean*

0 Miles   300

0 Kilometers   300

© 2012 Jeffrey L. Ward

he hoped to end "dollar diplomacy" in the hemisphere and make a fresh moral start. "President Wilson has served plain notice that foreign interests and concessions are no longer to be the first consideration in the relations between the U.S. and the Southern Republics," a journalist paraphrased Wilson after interviewing him. "Foreign interests" meant American as well. Since the late nineteenth century, Mexico had become a satellite of the United States, which used it, the wife of an American diplomat stationed there wrote, "as a quarry, leaving no monument to God nor testaments to man in place of the treasure that we have piled on departing ships or trains." Challenging the grip of the "special interests" at home, Wilson took a wider view of his responsibilities than to serve as their political arm in Mexico. "If American enterprise in foreign countries . . . takes the shape of imposing upon and exploiting the mass of the people in that country, it ought to be checked," he declared in his 1914 Fourth of July oration in Philadelphia. He was "willing to get anything for an American that money and enterprise can obtain, except the suppression of the rights of other men." If Americans lost property in Mexico, if some were killed in the revolution, that was of course regrettable, "but back of it all is the struggle of a people to come into their own."

The blood and obloquy of Veracruz has obscured both the lost story of an American president arming a popular revolution in Latin America and the long reach of Wilson's decision and its lasting consequence. Entering the Mexican labyrinth as a hemispheric hegemon, the United States would exit it as a world power.[6]

From the Stone Age to the Age of Capital, the history of Mexico was a violent struggle for the land of Mexico. In the century before the Spanish Conquest in 1520, the Aztecs exploited peasant revolts against local elites to build their empire. Expropriating land as they conquered it, they forced subject peoples to work in the fields for the Aztec state. "Every year many of their sons and daughters were demanded of them for sacrifice, and others for service in the houses and plantations of their conquerors," the ruler of a Totonac town complained to Hernán Cortés.

Revolts were frequent, and savagely repressed. Prisoners taken in battle had their beating hearts ripped out to propitiate Huitzilopochtli, the Aztec war god. The conquistadores arrived during an anti-Aztec revolt, and exploited it to supplant the Aztecs as Mexico's rulers. The pattern of revolt was set for the next five hundred years. Aztec emperors, rebellious Indian aristocrats, Spanish conquistadores, the bourgeois political leaders of both the war of independence and the revolution—elites rode the peasants into power, then betrayed them.[7]

Greeted as liberators, the Spaniards soon recognized the utility of slavery, modeling the *encomienda* system of forced Indian labor on the grimmest features of the Aztecs' "despotic tributary regime." Slaves were branded with their owners' initials like cattle—on the face. The gold and silver mined by the pre-Conquest peoples under the Spanish lash financed the commercial revolution of the Age of Discovery. The money god proved hungrier than Huitzilopochtli. In central Mexico, out of an aboriginal population estimated at eleven million in 1500, by 1650 only a million and a half had survived the fatal impact of European colonization.[8]

Using the Indians up in the mines, the Spanish could not exploit their labor in the fields. Yet the growing colony had to be fed. So, by bestowing huge swathes of land on throne-connected grandees, the Spanish created the hacienda system, "the centre of gravity of the Mexican economy for the next two-and-a-half centuries." The haciendas first expropriated the land of exterminated Indians and then, with legal cover after the villages lost the protection of the Spanish crown, annexed the communal land of mixed-race settlers. Land seizures accelerated in the nineteenth century, provoking a hundred village revolts against haciendas and a score of regional and two national rebellions. One of these brought independence from Spain after 1810, another, the last and greatest, revolution in 1910.[9]

The hacienda was a feudal world with a workforce of debt-chained peons, farm laborers and sharecroppers, a priest to pacify the living, a cemetery to bury the dead, and a prison to punish the disorderly—a ministate ruled by the *hacendado,* who answered to no man for his appetites.[10]

In *The Old Gringo,* Carlos Fuentes's novel of the Mexican Revolution, General Arroyo, a character with a Villa-like biography, exposes to an American woman the secret wounds of life on the hacienda. An overseer ran it, he explains; the owners visited for recreation:

"The Torches" by Leopoldo Méndez. These peasants
appear about to set fire to a hacienda, the "Bastille of the
Mexican Revolution."

When the owners came, they got bored and drank cognac. They
fought the young bulls. They also went galloping through the
tilled fields, terrifying the peons bent over their humble Chihuahua crops, beans, wild lettuce, spindly wheat; they beat the backs
of the weakest men with the flat of a machete, and then lassoed
the weakest women and then raped them in the hacienda stables
while the mothers of the young gentlemen pretended not to hear
the screams of our mothers and the fathers of the young gentlemen drank cognac in the library and said, They're young . . .
They'll settle down. We did the same.

The owners might rape aloud; the help copulated in silence: "Here
they killed you if you made any noise in bed. If a man and a woman
moaned while they slept together, they were whipped . . . We made
love and we gave birth without a sound, *señorita*."[11]
Arroyo's picture of the hacienda's regime of submission reveals why
"in the oral tradition of many peasant soldiers the revolution itself
appeared as a series of hacienda-seizures rather than an overthrow of
state power," according to the Mexican historian Adolfo Gilly. The
hacienda was the "Bastille of the Mexican Revolution."[12]

During the reign of the military strongman Porfirio Díaz (1876–1910), nearly all of Mexico's villages lost land to state-promoted haciendas, representing an oligarchy of three thousand families. By 1910, they "owned over half of the nation's territory." Díaz also sold vast tracks of land and subsidized U.S. railroads to build five north-south lines twenty-five hundred miles into the interior. The lines bid up land prices, increasing the incentive for haciendas to annex fifty thousand villages.[13]

Connecting Mexico to the United States and world markets, the railroads created an export boom in cash crops—coffee, sugar, and fruits—but the production of staple crops, the original purpose of the hacienda system, languished. To feed its common people Mexico had to import corn and beans. As food prices rose, the Mexican diet deteriorated. Producing more, the field worker ate less. An old peasant,* a soldier in Villa's army, explained to the American journalist John Reed why men like him joined the revolution: "When [the revolution] is over, we'll never, ever, be hungry."[14]

Force protected Díaz's agrarian capitalist revolution from above against rebellion from below. To suppress local revolts, the *hacendados* furnished a semiofficial militia. Bigger trouble was contained by the Mauser-armed suede-dressed *rurales*; and by the army, its ranks thickened by the *leva* (impressment) of captured rebels and outlaws. Recalcitrants were deported to servitude on the hemp plantations of the Yucatán. The hardest cases were shot trying to escape; the *ley fuga*, a

---

* "The terms 'peasant' and 'peasant movement' are widely used to denote a particular rural social stratum and its purposeful self-organization. Peasants, however, have been so variously identified that a generally accepted definition has yet to be produced. Usually the term refers to rural producers who possess (but do not necessarily own) the means of producing their own subsistence and a marketable surplus—that is, smallholders, squatters, members of corporate Indian villages, service tenants, cash renters, sharecroppers and the like." John H. Coatsworth, "Patterns of Rural Rebellion in Latin America: Mexico in Comparative Perspective," in Friedrich Katz, ed., *Riot, Rebellion, and Revolution: Rural Social Conflict in Mexico* (Princeton: Princeton University Press, 1988), 22. "The driving force of the revolutionary upheaval of 1911–1916 was the rural peasantry and proletariat. To the dispossessed peasant small ranchero, Indian *cumunero*, or rural proletarian, the enemy—the landlord-capitalist—was still very much in evidence. To these people the solution was simple: take back the land and water, seize the mills, provide for self, family, and community rather than the boss." James Cockroft, quoted in ibid., 418, n. 2.

trial-saving expedient, claimed some ten thousand victims under Díaz. To muffle outrage Díaz relied on *pan o palo*, bread or the stick. Friendly newspapers received *pan*, subsidies; libel laws silenced the rest.[15]

Besides force and fraud, the Porfiriato rested on prosperity; when it vanished in the slump beginning in 1908–9, so did the aged dictator's hold on the urban middle and upper classes. One of them, Francisco I. Madero, scion of a wealthy *hacendado* family in the northeastern state of Coahuila, challenged Díaz in the presidential election of 1910. When Madero's call for "a real vote and no boss rule" won cheers wherever he spoke, Díaz jailed Madero for treason, sportingly permitting him to receive 183 votes in the seventh rigged election since 1884. After five months in a San Luis Potosí prison, Madero was paroled on his family's bond. Allowed the freedom of the city, he galloped away from his guards, rode to the border, and escaped across the Rio Grande. From San Antonio, the thirty-seven-year-old spiritualist, spurred into politics by a visitation from the shade of Benito Juárez (1806–1872), the great liberal reformer who in the late 1860s liberated Mexico from its French invaders and executed the mountebank emperor Maximilian, named himself provisional president. He called for an all-class uprising to oust Díaz commencing on November 20, 1910, and he issued a manifesto, the Plan of San Luis Potosí.[16]

The plan outlined a series of reforms appealing to Díaz's middle-class opponents—free elections, a free press, nonreelection of the president and vice president—and if it had stopped there, the revolution would have stopped, too. But Article Three changed everything.

"Through unfair advantage taken of the Law of Untitled Lands, numerous proprietors of small holdings, in their majority Indians, have been dispossessed of their lands," Madero wrote. "In all fairness, those lands . . . should be returned to their former owners." Mexico's landless poor now had a cause to fight for. Hundreds and then thousands rallied to the son of Mexico's fifth-richest family, suddenly leader of the greatest rural uprising in a century. "No organized party presided at its birth," Eric Wolf writes of the fire of revolution ignited by Madero's vague plan. "No intellectuals prescribed its program, formulated its doctrine, outlined its objectives." The peasants were in the saddle and rode Madero.[17]

★   ★   ★

At dawn on November 20, 1910, at the small Chihuahua ranch of La Cueva Pinta, armed men gathered around campfires to listen to the plan being read aloud. "As they heard the moving words," the reader, a Madero ally, recalled, "the faces of these simple peasants . . . showed enormous satisfaction . . . Some had suffered from the egotism of their masters their whole lives long . . . ; others had seen their small properties confiscated with the full sanction of the government; others had been persecuted . . . for having avenged the honor of their sisters or wives, violated by the rich and by corrupt authorities . . . Once the reading of the plan was finished, we all brandished our arms and hands and cried out, 'Down with the tyrants, long live freedom for all, long live Francisco Madero! . . .' They split into four companies and elected their officers. Voted 'First Commander' of the first company was one 'Francisco Villa.'[18]

Pancho Villa was of the people. Like so many of Mexico's poor, he had no schooling. "A rifle sight was the only spelling book I knew until I was a grown man," he told the *Los Angeles Times*, a line crafted for quotation. The oldest of five children, he was born Doroteo Arango into a sharecropping family on a Durango hacienda in 1878. One day, returning to his house from the fields, so the Villa legend goes, he found his mother confronting the *hacendado* for ravishing his twelve-year-old sister, Martina. "I went to my cousin Romualdo Franco's for the pistol he kept there," he wrote in his myth-making *Memoirs*, "and returned and fired at Don Agustin and hit him three times." Villa fled to the sierra and, at sixteen, took up the bandit life, "pursued, wanted dead or alive in every district." The *rurales* were on his heels; fame was close behind.[19]

The young progressive journalist John Reed reported on Villa's Division of the North for leading American magazines and newspapers in 1913–14, and, while documenting it, spread the Villa myth. "An immense body of popular legend grew up among the peons around his name," Reed wrote. "There are many traditional songs and ballads, celebrating his exploits—you can hear the shepherds singing them around their fires at night. For instance, they tell the story of how Villa, fired by the misery of the peons at the hacienda of Los Alamos, gathered a small army and descended upon the big house,

Pancho Villa. Though Woodrow Wilson called him a "patriot and an honorable gentleman," Villa was a bandit briefly elevated by a revolution that the president saw as "the struggle of a people to come into their own."

which he looted and distributed the proceeds to the poor." And more in that hagiographical vein.

Woodrow Wilson, a fan of Reed's work, spoke as if he had imbibed *pulque* and Villismo around those campfires when he told the British ambassador that his colleagues in Mexico City had Villa all wrong. He was no vicious killer but "a sort of Robin Hood [who] had spent an eventful life in robbing the rich in order to give to the poor." At worst a good bad man who had "even at one time kept a butcher's shop for the purpose of distributing to the poor the proceeds of his innumerable cattle raids."[20]

The part about the cattle raids was true. As pieced together from official records by Friedrich Katz in his monumental 1998 biography, Villa was a calculating bandit who, if he did not share his loot with the poor, at least did not rob them.

A member of a Durango gang, Doroteo Arango was first arrested in 1901 by a lawman notorious for administering the *ley fuga* but released by a judge likely bribed by a local "black marketer" Arango supplied with stolen cattle. Four days later he was arrested again, for assaulting a man and stealing his guns. Sentenced to the army, he deserted and quit Durango for the state of Chihuahua over the mountains to the north.

Taking up a new life under the name of the rich man who had sired his father, Villa found work as a miner, mason, brickmaker, and butcher. Foreign mining and railroad corporations hired him as a guard and mule driver. "I needed a good man to take charge of teams and drivers en route," an English silver miner recalled. "By good I mean good in a fight in case the drivers quarreled or the wagons were held up. I chose a tough specimen who gave me his name as Pancho Villa." None of the foreign businesses that hired Villa regretted trusting him with payrolls of seven hundred thousand pesos and shipments of precious metals.

But Villa had not renounced all his old ways. A graveyard for bandits, Chihuahua was a garden for rustlers. The landless country people resented the closing of the open range by fifteen haciendas covering twenty-two million hectares (one hectare equals roughly a hundred acres) owned by a single family. Rustlers were seen as "social bandits"— that is, in Eric Hobsbawm's classic definition, "peasant outlaws whom the lord and the state regard as criminals, but who remain within peasant society, and are considered by their people as heroes, as champions, avengers, fighters for justice, perhaps even leaders of liberation, and in any case as men to be admired, helped and supported."[21]

Before the revolution, then, Villa emerges as a tough, dependable young man and an outlaw on the side who acted out forbidden impulses, more Billy the Kid than Robin Hood, admired for his anarchic individualism, not for sharing his swag with the peasants. Nor had that side of Villa appeared as late as July 1910, when he made the most wanted list for murder. In broad daylight, in the crowded streets of Chihuahua City, and while eating an ice-cream cone, he shot a former gang member who had betrayed him to the police and then slowly rode out of town "with no one daring to follow." Here, at last, is the stuff of song and legend.[22]

Recruiting for the revolution, Madero's agent in Chihuahua offered Villa amnesty for his crimes, including murder. There was one catch: Madero had to win. Another version of Villa's baptism in revolution has Madero himself meeting with him at the Palacio Hotel in Chihuahua City and, after listening to Villa's tearful confession of his crimes, promising him absolution in the "Revolution." For a time, the revolution seemed to exalt Villa but with serial defeat in battle in 1915–16, his killings, stripped of their political alibi, became murders, and the murders massacres.[23]

Such was the path Villa had followed to La Cueva Pinta and the moment when the soldiers of Madero chose him as first commander of their first company, and, at thirty-two, he entered history. "In personal appearance," an American doctor who knew him well reported to U.S. military intelligence in 1914, "he is about 5 feet 10 inches in height, weighs about 170 lbs., is well developed in a muscular way; has a heavy protruding lower jaw and badly stained teeth; a rather dandified moderately heavy moustache of the heavy villain variety; crispy kinky black hair of the Negro type." As Villa's "most distinguishing features" a reporter singled out "his cruel mouth . . . and his eyes, bloodshot, protruding, and piercing. Another reporter who saw them blazing at Torreón described them as 'the eyes of a man who will some day go crazy.'"

Villa was a celebrated horseman, a crack shot, a surprising abstainer from tobacco, drink, or drugs, a marked man so fearful of poisoning that at official dinners he swapped plates with his neighbors, and an insatiable womanizer who made "scores of promises of marriage to girls all over Chihuahua" to seduce them and as souvenirs of the occasion sometimes left them with child.[24]

Politically, Pancho Villa was a virgin. After the revolution, discussing

John Reed with a radical Mexican painter who had just returned from Moscow bearing news of Reed's death, Villa remarked, "Johnny was a good man, a revolutionary . . . It was from him that I first heard the word *socialism*. I thought it was a thing, but then Johnny explained that it was a system in which there are no landowners and no capitalism; all men live as brothers and work for the common good." In 1914, Pancho Villa thought socialism was a *thing*. Unlike the other historic figure of the Mexican Revolution, Emiliano Zapata, a Morelos horse breaker, for Pancho Villa, returning the land of Mexico to its people was less a passion than a recruiting tool. Villa fought for amnesty, honor, and revenge.[25]

He quickly showed bravura as a guerrilla commander, raiding a hacienda in November 1910 (and killing its administrator), ambushing a party of federal soldiers at a train station, and, with forty men, rashly attacking seven hundred federals outside the state capital. A ruse saved his party from annihilation. They had set out a long row of sombreros on a nearby mountain top, and as the federals turned their fire on these phantoms, the real rebels made good their retreat.[26]

It took months of hard fighting, but by July 1911, Porfirio Díaz was residing in Paris. Madero had won—and promptly undid his victory. Repeating the pattern of the Mexican past, he rescinded the land plank of his Plan of Potosí, abandoning the peasants who had joined him for justice. Embracing his enemies in the federal army, Madero turned on his friends, ordering the revolutionary armies to surrender their weapons to officers they had just defeated. He allowed General Huerta to jail Pancho Villa on trumped-up charges; Huerta then put Villa before a firing squad for defying orders and only the last-minute intervention of Madero's brother saved him. Madero also dispatched a punitive expedition to crush Zapata's forces in the small southern state of Morelos. Madero wanted to destroy so-called Zapatismo before the lure of land etched in stone in Zapata's Plan of Ayala, framed by peasants "barely able to sign their names," sparked new revolts all over Mexico.

Just before the break with Zapata, his most loyal lieutenant in the southern campaign against Díaz, Madero sent a delegation to Morelos to offer amnesty to the Zapatistas if they gave up their arms.

"Madero has betrayed me as well as my army, the people of Morelos, and the whole nation," Zapata told Madero's emissaries. "Tell him . . . to take off for Havana, because if not . . . in a month I'll be in Mexico City with twenty thousand men, and have the pleasure of going up to Chapultepec castle and dragging him out of there and hanging him from one of the highest trees in the park."[27]

Madero turned right after leading a revolution from the left because like all the Mexican elite, Porfirian and revolutionary alike, he dreaded the messianic hopes stirred by his own plan—the "anarchy" below that threatened to pull his propertied world down. Peter Durnovo shared the same fear of the "unconscious . . . Socialism" of Russia's peasants, warning Nicholas that "the Russian masses, whether workmen or peasants, are not looking for political rights, which they neither want nor comprehend" but for "social revolution in its most extreme form."[28]

"Zapata" by David Alfaro Siqueiros

Madero's right turn won no praise from the right. On the contrary, the Mexico City papers demanded bloodier measures against Zapata, headlined THE NEW DANGER and THE ATTILA OF THE SOUTH. They urged Madero to undertake "an energetic purification" of Morelos, a state infected by "this amorphous agrarian socialism, which, given the low intelligence state of the Morelos peasantry, can only take the form of mindless vandalism." All over Mexico peasants and peons were standing up—driving an English estate owner off his Oaxaca hacienda after he threatened to fire peons for attending a victory parade for revolutionary fighters; striking for a shorter working day, the abolition of the company store, and payment in money instead of in kind at a hacienda in Durango. "The general situation is very bad," a Chihuahua *hacendado* wrote Porfirio Díaz in Paris in September 1911. "There is no respect for the constitution, for private property . . . but rather we have the rule of brutal force of the lower classes, armed with rifles, full of passion, with communist ideas and full of hatred of the upper classes."

That one of their own had distributed those rifles, licensed those ideas, whipped up that hatred, maddened such men. In an early 1913 letter to Woodrow Wilson, twenty "long-time American residents of Mexico" cast the rightist anger at Francisco Madero in terms the Southern-born president could understand: "Suppose a wealthy white man in Alabama had started in arming the Negroes a few years after the War, offering each a pure democracy, 40 acres and a mule, if they would make him governor. How long would the intelligent whites hesitate in stringing him to the nearest telegraph pole, especially if the Negroes there outnumbered the whites three to one? . . . That is exactly what Madero did, offering the peons a vote and a free distribution of land."[29]

Madero escaped lynching. He was shot dead in February 1913 following a coup, "the forerunner of the many similar twentieth-century coups in which reform-minded presidents, such as Romolu Gallegos in Venezuela, Jacobo Arbenz in Guatemala, and Salvador Allende in Chile, would be toppled by the military with varying degrees of covert or even overt support from foreign, mainly U.S., sources." Military cadets freed Félix Díaz, the nephew of the late dictator, from his Mexico City prison, and then marched on the national palace, where

Maderist forces repulsed them. There followed the Ten Tragic Days of fighting during which the heart of Mexico City was torn open by exchanges of artillery fire between the Maderists under General Huerta and the cadets under Díaz. Encouraged by the American embassy, Huerta changed sides, joining forces with Díaz to oust Madero. Surviving the assault on the palace, he was taken prisoner, and ordered killed by Huerta, who blamed Madero's death on supporters trying to rescue him. Defying the Taft State Department, Ambassador Henry Lane Wilson, who loathed Madero for failing to impose "order," had orchestrated the coup, and when his wink could have saved Madero's life did not wink.[*][30]

The news of Madero's death reached Villa in El Paso. With the help of former Porfirian officials who hoped he would lead a rebellion against Madero, on Christmas Day 1912 he had sawn through the bars of his cell in a Mexico City prison and after a harum-scarum journey found refuge in the United States. The proprietor of an El Paso club, a revolutionary haunt, recalled Villa as a man "of unstable temper . . . who liked ice cream and got it almost every day at the elite confectionary. He was also fond of peanut brittle and always carried a supply in his pocket . . . Pancho said he had a very delicate stomach and had to almost live on squab. He kept a box of live pigeons in his rooms at my father's hotel."[31]

The pigeons were not for eating but for communicating with his friends in Chihuahua. From one of these, Abraham González, now governor of Chihuahua, who had recruited him for Madero in 1910, Villa received the summons to return to Mexico to oust the usurper and assassin Huerta. This was a fight Villa could warm to.

On March 6, with eight companions and nine rifles and on nine rented horses, Villa crossed the Rio Grande. From just inside Mexico, he telegraphed the local commander of Huerta's federal army:

---

[*] "The victory of the recent revolution is the work of American policy. Ambassador Wilson made the . . . coup; he himself brags about it," Paul Von Hintze, Germany's minister in Mexico, wrote to Berlin. From Friedrich Katz, *The Secret War in Mexico: Europe, the United States and the Mexican Revolution* (Chicago: University of Chicago Press, 1981), 108. Katz (on page 110) concludes, "[Lane] Wilson's attitude indicates that he not only wished to undertake no effective steps on Madero's behalf, but that he actually favored his execution."

"Knowing that the government you represent was preparing to extradite me, I have saved them the trouble. I am now in Mexico, ready to make war upon you. Francisco Villa." In less than a year he'd be back on the border, to attack El Paso's sister city Juárez, leading an army.[32]

While Villa, in his hotel room in El Paso, packed his peanut brittle to fortify himself for the hard ride into Chihuahua, in Princeton, Helen Woodrow Wilson was writing Jesse Woodrow Bones about their cousin Woodrow, like Pancho Villa poised to make history. Woodrow Wilson and his family had lived in Princeton since 1890, when he arrived as a young professor of jurisprudence and political economy. Helen had news of the small army of undergraduates following the former president of Princeton to Washington to serenade him at his inauguration as president of the United States:

March 1, 1913

The time for leaving Princeton has actually come; we start for Washington Monday morning . . . The morning of the 4th they march behind the carriage in which cousin Woodrow rides to the W. H. door. They wish to sing "Old Nassau" as a good-bye; that depends on Mr. Taft's feeling about it. I rather think he'll let them do it, he's such a dear old soul—and if he doesn't let them their hearts will be broken.

The author of these gushing lines inhabited a different moral universe from Pancho Villa. Cousin Woodrow, raised a minister's son, lived in a genteel society. Yet Woodrow Wilson was not genteel. When traces of the knight still survived in the idea of the gentleman, he was a gentleman. It does not fit the received image of Woodrow Wilson, for example, to find him warning reporters that only his position restrained him from "thrashing" them for buzzing over the romantic lives of his daughters. Like Pancho Villa he tried to live by a code of honor, which lent unexpected steel to his character. "In fact, arguments, however soundly reasoned, did not appeal to him if they were opposed to his feeling of what was the right thing to do," Robert Lansing, his future secretary of state, wrote of him. "He once

Taft hands Mexico to Wilson, from *Puck*, March 5, 1913.

said to me," a Princeton contemporary remembered, 'I am so sorry
for those who disagree with me.' When I asked why, he replied, 'Because I know they are wrong.' "[33]

On February 8, 1913, General Huerta had "the honor to inform"
President Taft "that I have overthrown this government." Huerta
expected diplomatic recognition. Taft wanted to trade recognition
for Huerta's agreement to settle long-standing American economic
and territorial claims, but before a deal could be reached his term
expired. Recognition became Woodrow Wilson's decision.[34]

Since the days of Thomas Jefferson, the United States had applied a de
facto principle of recognition—that "the mere existence of a government was sufficient for recognition." Mere existence was rarely good
enough for Woodrow Wilson.* The United States had the right "to

---

* On this point, commenting in his paper "L'Homme Enchainé" on Wilson's message of January 22, 1917, proposing "peace without victory," Georges Clemenceau

inquire fully whether [a foreign government] had come to power because its leaders were motivated by personal interests and ambitions,"
Wilson maintained in a speech a week after taking office.[35]

Requiring new foreign governments to prove the purity of their
motives before the United States favored them with an ambassador—
this novel test of legitimacy harmonized with the moralism of Secretary of State William Jennings Bryan, who helped Wilson draft the
speech. Bryan owed his unlikely job to delivering party regulars to
Wilson at the 1912 Democratic National Convention. The three-time
Democratic presidential candidate "was endowed with such an excess
of virtue that he found it difficult to recognize evil in other men."
Still, Bryan and his chief saw Huerta for the "murderer" he was, and,
overruling the State Department, refused to recognize his government.[36]

Huerta exceeded their worst expectations. By the end of 1913,
at least thirty-five of his political opponents had been assassinated,
including a member of the Chamber of Deputies who, "after providing for the future care of his son," had attacked Huerta as one "who
snatched power by means of treason." A March exposé in the *New York
World* of Ambassador Lane Wilson's role in the coup had only strengthened *Woodrow* Wilson's conviction that Huerta must go. That European powers with economic interests at stake in Mexico recognized his
government proved their iniquity. "The force of America is moral
principle," Wilson declared. "There is nothing else . . . for which she
will contend."[37]

In early 1914, Wilson asked his diplomats to canvass foreign opinion on the Mexican crisis. The chargé d'affaires in St. Petersburg reported that the tsar believed "the only satisfactory solution is [U.S.]
annexation, and this action Russia would see with approval." Nicholas's
imperial solution was shared by the American Smelting and Refining

---

wrote: "Never before has any political assembly heard so fine a sermon on what
human beings might be capable of accomplishing if only they weren't human . . .
He leaps forward far beyond the limits of time and space . . . way above material
things, whose inferiority resides in the mere fact of their existence." See the essay
by Jean-Baptiste Duroselle in J. Joseph Huthmacher and Warren I. Susman, eds.,
Wilson's Diplomacy: An International Symposium (Cambridge, MA: Schenkman Publishing, 1973), 21.

Company (ASARCO), one of whose directors openly called for the United States to absorb northern Mexico. The financier Otto Kahn would have settled for the north becoming a separate country. Robert Lansing, then counsel to the State Department, warned that with nonrecognition and the lifting of the arms embargo the United States was on a path to war with Huerta. Annexation—of California and the Southwest—had crowned victory over Mexico in the 1846–48 war, and history might repeat itself in 1913–14. Woodrow Wilson confessed his shame over the Mexican War and in a major speech on Latin America before the Southern Commercial Congress in Mobile pledged that the United States would "never again" seek "one additional foot of territory by conquest." Yet his anti-imperialist policy, twisted back on itself by contact with the tenebrous reality of Mexico, seemed headed toward war and conquest.[38]

If not Huerta, who? In 1913, Wilson sent "executive agents" to Mexico to find out. Washington suspected the leader of the so-called Constitutionalist rebels, Venustiano Carranza, a *hacendado* and former governor of Coahuila, of anti-Yankee nationalism. Pancho Villa hid his nationalism under a mask of subservience calculated to flatter Americans' belief in their superiority over "half-breed" Mexicans like him. "In Villa they have an intrepid and resourceful general. He is the highest type of physical, moral, and mental efficiency that the conditions—and the environment—could reasonably be expected to produce," the most influential of Wilson's agents, former Minnesota governor John Lind, reported to Bryan. "An aristocrat ruined his sister; [Villa] killed him . . . Pictured as a demon in the Mexico City press principally because he executed some officers and some spies . . . employed by Huerta to assassinate him." Though Villa admittedly shot prisoners, "the Federals shot over 30 rebels in their cots in the hospital at *Gomez Palacio* in the presence of an American doctor."[39]

If Villa impressed Wilson's agents, he seduced American reporters. Favorites traveled in a "luxurious" sleeper in Villa's private train, refreshed themselves in a salon car, and enjoyed the services of "Fong," our "beloved Chinese cook," the well-fed John Reed testified. With funds raised by selling cattle from confiscated haciendas, Villa bribed journalists, funded American and Mexican papers, hired American publicists, and sold his life story to Hollywood along with the rights to film his battles. "No great man in the public eye at present understands the value of publicity to greatness better than Francisco Villa," the *New York Times*, which thrived on front-page stories about Villa, observed in February 1914. In Pancho Villa's story, as related by his agents in Mexico and romanticized by publicity, Woodrow Wilson saw the history of Mexico.[40]

Throughout 1913 Wilson took no side in Mexico's revolution, his policy one of "watchful waiting." In vain had he waited for Huerta to hold elections, even offering what Mexico's foreign minister condemned as "a bribe" if Huerta agreed not to run. After nearly a year of ignoring the Constitutionalists, Wilson in late 1913 began waiting for them to commit to holding elections as a condition of lifting the embargo. Carranza, the "First Chief" of the revolution, sought through a skillful Washington envoy, Luis Cabrera, to disabuse Wilson of his "foolish hope of settling a revolution with an election." And by degrees Wilson shifted toward the Constitutionalist position that the only way forward for Mexico, in his own hard words, was "civil war carried to its bitter conclusion."[41]

"He had come to the conclusion that the real cause of the trouble in Mexico was not political but economic," Cecil Spring Rice, the British ambassador in Washington, summarized the president's thinking to Edward Grey, the foreign secretary. "So long as the present system under which whole provinces were owned by one man continued to exist, so long would there be perpetual trouble in the political world." Wilson had felt his way into Mexican history, into the struggle for the land that in John Reed's words, "had been smoldering since the Spanish crown gave Cortez a province for a garden," and in that struggle the American president sided with the Mexican peasant. "This . . . was a fight for the land—just that and nothing more," Wilson told a *Saturday Evening Post* interviewer. "My ideal is an orderly and righteous government in Mexico, but my passion is for the submerged eighty-five per cent of the people of that Republic." As he said this, he slammed a clenched fist on his desk, and "a few open letters stirred a bit from the jar of the blow."[42]

By January, Spring Rice was sadly informing Grey that "Mr. Bryan considered Villa was now the only alternative to Huerta." Villa was unacceptable to the British, whose substantial oil concessions in Mexico, a source of the fuel for the newest ships in Winston Churchill's navy, were put at risk by the fighting and menaced by the revolution.

In February, the secretary to Britain's legation in Mexico City, T. B. Hohler, sought to set Wilson straight about Villa. In a two-hour White House meeting, the diplomat instanced the killing of a Huerista messenger as proof of Villa's barbarism. "Mr. Wilson interrupted me and said that the messenger had come to move Villa from his allegiance to his chief [Carranza] and to his duty." Wilson pressed on. "Supposing a man came into this room at this moment and offered him a million dollars to desert . . . the best interests of his country, would [the president] not kick him out?" "Yes, I said, . . . but hardly into the next world." Indeed, Wilson, joined by the virtuous Bryan, insisted, into the next world. There was a war on; the messenger was a traitor. A thug and killer to Thomas Hohler, Villa was "a patriot and an honorable gentleman" to Woodrow Wilson.[43]

Extenuating murder, Wilson had left behind the genial moral code of Cousin Helen's world to endorse revolutionary morality, as defined by General Arroyo in *The Old Gringo*, the necessity of "the new violence to end the old violence."

By the turn of the year, Woodrow Wilson had watched and waited long enough. Dropping his condition of elections first, he lifted the arms embargo on February 3, 1914. No sooner had the president reassured a doubting senator that this step would not trigger a "bloodbath" than Pancho Villa bathed his name in blood.[44]

On February 17, 1914, William Benton, a belligerent English *hacendado*, entered Villa's home in Juárez to demand payment for cattle that villagers (or Villa's men) had rustled from land taken by Benton on the eve of the revolution. At the Villa residence, a British soldier of fortune, Francis Michael Tone, was inventorying weapons in a room adjoining Villa's office when he overheard Benton and Villa shouting. From Tone's account:

MR. BENTON: Give me money for my cattle, sir.
VILLA: Mañana, hombre.

BENTON (IN ENGLISH): I am a damned sight better man than you,
    any way you'd like to take it.
VILLA: No, muchacho.

A second or two later a shot was fired and . . . I rushed through
the folding doors . . . into Villa's office . . . Benton was lying in front
of [Villa's] desk . . . Blood was coming from a wound in his right
breast, he appeared to be dead.[45]

At first Villa claimed that Benton started to draw his pistol but that
Rudolfo Fierro, Villa's psychopath in residence, shot him before he
fired. Tone saw only Villa and Benton in the room. After sifting a
welter of conflicting stories, Friedrich Katz believes Villa shot Benton, possibly through his desk, citing Villa's admission months later
that Benton had been reaching for his handkerchief, not his gun.

Benton's death made no end of trouble for Villa, the *London Times*
detecting a growing belief in Washington "that intervention to restore order is practically inevitable." Benton also bedeviled Wilson,
branded "obstinately stupid . . . and obstinately wicked" by the *Los
Angeles Times* for lifting the arms embargo on the "bandit and murderer." The Asquith government faced questions in Parliament. Since
the United States had "undertaken the obligation of protecting British subjects in those places in Mexico at which we have no Consular
representatives," the *Times* maintained, British opinion expected the
American government to "secure the just punishment" of Benton's
killer. Fanning the tension between London and Washington, *Le
Temps* in Paris warned that "Mexico is on the eve of European intervention because President Wilson and Mr. Bryan have prevented the
re-establishment of order."[46]

An impetuous bullet had imperiled Villa's one foreign policy objective: by pro-American acts and pro-Wilson rhetoric ("You have
the greatest government in the world and your president is the best")
to get the arms embargo lifted, and win American support for the
rebels. Though he assured American reporters that "I know I am not
competent to hold high office because of my lack of education," Villa
undoubtedly also nurtured dreams of being Mexico's next president.

To give himself—and Woodrow Wilson—political cover, Villa

concocted a story for American consumption. Benton, he told a U.S. envoy, had pulled a gun on him; he was disarmed, given a court-martial, for which Villa produced the bogus transcript, and executed by a firing squad. When the Americans asked to see the body ("An examination would . . . prove whether he was killed by a firing party or by a revolver bullet," the *Times* pointed out), Villa ordered Fierro to dig it up and shoot it full of holes.[47]

Woodrow Wilson had to accept Villa's story. To do otherwise would have licensed calls to intervene, which Villa energized when he declared that "out of respect for the dead" he would not disinter Benton after all. Benton's posthumous execution, Villa had concluded, would not disguise the cause of death from the American surgeons sent by the State Department to examine the body. When, at a February 26 press conference, a reporter asked Wilson's opinion of Benton, the president impugned the dead man's character: "He seems, so far as I can gather, to have been a very aggressive sort of person," who got, Wilson implied, what he asked for. The alliance of choice arranged by necessity between the president and the bandit had survived the Benton controversy—and U.S.-purchased arms flowed across the border to Villa's army.[48]

Drawn to Villa by his success, by the promise of land, and by exploits like "stealing pretty women" that "have brought [him] a renown among Mexicans like the old legends of Robin Hood or Dick Turpin," in the words of a U.S. military intelligence agent, Villa's band of eight, in the year since crossing the dark river, had multiplied into an army of ten thousand. Villa's strategy had correspondingly expanded from raiding communications to attacking federal garrisons. In November 1913, he had pulled off the exploit of his career: capturing the fortified border city of Ciudad Juárez.

Fresh from a serious repulse at Chihuahua City, where machine guns and shrapnel shells had decimated his cavalry, Villa moved on to Juárez, which was also defended by machine guns and artillery. Since Juárez backed up to the Rio Grande, Villa knew a frontal attack might harm property and people in El Paso. Collateral damage in the United States risked alienating Woodrow Wilson. Yet Villa needed a victory to sustain the morale of his troops and attract recruits. He got his victory and with it won overnight fame. Capturing a train that ferried supplies between Chihuahua City and Juárez, Villa forced the conductor to wire Juárez that Villa was in the vicinity: *Please advise.*

Federal headquarters ordered the conductor to return immediately, stopping at stations along the way to confirm his unmolested progress. Villa loaded two thousand men on the train and aimed it at Juárez. At each station, a Villista soldier held a gun on the telegraph operator while, with a Villa telegrapher listening, he reassured Juárez that Villa was nowhere to be seen. An *El Paso Times* reporter described what happened when the Trojan train reached its destination: "Shortly after two o'clock this morning, a freight train rolled into the Juárez yards over the Mexican Central, and from it poured hundreds of rebels. That the surprise was complete is proved by the fact that not a shot was fired until the rebels had penetrated into the very heart of the city . . . The federal garrison made but little resistance."[49]

With only isolated pockets of federals left in Chihuahua, Villa turned from war to politics by appointing himself "military governor" of Chihuahua, Huerta's thugs having assassinated the elected Maderist governor Abraham González. During his six months in prison, Villa had befriended a Zapatist intellectual, who tutored him in agrarian radicalism. Thereafter Villa professed devotion to Zapata's Plan of Ayala. In the four weeks he could spare as governor before leading the drive south toward Mexico City, "hopelessly perplexed with the piles of paper that were presented to him and longing to get back among his soldiers," he managed nevertheless to confiscate the Chihuahuan oligarchy's million-acre estates, or, rather, those belonging to his opponents. Villa's radicalism was personal, arbitrary, animated by score settling, not ideology. By his decree, the lands would be divided among veterans of his army, among the villages dispossessed by the *hacendados*, and, in the form of pensions funded by land sales, among the widows and orphans of the fallen—this social revolution to occur "after the victory of the revolution." Until then, Villistas would run the estates to raise money for the army.[50]

To meet Huerta's demands for cannon fodder, press gangs were kidnapping Mexico City servants, messenger boys, and fans leaving bullfights, dressing them in uniforms, and packing them into northbound trains. Villa's volunteers went south to meet Huerta's conscripts believing that if they survived the battles ahead they would own land and if they died their dependents would receive pensions.[51]

Villa led by fear as well as hope. He assigned fear to a former collection agent named Manuel Banda. "What is your role?" an old friend asked Banda. "To force people into battle at the point of a gun . . . In some battles I may have killed as many of our men as the federal troops have done . . . They know me, and they are gripped by panic when they see me on my motorcycle with a pistol in my hand . . . That's the system of General Villa."[52]

Villa wanted the enemy to be as afraid of him as his men were of Banda. His reputation for killing captured federal officers and sparing the men (if they agreed to switch sides) motivated retreats, surrenders, and mutinies. From the first battle of the new war against Huerta, Villa earned his reputation. The Villistas took prisoners; Villa's autobiography recorded their fate: "I formed the sixty prisoners in files three deep and had them shot in that formation, to save ammunition by killing three with one shot." It sounds comical and then you picture it.[53]

The professional European armies of the late nineteenth century banned women and children from following soldiers to war. But in the wars of the Mexican Revolution, women did everything, including spying and fighting. The federal army depended on wives and girlfriends to feed their men and nurse the wounded—and to keep conscripts from deserting. Reports in the American press bear out the sensational charge made by John Lind that men without women were also provided for. "Huerta is capturing women as well as men for the army," Lind wrote to the president in January. "Some of them are undoubtedly decent women, but many of them vile. These are assigned to the conscripts as soon as they commence to 'make good.'" Dr. Louis Duncan, who set up a field station in Presido, Texas, to treat federal soldiers wounded in a border battle, reported that half of his patients had carnal diseases.

Villa did not require *soldaderas* to perform military functions. A quartermaster corps fed his soldiers, sixty American and Mexican doctors housed in a forty-car hospital train cared for the wounded, and Banda discouraged deserters. Still, Villa understood, as one of his officers put it, that "we had to have *soldaderas* if we wanted to have soldiers."[54]

An American mercenary painted a scene of Villa's camp on a day of battle:

> The men were told to eat and be ready to march at dawn . . . and "without women." Rumors . . . spread of a large enemy force marching against us and not far distant. The men accepted the news with calm and austere fortitude . . . Just before sunrise, this ill-equipped little rebel force of about 5,500 men, with bandoliers three-quarters empty, moved out. Some didn't even have a gun, but proudly carried their machetes . . . The women camp followers had orders to remain behind, but hundreds of them hanging onto their stirrups followed their men on the road for a while. Some other women carrying carbines, bandoleers, and who were mounted, managed to slip into the ranks and fight with us. These took their places in the firing lines and withstood hardship and machine gun fire as well as the men. They were a brave worthy lot.[55]

Millions marched to war in 1914 and a million died, but only in Mexico for justice and dignity. The great French socialist Jean Jaurès assigned different moral weights to the violence of war and revolution: "In the Europe of today, it is not by means of international war that the work of freedom and justice will be accomplished . . . If we have a horror of war, it is not at all because of a weak and enervated sentimentality. The revolutionary resigns himself to human suffering when it is the necessary condition of a great human advancement, when by it the oppressed and exploited rise up to freedom."

That describes one face of Mexico's violence in 1914 and suggests why it frightened the ruling classes of Europe and why they wanted "order" restored in Mexico. European governments risked alienating the Wilson administration by recognizing General Huerta not only because he protected their industrialist's mines and oil fields from nationalization by the rebels but because the "Mexican Revolution represented the first serious challenge to the international order established by the industrial nations in the mid-nineteenth century." The world had yet to witness a successful nationalist revolt of a brown-skinned people against a dictatorship serving the interests of imperial powers.

"Mexico's Two Strong Men"

When Britain's *Morning Post* called for a joint Euro-American occupation of Mexico, writing that the Americans needed to learn "the meaning of the white man's burden" in places of "un-civilization," it voiced a shared European anxiety about the contagion of Mexico's example.[56]

Torreón—the "Chicago of Mexico," rail hub of the north-south, east-west trunk lines, a third of the way between the Texas border and Mexico City—was a strategic prize. For three years its people had been war's playthings, with each new occupier settling scores with supporters of the old. Seizing the city in May 1911, Maderist troops went on a xenophobic rampage—massacring hundreds of Chinese immigrants and sacking their stores. With an American consular agent watching over his shoulder, Villa had controlled his troops during his October–December 1913 occupation of Torreón, which ended when

Villa redeployed to Chihuahua. Now, in March 1914, he meant to return. Two other rebel armies were moving against Huerta's stretched forces, one down the Pacific coast, the other in the northeast; but Villa in the middle, descending on Torreón, constituted a mortal threat. Huerta responded to it, sending his best troops and generals to hold Torreón. "Their soldiers numbered no less than ten thousand," Villa writes. "They had twelve cannons, an enormous number of grenades, and plenty of supplies. They had machine guns mounted on permanent emplacements and many good officers to direct them."[57]

In mid-March 1914, Villa's Division of the North flowed south on long trains—including an armored flatcar carrying the celebrated cannons El Niño and El Chavalito, the hospital train with its staff of one hundred, and Villa's own train with a car for the machine guns and the automobiles, a sleeper and a salon car for the journalists and the movie men,* and Villa's private car, a chintz-curtained red caboose. Above their heads, above the machine guns and the artillery, on the flat roofs of the boxcars, sprawled the soldiers of Villa's peasant army and their women and children. Some *soldaderas* were baking tortillas over mesquite twig fires "so that it seemed as if each boxcar had a chimney"; some, hanging out their washing to dry in the desert air. Others rode beneath the cars on planks held by ropes; yet others, on the cowcatchers of the locomotives. When the trains stopped, the *soldaderas*, children strapped on their backs and babies clasped to their breasts, climbed down from the cars, lit fires, and cooked while the men gathered over the steaming pots—for at least five hundred fighters of the Northern Division, perhaps their last meal with their women.[58]

Many of Villa's soldiers were boys—twelve- to sixteen-year-olds; most were of mixed blood; but some were pure Apaches, Tarahumaras, and Tepehuanes. "They are able to bear the pain of wounds with the patient insensibility of animals," the London *Times* ineffably observed. Besides peasants fighting for their own land, others fought for village autonomy against the local jefe; cowboys, laborers, and drifters joined for the regular pay with bonuses for victory. "What are you fighting for?" John Reed asked one soldier. "Why, it is good fighting,"

---

*For twenty-five thousand dollars and 20 percent of the gross, they had a commitment from Villa to stage a day battle for the cameras.

Soldaderas. They traveled with all the armies in Mexico. Since the
Spanish king gave Cortés "a province for a garden," the history of Mexico
had been a struggle for the land of Mexico. Women like these fought beside
their men for the land stolen from their Indian ancestors.

he replied. "You don't have to work in the mines." The soldiers wore
khaki uniforms made in a Chihuahua textile plant, and carried Mausers and Colts. They included descendants of the old military colonists
in the north, given land by the Spanish crown if they agreed to fight
the Apache; and their Villista sons and grandsons, raised to shoot from
the saddle, made superb cavalry.[59]

Villa led cavalry charges at desperate moments outside Torreón, but
the eleven-day battle belonged to soldiers fighting on foot. In night
attacks they hurled themselves at federal strongpoints on three hills
outside Torreón. In Villa's words, "[The federals] were dying in order to save those positions; we were dying in order to seize them."
Pounded by federal artillery, sited by French and German gunners,
and counterattacks, the Villistas gave ground by day only to renew
the attack at night. Seven rings of dead circled the Hill of the Cross.
"Each receding tide of the attacking force left a gruesome flotsam of
dead and dying, weltering in stagnant eddies of blood," a *Washington
Post* correspondent reported.

When they broke into Torreón the Villistas exacted revenge.
In hand-to-hand fighting, they hacked the federal conscripts with
machetes, clubbed them with rifle butts, and blew them up with

homemade grenades flung by leather slings. Facing mutiny from soldiers petrified by Villa's reputation for killing prisoners, the federal commander ordered a retreat. The cameramen for the Majestic Motion Picture Company shot two hundred feet of street fighting, including a bayonet charge. Having persuaded Villa to don a general's uniform, they were pleased with their star's close-ups.[60]

A U.S. Army intelligence officer disguised as a war correspondent was "filled with admiration" for the will to fight displayed by soldiers motivated by Villa's promises and threats. "I saw many instances of men who were quite seriously hurt—shot through the shoulders or elbows or hands or wounded in the head—who held their places in

"The Trench" by José Clemente Orozco

the line, refusing to go to the rear." And he pronounced "notably heroic" the conduct of the "women who came along on the railway trains . . . many of whom accompanied their men into the firing line around Torreón." In contrast, fifteen hundred federals either deserted or switched sides. The corpses of the dead—roughly a thousand federals and five hundred Villistas—were piled on wooden pyres on the hillsides and burned, suffusing Torreón with an evil smell. Reporters found Villa "cheered as the military genius of modern Mexico" at the Hotel Salvador, "smiling through his black uneven teeth like a boy who had obtained the toy he wanted."[61]

On July 17, the German cruiser *Dresden* conveyed General Huerta to Jamaica, her captain reporting that "Huerta had roughly half a million marks in gold with him [and] a much greater amount in checks and other paper." The British minister in Mexico City traced the three-month unraveling of Huerta's rule to "the utter demoralization of the federal army since the fall of Torreón." In his farewell message, Huerta ascribed his defeat to "scarcity of funds as well as to the manifest and decided protection which a Great Power on this continent has afforded to the rebels," that is, to the team of Wilson and Villa.[62]

Just when the Constitutionalist rebels were everywhere prevailing against a federal army whose officers hid casualties to pocket the pay of dead soldiers, just when Wilson's policy of permitting the rebels to buy arms in the United States was achieving the results the president had hoped for, in short, just when events had obviated U.S. intervention against Huerta, the United States intervened against Huerta.[63]

Wilson's assessment of Mexican realities was skewed by his agent, John Lind. The significance of Villa's victory at Torreón had failed to register on Lind when he left Mexico to confer with Wilson in Washington in early April. His pessimism conditioned by the Huertista press, Lind had been writing from Veracruz that the rebels were "a lost cause," and that ridding Mexico of Huerta might take U.S. action. "The temporary taking of Mexico City" to force out Huerta "should not be regarded as intervention in the offensive sense." That semantic torture ought to have impeached Lind's judgment that "it is not believed that . . . any resistance [would] be offered to the expedition this side of Mexico City."[64]

On April 6, Lind left Veracruz for Washington aboard the presidential steam yacht *Mayflower*. April 9 brought the "Tampico incident," the most discreditable episode in Wilson's eight-year stewardship of American foreign policy.

In the port of Tampico, where American ships were standing by to evacuate refugees from the encroaching fighting and to protect the nearby oil fields, a party of American sailors trying to obtain gasoline for their admiral's launch was briefly detained by an overzealous federal officer rattled by recent rebel attacks. Within minutes his commander set the sailors free, jailed the errant officer, and apologized to the American admiral. That did not satisfy Rear Admiral Henry T. Mayo, a martinet restive from months of standing by "with his big fleet there away on the horizon and the ordinary Mexicans . . . utterly oblivious to its presence." Without informing the State Department or his immediate superior, Mayo threatened fire and blood unless the Mexican authorities raised the American flag over a prominent government building and delivered a twenty-one-gun salute to atone for the "insult" given the flag. The Mexicans demurred, agreeing only if Mayo promised in writing to answer the salute "gun by gun, instead of by 21 shots after the Mexican salute." Mayo appeared ready to accept this condition, but, incited by Lind's militancy, Woodrow Wilson demanded unconditional compliance.[65]

Projecting his gentleman's code onto Tampico, Wilson magnified a mistake into a calculated affront. In an April 20 address to Congress, he gave a mendacious account of the Tampico and similar incidents as manifesting Huerta's "disregard for the dignity and rights of this Government." With a "rebel yell," the House voted him authority to use force to settle what the president called "an affair of honor."*[66]

Wilson decided to capitalize on "the psychological moment" of Tampico for reasons he explained to John Reed, of all people. ("I

---

*"The present writer feels obliged to say that this was a misrepresentation of the facts. Huerta and his subordinates had acted with studied courtesy toward the U.S. government and its representatives and shown an extraordinary concern in protecting American citizens and property in Mexico . . . Wilson was . . . manufacturing charges against the [Huerta] government to justify the use of force." Arthur S. Link, *Woodrow Wilson: The New Freedom* (Princeton: Princeton University Press, 1956), 398.

opened my mind to him completely," Wilson told his press secretary.) After Reed sent him a copy of an article based on their White House interview, Wilson forbade its publication, likely on account of this passage:

> President Wilson did not send the army and navy to [Tampico and] Veracruz to force Huerta from the dictatorship. He sent them to prevent war . . . For a long time it was known that Huerta was . . . trying to create irritation between the Mexican people and the American people so that he might unite the Mexicans behind him. If he could . . . bring about an act of retaliation, he might become . . . the representative of a united people . . . But the President saw what he was trying to do and called his bluff before he was ready to act.

Huerta might have occupied Galveston, "hurl[ing] us, on a wave of popular emotion, into a bloody war." So Wilson retaliated before Huerta could provoke him to retaliate. This specious stratagem nearly caused what it was intended to prevent—the unification of all Mexico behind Huerta. Wilson was right to deny Reed's request to publish. Statesmen claiming not merely to have divined but surprised the flow of events invite ridicule.[67]

Meanwhile, news arrived that a German merchant ship, the SS *Ypiranga*, was about to land an arms shipment at Veracruz, three hundred miles to the south.[68]

The saga of "the arms of the *Ypiranga*" is the stuff of spy fiction, except that no one would believe it. In late 1913, Huerta had bribed the vice consul of the Russian embassy in Mexico City, Leon Rast, to travel to New York under his diplomatic passport carrying a million and a half pesos in Banco Nacional bills. Rast conveyed this sum to an American middleman, a legitimate importer, who delivered it to the general sales agent of the Colt Automatic Arms Company in Hartford, who handed over twenty machine guns to the importer. These were added to weapons already stockpiled in New York and, to disguise their destination from the U.S. government, shipped to Veracruz by a continent-scrambling route. Rast had them sent first to Odessa via Constantinople, the arms for Huerta passing the Bosporus

"A Sort of War" from *Punch*
President Wilson: "I hope you are not shooting at my
dear friends the Mexicans?"
U.S. Gunner: "Oh, no, sir. We have strict orders only to aim at one
Huerta."

as Liman von Sanders was arriving in that city. At Odessa, Nicholas's
security men, thinking the guns were for Armenian rebels, im-
pounded them. Two weeks passed before they could resume their
journey to Mexico, via a dogleg to Hamburg. There the Mexican
agents shepherding the guns briefly inspected a ship that would soon
be laden with a clandestine cargo of arms for the Ulster rebels before

settling on the Hamburg American line's *Ypiranga* to complete their eighteen-thousand-mile passage to Veracruz.[69]

According to his press secretary, Joseph Tumulty, Wilson feared Huerta would use the arms "against American boys." Wilson may also have believed that "he was forestalling 'outside' intervention in support of Huerta." A British diplomat had cautioned Bryan that "public opinion in England would take a very serious view of the menace to immense British interests" if Huerta's forces withdrew from the Gulf oil fields, which contained "practically the Navy's whole supply." The *New York Times* was thinking along similar lines when, writing two days after the occupation of Veracruz, it editorialized that "if nothing [was] done" after "the insult to the flag" "our European friends might conclude that the United States could not look after anybody's interests in Mexico" and that they had better do the job themselves. Stopping the *Ypiranga* at sea risked a diplomatic row with Germany. So Wilson ordered the navy to seize the customs house at Veracruz.[70]

Lind had predisposed Wilson to believe that the eight hundred American invaders would be greeted as liberators from Huerta's levas

Bluejackets at Veracruz. The occupation of Veracruz has gone down as imperialism. Pancho Villa was the only Mexican leader (maybe the only Mexican, period) who defended it, telling reporters, "Your president is the best."

and punishing taxes. When the bluejackets were instead not only resisted by Huertista troops but also sniped at from rooftops and windows by outraged citizens of Veracruz, the president was "profoundly unnerved." Huerta was emboldened. "Mexico," he vowed, "will fight to the extreme limit of her power against the colossus." He called on "all able-bodied citizens to bear arms" to repel the invader. A member of the Mexican house expressed the national passion with eloquence:

> Gentlemen, at this time I have only curses on my lips, rage in my heart, and blows on my fists for the blond thieves who struck at Veracruz with a coward's naval assault . . . Who are these Yankees, the same ones . . . , the eternal highwaymen, the eternal thieves; they are the same as those who blew up the Maine; the same ["Death to the thieves of 1848!" someone shouted] that committed the crime of the Philippines; the same that committed the crime of Nicaragua; the same that committed the crime of Cuba. They are guilty of all those crimes and today they begin the crime of Mexico.[71]

"Three years of fratricidal war was forgotten in a day," the *London Daily Telegraph* reported from Mexico City, where factory workers were drilling during their lunch hour and government clerks in military uniforms parading before Huerta. In the Huertista press, Mexico's railroad workers were pledging Huerta 150,000 men, the beggars of Guadalajara mobilizing, and the pupils of a school for the blind offering "their bodies to build defenses." Huerta sent emissaries to the Constitutionalists and to Zapata to join his crusade against the "pigs of Yanquilandia."* Zapata had them shot. In Juárez, Villa warned his soldiers that anyone trying to start an anti-American demonstration would suffer the same fate.[72]

---

*In Latin American anti-imperialist invective of the era, Yankees are blonds or pigs and sometimes both. When Major Smedley Butler, leading a force of 350 U.S. Marines, intervened in Nicaragua to prop up a threatened ruler in 1912, a Nicaraguan journal condemned "the blond pigs of Pennsylvania advancing on our garden of beauty." See Walter LaFeber, *Inevitable Revolutions: The United States in Central America* (New York: Norton, 1993), 50.

Outside Villa-controlled Mexico, anti-American demonstrations were the order of the day. Huerta's son led a Mexico City mob that tore down a statue of George Washington. Circulars passed out in the capital called for all Americans to be shot. Americans in Tampico were afraid for their lives—and, the American fleet having sailed to Veracruz, the captain of the *Dresden* was obliged to send German marines ashore to evacuate American civilians. Of grave political concern to the Wilson administration was the reaction of Villa's boss, the "First Chief of the Constitutionalist Army in Charge of Executive Power," Venustiano Carranza, who threatened war if Wilson did not evacuate "our territory."[73]

European reaction was scalding. "For the first time the veil is torn away from the pretence behind which the designs of American imperialism have been hiding," the *Paris Journal* thundered. "Its conquest of Mexico has begun." How valid was this charge of Yankee imperialism?[74]

John Reed asked readers of the *New York Times* to imagine the rage felt by the people of Veracruz seeing their streets shot up "because some foreign businessmen they had enriched were not satisfied and wanted it all." John Mason Hart, a leading scholar of the Mexican Revolution, shares that view: Wilson intervened to protect U.S. businesses in Mexico, which had prospered in the Díaz years to the point where "Mexico had passed into the hands of foreign economic interests," of which American railroad, mining, and oil companies represented the largest share. "The preparation for U.S. intervention at Veracruz began in November 1913," Hart writes, "when William F. Buckley, Sr., wrote to [Colonel Edward M.] House as the chief legal counsel for the Texas Company in Mexico and an old friend." In a sixteen-page letter to House, his Austin neighbor and Woodrow Wilson's confidant, Buckley enumerated the damage the rebels had inflicted on American oil companies along the Gulf Coast and sundry other businesses across Mexico. Speaking for companies weary of paying protection to the rebels and afraid lest their oil fields become battlegrounds, Buckley demanded intervention.[75]

In January 1914, according to Hart, an irresistible cabal made up of Colonel House, the Texans in Wilson's cabinet, New York investors in Mexico, and major campaign contributors to the Democratic Party convinced Wilson to take military action. But unless Colonel House lied to his diary, he opposed intervention, and he told Wilson as much the same month Hart has him caballing for it. ("I urged him to do what he could to settle the matter without intervention.") Alan Knight, author of a two-volume study of the revolution, finds "little evidence" that either economic or military imperialism—the "conquest of Mexico"—motivated Wilson, the latter because it was beyond the capacity of the American military.[76]

The German General Staff reckoned that since an American attack would "unite the belligerent parties of Mexico . . . 150,000 men would hardly suffice to crush Mexico," but the U.S. Army had only 31,500 men under arms while the 120,000-man National Guard was "raw" and "scantily trained." At the president's request, the army prepared can-do war plans to invade Mexico. But the army *couldn't* do. General Tasker Bliss drew up an Alternative Plan for which the forces did not exist. A U.S. invasion of Mexico? As the general pointed out to Washington, the number of U.S. troops on the border was "trivial" compared to the Mexican armies, federal and Constitutionalist, across from them; therefore, a successful local *Mexican* invasion of the United States was a "foregone conclusion."[77]

Critics who did not arraign Wilson for imperialism scored him for shedding blood over a "trivial point of honor." Writing in *Homme Libre*, Georges Clemenceau denounced "the pacifist jurist, President Wilson, [for] knocking down [Mexican] houses with his shells" for a slight to the flag. Wilson had invited that criticism by claiming that he sent in the marines to vindicate the American honor allegedly insulted at Tampico, not to prevent arms from reaching the dictator Huerta. The arms of the *Ypiranga* disappeared behind the cloud Tampico cast over Veracruz. "By singling out this incident as an excuse for war," Britain's liberal *Nation* lamented, "Dr. Wilson has done more to lower the standard of international morality than all his fine utterances in the past have done to raise it."[78]

At home progressives, pastors, and Andrew Carnegie joined the foreign chorus against what the editor of the *Nation*, in a letter to Wilson, called "the untenable and immoral position in which we find ourselves in Mexico." Such high-minded criticism got under Wilson's thin skin. At a May 11 memorial service for the American dead held in the Brooklyn Navy Yard, the president displayed wounded narcissism when he declared, "I fancy that it is just as hard to do your duty when men are sneering at you as when they are shooting at you."[79]

Wilson had as much to regret in his supporters as in his critics. The Confederate veterans of Huntsville, Alabama, wanted it known they were available to serve, as was Theodore Roosevelt, who volunteered to raise a brigade of Rough Riders to invade Mexico. In a preview of scenes soon to be enacted in London, Paris, Berlin, Vienna, and St. Petersburg, men were reported "standing in lines a block long at Army and Navy recruiting stations" in Chicago, an example of a widespread "rush to enlist in the Army."[80]

American xenophobes exercised their patriotism on Mexicans and labor radicals protesting the intervention. In New York a mob pulled two Mexican Americans off a streetcar and a Mexican American baseball player was killed by his YMCA teammates. At Notre Dame, eleven Mexican boys were thrown into a river. Students at a Topeka high school forced Mexican railroad workers to salute the flag. Appleton, Wisconsin, youth marched in a torchlight parade under banners reading AVENGE THE FLAG! Wilson received a string of letters urging him, in the words of a Philadelphia piano tuner, to "let Uncle Sam take off his coat, roll up his sleeves, and pitch into those Mexicans . . . and teach them to behave themselves." Senator William E. Borah, a member of the Foreign Relations Committee, evoked Manifest Destiny: "Once the U.S. forces enter Mexico as an armed body, we are starting on the march to the Panama Canal."[81]

Wilson recoiled from the jingoism incited by his demagogic address to Congress. "I had a feeling of uneasiness as I read the papers this morning as if the country were getting on fire with war enthusiasm," he remarked at a press conference. "I have an enthusiasm for justice and for the dignity of the United States, but not for war." The army had "plans" to march on Mexico City from Veracruz, but he would not hear of that now; wiser by experience, the president who had tried to outsmart tomorrow in Mexico said, "Events must take their course." When Argentina, Chile, and Brazil offered to mediate the conflict, he accepted with alacrity.[82]

His Mexican ally had other ideas. "Asked if he will accede to an armistice requested by the ABC powers," the *Times* reported, "Villa says he had never heard the word." Told what it meant, he pointed toward Mexico City "and said only when he's there and Huerta's gone would he consider an armistice." Villa wanted to be the first rebel commander to occupy the capital, but after his victory at Torreón, Carranza, to stop his general from converting his military fame into political power, ordered him to clean out federal army redoubts in the north. By July, though Huerta was in Havana, the fighting in Mexico was just beginning.[83]

Villa was the big loser from Veracruz. After Carranza's bellicose response to U.S. intervention, the State Department reimposed the arms embargo on the Constitutionalist rebels; the embargo blocked arms shipments by land but less effectually by sea, hurting Villa, not Carranza, who held the Gulf Coast throughout the "war of the winners" that broke out between the rivals in 1915.

The *Ypiranga* eventually landed its arms at Puerto Mexico on the Yucatan Peninsula and Huerta received them before his final collapse. "It was to the Navy like a blow in the head," Wilson's navy secretary Josephus Daniels wrote. "Our chief incentive in seizing the customs house was to prevent the [arms] . . . from becoming available to the unspeakable Huerta." The Americans did find warehouses of arms stockpiled at Veracruz and kept *these* out of Huerta's hands, turning them over instead to Carranza's Constitutionalist army. The Constitutionalists used the arms of Veracruz first to defeat Villa in three big battles in 1915 and then to subdue Zapata in 1918–19: "The Americans' transfer of the arms stored at Veracruz to the Constitutionalists in November 1914 turned the tide of the revolution." Administering the coup de grace to Villa, Wilson granted de facto recognition to Carranza's government in October 1915.[84]

The defeat of Villa and Zapata ended Mexico's peasant revolution. As from time immemorial in Mexico, the revolutionary elites betrayed the peasants after riding them into power. They had "forced their way into a history that had previously unfolded above them," and then history closed over them again and over Woodrow Wilson's solidarity with them. The peasant armies had fought for land, but whereas in 1910 haciendas of over a thousand acres occupied 71 percent of the land, in 1920 they occupied 77 percent. A peasant-soldier expecting land would have to wait twenty years for the reforming government of Lázaro Cárdenas. While "the power and legitimacy of the landlord class—which had underpinned Porfirian rule—never recovered," after the revolution an elite of Constitutionalist generals and officials replaced it, their status legitimized by the protective mystique of the revolution. Pancho Villa himself, ending his days as a *hacendado* ruling Canutillo, a 163,000-acre government-supplied estate at the headwaters of the Río Conchos in Durango, was a symbol of the new order.[85]

After a Constitutionalist army led by Álvaro Obregón shattered the Division of the North in 1915, Villa waged a guerrilla campaign against the Carranza and Obregón governments. To destabilize Carranza, he staged his notorious March 8, 1916, raid on Columbus, New Mexico. Woodrow Wilson rose to Villa's bait, dispatching General Pershing's Punitive Expedition to find Villa—and triggering a war crisis with the Carranza government.

Stung by Villa's charges in the villages of Chihuahua that he was a tool of the "*gueros*," Carranza demanded that the Americans leave Mexico. A skirmish at Carrizal inflicted one hundred casualties on both sides. With war appearing imminent, Carranza sent "a plea for help . . . to the Germans."[86]

To keep the United States embroiled in Mexico, Germany had considered supporting a 1915 attempt by General Huerta to regain power. It had shipped arms to Villa for the Columbus raid and there are suspicions that his German-born physician and translator manipulated his illiterate patient into the raid by falsifying a bank statement to make it look like the Columbus State Bank was cheating Villa, who maintained an account there. Then, when it seemed that Carranza would make more trouble than Villa for the Americans, the Germans courted *him*. For his part, Carranza had played Germany off against the United States, hinting in August 1916 that Mexico would provide a submarine base to Germany if it declared publicly against American intervention.[87]

In January 1917, a new German foreign minister, Arthur Zimmermann, answered Carranza's plea with his infamous telegram proposing that Mexico join with Germany in a war against the United States, in fantastic return for which Texas, New Mexico, and Arizona would be restored to Mexico. Achieving the war's greatest intelligence coup, Britain's code breakers at Room 40 of the Admiralty had intercepted the telegram and given it to Washington. According to Ray Stannard Baker, the journalist Wilson chose to write his biography, "No single more devastating blow was delivered against Wilson's resistance to entering the war"—not even Germany's February 1, 1917, declaration of unrestricted submarine warfare on American vessels.[88]

Neither had unleashing the U-boats swung majority American opinion toward war with Germany. "The mass of Americans, who never saw a seacoast, could not be worked into a war fever over an international lawyer's doctrine [the rights of neutral vessels] nor aroused to a fighting mood over persons who chose to cross the ocean on belligerent boats in wartime . . . It was all very confusing and—to the majority of the country—remote," Barbara W. Tuchman explains. "But the Prussian Invasion Plot, as the newspapers labeled the Zimmermann telegram, was as clear as a knife in the back and near as next door." Heartland papers like the *Chicago Daily Tribune*, the *Cleveland Plain Dealer*, and the *Oshkosh Northwestern* that since August 1914 had called for U.S. neutrality in the European conflict now declared, with the *Detroit Times*, "It looks like war for this country." If Wilson had recognized Huerta in 1913, Zimmerman would not have sent his telegram. Would the United States have gone to war? If it had it would have been as a more divided country. On March 17, the *Literary Digest* summed up editorial comment on the telegram in the headline HOW ZIMMERMANN UNITED THE UNITED STATES.[89]

In eleven months of searching, Pershing's horse soldiers never found Villa, a failure that had a "profound effect . . . on world history," Friedrich Katz, citing German sources, contends. "The military incompetence of the United States has been revealed by the campaign against Villa," the press office of Germany's armed forces concluded. "The United States not only has no army, it has no artillery, no means of transportation, no airplanes, and lacks all other instruments of modern warfare." This scathing assessment helped the military persuade the kaiser that Germany had little to fear in loosing its U-boats on American shipping, Britain's lifeline. At the January 9, 1917 session of the kaiser's Privy Council that decided for unrestricted submarine warfare, the admirals predicted that within six months Britain would be starved into submission; meanwhile, U-boat "wolf packs" would feed on American troop transports. Inevitably some American units would reach the continent but the American army was not a serious fighting force, Field Marshal von Hindenburg told the kaiser (a viewpoint adopted by German cartoonists, who depicted American soldiers as cowboys and billionaires riding sea horses). Ineffectual as ever, rightly afraid for his job if he resisted, Chancellor Bethmann Hollweg acceded to a policy that as a friend noted spelled "*finis Germaniae.*"[90]

As for Pancho Villa, the bandit whose 1914 alliance with the president tangled the United States in the toils of the Mexican Revolution, the now "angry, beaten, rheumatic bushwacker" remained at large, reverting to terror and banditry. Finally Obregón had enough and bought him off with Canutillo.[91]

Villa shared his life there with a rotation of wives and a sample of his progeny. He founded a school for Canutillo's three hundred children, and a night school to teach their parents to read and write. "Ah, friends, if my parents had only educated me," he was heard to say. In its Villa obituary, the *New York Times* seconded his regret: "An educated Villa might have been president of the republic." Villa ran his hacienda on military lines, assuring the teachers he imported from Mexico City, "Look, here in Canutillo nothing is lost, for if anyone steals I have him shot." His constant worry was that he'd be shot; he had so much to be shot about.[92]

From a catalog of atrocities, one from 1916 stands out. After overwhelming the Carrancista garrison of the city of Camargo, Villa was approached by a woman who tearfully pleaded with him not to execute her husband, a paymaster in the garrison. When a subordinate informed Villa that the man was dead, the woman cursed Villa; enraged, he pulled out his pistol and shot her. "But this was not enough to assuage his fury." So he ordered the ninety other soldadera attached to the Camargo garrison to be shot as well. Villa's secretary was long haunted by the memory of an infant playing in his mother's gore.[93]

On July 20, 1923, on a visit to Parral, Pancho Villa was shot nine times by assassins who left town much as he had done years earlier after putting aside his ice-cream cone long enough to shoot the informer in Chihuahua City—that is, riding slowly, as if, a witness reported one saying, they "had no reason to run."

The Mexican government "probably organized" Villa's assassination. Obregón sought full diplomatic recognition from the United States. According to a theory Mexican intelligence agents found current in Mexico City, the Americans, seeking revenge for the Columbus raid, "had informed Obregón that one stumbling block to recognition was Pancho Villa and that the sooner they removed him the sooner recognition would be extended."

What is certain is that, three weeks after Villa's death, the Warren Harding administration granted de jure recognition to the Obregón government. Thus ended the dance of recognition, ten years after Woodrow Wilson spurned Huerta and, seeking a worthier recipient of American favor, embraced the Mexican Revolution, the Constitutionalist rebels, and Pancho Villa.[94]

A visitor to Canutillo once asked Villa if he planned to send his children to the United States for higher education. "No Señorita," Villa answered. "Not to the United States. The first thing I am teaching my children is to hate the enemy of my race." He never got over Woodrow Wilson's betrayal—the cause, he felt, of his defeat—and named a mule President Wilson.[95]

5

AUSTRIA-HUNGARY

FRANZ FERDINAND LIVES: A COUNTERFACTUAL

So first of all an energetic internal clean-up and external peace for us . . . That is my profession of faith, for which I will work and struggle for as long as I live.

—Archduke Franz Ferdinand,
February 1, 1913

FOR THE MAN who started World War I, death came violently when it came at all. That was the family history of Francis Joseph, emperor of Austria and king of Hungary. His younger brother was shot by a Mexican firing squad, his son was a suicide, his wife was stabbed to death, his nephew and heir apparent assassinated. In 1853, five years into his sixty-eight-year reign, while taking his constitutional in Vienna, Francis Joseph was himself stabbed in the neck, the thick golden embroidery on the stiff collar of his uniform saving his life. At a Bosnian railway station in 1910 a would-be assassin armed with a revolver was close enough to touch the emperor; but in a tragedy for humanity, he lost his nerve in the royal presence. Francis Joseph seemed to court death by walking alone through the streets of Bad Ischl, the resort town outside his summer villa—but death would not come. "All are dying, only I cannot die," he complained in his early eighties. While he lived to die, millions died because he lived.[1]

The debate over German "war guilt," codified in Article 231 of the

Versailles Treaty, has obscured Francis Joseph's primary responsibility for the war. "Austria-Hungary has escaped the scrutiny of many historians for far too long," Annika Mombauer wrote in 2007. In particular, "German historians have been duped . . . by the Austro-Hungarian attempt to pass the blame for the outbreak of the war onto Berlin" when "the initial decision for war . . . was made in Vienna, not Berlin." Yet Vienna chose war with Serbia with the "blank check" it received in Berlin; history did not run an experiment in which it came away empty-handed. That consideration casts a thin shadow of ambiguity over statements like "Vienna independently made the crucial deci-

"The Empire of Death," by Alberto Martini. This Italian postcard is tough on the "old gentleman," but then he did start World War I. The skeleton in Francis Joseph's left eye socket is Franz Ferdinand assassinated in Sarajevo by the skeleton in the right socket, Princip. Hanging from the emperor's ears are victims of post-assassination reprisals against Bosnian Serbs in Austria-Hungary and Serbs in the Balkans. From the right ear, "Trento" and "Trieste," Austrian provinces coveted by Italy; from the left, "Serbia."

sion to go to war in July 1914," the conclusion reached by Samuel R. Williamson Jr. and Ernest May in a major review essay surveying the scholarship on the war's origin written over the past generation.[2]

Francis Joseph's military aide, Baron Margutti, asked the central question: "How could it possibly have come about that the peace-loving old Emperor, of all men, should have lighted the torch that set the world aflame?" There is a big-picture answer.[3]

Austria-Hungary was the memory of a Great Power, spending three times as much on beer, wine, and tobacco as it did on defense. "Let the others wage war," the Emperor Charles V declared in the fifteenth century, "you, faithful Austria, marry." The Habsburgs—Francis Joseph's thousand-year-old dynasty—had conquered by the bed, not by the sword; their empire was an artifact of strategic marriage. When Napoleon married Marie Louise, the sister of Francis I, a cynical prince summed up Habsburg diplomacy: "Better an Archduchess should be *foutue* [fucked] than the monarchy." Since losing midcentury wars to France and Prussia, Austria-Hungary had been living on bankrupt repute. In the days after the assassination in Sarajevo of Franz Ferdinand by a Bosnian Serb student with ties to Belgrade, its leaders feared that, if upstart Serbia got away with conspiring to murder its next ruler, not just big powers like Russia but small ones like Italy and pups like Montenegro would pick the empire apart. A show of power was imperative to maintain the shield of prestige.*[4]

Such was the first requirement of deterrence according to the influential Prussian historian Heinrich von Treitschke. Sounding like

---

*Recent American history has opened a new perspective on the Austrian decision to go to war over the murder of its archduke. "State sponsored terrorism that struck at the Monarchy's heir apparent went beyond the bounds of acceptable international behavior," Samuel R. Williamson Jr., a leading historian of Austria-Hungary, writes. "[The Serbian government's] failure to investigate any Serbian links to the murders and the glee of the Belgrade press over the deaths at Sarajevo provided additional incentive and anger. In a post 9/11 world, Vienna's response becomes possibly more understandable than it would have been for previous generations of historians. Sometimes enough is felt to be enough, whether or not that feeling is wise." Samuel R. Williamson Jr., "Aggressive and Defensive Aims of Political Elites? Austro-Hungarian Policy in 1914," in Holger Afflerbach and David Stevenson, eds., *An Improbable War? The Outbreak of World War I and European Political Culture before 1914* (New York: Berghahn Books, 2007), 72.

North
Sea

SWEDEN

DENMARK

•Copenhagen•

THE
NETHERLANDS

AUSTRIA-HUNGARY
1914

Berlin•

GERMAN EMPIRE

Warsaw•

RUSSIAN EMPIRE

Rhine R.

•Prague
BOHEMIA

•Kracow

Danube R.

Munich •

Vienna•

SWITZERLAND

•Budapest

AUSTRIA-HUNGARY

Milan •

Venice •

CROATIA
AND SLAVONIA

ROMANIA

ITALY

BOSNIA
AND
HERZEGOVINA

•Belgrade

Bucharest•

DALMATIA

•Sarajevo

Danube R.

SERBIA

CORSICA

Adriatic Sea

•Dubrovnik

MONTENEGRO

BULGARIA

•Sofia

Black
Sea

• Rome

•Constantinople

SARDINIA

• Naples

ALBANIA

Tyrrhenian
Sea

TURKEY

0 Miles   100   200

GREECE

Aegean
Sea

0 Kilometers   200

SICILY

Ionian
Sea

•Athens

TUNIS

Mediterranean Sea

© 2012 Jeffrey L. Ward

Woodrow Wilson brandishing battleships at General Huerta for refusing to salute the stars and stripes, Treitschke held that "if the flag of the state is insulted, it is the duty of the State to demand satisfaction, and if satisfaction is not forthcoming, to declare war, however trivial the occasion may appear, for the State must strain every nerve to preserve for itself the respect which it enjoys in the state system." Great Powers had to be willing to fight to uphold their independence, territorial integrity, and standing. Austria-Hungary was willing because Francis Joseph was. He was it. For him, "taking up the sword" against Serbia amounted to "an affair of honor," as Wilson dignified American truculence over Tampico. In the war manifesto of July 29, 1914, the emperor used the pronoun "I" twenty-six times and referred to "my House," "my monarchy," "my peoples," and "my army," casting Serbia's challenge to Austria-Hungary as a personal affront, something he would have settled with a duel if he were not aged and did not have an army for an arm.[5]

A second, more speculative answer to Margutti's question may lie in Francis Joseph's bleeding biography. Francis Joseph would not have been human if he were not prey to dark wishes that all should suffer as he had. "If the monarchy is doomed to perish," he remarked when he decided for war, "let it at least perish decorously." The law knows that as "depraved indifference to human life." To the hard deposit of tragic experience, Francis Joseph's great age added the apathy of the failing grip. Whereas during the Franco-Prussian war in 1870, he led five ministerial conferences in twelve days, in the three years before July 1914 he missed all thirty-nine meetings of his Council of Ministers.

After ascending to the throne at eighteen—"Farewell to youth," he commented—Francis Joseph did not read a single book for pleasure, starving his moral imagination. By 1914 his self had long since been "crushed" under the weight of his throne. In the dual monarchy empathy went up, from subject to emperor, not down.[6]

The emperor gave at the foot washing on Holy Thursday. Standing in for the apostles at this annual ritual were twelve old men rounded up from Vienna's almshouses, cleaned, and installed in chairs in a ceremonial hall of the Hofburg palace. Francis Joseph served them meat, and the archdukes cleared away the dirty dishes. Then, while a priest read from the New Testament, he knelt before them and "touched

Francis Joseph (1830–1916). His suffering propped up his rule.
People felt sorry for him. He felt sorry for himself.

their bare feet with a napkin dipped in water from a golden basin."
The gesture only appeared humble: The emperor was imitating the
Son of God.[7]

On the feast of Corpus Christi in May crowds gathered in St.
Stephan's Square to witness the emperor's arrival for another ceremony of humility. Marching ahead of him came soldiers and officials
of an empire, extending from the Swiss border to Russia, that required
the mobilization orders issued in July 1914 to be printed in fifteen different languages:

> The light-blue breeches of the infantry were radiant . . . The
> coffee-brown artillerists marched pass. The blood-red fezzes on
> the heads of the azure Bosnians burned in the sun like tiny bon-
> fires lit by Islam in honor of His Apostolic Majesty. In black-
> lacquered carriages sat the gold-decked Knights of the Golden
> Fleece and the black-clad red-cheeked municipal councilors.

After them . . . came the horsehair busbies of the bodyguard
infantry . . . The Imperial and Royal anthem . . . floated over all
heads, a sky of melody, a baldachin of black-and-yellow notes . . .
The loud fanfares resounded, the voice of cheerful heralds: Clear
the way! Clear the way! The old Kaiser is coming!

And the Kaiser came; eight radiant-white horses drew his carriage. And on the white horses rode the footmen in black gold-
embroidered coats and white periwigs. On each side of the carriage
stood two Hungarian bodyguards each with a black-and-yellow
panther skin over one shoulder . . . The Emperor wore the snow-
white tunic known from all the portraits in the monarchy, and an
enormous crest of green parrot feathers on his hat.

The procession began at seven A.M. and lasted nearly three hours.
Its cynosure was the Eucharist. The dynasty rested on a foundation
myth centered on this symbol of Christ's body and blood. Hunting the
stag, the first Habsburg, Rudolf I (1218–94), met a priest bringing the
Host to a dying man. A swollen stream barred the way. But Rudolf
lent the priest his horse, who carried him across. In return, the grateful (and connected) priest promised Rudolf's descendants "a worldly
Empire mandated and protected by God." The House of Habsburg
thereafter styled itself God's chosen House. God never denied it.

In 1898, concurrent with the celebration of its longest tenant's fifti-
eth year on the throne, the monarchy's publicists topped Rudolf as the
Good Samaritan by identifying Francis Joseph with Christ. This medi-
evalism had a political purpose—to highlight Francis Joseph's divine
claim to legitimacy at a time of empire-shaking controversies over
language and nationality. From two years before the twentieth century, Francis Joseph was "Christ in the noblest meaning of the word,"
or so an article printed by the Imperial and Royal Court and State
Press impiously asserted.

The Corpus Christi procession evoked this dragooning of God in
aid of State. Members of the high nobility held a balduchin over the
cardinal archbishop of Vienna carrying the Host in his monstrance.
Bareheaded, his plumage tucked under his left arm, his white trident
beard extending his long thin face, Francis Joseph came next. Holding a burning candle emblemizing the light of faith, he followed the

Host along a path of boards strewn with fir branches through the city of Freud and Wittgenstein.[8]

On Francis Joseph's last Corpus Christi circuit in 1913 the press chivalrously remarked on "the Emperor's youthful step." People felt sorry for their emperor. "'Surely you can't do that to the old man,' was one of the standard expressions in the Dual Monarchy's public life." As an 1898 biography had it, wasn't the emperor, for all his body-guards in panther skins, "one of the most sorely tried bearers of human pain"? "The Emperor Franz Joseph succeeded at an early age in acquiring the deep personal attachment of his subjects," the *Times* of London Vienna correspondent, Wickham Steed, reported in 1902. "In the course of time this feeling was enriched by the sympathy aroused by his participation in the national misfortunes and by his terrible family afflictions."[9]

Those afflictions left Francis Joseph alone with his duty. After his wife, Elizabeth ("Sisi"), was murdered by an Italian anarchist in front of her Lake Geneva hotel in 1898, "Apart from his youngest daughter, who with her numerous children gave him something of the warmth of family life, he would not have had a single creature about him who treated him as a human being." The sole exception to this mean rule was Francis Joseph's thirty-five-year bond with the actress Katharina Schratt. Unable to abide life in the gilded cage of royalty ("I like the emperor so much," she remarked at fifteen when he was courting her. "But if only he were not emperor!"),[10] the peripatetic Sisi had encouraged their relationship.

It was certainly an upgrade over the emperor's thirteen-year affair with Anna Nahowski, whom he encountered during an early morning walk near his Schönbrunn palace. At sixteen, Anna was blond, plump, and mercenary. She and her husband, an accommodating railway official, were set up in a house overlooking Schönbrunn Park, and in time in a summer home in the Styrian Alps, where the emperor vacationed. This arrangement only came out after a hundred years.[11]

In contrast, Francis Joseph's affection for Frau Schratt, a single mother abandoned by her debt-fleeing Hungarian husband, provoked gossip from the beginning. In a St. Valentine's Day "letter of medita-

tion," she once offered to become his mistress. Though flattered—
"especially when I look in the mirror and my old wrinkled face
stares back at me"—Francis Joseph gallantly declined. "I love my
wife and do not wish to abuse her confidence and her friendship
with you," he replied in the most intimate of his more than five
hundred letters to her. "I am too old to be a brotherly friend, but
treat me as a fatherly friend." Without her he would have been un-
bearably alone.[12]

A political diary kept by Joseph Baernreither, a former minister
and senior civil servant, highlights a conspiracy to isolate Franz
Joseph: "He is surrounded by a ring of advisors, domestic, military, and
medical . . . For them, there is one law only—to spare the Emperor, to
save him from every unpleasantness, to put no difficult decisions before him. Hence they wash their hands and keep their places." Observers noted this "system of palace sanitation" as early as 1881, when
it came out that the emperor "read only the sections marked by his
officials in red" in the newspapers and so believes "that we are enjoying one of the happiest epochs of Austrian history."[13]

Palace sanitation figured in the confrontation with Serbia that began
the world war. In December 1912, his government rebuffed overtures
from Serbia's prime minister for direct talks in Vienna, but no one told
the emperor. And, just before declaring war on Serbia on July 28,
1914, he was falsely told that Serbian troops had invaded Bosnia and
Hungary.[14]

Rural folk believed that whenever "something happened to the
detriment of one of his subjects, it happened without his prior knowledge and against his will, and they were convinced he would remedy
any grievance if only his bad or wicked advisors would let him do
so." They were not so far wrong.[15]

"The great tides of life of our time hardly reach[ed] his ear as a distant echo," Baernreither wrote of the aging, isolated, incurious emperor who resisted bathrooms in his palace (a bucket was good enough
for *him*) and saw no need to equip the empire's civil servants with
telephones or, lest they scare the horses, the army with armored cars.
An Austrian invented the tank in 1911, but the General Staff, in the
emperor's spirit, rejected it as unworkable. Entertaining Theodore

Roosevelt in 1910, Francis Joseph declared, "You see before you the last monarch of the old school."[16]

Yet with subjects from eleven nationalities and multiple religions, he stood for a principle a century ahead of its time—the "Austrian idea." Children were taught that Austria-Hungary was a state of a "higher order—one that had or could overcome the tribal instincts of nationalism and serve as a model for the transnational European future." Removing his shoes to visit mosques and attending High Holiday services at Jewish temples, Francis Joseph was a multicultural ruler. Such bows to pluralism were well judged in an empire in which, out of every one hundred soldiers, twenty-five were Germans, twenty-three Magyars, thirteen Czechs, nine Serbs or Croats, eight Poles, eight Ruthenes, seven Rumanians, two Slovenes, and one lonely Italian.

The emperor's gestures to diversity, however, could not reliably contain the fissiparous pressures of nationalism and irredentism mounting within Austria-Hungary. An analogy captures the scope of the challenge: "A great power can endure without difficulty one Ireland, as England did, even three, as Imperial Germany did (Poland, Alsace, Schleswig [seized from Denmark in 1864]). Different is the case when a Great Power is composed of nothing else but Irelands, as was almost the history of Austria-Hungary." Haunting its future was the question whether the mystique of Francis Joseph as the protector of peoples, in his own words, "too weak to remain independent if left to their own devices" would attach to the empire after the emperor was dead.[17]

In 1910 fewer than a million of his nearly fifty million subjects could remember a time when Francis Joseph, who ascended the throne in 1848, was not emperor. His image was ubiquitous, appearing on banknotes, stamps, and coins, as well as on the kitsch of empire—busts, vases, cups, ashtrays, aprons, jackknives, scissors, and rubber balls. The Interior Ministry put its foot down when a company requested permission to display his likeness on crates of fish.* Otherwise there

---

* Compare Bismarck: "His name was to be found . . . on streets, squares, bridges, tunnels, obelisks, towers, ships . . . a mountain peak, a dye (dark brown), a vodka, a rose, a jelly doughnut . . . and a pickled herring." See Otto Pflanze, *Bismarck*

Franz Ferdinand handing a bouquet to his uncle.
Francis Joseph was relieved when he learned of his nephew's assassination on
June 28, 1914. In Vienna's parks the bands played on. Sunday promenaders
on the Ringstrasse showed little grief. Franz Ferdinand lacked charm;
case closed for the Viennese. He also had crazy ideas. One was to save
the empire with a template borrowed from the United States.

was no escaping his vacant mien: "Above the bed was a portrait hanging of the all-illustrious monarch. During all the primogenitive acts
(and there were quite a number of them) Mrs. Stukla kept her eyes
fixed on this picture—a fact that displeased Mr. Stukla, the more so
as he with good reason demanded of his spouse active participation in
pursuing an operation designed to increase the subjects of the Austro-
Hungarian monarchy."[18]

The great fear of Francis Joseph's old age was that his nephew's
children would foul the lineage of the seven-hundred-year-old empire. That accounts for the hard words attributed to him when, on the
evening of June 28, 1914, he read the telegram reporting the murder
of that nephew, Franz Ferdinand, and his wife in Sarajevo.[19]

"Horrible! The Almighty does not allow himself to be challenged
with impunity . . . A higher power has restored the old order which
I unfortunately was unable to uphold." The higher power had waited
exactly fourteen years. Yielding, by one account, to Franz Ferdinand's
threats to shoot himself (like Crown Prince Rudolf, Francis Joseph's

only son) if forbidden to marry the woman he loved, on June 28, 1900, the emperor officially sanctioned Franz Ferdinand's union with Sophie Chotek, a member of the minor nobility.[20]

Francis Joseph's life was regulated by the exacting Spanish Court Ceremonial of his ancestors. On July 25, 1914, the day he approved the ultimatum to Serbia, for example, in a handwritten note to his chief aide he "prescrib[ed] the dress to be worn by the wait staff that night." This stern code required him to exact a price for allowing Franz Ferdinand to marry beneath him—renunciation of his unborn children's rights to succeed him on the throne.[21]

Ever since yielding to his nephew as "a new proof of my special affection" the old man had ruminated that Franz Ferdinand would break the contract and bequeath the House of Habsburg to Sophie's inferior spawn. Via assassination the Almighty had lifted that cloud over his mind. To his daughter, who found "Papa amazingly fresh" the day after Sarajevo, he confessed, "For me it is a relief from a great worry."[22]

Franz Ferdinand's body was spared the interment ritual prescribed for archdukes—that is, his corpse was not deposited in the vaults of the Capuchin Church, nor his heart conveyed to a silver urn at St. Augustin's, nor his intestines stored in a silver vat at St. Stephen's cathedral. After a "third-class funeral" lasting fifteen minutes, during which, one of the deceased's aides recalled, Francis Joseph glanced around the Hofburg chapel "with complete indifference," Franz Ferdinand and Sophie were buried together at Artstetten, their estate in lower Austria.

The barbarous ritual of dispersing parts of the royal body deserves comment. Like the Corpus Christi procession through Vienna's Old City, it is redolent of Europe's feudal ethos, a cursed inheritance of " 'premodern' elements [that] were not the decaying and fragile remnants of all but vanished past but the very essence of Europe's incumbent civil and political societies." From this culture of the undead proceeded the self-destruction of an ancien régime that, a century after the French Revolution, still practiced power politics by a code of honor that put "courage above survival" and still held otherwise modern nations in its death grip. Count Ottokar Czernin, a Franz Ferdinand ally and Austria-Hungary's last foreign minister, spoke

not just for the Habsburg monarchy but for Europe's aristocratic order when he said, "We were at liberty to choose the manner of our
death, and we chose the most terrible."[23]

Besides anxiety over bad blood tainting his line, Franz Ferdinand's
death relieved Francis Joseph of a threat to the empire's cornerstone,
the Augsleich—the 1867 Compromise with Hungary—that Franz
Ferdinand abhorred as the empire's curse. Farsighted contemporaries
agreed. Writing in 1911, the British Balkan hand Hugh Seton-Watson
called "the fatal dual system" with Hungary the "ruin of modern
Austria." For Joseph Redlich, a liberal parliamentarian and Francis
Joseph biographer, "Hungarian policy . . . had long constituted the
root evil from which the whole body of the realm was sickening."
Baernreither hoped that Franz Ferdinand would live up to the claims
made by his allies and reform dualism once he became emperor: "For
him, and for us, it is a life and death question."[24]

From the 1500s until Napoleon abolished the "union of crowns" in
1806, Austria and Hungary were equals under the Holy Roman Empire. The successor Austrian Empire absorbed Hungary, which nearly
broke free in 1848–49, but Austria suppressed the revolt with Russian troops. After Bismarck, in the second of his wars of German
unification, defeated Austria in 1866, Francis Joseph, to secure his
realm for a new war on Prussia, agreed to Hungarian demands to
restore the union of crowns. Under the Compromise, each country
had its own prime minister and parliament, with the "common monarchy" made up of the emperor-king, and Vienna-based ministries of
foreign affairs, defense, and finance.

"The mysteries of this Dualism (the technical term for it) were at
the very least as recondite as those of the Trinity," Robert Musil
noted in a passage of *The Man Without Qualities*, a Viennese epic set
in the last days of Austria-Hungary, that encapsulates the comic civic
punctilio exacted by the hyphen:

The Austro-Hungarian state was so oddly put together that it
must seem almost hopeless to explain it to anyone who has not
experienced it himself. It did not consist of an Austrian part and
a Hungarian part that, as one might expect, complemented each

other, but of a whole and a part: that is, of a Hungarian and an Austro-Hungarian sense of statehood, the latter to be found in Austria, which in a sense left the Austrian sense of statehood with no country of its own. The Austrian existed only in Hungary, and there as an object of dislike; at home he called himself a national of the kingdom and lands of the Austro-Hungarian Monarchy . . . meaning that he was an Austrian plus a Hungarian minus that Hungarian.[25]

Francis Joseph never got his war of revenge on Bismarck; Hungary vetoed it. And every ten years, when the Compromise came up for renewal, the Hungarians threatened to secede unless he met their demands.

Many were trivial. Budapest objected to substituting the article "and" for the hyphen in naming government departments like "The Bureau of Standards for Austria *and* Hungary." It lodged a "vehement protest" to a grieving Francis Joseph to add the legend "QUEEN OF HUNGARY" to "EMPRESS OF AUSTRIA" on Sisi's coffin.[26]

Two demands, however, were serious. Hungary was increasingly unwilling to provide recruits for the Imperial Army. In 1903–06 the Hungarian Independence Party went further, calling for a separate Hungarian army. To head this off, Francis Joseph seriously considered a military coup against the Budapest government but decided in the end to play the democracy card.

Hungary was run by and for its Magyar landed gentry. In the Budapest parliament, 392 deputies represented the 8.5 million Magyars; 21 deputies the 8 million non-Magyars. To break the Magyar monopoly of power, Francis Joseph threatened to decree universal suffrage in Hungary. Stephen Tisza, the Magyar leader, said *that* would amount to "castrating the nation." The Magyars blinked, agreeing to maintain a common army though dragging their feet and making a row over the language of command. Francis Joseph had long since blinked over their second demand, to Magyarize Hungary's non-Magyars—Germans, Slovaks, Serbo-Croats, Ruthenes, and Rumanians.[27]

To Joseph Redlich this was the emperor's "gravest political sin." The Magyars ruled the minorities at bayonet point and suppressed their languages and cultures. When their representatives complained to the emperor, he turned them away. "Any appeal to him as Austrian emperor about Hungarian matters was prohibited, for that was the Hungarian king's responsibility." But Francis Joseph was the Hungarian king. Nevertheless, "he refused to interfere in Hungarian affairs—if it was on behalf of his other peoples." Though it made a mockery of "the Austrian idea," he stood with the Magyars. Not only did he refuse to meet with three hundred Rumanian delegates protesting Magyarization, he allowed them to be prosecuted for treason. Preserving the Compromise required it.[28]

Exaggerating truth, Franz Ferdinand shared with Kaiser Wilhelm his conviction that "all the difficulties that we have to face in the monarchy have their origin with the Magyars.* Who is behind the Slav danger? [The separatist agitation of the Bohemian Czechs, Bosnian Serbs, and Hungarian Croats.] Where is the core of this evil? Who has been the teacher of all those elements that succeed by revolutionary . . . excess? The Magyars. The Slavs act that way only because they imitate the conduct of the Magyars and because they see how the Magyars get all they want by their shameless conduct."[29]

Rancor inflected that acute political judgment. Just as Pancho Villa named his mule "Wilson," so to mark the thousand-year anniversary of the Magyar conquest of their Danubian lands, Franz Ferdinand rebaptized his "Boreo" (borro) to "Millennium." The archduke had seen the Magyar supremacy at work among the 3.2 million Transylvanian Romanians in Hungary. "Rumanians have been persecuted and oppressed with cynical disregard for justice in Hungary under every Ministry . . . in matters of education, constant imprisonments, and arrests," he wrote to Count Berchtold, the foreign minister of Austria-Hungary. "I will never forget the time when I paid an official

---

*By treating Sophie with the respect due a future empress of Austria, the kaiser endeared himself to her husband. Their relationship began unpromisingly, however. Franz Ferdinand was "*terribly,* terribly offended" after their first meeting at a Berlin railway station, when Wilhelm greeted him with, "Don't imagine I've come to *your* reception—I am expecting the Crown Prince of Italy." See John C. G. Röhl, "The Emperor's New Clothes: A Character Sketch of Kaiser Wilhelm II," in John C. G. Röhl and Nicholas Sombart, *Kaiser Wilhelm II: New Interpretations, The Corfu Papers* (New York: Cambridge University Press, 1982), 34.

visit to Romania and at every station our indigenous Romanians in southern Hungary and Transylvania wanted to welcome my wife and me and bring us flowers." But "they were driven off the train platform by local authorities and guards with bayonets . . . It is easy to conceive the population's legitimate bitterness at being prevented from bringing flowers to their next ruler by Magyar bayonets." The flowers were eventually delivered. At the short requiem service held in the Hofburg chapel on July 2, 1914, representatives of the Hungarian Romanians laid floral wreaths bearing the legend TO OUR LAST HOPE, IN LOYAL DEVOTION on the catafalque of Franz Ferdinand.[30]

Was he worth their loyalty? Unpopular in life and unmourned in death, "Franz Ferdinand lacked everything that counts for real popularity in Austria; amiability, personal charm and easygoingness," recalled Stefan Zweig, who observed the archduke, "with his bulldog neck and his cold staring eyes" and his wife in their box at the theater, "never casting a friendly glance toward the audience or encouraging the actors with hearty applause." The couple "had no friends" and "the old Emperor hated him with all his heart because he did not have sufficient tact to hide his impatience to succeed to the throne." Franz Ferdinand was in a hurry in a country where nothing happened fast ("red tape was legendary: at Vienna twenty-seven officials handled each tax payment"), and the old emperor never died. Convinced that no one liked him, Franz Ferdinand gave up trying to be liked. Tetchy, he was notoriously sensitive to slights, especially to his wife.[31]

The chamberlain of Francis Joseph's court, Prince Montenuovo, saw to the slights. As curator of the Spanish severities, he tried to prevent the marriage by circulating a photograph of Sophie touched up to make her look like an aging slattern. "The Emperor did what he could to mitigate the situation by creating her the Duchess of Hohenberg," Rebecca West wrote. "But the obsessed Montenuovo hovered over her, striving to exacerbate every possible humiliation, never happier than when he could hold her back from entering a carriage or cutting down to the minimum the salutes and attendants called for by any state occasion." Franz Ferdinand avoided Vienna to spare her these insults.[32]

Slaughtering animals purged some of his anger—on a record day at a Czech castle he "bagged" 2,150 pieces of small game—but he was always molten. "He was capable of flying out at people and terrifying them [so much] that they lost their heads completely," wrote Count Czernin. Franz Ferdinand could sound terrifying. "When I am Commander-in-Chief I shall do as I will; if anyone does anything else, I shall have them all shot," he remarked to General Conrad von Hötzendorf, the chief of staff, whose chronic agitation for war with Serbia (and Italy!) antagonized the archduke.[33]

Franz Ferdinand's letters reveal him as an irascible reactionary dreaming of an alliance of the three dynasties—Habsburg, Hohenzollern, Romanov—against modernity. They also reveal him to be an anti-Semite. So was Kaiser Wilhelm. But the archduke possessed what the kaiser lacked—vision. Historians agree that he was an unpleasant personality. There is less consensus over whether his vision, by offering the minorities their "last hope," could have held together an empire made up of nothing but Irelands. His death, Joachim Remak asserts, "was more than an excuse for war; it was one of its major causes." If he had lived, would the war, too, belong to the lost history of 1914?[34]

"There are three possible political systems in Austria—Centralism, which gives the hegemony to the Germans; Dualism, which divides it between the Germans and the Magyars; and Federalism, which secures equality of rights to all the races of the Empire," a prewar Bohemian historian wrote. Franz Ferdinand, who as a young man crossed the United States by train, sought an American solution for the monarchy— Centralism, plus Federalism. In a 1906 essay, "The United States of Greater Austria," a member of his inner circle presented the autonomy enjoyed by American states in domestic matters and Swiss cantons as a template for the empire's regions and nationalities.[35]

The American solution was Franz Ferdinand's answer to the so-called South Slav Question, the empire's greatest challenge. In 1908, Austria annexed Bosnia-Herzegovina from Turkey, saddling Austria with a restive Slavic population—the Bosnian Serbs—who looked upon the Kingdom of Serbia just across the Drina River from Bosnia as the homeland of their religion, language, and culture. Secret societies in Serbia fanned this sentiment in Bosnia, eventually "exasperating Austrian policy enough to start a world war." The alternative to the American solution was war with Serbia.[36]

"I stand or fall by a Habsburg federal Empire," Franz Ferdinand told Baron Margutti. He went on: "It would mean that the Slav problem would solve itself. The Czechs would be separated from the Germans of Bohemia and enjoy autonomy. So would the Croats, the Slovenes, and the Hungarian Serbs. Then all these peoples would exercise so strong an attraction—by their very mass—on the Serbs of the Kingdom that the latter would seek national unity within the Monarchy, i.e., in a centripetal sense, and not in a centrifugal sense by the incorporation of our South Slavs with the Serbs of the Kingdom."[37]

Was federalism *the* answer? Seton-Watson thought it might be. "I had pinned all my hopes for the future upon him," he wrote just after the assassination but before its cataclysmic sequel. "He represented a progressive idea in the Europe of today, and all Europe is the loser by his death." The Magyars, the emperor, and the Serbs all feared it might be.[38]

At the time of the annexation of Bosnia, a Hungarian politician recognized the impetus it would lend to the archduke's anti-Magyar campaign:

Thus Bosnia and Herzegovina must be regarded as the nucleus of a future Southern Slav Kingdom and as a third part of the Monarchy—namely, the foundation upon which 'Greater Austria,' the favorable scheme of the Heir Apparent, is to be erected . . . The equality of rights enjoyed by Hungary will obviously be curtailed when she will be compressed between the Slavs of Bohemia in the north and the Slavs in the south . . . I regard the annexation as a second Mohacs, the battle at which the independent Kingdom of Hungary was destroyed by the Turks in 1526.[39]

Regarding it as a second Mohacs, the Magyars were the stumbling block to Franz Ferdinand's American solution to the South Slav problem. As the archduke wrote to Kaiser Wilhelm, it followed that "to conduct a vigorous foreign policy, beneficial to all the peoples . . . there is only one remedy and one requirement; that is to break the *predominance* of the Magyars." By "break" he meant use force: "Very well. Hungary will have to be conquered once again at the point of a sword. I do not see how it would be possible to escape from this necessity."[40]

Francis Joseph dreaded the chaos the archduke's reform plans would wreak. In his eyes the Compromise had preserved Austria as a Great Power. The American solution would be the shipwreck of his life's work. A contemporary Austrian historian agrees: Franz Ferdinand's extralegal measures against Hungary "could have called forth . . . a dangerous external crisis . . . It would have needed no world war to blow up the monarchy." Franz Ferdinand's death had relieved Francis Joseph of that "great worry."[41]

The seven teenage Bosnian Serb terrorists stippled throughout the crowd lining Sarajevo's Appel Quay to welcome Franz Ferdinand on June 28 plotted to kill him to prevent his American solution. "I have no regrets because I am convinced that I have destroyed a scourge and done a good deed," Gavrilo Princip, his nineteen-year-old assassin, said to investigators. "As future Sovereign he would have prevented our union [with Serbia] and carried out certain reforms which would have been clearly against our interests." His fellow conspirator, Nedjelko Carbrinovic, concurred: "The Archduke proposed the creation of a federal monarchy which was . . . a danger to . . . Serbia."

The assassins were trained and armed in Belgrade by the Black Hand, an underground terrorist organization, led by one Colonel Dragutin Dimitrijevic, aboveground the chief intelligence officer of the Serbian army. And Dimitrijevic, too—codenamed "Apis," the sacred bull of Egypt, by his fellow conspirators—regarded the archduke's plan as a threat to the project of Greater Serbia, the drawing in of the South Slavs into a Yugoslav state led by Serbia. Apis, his nephew told the historian Luigi Albertini, "had grasped all the danger of the Archduke's plan. Austria meant to bring about a Southern Slav union within the framework of the Danubian monarchy." Apis "was seriously perturbed by the information, continually brought to him by Serbs and Croats from the Monarchy, of the growing sympathy which that program roused among the Slav subjects of Austria.

That was why he decided to seize the first occasion to eliminate Francis Ferdinand."[42]★

Against the testimony of contemporaries about the mortal danger Franz Ferdinand's American solution posed to Magyar hegemony, the Dual Monarchy, and Serbian nationalism, one must set the doubts of historians whose recoil from Franz Ferdinand the man magnifies their contempt for his ideas. "Recent historiography is skeptical about the possibility of realizing any of" Franz Ferdinand's plans, one Austrian scholar concludes. The archduke was "a federalist only when it gave promise of breaking Hungarian particularism." Another says that his federalism "did not mean any . . . improvement of the position of the nationalities." What the archduke sought was not the "equality of nations but their equal non-equality" under a "neo-absolutist" central government in Vienna." "Franz Ferdinand," A. J. P. Taylor asserts, "was one of the worst products of the Habsburg House: reactionary, clerical, brutal and overbearing, he was also often insane." A Francis Joseph biographer agrees: "It is hard to escape the feeling that he would have become a disastrous Emperor if he had lived."[43]

Perhaps, but that "what if" is of interest chiefly to Austria-Hungary scholars. We care about a different one: "If he had lived would World

---

★The Serbian government accepted most of the demands made on it by the Austrian ultimatum, but, knowing any inquiry would lead to Apis, would not agree to permit Austrian police to go to Belgrade to investigate the assassinations. Serbia's rejection of this demand triggered Austria's declaration of war. If the zero-sum diplomacy of imperialism had not eclipsed the diplomacy of European Concert that had kept the peace for decades, "Europe acting in concert" could have asked "Austria-Hungary to turn its cause and demands over to them, and then carr[ied] through seriously on an investigation and any required sanctions . . . Russia was more than once required in the nineteenth century to turn its cause and honor in the Balkans over to the European Concert to defend . . . The fact that this procedure did not always work or was not always tried makes no difference. It was there, it could and did sometimes work, and in some instances like this one it was the only thing that could have worked." See Paul W. Schroeder, "Embedded Counterfactuals and World War I as an Unavoidable War," in David Wetzel, Robert Jervis, and Jack S. Levy, eds., *Systems Stability and Statecraft: Essays in International History* (New York: Palgrave, 2004), 39 (Web version).

War I have happened?"* On that "counterfactual," F. H. Hinsley, a British historian, voices the unspoken assumption shared by generations of historians: "If the Sarajevo crisis had not precipitated a particular great war, some other crisis would have precipitated a great war at no distant date." War was inevitable. Some wars look that way in retrospect. If rebels had not fired on Fort Sumter in 1861, they would have attacked Fort Pickens or some other federal facility in the South, and that place would be as famous as Fort Sumter. The shelling of Fort Sumter was the catalyst of the American Civil War, not its cause. Franz Ferdinand's assassination was an event of a different order. It satisfied so many of the conditions necessary for the war that the "what if" above cannot be dismissed with Hinsley's bluff confidence in destiny.[44]

Consider the difference Franz Ferdinand's absence made in Austria. Between December 1912 and July 1914 Austria-Hungary "went to the brink of war" four times over territorial aggrandizement by Serbia or Montenegro stemming from their victories over Turkey and Bulgaria in the Balkan Wars—but went over it only once. Franz Ferdinand was the most forceful advocate of peace on two of the three occasions, reinforcing the clement inclinations of Francis Joseph. On the third, spooked by the military's "worst-case" analysis of December 1912 that Serbia might attack Austria-Hungary, he wavered briefly, before recovering the prudence that made him "as cautious in foreign affairs as he was impetuous in domestic policy." On the fourth, he was dead, and Austria-Hungary declared war.[45]

The historian Samuel R. Williamson Jr. invites us to speculate on what might have happened if, instead of Franz Ferdinand, Princip had killed the governor general of Bosnia, Oskar Potiorek. It could

---

*The following analysis closely follows Richard Ned Lebow, "Franz Ferdinand Found Alive: World War I Unnecessary," in Philip Tetlock, Richard Ned Lebow, and Geoffrey Parker, eds., *Unmaking the West: Counterfactual Thought Experiments in History* (Ann Arbor: University of Michigan Press, 2006). Also see Richard Ned Lebow, "Counterfactual Thought Experiments: A Necessary Teaching Tool," *History Teacher* 40, no. 2 (2007): 1–17. I am indebted to Professor Lebow. For a robust theoretical defense of counterfactual history, see Niall Ferguson, "Virtual History: Towards a 'Chaotic' Theory of the Past," in Ferguson, ed., *Virtual History: Alternatives and Counterfactuals* (New York: Basic Books, 1999), 1–90.

easily have happened. Just as Princip pointed his automatic at the archduke, whose open touring car, having taken the wrong turn, had stopped to reverse five feet away, a policeman lunged at his hand— too late (by one account, an accomplice hit the policeman). Speed up the policeman's arm by a millisecond, the Armageddon blink, and the bullet might have struck Potiorek, sitting in the front seat.* Franz Ferdinand, unscathed, would have been whisked away—and been in Vienna to shape Austria-Hungary's response to Potiorek's assassination.[46]

As he had in the three earlier war crises, as he did twenty-five times in 1913 alone, Chief of Staff Conrad von Hötzendorf, an army modernizer popular with junior officers, and "possibly, the single most important military figure in Europe's rush to war," would have demanded war with Serbia. Franz Ferdinand had pushed for Conrad's appointment to chief of staff in 1906 partly on the strength of the general's anti-Magyar convictions. Conrad's war-mongering made him regret this, and in 1911 he had prodded Francis Joseph to relieve Conrad only, bowing to pressure from the army, to turn full circle and urge his recall a year later.[47]

Against Conrad's call for war in July 1914, in our counterfactual scenario, Franz Ferdinand would have pressed argument like this one from a 1913 letter to Count Berchtold: "Suppose we wage a separate war against Serbia? In no time at all, we will overthrow it, but what then, and what good will it do us? . . . God save us from annexing Serbia; a country over its head in debts, brimming with regicides [!] and scoundrels, etc. As it is we cannot even cope with Bosnia . . . And Serbia will be far worse! We can throw away billions there and still be faced with terrible *irredenta*." Cross-examination of Conrad would have educed that the army had no plans to occupy Serbia: "In the most favorable case, the Austro-Hungarian Army would march into Serbia; it would extract promises of good behavior from the Serbs; and then it

---

*In another account, Princip shot the archduke, then shifted his aim to Potiorek and would have shot him "had not Sophie thrown herself across the car in one last expression of her great love, and drawn Franz Ferdinand to herself with a movement that brought her across the path of the second bullet." Rebecca West, *Black Lamb and Grey Falcon: A Journey Through Yugoslavia* (New York: Penguin Books, 2007), 349–50.

would leave." Austria-Hungary wanted, Franz Ferdinand once told Conrad, "not a single plum tree or a single sheep" from the Balkans. Why, to mount a punitive raid on Serbia, start a war with Russia?[48]

For, Franz Ferdinand would have reminded Conrad in front of Francis Joseph, Serbia *was* Russia. "If we take the field against Serbia, Russia will stand behind her, and we will have the war with Russia," he had written to Berchtold. Could Austria hope to prevail when Russia fielded ninety-three divisions to Austria's forty-eight and spent three quarters more on armaments than she did? "War with Russia will mean the end of us . . . Should the Austrian Emperor and the Russian tsar topple one another from the throne and clear the way for revolution?" Incredibly, during the Common Ministerial Council of July 7 that set Vienna's strategy, nobody raised Franz Ferdinand's questions about the foreseeable consequences of war with Russia, which all assumed Germany would deter.[49]

Finally, Franz Ferdinand would have played the nationalities' card against Conrad, who advocated war as a domestic political imperative. "Two principles stood in sharp conflict," Conrad wrote in his memoirs, "the preservation of Austria-Hungary as a conglomerate of different nationalities . . . ; the rise of separate independent national states which would attract their co-nationals in Austro-Hungarian territory and bring about the disintegration of the Monarchy . . . That and not expiation of the murder was the reason why Austria-Hungary was forced to unsheath the sword against Serbia." War, he believed, would weld the national minorities to the empire. It was all that would. To stay together, Austria-Hungary had to risk breaking up under the hammer of war.[50]*

---

* "This old idea is often referred to as the scapegoat or diversionary theory of war, for political elites can use a foreign war to divert popular attention from internal social, economic, and political problems . . . The scapegoat theory is based on the in-group/out-group hypothesis in sociology. [Georg] Simmel, in the first systematic treatment of the subject, argued that conflict with an out-group increases the cohesion of the in-group, and generalized to international relations: 'war with the outside is sometimes the last chance for a state ridden with inner antagonisms to overcome these antagonisms, or else to break up definitely.'" Jack S. Levy, "Domestic Politics and War," *Journal of Interdisciplinary History* 18, no. 4, "The Origin and Prevention of Major Wars" (Spring 1988): 667.

Based on his known views, Franz Ferdinand would have retorted that the risk was too great, the centripetal forces generated by war too strong. Incited by Russia, the minorities would revolt, trading their subordinate status in a German–Magyar-dominated "nation of nationalities" for independence as "nation states." That danger was familiar to Conrad. In the event of a prolonged German–Slavic (Russian) war, he wrote to General Helmuth von Moltke, the German chief of staff, in 1913, "we can hardly count on the enthusiastic support of our Slavs, 47 percent of our population." Could this advocate of war to save the monarchy have met the more plausible argument that war would destroy it? Conrad was coolly rational in his memoirs; in 1914 he was fatalistic. The night of Sarajevo, in a letter to his mistress, he expressed a desperate pessimism: "It will be a hopeless struggle but nevertheless it must be because such an ancient monarchy and such an ancient army cannot perish ingloriously." Could this doomsayer have given a convincingly positive answer to Franz Ferdinand's simple, devastating question, Can we *win*?[51]

Auspiciously, Franz Ferdinand and Stephen Tisza, the Hungarian prime minister, would have been on the same side in July 1914—against war. This would have "carried considerable weight because the two men were otherwise always at odds," the political scientist Richard Ned Lebow writes. "With Franz Ferdinand urging moderation, Berchtold, a weak personality, would also have pursued a cautious line, and Francis Joseph, cross-pressured in 1914, would probably have sided with them instead of with Conrad." The Franz Ferdinand biographer Robert A. Kann concurs: "Berchtold's policy was largely dictated by the Heir Apparent." With Franz Ferdinand gone, Berchtold, using the same words at roughly the same time as the Russian foreign minister Alexander Serge Sazonov in St. Petersburg, declared, "Failure to act decisively" would be "the renunciation of our Great Power position."[52]

At the council meetings what Vienna journalists called "the war party" was led by Conrad and General Oskar Potiorek, lamentably alive. Potiorek wanted to bury in the rubble of war his responsibility for the lax security in a city hung with Serbian flags (commemorating the battle of Kosovo in 1389) until authorities removed them just before the archduke's arrival. Conrad wanted war to impress his girlfriend.

Frustrated from sharing the favors of Gina von Reininghaus with her husband, Hermann, the beer king of Austria-Hungary, Conrad imagined that if he led the army to victory a bedazzled Gina, twenty-eight years his junior and the mother of six, would sue for divorce while a grateful emperor would persuade the Vatican to permit them to marry in the church. In the first months of the war when he was trying hard to wow Gina and before she converted to Protestantism, Conrad's judgment was rushed and rash. An example came as early as August 3 when he cited a report from the military attaché in London to argue "that there is no desire [in England] for war for the time being, taking into account the Ulster crisis and the civil war." The next day, England declared war on Germany and, eight days later, on Austria-Hungary.[53]

Franz Ferdinand, a strict Roman Catholic, censured Conrad's romance with Gina, at one point ambiguously warning Berchtold that Conrad's personal stake in war endangered the monarchy. In our counterfactual argument in Vienna over whether to attack Serbia for Potiorek's assassination in Sarajevo, the archduke might well have impeached Conrad's war mania by surfacing its, in the circumstances, grotesquely selfish motives.[54]

Historical analysis arrives at the same destination as counterfactual speculation. Comparing the Habsburg elite's attitude toward war with Serbia before and after the assassination, Holger Afflerbach and David Stevenson conclude that "Sarajevo really was the decisive moment: without the murder of Franz Ferdinand and his wife, there would have been no decision for war in Vienna, and therefore no general conflict."[55]

The latter point shifts the focus to Berlin. In a brilliant paper, "Franz Ferdinand Found Alive: World War I Unnecessary," Lebow argues that the assassination "created the necessary psychological environment for kaiser and chancellor to overcome their inhibitions about war." The murder of "Franzi," his friend and fellow-crowned head, whom he had seen in Bohemia two weeks earlier, shocked Wilhelm. He had not taken seriously Vienna's obsession with the Serbs; he did now. In Bethmann Hollweg Sarajevo crystallized a "gestalt shift" from brooding on Russian power to being willing to risk war with Russia. The politics of the assassination were fortuitous for the chancellor. Princip's Serbian connection kindled Socialist Russophobia into a unanimous SPD vote in the Reichstag for war credits, satisfying the domestic precondition for war. Altogether, Sarajevo belonged to a special category of incidents that are at once catalysts and causes of war. President Lyndon Johnson's national security advisor, McGeorge Bundy, termed them "streetcars," referring to the February 1965 Vietcong attack on the American adviser's barracks in Pleiku. Washington could count on such streetcars to provide the pretext to escalate the Vietnam War. The assassination of Franz Ferdinand was Berlin's streetcar to preventive war against Russia.[56]

If he had lived, would another streetcar have come along? The hour was late; the line shutting down. The day Franz Ferdinand became emperor his military staff planned to move against Hungary. That would have been in 1916, after Francis Joseph's death. From that date Austria-Hungary would be embroiled in civil strife. It could not start a war with Serbia; Berlin would wait in vain for that streetcar. By 1917, Russia's railways to the German border would be completed; so would the Great Program military buildup begun in June 1914 in reaction to the Liman von Sanders affair. This would expand Russia's peacetime army to two million men. Germany's strategy for a two-front war, to defeat France before Russia could mobilize, would be obsolete when Russia could mobilize rapidly. German officials saw this coming. "The future belongs to Russia which is growing and growing and is becoming an ever increasing nightmare to us. After the completion of her strategic railroads in Poland our position will be untenable," Bethmann Hollweg confided to his aide Kurt Riezler at the beginning of the July Crisis. Germany had a three-year window in which it could risk a war with Russia and France. After that, the German generals, Lebow writes, "would . . . no longer have an incentive to launch a preventive war or preempt in a crisis, and to the extent that they were fearful of Russian military capabilities, they might even have become a force for preserving the peace."[57]

Counterfactual history reminds us that great events can be both massively overdetermined—see Lebow's table on the Underlying Causes of War, each one representing a mountain of scholarship—and contingent, as Herodotus has it, on things that don't happen or hap-

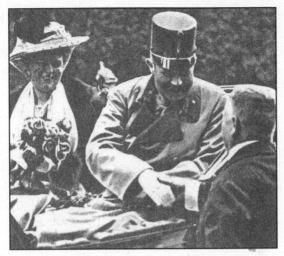

The happy couple arrives in Sarajevo.

pen at the wrong time. All the big causes swirled around Franz Ferdinand in June 1914, but none decided him to go to Sarajevo.*

Francis Joseph was stricken with severe bronchitis in April. He had inflammation of the lung, and his life hung in the balance. For the last ten days of the month, Franz Ferdinand kept an engine under steam at a station near his Bohemian castle to take him to Vienna at a moment's notice should his uncle's condition worsen. But the old man rallied. The talk in Vienna, the *Times* reported, was that his recovery was spurred "by his keen desire to spite his nephew and delay his accession to the imperial throne for as long as possible."

---

*"It is worth considering the somewhat counterintuitive proposition that there may be no relationship between the number and intensity of underlying causes and the probability of an outcome . . . Social scientists err in thinking that major social and political developments are invariably specific instances of strong . . . regularities in social behavior. These developments are sometimes the result of accidental conjunctions . . . The concatenation of particular leaders with particular contexts, and of particular events with other events, is always a matter of chance, never of necessity." Richard Ned Lebow, *Forbidden Fruit: Counterfactuals and International Relations* (Princeton: Princeton University Press, 2010), 133. From a chapter coauthored with George W. Breslauer.

On June 4, Franz Ferdinand met with him in Vienna and, pleading the extreme heat, asked to be excused from attending, in his capacity as inspector general of the army, long-scheduled maneuvers in Bosnia later that month. Francis Joseph replied that it was of course his choice—"but added that, if he went, Sophie might accompany him officially to Sarajevo on June 28—the anniversary of their pact of marriage." Officially: Meaning Sophie could be treated, for that trip, as his equal. Franz Ferdinand loved his wife. He changed his mind.[58]

6

FRANCE

THE WAGES OF IMPERIALISM

Agadir was the most arduous adventure that France had known.

—Joseph Caillaux, *Agadir*, 1925

*I agree, too, that Caillaux is the man to bring it off, and, if this war
materializes, I rather think the historians—who've made so much of
Cleopatra's nose—will ascribe its due importance to the tragic
revolver shot at the Figaro offices when they're unraveling the causes
of the war . . . One thing for sure, my boy: if he had stayed in
power, things wouldn't have come to the pass they've got to now.*

—A character in *Summer 1914*,
a novel by Roger Martin du Gard

MILLIONS OF BULLETS were fired in 1914 but only two
changed history: The bullet fired by Princip's Browning automatic that pierced Franz Ferdinand's uniform collar and entered his
neck, and the bullet fired by Henriette Caillaux that killed Gaston
Calmette, the editor of *Le Figaro*, whom she believed was about to expose the intimate secrets of her marriage. Except for the bark of *her*
Browning, Henriette's husband Joseph Caillaux would have been
France's premier in July 1914. His elevation from finance minister
would have incalculably affected German opinion. "If Monsieur Caillaux had remained in office, if Madame Caillaux's gesture had not

been made," the *Kölnische Zeitung* observed months into the war, "the plot against the peace of Europe would not have succeeded," Caillaux would have eased the pressure of that paranoia. Vienna and Berlin made the plot against the peace, but in the story the German public was told it was hatched in St. Petersburg and Paris, by Nicholas II and French president Raymond Poincaré, a Lorrainer who schemed to recover by a new war the two provinces, Alsace-Lorraine, lost to Germany in the Franco-Prussian war of 1870–71. Caillaux, born in Le Mans, was not from one of the Lost Provinces. As premier in 1911, he had defused a crisis with Germany by back-channel negotiations through the German embassy in Paris. He was a known critic of France's ties to England and of the machinations of Russia's ambassador to France, Alexander Izvolski, who to revenge himself on Austria-Hungary for his humiliation in the Bosnia crisis of 1908 worked for war with the Central Powers. The man who would have been Caillaux's Foreign Minister in July 1914, the Socialist giant Jean Jaurès, was a passionate critic of France's military alliance with Russia and the most famous ant-militarist, if not pacifist, in Europe. At a minimum, with Caillaux as premier and Jaurès as foreign minister Berlin would have had a significantly harder time selling the war to Germany's socialist workers, who knew Jaurès as a voice for fraternity between the German and French working classes. The Social Democrats were the largest party in the Reichstag, and without their support Bethmann Hollweg would have hesitated to risk war.

In the weeks after Franz Ferdinand's assassination, would imponderables like these have moved Berlin to restrain Vienna? The case for the desirability of war undoubtedly would have encountered friction among the coterie of German decision makers. Somehow, in some way, things would have been different—perhaps different enough to slow or stop the war.

In *Summer 1914*, the last volume in Roger Martin du Gard's chronicle of the Thibault family, two friends are discussing the slide to war during the last days of peace. One of them challenges us to think anew about the inevitability of World War I: "If this war materializes, I rather think the historians—who've made so much of Cleopatra's nose—will ascribe its due importance top the tragic pistol shot at the Figaro offices when they're unraveling the causes of the war. One thing's for sure, my boy, if Caillaux had stayed in power things would not have come to the pass they've got to now."

According to the American ambassador to Germany, James W. Gerard, as late as July 1914 the German Foreign Office believed the British were "so occupied with the Ulster rebellion and unrest in Ireland that they would not declare war." There was no French Ulster; the Germans knew the French would fight but doubted their staying power. Field Marshal von Moltke was confident that "once France is defeated in the first big battles, then this country, which does not have great reserves of people, will hardly be able to continue a long war."[1]

France's "decline"—its low birthrate, lagging economy, and chaotic republican politics—was a cliché of German commentary on foreign affairs. A 1910 memorandum prepared by the German General Staff contrasted Germany's population surge since 1880—from forty-two to sixty-two million—to France's blip from thirty-seven to thirty-nine million. That birth dearth required the French to draft 80 to 85 percent of young men. Many were "inferior defenders of the fatherland." Some weighed as little as eighty pounds. To fill out the army the government recruited soldiers from France's overseas empire, but in German eyes, these were even poorer specimens. "A Picture of the Future," a 1911 cartoon in the satirical journal *Kladderadatsch*, showed a line of snarling gorillas dressed in French uniforms.[2]

France's reproductive funk chiefly accounted for the slow growth of an economy hobbled by a chronic "deficiency of aggregate demand"—that is, a static supply of consumers. Between 1870 and 1914, the German economy grew almost two times faster than the French. Coal production went from two to five times greater in Germany, pig iron from parity to three times greater, steel from nothing in both countries to four times greater. The post-revolutionary inheritance laws and the *morcellement* of territory to peasant proprietors limited the size of the French farm, while the national preference for aesthetically pleasing labor-intensive goods had a similar effect on the French firm. German big business, the industrialist Hugo Stinnes was confident, had nothing to fear from French competition: "They are a people of small rentiers."

German critics of republican politics noted the instability of French

"Parisian Sigh," *Simplicissimus*, July 8, 1912.
"Have you heard that in Germany they have found a
way to get babies without men?"
"*Mon dieu*, and we don't even get them with men!"

governments—eleven between 1909 and 1914, four in 1913 alone—
and traced it to a fundamental instability. A century after the great
Revolution, the French remained divided over the terms of their
polity. The Catholic Right hated the secular Republic; the socialist
Left was uneager to defend the bourgeois Republic. On the fringes
of politics, Bonapartists and monarchists schemed to undermine the
revolutionary Republic. Fifteen years on, the Dreyfus Affair, recom-
bining these antipathies in new polarities, still divided Frenchmen—
and French soldiers. "One must ask oneself if an army which contained
so many contradictory elements . . . will be united enough to succeed
against an external enemy," the retiring chancellor Bernhard von
Bülow wrote his successor, Bethmann Hollweg, in 1909.[3]

Packing decades of derogation into a sentence, a German essayist
observed: "A people whose men do not want to be soldiers and
whose women refuse to have children, is a people benumbed in their
vitality . . . fated to be dominated by a younger and fresher race."[4]

The Germans can hardly be blamed for getting the French so wrong.
No moral seismograph could have revealed to them how the French
would rally to their Republic on August 1, 1914. When at three fifty-
five P.M. mobilization orders were wired to every *marie* in France and

the notices kept for the occasion went up in the town squares, 3.7 million men, republicans, socialists, Catholics, monarchists, and Bonapartists alike, left for their regimental depots. Whereas the French General Staff had predicted that 10 percent of conscripts might not answer the call of mobilization, in the event only 1.5 percent failed to show up. Overnight, it seemed, what President Raymond Poincaré called the "Franco-French war" had been suspended. "So, this is it, then, Monsieur le Curé," a lay schoolteacher in an Alpine village remarked to his long-time enemy. "Well, we are friends, we only hate the invader now."[5]

Historians are still probing the riddle posed by Jean-Jacques Becker in *The Great War and the French People* (1986): "How and why . . . did the French of La Belle époque, those people who were said . . . to be easy-going, fun-loving, and without ideals, bear and accept fifty-one months of sorrow and destruction?"[6]

One answer is because pleasure *was* their ideal: Love, conversation, the table, the grape, the countryside, the light, these blessings of the good life were worth fighting for.* In absolute terms, France boasted the highest standard of living on the continent. The birthrate was low partly because French men and women wanted to enjoy life and prized belonging to a society whose genius that was. "Many of them knew and the rest felt," André Maurois wrote of the men who without incident gathered at the depots and boarded the trains to war, "that the civilization they were about to defend was one of the loveliest and the happiest in the world."[7]

Another answer to Becker's riddle is that for the duration of the war "barbarian" invaders exacted tribute in labor and treasure and sex from the people of the northern *departments* of France overrun by the German army. Outraged at newspaper accounts of Frenchmen shipped to Germany as forced labor and at propaganda drawings of simian boche debauching French girls, Frenchmen held out because the Germans held on to one fifth of their country. Not until France

---

* "Giving pleasure, after all, is France's unique selling proposition. The country has for centuries created beguiling things to eat, drink, smell and wear. When my Paris landlord arrived with an old chair that the tiny apartment did not need, he explained that it was 'for the pleasure of your eyes.'" Donald Morrison, "Je t'aime . . . moi non plus," *Financial Times*, Life & Arts, June 18, 2011, 19.

bled itself white defending Verdun in 1916 would "They shall not pass" become a national credo, but from August 1914, the French lived and died by it.[8]

In August 1914 the government ordered newspapers not to print the name of Joseph Caillaux lest it remind the French of the road not taken—the road to peace. The German invasion had swept away the Caillaux scandal, which had transfixed France since Henriette Caillaux shot Gaston Calmette on March 16 up to her trial, which only ended days before the war began.

"Sous La Botte" (Under the Boot) by Théophile Alexandre Steinlen

Surveying opinion in the days following the crime, the *Times* of London judged that "Not since the Dreyfus Affair has any event in French history stirred the imagination of the French people as has the shooting of Gaston Calmette." Germans viewed the publicity surrounding the July trial, unfolding during a grave international crisis, as evidence that the French were terminally frivolous.[10]

Venomous politics lay behind *affaire Caillaux*. In the spring 1914 elections, Joseph Caillaux's Radical-Socialist Party, allied with the socialists in a puissant coalition, was likely to win a parliamentary majority. Once in power, Caillaux pledged to move toward détente with Germany. To prevent this, between December 1913 and March 1914 Gaston Calmette published 110 articles, anecdotes, and cartoons attacking Joseph Caillaux as a thief and "traitor"—the former for abusing his power as finance minister to benefit himself and his friends, the latter for pursuing secret negotiations with Germany as premier during the Morocco crisis of 1911. Extending from President Raymond Poincaré, who talked of Caillaux in private in terms as bitter as those used by Calmette in *Le Figaro*, to the protofascists of the Action Française, who mounted violent street demonstrations against Caillaux on the night of Calmette's murder, the French right hated and feared Caillaux for speaking to the self-interest of the French to their desire to curb a tax-eating arms race with Germany that fueled an 85 percent increase in French military spending, which absorbed over half the total budget.[11]

"[Caillaux] knows his countrymen through and through," Belgium's ambassador in Paris reported to Brussels in January 1914, "and is well aware that outside the official political cliques and a handful of chauvinists . . . by far the greater number of Frenchmen, the peasants, shopkeepers and industrialists, are impatient under the excessive expenditure and personal liabilities imposed on them." The ambassador added, "Caillaux's presence in power will lessen the acuteness of international jealousies and will constitute a better base for relations between France and Germany." Such views were rarely heard in "official Paris" where "everybody that you meet tells you that an early war with Germany is certain and inevitable."[12]

Joseph-Marie-Auguste Caillaux was born, just below the top, in 1863. His father, Eugène, an engineer and high civil servant, served as minister of finance in the cabinet of the royalist Marshal McMahon and Joseph lived briefly in the Ministry, then housed in the Louvre. Joseph spent his childhood on the family estate at Mamers, near Le Mans. The Caillaux family had acquired its wealth after the Revolution by speculating in land seized from *aristos*. Joseph's mother's ancestors were Huguenots persecuted for their faith, and, a biographer surmises, "Joseph grew up craving convictions of his own to suffer for."[13]

The mature Caillaux refused to suffer for his infidelities. He lived by a code of untrammeled desire, juggling wives and mistresses with defiant unconcern for public opinion. He thought "no rule was made for him," a journalist observed. Yet Republican politicians were expected to live by the rules, to wear masks of dignity, and to keep their transgressions private. French society was under intense pressure to change from workers, students, feminists, artists, and "it was as if the elites believed they could be unorthodox only when the masses were orderly." Caillaux caught the difference between the republican style and his own in his memoirs when telling of a trip he and Raymond Poincaré took to Italy with their mistresses—"mine I displayed, his he kept hidden." In a 1905 Chamber of Deputies debate over the silk tariff, he talked knowledgeably about women's changing taste in underwear, contrasting the "rich fabrics of thick silk, fabrics that hung heavy on the body" of "ten, twenty, thirty years ago," and the "soft and supple silks, *mousselines*" that "have since become the favored materials of dresses as well as undergarments (applause)."[14]

Contemporary profiles of Caillaux betray an envious incredulity. "What a man!" a 1918 biographer exclaimed. "Businessman, ladies' man, political man. He's excessive and rash in all he does, from finance to love to politics . . . This bald Don Juan . . . insolent as a tax farmer of the *ancien regime*, . . . acknowledges the acclamations of Jacobin revolutionaries, while counting the votes of his elegant female followers watching from the reserve gallery above."[15]

Caillaux studied economics while earning a law degree, served as an inspector of finance examining municipal government books, wrote "the definitive work" on France's byzantine tax system, and taught at the École Libre des Sciences politiques—all that before, in 1898, winning a seat in the Chamber of Deputies, France's House of Representatives. Campaigning around Le Mans on a bicycle, the thirty-five-year-old candidate did not dispel the impression among the peasants that he was his father, nor the hope among the royalist gentry that like his father he rejected the Republic. French politicians tended to be lawyers and journalists. Caillaux was an expert in public finance. It was enough, a year after entering the Chamber, to elevate him to the cabinet as minister of finance.[16]

By inheritance Caillaux was of the right, but his interest in rationalizing French taxation, three fourths dependent on indirect taxes discouraging to economic growth, made him champion a graduated income tax, a cause of the left. He first brought it forward in 1901, but the time was not ripe and, as he wrote his mistress at the time, Berthe Gueydan, "I crushed the income tax while seeming to defend it." She kept his letter, signed "Ton Jo" [Your Jo]. Gaston Calmette printed a photographic reproduction of it on the front page of *Le Figaro* on March 13, 1914; three days later, certain that Joseph's letters to her were about to receive the same treatment, Henriette Caillaux pulled a pistol from her muff and shot him.[17]

In 1904, Gueydan, a notable beauty, divorced her husband to marry Caillaux. Soon Caillaux discovered that he had mistaken the frisson of illicit passion for love. Moreover, while French political society was still buzzing over Berthe, his restless eye had already fallen on another married woman, Henriette Claretie. "The case of Caillaux seemed . . . shocking," a historian of the Republic's elite writes. "To marry a former mistress after her own divorce was hardly acceptable to the public opinion of 1906." Yet his constituents kept voting for him. At Le Mans' train station, "the stationmaster himself always hurried to meet me," Caillaux recalled. He did not want to give the honor of carrying my bags to anyone else." Nor did Caillaux's amours discourage Georges Clemenceau, whose notorious love affair with an American woman had slowed his rise to the premiership, from appointing Caillaux as finance minister in his new government.*[18]

---

*On Clemenceau: "He had a gay time with women, he was fond of actresses, but he would not tolerate any liberty in his wife. He obtained divorce by taking a policeman with him to catch her in a compromising situation. He had her convicted to 15 days imprisonment for adultery, and then expelled from the country, like a common criminal." Theodore Zeldin, *France 1848–1945*, vol. 1 (New York: Oxford University Press, 1973), 703.

A friend had warned him about Clemenceau, quoting Léon Gambetta, the great public man of the early Republic: "Where Clemenceau has set his foot the grass never grows again." They served cordially together in government (1906–09), Clemenceau remarking to a colleague that Caillaux "was one of those rare people with whom he did not have an argument." Clemenceau became Cailluax's nemesis later, over Germany.[19]

In 1909, anticipating that Joseph would divorce Berthe, Henriette Claretie divorced her husband. But Berthe would not go quietly. Breaking into Joseph's desk, she discovered a letter he had written to Henriette, who returned it at his urging lest it fall into the wrong hands, promising to divorce Berthe after the coming election campaign. "There is only one consolation," Joseph wrote and Berthe read. "It is to think of my little one, to see her in my arms as at Ouchy (God, what delicious moments!) . . . A thousand million kisses all over your adored little body."[20]

The political calendar gave Berthe the upper hand. A second "divorce scandal could easily turn [Joseph's] peasant constituents against him." During Henriette Caillaux's trial, Berthe testified that she "had never suspected that my husband had a mistress." She first knew it "when he threw himself at my knees and asked my pardon. He humbled himself and I pardoned him . . . I believed that the evil surrounding my home had gone, for I thought I saw the bottom of his heart in his tears." Joseph begged her not to divorce him. She agreed, exacting his pledge to break with Henriette ("only the day after he returned to this person") and insisting on a second honeymoon. He required Berthe to burn the incriminating letters (two more had come to light) in front of his lawyer. She complied, but not before mailing them to her sister, who had them photographed.[21]

Reelected, Joseph walked out on Berthe. Addressing her in court, he explained why: "Between a man to whom everyone grants authority, vigor, and power and you in whom these qualities are overdeveloped as well, it was impossible that things would last." Edward Berenson suggests that Caillaux's acknowledgement of his "candid desire for intellectual and emotional precedence over the woman he married" was calculated to appeal to the desires of the all-male jury. "Demoralized by the acceptance of defeat," in the words of Le Gaulois,

Berthe Gueydan testifying at the trial of Henriette Caillaux.
Their marriage foundered on your "vigor and power," Joseph
Caillaux told her in court. Men of the Third Republic needed
soft women like Henriette (who was hard enough to take target
practice before shooting Gaston Calmette).

Frenchmen of the Third Republic needed boosting. To expunge the
memory of Germany's conquest of France in the war of 1870–71, they
conquered colonies abroad and wanted wives who made them feel
like conquerors at home—wives like Henriette, who, Joseph declared
in court, possessed "a character and a nature I could attach myself to."
They were married on October 31, 1911. Joseph was premier.

Nineteen eleven would have been his triumphant year if imperialist rivalry had not brought France closer to war with Germany than at any other time since The Defeat of 1870, where the road to Morocco begins.[22]

In his memoirs, Charles de Gaulle evoked the desolate France of 1870–71, its army routed, Paris torn by fighting between Frenchmen, the king of Prussia crowned emperor of Germany at Versailles: "An immense disaster, a peace made of despair, loss of life that nothing compensated, a state without foundations, no army other than that which was leaving the enemy's prisons, two provinces torn away, billions to be paid, the victor's troops garrisoned in one-fourth of the territory, the capital streaming with blood in a civil war, a Europe ice cold or ironic: Such were the conditions in which a vanquished France resumed the march to its destiny."[23]

Following Gambetta's admonition, the French thought of revenge "always" but spoke of it "never." In school classrooms a swag of black and purple cloth covered Alsace-Lorraine, the two provinces torn away by Bismarck, on the map of France. "You have no idea of the somber atmosphere in which we grew up, in a humiliated and wounded France—bred for bloody, inevitable and perhaps futile revenge," the novelist Romain Rolland recalled. The young de Gaulle wrote a story set in 1930 in which, as "General Charles de Gaulle," he liberated Lorraine.[24]

"Must we hypnotize ourselves with the lost provinces, and should we not take compensation elsewhere?" Premier Jules Ferry asked a leading *revanchard*. Beginning under Ferry in the 1880s, France embarked on a distinctly military form of imperialism, the "vile scramble for loot" that, between 1876 and 1915, saw six industrial powers carve colonies out of roughly one in every four acres of the earth's surface. The inhabitants of those acres were pretty well carved up themselves. Writing in 1890 and of Africa only, a British observer estimated that "twenty millions of human beings underestimates the number killed or captured for European gain."[25]

For France, a Republican politician declared, to fail to "carry wherever she can her language, her way of life, her flag, her arms . . . would be the high road to decadence." Unable to extrude the enemy from Alsace-Lorraine without war, the French army conquered lesser

"The Capitulation of Sedan," 1870, by Honoré Daumier.
That helmet again. Here it crowns the worst defeat of
French arms since Waterloo—the surrender of an army at
Sedan. Bismarck was there to arrange the terms of
humiliation with Napoleon III. From September 2, 1871,
Sedantag (Sedan Day) was a national holiday in Germany.

breeds without artillery. In this way the French way of life was brought
to Indochina, West Africa, Tunisia, and Morocco as earlier to Algeria.
Ferry might lament: "All that interests the French public about the
Empire is the belly dance." Still, Frenchmen avidly followed newspaper accounts of colonial adventures, which furnished anecdotes
against decadence. Conquest was therapy for the culture of defeat. For
General Lyautey, the hero of the conquest of Morocco, colonialism
was more than a cure. It was a cause: "North Africa is for our race what
the Far West is for America."[26]

It helped that the indigenous inhabitants fought in a poignantly
dated style. For example, in April 1908, fifteen thousand horsemen
from tribes in Morocco's Middle Atlas Mountains massed before a
blockhouse held by seventy-five French soldiers—French officers and
black African enlisted men—supported by two 80 mm cannon. Before attacking, Moroccans sent this proposal to the French:

To the chief of the French "fraction" at Boudenib. May Benefi-
cence be on those who humble themselves before merciful God

EDUCATION

— Tas de brutes! On ne peut rien leur faire entrer dans la tête!...

"Éducation." British historians still defend British imperialism. It
brought law and trains to India. Sorted out the tribes in Africa. There
was less to be nostalgic about in French imperialism, an affair of
soldiers and adventurers not of sons and heirs. Celine was right wing,
but his *Journey to the End of the Night* (1932) is scalding on the moral
regression of the French in West Africa, where he was stationed during
the war. "Éducation" represents the left-wing view of what Europe's
"apostles of pity and progress" were up to in the tropics.

and seek justice. Know that, since your arrival in the Sahara, you
have badly treated weak Muslims. You have gone from conquest
to conquest. Your dark soul fools you by making you rush to your
destruction. You have made our country suffer intense harm,

which tastes as galling to us as the bitter apple. The courageous and noble Muslim warriors approach you, armed for your destruction. If you are in force, come out from behind your walls for combat.

For the mujahideen, "Brave men fought openly, offered their breasts to bullets." They assumed the French would come out and be massacred. But the French hadn't fought that way since Charles Martel defeated an invading Muslim army at Tours in 732. The soldiers stayed behind their walls; the Moroccans charged and charged again. This went on for eighteen hours. No Frenchmen appear to have been killed. Many Moroccans were.[27]

In Morocco no single leader emerged for the tribes to unite behind, no Mahdi, who, after annihilating General Gordon and his Anglo-Egyptian army in Khartoum in 1885, kept the Europeans out of the Sudan for nearly fifteen years. Consequently, "Moroccan armed resistance was the least of [France's] problems."[28]

Certainly that was true compared to Morocco's European complications. In vain had the French searched for the "French India" ("the last great prize to keep France even in the Anglo-Saxon world of the 20th century") in Algeria, Mexico, Indochina, and West Africa. Now they sought it on the red-brick plains of Morocco. But the masters of the real India, the British, had got there ahead of them. Having opened Morocco to European exploitation in the 1850s, Britain had since run much of it as a "puppet state." Professing to be friends of Moroccan independence, the British warned the sultan to beware: Morocco might suffer Algeria's fate—annexation by France.[29]

Across Africa, agents of French imperialism, seeking "to arrive first wherever African territories were still unclaimed," kept running into wily Englishmen in weathered pith helmets. French Anglophobia was aroused. In 1882, public fury forced the Freycinet government to resign when, under British diplomatic pressure, it curtailed France's "influence" over Egypt. In 1894, the French invaded Madagascar "to teach the English a lesson." Four years later, after a three-thousand-mile march from the mouth of the Congo River across the heart of Africa to the Nile, a French column of six officers and 120 men under Captain Jean-Baptiste Marchand raised the Tricolor over Fashoda, a swampy village in the Sudan. The French hoped that a garrison "in the Egyptian hinterland would force London to come to terms with France's 'historic claims' on the Nile." They failed to reckon with General Kitchener.[30]

Fresh from slaughtering ten thousand of the Mahdi's followers in two hours at the battle of Omdurman ("Whatever happens, we have got/The Maxim gun, and they have not"), Kitchener came down the Nile to Fashoda to dislodge the French. Employing psychological warfare, he presented the French officers with a bundle of newspapers; from these they first learned of the Dreyfus Affair convulsing French society and staining the French Army. They wept and, their government bowing before a British ultimatum, quit the Sudan.[31]

Over the retreat from Fashoda "the wild desire for vengeance" in France was greater than over the loss of Alsace-Lorraine, the *Daily Telegraph* reported. "Germany is the accidental enemy," a Catholic paper editorialized, "while England is the eternal enemy."[32]

After Fashoda, Anglo-French relations briefly warmed only to cool during the Boer War. As late as 1902–03, when shouts of "Vive Fashoda!" greeted King Edward VII as he alighted from his train at the Bois de Boulogne station, French intelligence agents were in Ireland mapping possible invasion sites and sounding out nationalist boyos "on the chances of success of a Franco-Russian landing in Ireland"![33]

For her part, between 1895 and 1901, Britain "had proposed to Germany a partition of Turkey, a partition of Morocco, and ultimately an out-and-out alliance." Spurned by Germany, and determined to end its policy of "splendid isolation," Britain "rather reluctantly" turned to France.[34]

The *Entente cordiale* was "born without grandeur in the midst of bargains." France promised England a free hand in Egypt—there would be no more Fashodas. England abandoned Morocco to France. The powers sealed the bargain with a pledge to support each other's claims in these countries. Neither realized the implications of that sweetener until, on a stormy March 31, 1905, the German liner *Hamburg* appeared in the Bay of Tangiers. On the bridge stood a serious European complication, Kaiser Wilhelm II.[35]

The French sought *their* India to balance the lost provinces. Bismarck

had encouraged them to pursue empire to divert them from the continent's bitter vistas. But, when the kaiser's call on Tangier created a crisis
heavy with war, it seemed that "for the French as for Bismarck, their
map of Africa was really a map of Europe" after all.[36]

Pleading the rough sea but really fearing assassination by Spanish an-
archists, Wilhelm decided not to come ashore at Tangier. He had to
be argued into it by the chargé d'affaires, acting for Chancellor von
Bülow, who had pushed the mission on the reluctant monarch. As it
was, landing the kaiser in the chop proved challenging: Two German
sailors had to plunge into the water and carry him the last few yards
to the quay. Through streets French nationals had festooned with blue,
white, and red, and to the sound of beating drums and ululating
women, Wilhelm was led on a white horse to the German legation.
He mounted this strange animal, he complained to Bülow, despite his
withered arm, and for the whole ride was "within an inch of a fatal
fall." His Wagnerian regalia—silver helmet, red gloves, hanging
saber—contrasted with the white djellabas of the Moroccan officials
waiting to greet him. After paying his respects to them and to the as-
sembled foreign diplomats, he said something in German to the sultan's uncle, who did not speak the language, and left as he had come.
The next day the embassy announced the purpose of his visit: to dem-
onstrate Germany's support for Morocco's independence.[37]

The diplomats in Paris and London had spread around the *solatium*,
to use the argot of imperialism. Italy was bought off by recognizing
her claims to Tripoli, Spain by secret promises of a succulent piece of
northern Morocco if the sultanate should lose its independence. But
where, Bülow complained, was Germany's slice of "the Moroccan
cake"? "To make matters worse," he wrote his ambassador in Paris,
"the settlement regarding Morocco has been reached without our being consulted."[38]

The table of the world was almost picked clean when Germany
arrived at the imperialist banquet. Bülow touched on this in the
memo to his ambassador: "Considering the steadily declining number of countries in which free trade and unhindered economic activity are still possible, Morocco's importance for us should not be
underestimated." The kaiser got to wear his admiral's uniforms to

"The Kaiser Woos Morocco" (Tangier, March 31)
From *Punch*, 5 April 1905
Kaiser Wilhelm (as the Moor of Potsdam) sings:
" 'Unter Den Linden'—Always at Home,
'Under the Lime-Light' Wherever I Roam!"

the Zoo-Aquarium, but during his reign Germany had not translated its naval power into empire—colonies, coaling stations, bases. *Welt-politik* had yielded a "paltry" two thousand square miles of territory, mostly islands and atolls in the South Pacific. Fewer than six thousand Germans had migrated to the colonies in Oceania, Africa, and China. And it was getting late; with the Americas off the table, there was not world enough left to take.[39]

In his 1916 pamphlet on imperialism, Lenin contended that the shrinking globe intensified rivalries among the powers for the few exploitable places, like mineral-rich Morocco, as yet unclaimed for civilization, accelerated the arms race, and led to "a war for the division of the world . . . an annexationist, predatory, war of plunder."[40]

Whether or not Morocco was worth a war, for Pan-German opinion, which "demanded that the entire Atlantic coast with its hinterland should be seized," it was worth a crisis. Pressured by the German
right, lobbied by Krupp, which supplied arms to the sultan, and
alarmed by calls in the French press for annexing Morocco, Bülow
decided to act.[41]

With France's ally, Russia, engulfed by war and revolution, Germany had rare leverage to humiliate France. Under threat of war, it
forced her to refer the Morocco question to a conference of the powers
who had signed the Treaty of Madrid in 1880 on the future of the
sultanate. In his memoirs, Bülow said he intended merely "to confront [France] with the possibility of war" and, when she asked her
new friend for help and England said it would not fight for Morocco,
to break up the *entente cordiale*. Held at Algeciras, a port on Spain's
Mediterranean coast, between January and April 1906, the conference boomeranged on Bülow. Germany won the point that France
was not the only power concerned in Morocco, and its economic
rights there were vindicated. But the powers—Britain, Italy, Spain,
Russia, and the United States—supported French claims to operate
the state bank, administer the customs, police the Algerian-Moroccan
border, and train Moroccan police in the ports. As bad, Germany
was isolated at Algeciras, Austria-Hungary refusing to back its ally
in an exotic dispute. Worse, far from destroying the *entente*, German

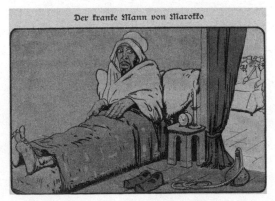

"Der kranke Mann von Morokko" (The Sick Man of
Morocco) from *Der Wahre Jacob*, March 1906. A
depiction of the powers dismembering Morocco at the
Algerciras Conference of 1906.

bullying forged what Churchill termed "an exceedingly potent tie" between France and Britain, the military talks between their General Staffs that beginning in 1906 transformed the *entente* from a colonial barter into a continental alliance in all but name. The kaiser was right to resist braving storm-tossed waters to land in Tangier; the very elements warned him to stay out of Morocco.[42]

Still, defying the elements a second time and spoiling Joseph Caillaux's debut as premier, in July 1911 Germany dispatched a gunboat to Agadir, a port at the southern end of Morocco's long Atlantic coast, precipitating another crisis over Morocco, one of the series of tocsins in the years before 1914 when death rattled impatiently in its chains.

The SMS *Panther*'s mission, Bethmann Hollweg told the Reichstag, was to protect "endangered" German subjects. "Roars of laughter" greeted this assertion. No one believed it. "Agadir was a closed port, and the nearest German was at Mogador. He was instructed to go to Agadir in order to be endangered."[43]

Bethmann revealed the social-psychological motive of Agadir in a later comment to Paul Cambon, the French ambassador: "For forty years, France has pursued a grandiose policy. It has secured an immense empire for itself in the world. It is everywhere. During this

SMS *Panther* at Agadir

time, an inactive Germany did not follow this example and today it needs its place in the sun."[44]

The German secretary of state for foreign affairs in 1911, Alfred von Kiderlen-Wächter, was hostage to a high-risk formula of success. Two years earlier, he had drafted the ultimatum that forced Russia to accede to Austria's annexation of Bosnia, a humiliation that the tsar vowed he would remember. "I knew the Russians were not ready for war," Kiderlen boasted to a Rumanian diplomat, "that they could not go to war in any case, and I wanted to make what capital I could out of this knowledge." Bluff had worked with Russia; he would try it with France. He instructed the kaiser to regard the warships— originally a second ship was to anchor up the coast at Mogador—as "pawns." If "France will offer us adequate compensation from her colonial possessions . . . we could then withdraw from the ports." Kiderlen advised Cambon: "Bring us back something from Paris."[45]

The *Panthersprung*—the leap of the *Panther*—was a reckless yet justified act. France, not Germany, initiated the Second Moroccan Crisis.

Though in the Act of Algeciras and a 1909 accord with Germany, France professed fealty to the independence of the sultanate, the colonial lobby agitated for France to dominate North Africa with the conquest of a few hundred thousand more square miles of sand and sky; and it was adept at orchestrating faits accomplis to get what it wanted. Reporting to Brussels, Belgium's minister to Berlin conveyed Germany's bill of complaint: "Every illusion that [Germany] ever entertained on the value of the Algeciras Act, which France passed with the firm conviction of never observing, must long since have vanished. She has not ceased for one moment to pursue her plans for annexation; either by seizing opportunities for provisional occupations, destined to last forever, or by extorting concessions which have placed the Sultan in a position of dependence on France."[46]

Encouraging the sultan to borrow heavily, the French yoked Morocco to debt, "a time-honored tactic of predatory imperialism." When the sultan tried to exact revenue from his subjects to service the debt, it sparked tribal revolts. Punitive expeditions, strengthened by French military advisers and artillery, proved equally counterproductive. The sultan sat on a gold–and–velvet throne, but his relish of torture—he fed the leader of one rebellion to a lion—pricked the European conscience, quick to indignation over "barbarism." The brute needed civilizing. Morocco needed good (French) governance. Outrages against Europeans furnished pretexts for occupying Casablanca, Marrakech, and Rabat. For this, and for "killing thousands of his subjects," France billed the sultan 2.4 million francs. His exactions increased. Unrest increased. The cycle of misrule spun toward French intervention.[47]

Joseph Caillaux was breakfasting at a London hotel when he opened the *Times* for April 23, 1911, and read that troops from France's Armée d'Afrique were marching from Casablanca to relieve a rebel siege of Fez, the sultan's capital, brought on when the French military mission there ordered the execution of two Moroccan deserters. "Pictures were painted with an African riot of color, of the atrocities committed, of the . . . perils of the Europeans shut up in Fez . . . 'Civilization' was in danger, barbarism had risen." Stirred to action by such representations from the tiny but clamorous *parti colonial*, three cabinet ministers had approved the expedition while their colleagues were away on vacation.[48]

Caillaux was the finance minister. The *Times* story was the first he had heard of the march to Fez. He was "thunderstruck." The rescue mission amounted to a repudiation of Algeciras. Occupation would follow rescue; a French protectorate would follow occupation.[49]

What would Germany do? The answer came on July 1—Agadir. By then, Monis had fallen and, when the musical chairs of Third Republic politics stopped, Caillaux was premier. What would *he* do?

France's colonial minister, its diplomats in Morocco, and the French officer on the spot had manufactured a plausible emergency at Fez. The theater of imperialism specialized in such productions. "The whole story was a myth," the Belgian consul in Tangier reported. The siege at Fez parted to admit the delivery of mail "fairly regularly." The fighting was "more noisy than murderous." A French diplomat told him that the city was safe from attack, the rebels lacking artillery.[50]

Still, dissension was rife behind the high brown ramparts; if the siege endured, mutineers inside might well have joined forces with rebels outside. And the Fez garrison was running low on ammunition. The Europeans in the city had reason to worry and someone to blame.

Colonel Mangin, one of the sultan's military advisers, had put them in danger by leading most of the sultan's force on a punitive expedition, "encouraging the [rebels] to besiege Fez," according to a candid French officer. But by the time Caillaux took power it was too late to investigate the stage management of the siege. The sultan's request for French troops to rescue his denuded command had been back-dated "to make it appear as if it has preceded, rather than followed, the French movement," but it was too late to check the paperwork.[51]

The siege had been lifted; the sultan had agreed to make Morocco a French protectorate; exercising its rights under a secret annex to the *entente cordiale*, Spain had grabbed up more of Morocco's Mediterranean coast. The independent country recognized at Algeciras had ceased to exist. Once more Germany had received no *solatium*. But the *Panther* was at Agadir, and in Berlin, Kiderlen was still waiting for Cambon to bring him back something from Paris.[52]

Caillaux dared not let France's diplomats sort out the crisis. Of the new foreign minister, Justin de Selves, "it can safely be said that his only mark of distinction was his high-sounding name." The French Foreign Ministry, the Quai d'Orsay, was a nest of Germanophobia; after Caillaux signed the agreement with Germany ending the crisis, its press spokesman told reporters with regret, "It was war that we needed."[53]

To cover himself, Caillaux was especially careful to check the war box, asking the army's commander in chief, Joseph Joffre: "General, they say Napoleon waged war only if he thought he had a 70–30 chance of winning. Have we a 70–30 chance?" Just appointed, Joffre could not be held responsible for his answer, "Non, monsieur le president."[54]

Caillaux resolved to negotiate. As Germany's price for ceding Morocco to France, Kiderlen demanded the whole French Congo. That was too much. Jungle or desert, no real interests were at stake in either place. Agadir was a crisis of prestige. Neither side could lose. Neither dared to win.

Caillaux sounded France's allies. Russia's ambassador was the redoubtable Izvolski, last seen blundering into the Bosnian crisis of 1908 in pursuit of the Turkish Straits; he told Caillaux that Russia was not ready for war. Caillaux publicly insulted him at the Paris Opera, claiming that the single-minded diplomat asked for the Straits as "compensation" for Russian diplomatic support on Morocco![55]

The British were at first no firmer, Edward Grey, the foreign secretary, suggesting that perhaps Germany should keep Agadir. Caillaux was alarmed. If the British deserted their *entente* partners in the crisis, he let it be known, France might be compelled to make territorial sacrifices to Germany opposed to British interests. Finally, after waiting fruitlessly for weeks for the Wilhelmstrasse to say what it was up to in Morocco, Lloyd George, the chancellor of the exchequer, reputed to belong to the pacifist wing of the Liberal cabinet, delivered a belligerent anti-German speech at Mansion House. As Churchill wrote his wife, "The Germans sent their *Panther* to Agadir and we sent our little Panther to the Mansion House."[56]

In a "stormy interview" the following day, the German ambassador branded Lloyd George's speech provocative and warned Grey that if France did not offer compensation, "German dignity as a great power" would require it to secure "if necessary alone, full respect by France for German treaty rights." Grey heard that assertion of German prestige as an ultimatum. Shortly, panic gripped Whitehall when the admiralty lost track of the German fleet. Grey had the Royal Navy move to "high readiness," an unprecedented militarization of a diplomatic conflict, heightening the risk of inadvertent war. This "naval alert" prompted Germany to increase the size of its fully manned battle fleet from two to three squadrons and Churchill, the first lord of the Admiralty, to respond by redeploying British warships from the Mediterranean to home waters as part of an agreement with France that, as we saw earlier, morally bound Britain to defend France's Atlantic coasts from German attack. Thus did the jockeying for prestige in Africa raise the odds of war in Europe.[57]

As tensions peaked, Caillaux found a path to settlement. It led through back-channel negotiations with the German embassy in Paris from which he excluded de Selves and the Quai d'Orsay. The German ambassador, Wilhelm von Schoen, cabled Berlin that Caillaux "would rather make a large-scale settlement of all the differences that have arisen between us in recent years. Such a settlement would help him justify before the public the cession of colonial territories." Schoen included a list of potential concessions to Germany selected from France's world portfolio, including the irresistible "possibility of ceding French possessions in Oceania." The cable concluded, "[Caillaux] asks us urgently not to let Cambon know about his offers."[58]

The next morning de Selves presented Caillaux with a deciphered version of the telegram—the French had cracked the German diplomatic code. Caillaux laughed off the bit about not telling Cambon, suspecting that Schoen put this invention into the cable to test the code's integrity. A rift between Caillaux and Cambon might have betrayed a breach in security. Taking no chances, Caillaux dispatched a messenger to Cambon in Berlin to report on his back-channel talks.[59]

The French also gained an edge by reading Kiderlen's letters to his mistress, a Russian baroness living in France. They recorded his disgust with "the two old women," Bethmann and Kaiser Wilhelm, who flatly told Kiderlen that Germany would *not* go to war over Morocco. Knowing this, Caillaux could safely resist Kiderlen's maximal demands.[60]

But the kaiser could not long be expected to remain in the posture of an old woman. In August, a misunderstanding set him off. To his intermediary with the German embassy, the financier Hyacinthe Fondere, Caillaux remarked in passing that unless progress was made on an agreement it would be hard for him to restrain hotheads like de Selves, who was advocating sending French warships to Agadir. When Fondere repeated this at the German embassy, Berlin heard it as a threat from Caillaux. Wilhelm reacted in character, personalizing a matter of state. In the margin of Kiderlen's report to him, he demanded that "the intermediary is to go at once to see M. Caillaux and to let him know that he is to apologize for having treated Me insolently, otherwise I break off negotiations!" When, next day, no apology had arrived, he wired Kiderlen to demand "the *reparation d'honneur* due to Us." If Caillaux had not promptly assured Schoen that "he had not the slightest desire for this remark to be passed on to the German embassy," the crisis might have escalated, for in his wrath the kaiser had requested "proposals for expediting a naval concentration" off Morocco to counter the imaginary French ships.[61]

The breakthrough came in late September: "In return for a little over one quarter of the Congo . . . Germany recognized the equivalent of a French protectorate in Morocco." The 120,000 square miles of "primeval forest" gained by Germany was at best a place in the shade. There was no wider rapprochement. The Pan-German League decried the agreement as a "a Jena without war." Germany's colonial minister resigned. Kiderlen needed a *solatium* from his baroness.[62]

"Caillaux had won the game," concluded the diplomatic historian C. P. Gooch. Making a cryptic comparison to Disraeli at the Congress of Berlin, Prime Minister Asquith instructed his ambassador in Paris to "tell Mr. Caillaux he comes back from Berlin like Lord Beaconsfield bearing on his flag, 'Peace with honour!' " Violating an international treaty and a separate bilateral agreement with Germany, France had ginned up a crisis at Fez to justify sending an army there to fasten a protectorate on the sultan. Caillaux inherited the angry German reaction and got France off the hook without war and without serious loss of face or territory. Yet Germany had got *something* out of the negotiations: Caillaux understood that France could not avoid war if he refused to deal, and the sacrifice of even a fly-infested jungle to the occupiers of Alsace-Lorraine affronted nationalist opinion. Gaston Calmette's calumnies of 1914 were recycled from 1911, when even the sober *Journal des Débats* blamed "Caillaux's secret negotiations . . . for the dismemberment of the French empire in Africa." The sardonic observation of a Caillaux biographer captures the dynamic of Hun bashing: "Politics in France is largely a matter of competitive patriotism; in a crisis a Frenchman who hates Germans unreasonably can make one who hates them reasonably look like a traitor."[63]

Nevertheless, Caillaux might have held on if he had not been caught out in a lie by Clemenceau. The "Cabinet-breaker," the *Times* reported, "knew the time had come to strike, and when he struck the blow was deadly."[64]

The Chamber of Deputies adopted the treaty solemnizing the agreement on December 21. The vote was 393–36, with a fourth of the deputies abstaining. On January 10, the Senate held a hearing on the treaty. Caillaux and de Selves were on hand to answer questions. "Spying Clemenceau, Poincaré, and Stephen Pinchon giggling in a

Clemenceau as "The Tiger"

corner of the hearing room, Caillaux had a fit of bravado." On his
"word of honor" he denied pursuing "unofficial negotiations" with
the German embassy. At this the tiger pounced.

CLEMENCEAU: Perhaps the Minister of Foreign Affairs has something to say on the subject.

M. DE SELVES remained silent.

CLEMENCEAU: But, Monsieur le Ministre you have something
to say.

M. DE SELVES: I have always been inspired by regard for truth and
for the superior interests of our country.

CLEMENCEAU: Were you and M. Cambon kept informed on all
the negotiations between Paris and Berlin?

M. DE SELVES: I cannot answer that question.

CLEMENCEAU: You may give that negative answer to any one you
like . . . , but you cannot give it to me.

CAILLAUX (interjecting): I maintain my declaration. [Clemenceau
replied that he had not addressed his question to the prime
minister but to the foreign minister.]

M. DE SELVES: I cannot reply, because I stand between two duties—
the duty of telling the truth and the duty of maintaining the
solidarity of the Ministry.

CLEMENCEAU: You may say this to anyone else, but not to me.
(Lowering his incongruously squeaky voice): Because you have
told me the contrary.

The room erupted; the hearing was adjourned. Within hours, de Selves resigned. The next day, unable to form a cabinet, Caillaux joined him. The *Journal des Débats*, which had been attacking Caillaux since September over his domestic reform program, saw him out with this: "We can understand the regret manifested this morning by Berlin and Vienna journals at the news of the fall of their great French Minister. For France his fall is the end of a nightmare."[65]

"I broke with my generation [in 1912], or rather it broke with me," Caillaux wrote in his memoirs. By generation, he meant "his political and social class." His class gravitated toward the Republican and Democratic Alliance (ARD), a Right-Center formation that in a society in which the number of strikes had tripled between 1901 and 1911 stood for a business nirvana: "The tranquil possession of this day's profit and of that of the day before." The Alliance opposed strikes, social spending, antitrust legislation, and the graduated income tax. Claims to be above party politics—to represent the "national interest"—disguised its class program. Its leading spokesman, Raymond Poincaré, advocated "nationalism"—"an anxiety for French unity and power and preparedness" seen by some historians as a political tactic, a way to "obliterate internal differences" and cover over existing social arrangements with a haze of consensus.* Postwar Fascism exploited fear of revolution to gain power; prewar conservatism exploited fear of war to retain it.[66]

Caillaux's income tax crusade, his moderate social reformism, found few followers in Poincaré's Alliance, which frustrated his domestic program during his brief premiership. Whether he broke with his party or his party with him, before being tripped up by Clemenceau, he was moving Left, toward forming a new governing majority with the Radicals and the Socialists.[67]

Caillaux adumbrated his break with Poincarisme in a January 1911

---

* "Recent scholarship suggests that the 'nationalist revival' in France from 1909 to 1914 was largely an outgrowth of, and perhaps even a smokescreen for, conservative attempts to dominate internal politics." See Frederic Seager, "Joseph Caillaux as Premier, 1911–1912: The Dilemma of a Liberal Reformer," *French Historical Studies* 11 (1979): 241.

speech in Lille. "One of the dangers of the present time is this renewal of the old Conservative harping on the theme of the unity of
all Frenchmen," he declared, alluding to a staple of nationalist apolo-
getics during the Dreyfus Affair. "I am well aware that the privileged
few are readily satisfied with the harmony of a universally accepted
status quo . . . These people . . . derive pleasure from their dreams of
blending and absorbing all the citizens of France in a single immense
Party . . . If political parties were to be broken up . . . the organized
force of established interests would be the only politically effective
power in the confusion that would inevitably result." And these established interests "would be sufficiently powerful to obstruct democratic reforms right up to the day on which violent uprisings would
break out."[68]

That is the voice of American Progressivism, of Woodrow Wilson
and Theodore Roosevelt and of British Liberals like Lloyd George.
Adjusted to national tonality, it is also the voice of Peter Stolypin and
Vladimir Kokovtsov in Russia, Francisco Madero in Mexico, and the
Social Democrats in Germany. In Europe and the Americas, democratic reformism was emerging as an alternative to a market society
organized for "the tranquil possession of this day's profit." A "swing
to the left" was evident in elections in Germany, Austria, and the
United States, while in Britain the Liberals and their allies held on
against an extra-Parliamentary assault from Unionist radicalism.

At the same time, the ascendant aristocratic classes used their political power in the state to resist changes to the status quo. As a result,
just as Caillaux warned at Lille, "all the countries of Europe stood
on the edge of civil strife."[69]

In France, Joseph Caillaux, his evolution from a vice president of
the Alliance to leader of the Radical Party complete, was at one with
this progressive moment. He had risen from the political grave of
January 1912, making himself over into what his rival Aristide Bri-
and called a "demagogic plutocrat." In the April 1914 elections he
would go to the country with a bold program: "It included stronger
government control over religious private schools, social reform
enacted with the Socialists, a peace initiative to Germany, the introduction of a progressive income tax, a return to two years military
service . . . and making the presidency of France as unpolitical as

[President] Poincaré claimed it should be—by removing Poincaré from office."[70]

The spring elections of 1914 would test the strength of the Radical-Socialist alliance. But unaffiliated voters in the broad middle of the electorate, fluid in their views and partisan loyalties, were swinging Left and Right, torn between toward "patriotic pacifism" and moderate nationalism, Joseph Caillaux and Raymond Poincaré.

"If looking for any one date from which to count the birth of nationalism as a widespread chauvinistic feeling," Eugen Weber writes, "I would pick the fourth of November, 1911, the date of the signing of the Franco-German agreement on Morocco." "Widespread" is misleading. "The German fife has rallied France," the ARD deputy Paul Deschanel asserted, but the sound did not carry beyond a "politically significant minority" that spanned the political classes—officials, deputies, and Paris journalists of the right and center-right. For these roughly twenty to thirty thousand people, Agadir was a fire bell in the night. Declared a senator submitting the agreement for ratification: "We negotiated under the cannon of Agadir . . . and a French government accepted this, forty years after the Defeat . . . It is the counterpart of Fashoda!" A provincial paper noted sadly that the "cession of territory in the Congo . . . recalls the loss of Alsace-Lorraine to the hearts of Frenchmen." In this nationalist mood the French made Raymond Poincaré the first premier from one of the lost provinces.[71]

During the Franco-Prussian War, Poincaré's family took temporary refuge in the French interior. When Raymond returned to his Lorraine home in Bar-le-Duc, a Prussian officer was occupying his bedroom. "Disgusting soldiers are in the house," the fourteen-year-old confided to his diary. "One paints a skull and crossbones on our sideboard, the other spits in our stew." In a 1920 article in the *University of Paris Review* Poincaré recalled that "in all my years in school . . . I saw no other reason to live than the possibility of recovering our Lost Provinces."[72]

In a January 1912 interview, soon after replacing Caillaux as premier, he signaled a tough new tone in France's relations with Germany: "Every time we have desired to show ourselves conciliatory toward Germany she has abused our good will; and on the other hand,

Raymond Poincaré. Leading American historians of the 1920s placed heavy blame for the war on Poincaré, French president from 1913 to 1920. His secret diplomacy encouraged Russia to be reckless—that was their line. Contemporary scholars, while fairer, have not completely abandoned it.

every time that we have showed ourselves firm toward her, she has given way." But what if Germany did not give way? That was the risk inherent in taking a firm line, and in an October speech in Nantes, Poincaré named it when he said the French were a people "which does not desire war but which nevertheless does not fear it."[73]

Put nation before self, Poincaré adjured his countrymen: "We should undertake a crusade in this troubled and disoriented country—to remind it that a great nation has reasons for existence other than material interests.

He established a national holiday honoring the symbol of French patriotism, Joan of Arc, and revived the *retraités militaires*, a weekly parade of troops through the streets of Paris, prohibited since the Dreyfus Affair. Poincaré's call for a "national renaissance" commanded the admiration of leaders of metropolitan opinion like the editor of *Le Figaro*, Gaston Calmette. The day after his murder, writing in his diary, Poincaré recalled Calmette's fulsome praise: "I don't have the right to forget [that] he was for me . . . before and after the pre-election last summer. Dining at the Elysee, he spoke to me with a sort of religious fervor. I had lifted the prestige of France, I was necessary for the country; he should watch over me, care for me, keep me . . . Who knows? Perhaps he thought he was doing a service for me [in attacking Joseph Caillaux] and defending me against the enemy."[74]

The election was the close January 17, 1913, vote in the Chamber that elevated Poincaré to the presidency. "The fog is dissipating," Calmette wrote when the outcome hung in the balance. "It is certain that M. Raymond Poincaré would be President of the Republic tomorrow if the country were consulted."[75]

Gaston Calmette's ardor for Poincarisme was sincere; it was also inspired by bribes. Rumored at the time, Russian subsidies to the Paris press were revealed in the 1920s by *L'Humanité*, the journal of the French Communist party, the Bolsheviks having supplied the editors with the tsarist documents. By 1912, the subsidies, administered by the French finance minister, M. Klotz, totaled more than two million francs a year. For this sum, Russia got favorable publicity for its railroad loan requests, for the presidential candidacy of Raymond Poincaré, and for his pro-Russian policies as premier and president.[76]

Always awkward, the Republic's alliance with tsarist autocracy became so close under Poincaré that a Toulouse paper could plausibly ask: "Is France Republican or Cossack?" After Russia signaled that it would not go to war over Agadir, Poincaré grew concerned that it might not fight for France under any circumstances. To prime Russia to honor its treaty commitments, he "implicitly" indicated to St. Petersburg that France would go beyond its own commitments. If, because of threats to Serbia, Russia were forced to attack Austria and Germany intervened to support her ally, France would stand by *her* ally. When Jean Jaurès, the great Socialist leader, called Poincaré "more Russian than Russia," he spoke truer than he knew.[77]

When Poincaré was still premier, Izvolski asked St. Petersburg to increase the "press fund" by three hundred thousand francs ahead of the upcoming presidential election. Prime Minister Vladimir

Kokovtsov took the matter up with Poincaré personally, writing, "If in your judgment a direct action . . . is indispensable in this matter, I will join in the opinion dictated by your great influence and judgment." After delivering this letter to Poincaré, Izvolski reported back to Kokovtsov: "I have reason to think that M. P. considers it desirable that we have recourse to this method." St. Petersburg wired the money, and tributes to Poincaré, like the one quoted above from Calmette, no doubt flowed from the presses. On Poincaré's election, Izvolski assured St. Petersburg that "we are therefore, for the period of his seven year term of office, perfectly safe from the appearance of such persons as Caillaux . . . at the head of the French Government."[78]

Besides conviction and cash Calmette may have targeted Caillaux over a woman. The day after Calmette's murder, the Swiss ambassador to France wrote to his government that "from the very beginning of Calmette's campaign in *Le Figaro* against M. Caillaux, everyone in Parisian high society has been saying that the campaign owed its origins to an *histoire de femme*." According to the gossip, Caillaux wanted to divorce his wife to marry a woman he was pressing to divorce her husband. Gaston Calmette was said to be "equally interested in this lady." While the ambassador did not credit these "slanderous" rumors, Madame Caillaux did and "lost her head" over them. But as Edward Berenson notes in his fascinating 1992 book, *The Trial of Madame Caillaux*, why would Henriette have "wanted to eliminate her husband's rival for possession of this other woman"? Why not eliminate her husband instead?[79]

"Madame Caillaux feared in 1914 that she would undergo the same fate as had Madame Gueydan [divorce]," according to the son of the Calmette's lawyer. A close friend, Louise Weiss, once asked Henriette what went through her mind as Calmette crumpled to the floor. She replied "that I did not love the president [Caillaux]," her use of the title, short for president of the council or premier, suggesting a chill formality in their marriage. Perhaps she felt that way because Joseph was no longer in love with her. In murdering Calmette, Berenson speculates, she may have been trying to murder Joseph politically or by killing for him to reclaim his love. "I was driven by a will that had taken the place of my own," she testified. If Henriette's fantasy was to bind Joseph to her, she succeeded but not in the way she hoped. "These pistol shots welded together two human beings who would soon come to hate each other," Weiss wrote. "Their marriage was their true punishment . . . [for] the trial had rendered it indissoluble."[80]

Caillaux himself lent the *histoire de femme* scenario some credibility, boasting that he had behaved honorably by excluding from the trial dirt obtained from Calmette's "mistresses" If the gossip was accurate, he knew at least one of them.[81]

The bad behavior of all concerned in the Caillaux affair presented an irresistible teaching moment for nationalists alarmed over the crisis of the French family. "When I heard Madame Caillaux say 'the first wife of my husband' or 'the son of my husband's first wife' I took my head in my hands, certain that this case represents nothing less than the trial of our secular society, of the rotten and immoral existence that the republic has inflicted on France," one right-wing journalist lamented. Nationalists believed the fate of France was tied to the family, "the essential foundation for the life of a nation and its necessary expansion," Yet the French family was notoriously barren (in 1895 more deaths than births were recorded). Blame fell on familiar targets.[82]

Nationalists arraigned "Anglo-Saxon cultural imperialism," carrier of the "plague of feminism." As early as the 1880s, a professor at the Paris Faculty of Medicine had disparaged "voluntary sterility"—birth control. And an economist was only half joking when he ventured that the best way to resist Germany would be to declare war on French abortionists. Divorce, championed as a guarantor of personal freedom by Radicals, came in for the severest strictures. "Divorce is at this very moment working to bring about the fall of the Third Republic," a woman writing under a pseudonym maintained in a *Figaro*-hosted debate. In the individualistic society held up to the national mirror in the Caillaux scandal, she argued, it was too risky for young women to start families. To nationalists Joseph and Henriette Caillaux, pursuing pleasure above all other values were symptoms of social narcissism. Others resented them for giving purchase to scolds.[83]

The months of publicity over the murder, hearing, and trial left Caillaux vulnerable. A parliamentary committee investigating Calmette's charges censured Caillaux for interfering in a judicial inquest on behalf of a swindler. When his opponent for the Mamers seat put up posters warning voters against becoming "accomplices to a crime,"

Henriette Caillaux in the dock.

Caillaux challenged him to a duel, fought without effusion of blood in the Parc des Princes in Paris. Unable to defeat him in electoral politics, his nationalist opponents felt they could end his career by wielding cultural politics against him. With Henriette in jail awaiting trial and the press opening their private life for public scrutiny, Caillaux and his party faced the electorate.[84]

"Reactionaries of all sorts had been confident of triumph," Caillaux wrote of the April elections. "But all their calculations were upset. The elections gave the parties of the Left, the Radicals, at whose head I stood, and the Socialists led by Jaurès, an irresistible majority; I myself was reelected by an enormous lead." If Caillaux's Radicals joined forces with Jaurès's Socialists following the second round of voting in June, a government of the Left would take power. Early in June, Caillaux and Jaurès conducted a long conversation on one of the settees lining the corridor of the Chamber. Caillaux made an unprecedented offer: Set aside the Socialist ban on serving in government and join my cabinet as minister of foreign affairs. "As soon as possible we must form a strong Leftist ministry which will press for a policy of European peace," Caillaux said.[85]

"The proposal was breathtaking," a Jaurès biographer writes. Consider its implications for Armageddon. Both men feared the alliance with Russia would drag France into a war over the infinitely remote Balkans, Jaurès asking, "Has [France] no other glory and no other purpose than to serve the rancors of M. Isvolsky?" On July 29, at the apex of the war crisis, Jaurès addressed an emergency meeting of the International Socialist Bureau in Brussels. French socialists, he declared, must "insist that it [the French government] speak with force that Russia may abstain" from mobilization. "If, unfortunately, Russia does not abstain, it is our duty to say, 'we do not know of any other treaty than the one which binds us to the human race.'" Had Jaurès been foreign minister at that decisive moment, would he have carried through on his threat to break the treaty with Russia to save the peace of Europe? That "breathtaking" question belongs to the alternative history of 1914.[86]

In their discussion in the Chamber corridor, Jaurès, who called Caillaux "the most capable man we have in France," agreed to join his government—with one stipulation. Mme. Caillaux must first be acquitted. "If his wife is condemned in the trial, which is about to open, that will be an obstacle to his return to politics," he explained to a German socialist.[87]

If her trial had been scheduled for June, the Caillaux-Jaurès ministry would have been in office during the July Crisis instead of the team of President Raymond Poincaré and his weak temporary premier, René Viviani. But the trial unfolded in late July, and Poincaré, during his three-day state visit to St. Petersburg in late July, stiffened Russia's will to stand up to Austria. Sazonov, the Russian foreign minister, summed up his discussions with Poincare this way: "France . . . is not inclined to tolerate a humiliation of Serbia unwarranted by the circumstances."*[88]

---

* The American historian Gordon Wright offers a decisive judgment on the consequences of Poincaré's unchallenged control of France's Russia policy: "The French people were dragged into a war which they did not want, over an incident which did not directly affect their interests. And the chains which bound their government had been forged in part by Raymond Poincaré." Gordon Wright, *Raymond Poincaré and the French Presidency* (Stanford: Stanford University Press, 1943), 149.

Courtroom sketches of Fernand Labori (Caillaux's lawyer), Berthe Gueydan,
and Henriette Caillaux

Did Madame Caillaux kill Gaston Calmette? On the evening of
July 29, five days before Germany declared war on France, eleven of
the twelve male jurors answered no. She had only intended to frighten
Calmette, who unfortunately fell to the floor where she aimed and
when she fired—that was her claim and the jurors believed it. They
also believed Henriette when she said she feared Calmette was about
to publish her "intimate letters"—the same ones Berthe Gueydan's
sister had photographed in 1909—and that this would disgrace her
before her young daughter, striking at her "woman's honor." Paris

juries favored leniency for women whose crimes—poisoning husbands who beat them, for example—accommodated that defense.
Jurors accepted her lawyer's picture of a woman overcome by volatile
emotions that her frail-sex reason was too weak to resist. Although
the shooting was a premeditated act (Henriette stopped at a gun shop
on the way to the *Figaro* offices and tested the Browning in the base-
ment), it was nevertheless a "crime of passion" in that Henriette was
"the victim of an inconceivable overexcitement."[89]

With newspaper hawkers outside the courtroom shouting that Austria had declared war on Serbia, with stray shouts of "To Berlin!"
heard on the streets, perhaps, too, the jurors were stirred by the closing appeal delivered by her lawyer, Fernand Labori, who had defended Alfred Dreyfus. Save your anger "for our enemies without,"
he told the jury. It was time for French men and women to "proceed
united as one . . . toward the perils that threaten us." To a nation at
war five days later, Raymond Poincaré echoed Labori's words. France
would "be heroically defended by all her sons; nothing will break
their sacred union" until the invader was driven from their land.[90]

The jurors were also swayed by Joseph Caillaux, who, speaking pas-
sionately for hours at a stretch, commandeered the eight-day trial. To
the *Daily Express* his "curious high-pitched voice," recalled "the voice
of Mr. Winston Churchill, but without the lisp." Stopping to dab his
eyes with his handkerchief, he blamed himself for ignoring Henriette's mounting fear that Calmette would expose their affair: "I failed
to realize the ravages Calmette's calumnies had made in the soul of
my wife." Responding to the gossip that he had tired of Henriette, he
declared that his marriage surpassed his hopes: "Never could I feel a
happiness more complete than the one I have found in this union . . .
We have lived and will continue to live in a close intimacy of heart
and spirit." Caillaux spilled out his feelings so nakedly that the British
reporters covering the trial could not believe their ears. Such words
would be spoken in England, one wrote, only in stage dialogue—in a
French play. Sitting in the defendant's box wearing a black dress, long
black kid gloves, and a mauve corsage, her blond hair edging a black
hat topped with a long blue ostrich feather, Henriette gasped and
cried and even fainted on cue.[91]

Caillaux on the stand. He commandeered the trial. The judge and jurors
were in his camp. Still, the verdict was shocking.

Caillaux the lover shared the stage with Caillaux the avenger. His
monocle bobbing on its black cord as he chopped the air with his
hands, he savaged the reputation of the victim, charging that Calmette
took bribes disguised as health spa advertisements from the government of Hungary. His emotionality, eloquence, and ferocity might
have persuaded any set of jurors. But these weren't any set of jurors.

Every month from a sealed wooden box containing the names of
three thousand Parisians a six-judge panel pulled seventy-two names
to sit as jurors. The box was then publicly resealed. On May 24, 1914,
the bailiff dropped the box as he carried it into the courtroom. When
he handed it to the judges, the seals were found to be broken. "No
one could recall such a circumstance. Had the seals broken when the
box hit the floor? Or had someone tampered with the names inside,
and then contrived the bailiff's accident?" After anxious discussion,

the judges decided to go ahead and pull the seventy-two names for July. Of those picked, court records reveal, "almost every one is identified as politically sympathetic to Caillaux." So was Judge Louis Albanel, a "close friend of the Caillaux's," who let Caillaux virtually conduct the trial by himself.[92]

The not guilty verdict after less than an hour of deliberation engulfed the courtroom in a "ferocious melee of shouts, howls, applause, raised fists," *Le Figaro* reported. "The roar of the crowd echoing like thunder in the corridors of the Palais [de Justice] already suggested the roar of distant gunfire." On the streets around the Palais, Caillaux haters shouted "As-sas-sin! As-sas-sin!" at Caillaux supporters, many of them "Corsican toughs" imported by Caillaux, who shouted back, "Vive Caillaux!" Outside Caillaux's house, where he was holding a reception for his friends, crowds chanted "Death to Caillaux!"[93]

Acquitted! Henriette embraces her lawyer

Before the trial, Poincaré conceded that if the jury returned a verdict of not guilty he would have no choice but to name Caillaux premier. But that was in an expired world. With Austria at war, Russia mobilizing, and German troops entraining for the Belgian and French frontiers, Caillaux, the man of peace with Germany, could not lead France in a war with Germany. Moreover, there was no place for the paladin of individualism in war's stern social order: "When France endeavored to recreate itself as one holy family . . . Joseph Caillaux had come to represent the antithesis of the values embodied in the *union sacrée*."[94]

Jean Jaurès by Félix Vallotton

Two days after the Caillaux verdict, Caillaux's putative partner in a new government, France's matchless orator and anti-militarist, Jean Jaurès, "exploded" before a group of journalists gathered in the corridors of the Chamber of Deputies, "Are we going to unleash a world war because Isvolski is still furious over Aehrenthal's deception in the Bosnian affair?" Early that evening, at the Foreign Ministry, he learned that Germany had given Russia two hours to cease mobilization; war was imminent. "Everything is finished. There is nothing left to do," a colleague said.

Jaurès, the Socialist of the will, would concede nothing to inevitability. "It will be like Agadir," he said. "There will be ups and downs but things will arrange themselves." That evening, his step slow, his massive brow creased, he walked to the offices of *L'Humanite* to prepare an appeal to the French people to save the peace. "I'm going to write a new *J'accuse*," he told associates, referring to Emile Zola's history-changing outcry against the persecution of Alfred Dreyfus. "I will expose everyone responsible for this crisis," he vowed, his voice charged with moral anger. He broke from his writing to enjoy a late dinner with colleagues at a café in Montmarte. It was a hot night and the café windows were open to the street. At nine forty, a young nationalist fanatic, Raoul Villain, crossed the street and shot Jaurès twice in the back. Minutes later he died. Villain belonged to a revanchard group allied with Action Française, whose newspaper, fixing a bull's eye on Jaurès, slandered him as a German agent. "One day in July, ignoble calumnies transformed an imbecile into an assassin," Anatole France wrote.[95]

After Calmette's murder, Villain had bought two revolvers. On the handle of one he carved the initial *J* and on that of the other *C*, for Caillaux.[96]

Agadir was "the most arduous adventure that France had known," Joseph Caillaux wrote in a postwar book detailing the secret negotiations with Germany through which he kept the peace. Agadir is remembered today in those terms, as a Great Power crisis, significant only as a place name, the port where the *Panther* and its relief ships, pawns in a test of wills with France, spent fourteen uneventful weeks.

Nothing happened there; nothing *there* mattered; nobody died at Agadir in 1911.[97]

Many died there in March 1912, but few remember Agadir for that. The victims left no mark on history. The battle of Agadir was an episode in the campaign to crush resistance to the French protectorate over Morocco. France, Premier Raymond Poincaré insisted in the Chamber, must never "give the natives the impression of weakness or timidity." They must be taught to fear the new "master of North Africa."[98]

In his haunting novel *Desert*, J. M. G. Le Clézio, winner of the Nobel Prize in Literature in 2009, depicts the lesson the French imparted at Agadir through the eyes of a young boy from the Smara, one of the last of the nomadic tribes pursued to their destruction by Colonel Mangin and the black soldiers of the Armée d'Afrique.[99]

"The soldiers of the Christians had slowly closed their wall around the free men of the desert." Occupying their wells, harrying them from the rivers, the French drove the free men to the coast, where a warship was waiting to shell them: "When they heard the sound of cannons for the first time, the blue men and the warriors started running toward the hills, to look out on the sea . . . Alone, off the coast of Agadir, a large battleship, like a monstrous slow animal, was spitting out flashes . . . In a few minutes, the high walls of red stone were no more than a pile of rubble from which black smoke rose." The inhabitants—men, women, children—poured out of the burning city, "bloody and screaming."

Now it was the turn of the warriors from the mountains to die. Three thousand horsemen rode in a giant circle, "churning up a large whirling cloud, raising the red dust up into the sky." They stopped to pray; then, shouting the names of their saints, they charged the position that the French infantry had prepared to trap them, counting on their impetuous zeal, after a long retreat, to fight. Waiting in the riverbed with four thousand riflemen and twenty machine guns, Mangin let the first spear-carrying riders through his lines, then lowered his arm, "and the steel barrels started firing their stream of bullets, six hundred a minute." The bodies fell "as if a large invisible wave were mowing them down."[100]

Mangin's Senegalese soldiers, in their turn, suffered terribly fighting in the "icy sleet" during the ill-fated French attack on the Chemin des Dames in April 1917. Before the war, Mangin had recommended their deployment in Europe. "In future battles," he argued in *La Force Noire*, "these primitives, for whom life counts so little and whose young blood flows so ardently, as if avid to be shed, will certainly attain the old 'French fury,' and will reinvigorate it if necessary." Recruited primarily from the Wolof, Serer, and Bambara tribes in a manner "all too reminiscent of the repudiated era of the slave trade," the 140,000 West Africans who fought on the Western Front were three times as likely to die in combat as their white infantry comrades, this because they were used as "shock troops," a role for which Mangin believed the "warrior" nature manifest in their "savage impetuosity with the bayonet" fitted them. On the Chemin Des Dames, "their hands were too cold to fix bayonets," a British military observer reported. "Paralyzed with cold, their chocolate faces tinged with grey,

"Marianne [symbol of France] Brings Civilization to Morocco"

they reached the assault-trenches with the utmost difficulty. Most of them were too exhausted even to eat the rations they carried. They advanced when ordered to do so . . . They got quite a long way before the German machine-guns mowed them down."[101]

"The Moors have lost their independence and their country," E. D. Morel, who had exposed Belgian atrocities in the Congo, wrote in the 1915 pamphlet "Morocco and Armageddon." "But, if it be any satisfaction to them, they have their revenge. For the legacy of international ill-will to which their treatment gave rise, must count as one of the most powerful originating causes of [the] war." In Churchill's metaphor, before Morocco the alliances stood side by side; after Morocco, face-to-face. The imperialist banquet was poisoned. In the years since the Fashoda Crisis of 1898, when Britain and France had nearly gone to war in Europe over territory in Africa, "an imperialism already red in tooth and claw abroad came to infect relations between European peoples and states." A European state system based on great power concert became "so warped by imperialist competition as systematically to reward conduct subversive of peace and stability." It was as the Muslim warriors wrote to the French soldiers holding the blockhouse at Boudenib: "Your dark soul fools you by making you rush to your destruction."[102]

7

THE VICTORY OF THE SPADE

And hope, with furtive eyes and grappling fist Flounders
in the mud. O Jesus, make it stop!

—Siegfried Sassoon

A LITTLE OVER A month after the end of the Caillaux trial,
German cavalry patrols roamed within eight miles of Paris. The
war happened in a world discontinuous with the one in which that
sordid little story counted as big news. The year split into before and
after, and contemporaries would never assimilate the totality of what
was lost on the far side. The dedication a Belgian poet wrote to a 1915
book, "With emotion, to the man I used to be," covered the experience of a generation.*

It was not only the inconceivable fact of war after a "century of
peace" and after Europe had achieved a degree of financial integration that a 1910 book that sold two million copies had made war

---

* "It is almost impossible even now to describe what happened in Europe on August
4, 1914. The days before and the days after the first World War are separated not like
the end of an old and the beginning of a new period, but like the day before and the
day after an explosion. Yet this figure of speech is as inaccurate as all the others,
because the quiet of sorrow which settles down after a catastrophe has never come
to pass. The first explosion seems to have touched off a chain reaction in which we
have been caught up ever since and which nobody seems to be able to stop." Hannah Arendt, writing in 1951 in *The Origins of Totalitarianism* (New York: Meridien
Books, 1958).

unthinkable; it was the immediate slaughter on a nuclear scale that shattered the compass of thought and feeling. Bull Run, the first full-scale engagement of the American Civil War, was fought three months after the shelling of Fort Sumter, and the death toll was light compared to Antietam and Gettysburg. The major battles of World War II happened years into it. But, though it lasted another four years, World War I was never bloodier than between August 1914 and January 1915, when over a million men died in battle.[1]

They were sacrificial offerings to a "cult of the offensive" that lent general staffs the nimbus of "strategy," wonder-working schemes sold to governments for winning on the quick. The cult of the offensive belongs to 19194's lost history. For while at least one of these strategies, Germany's Schlieffen Plan, is famous, their back story in institutional politics is forgotten, and why they failed with it.[2]

Militarily what the historian Stig Förster has written of Schlieffen also applies to the war plans of the other Great Powers—they made "no sense." In 1914 defense was dominant. That was the lesson taught by the Franco-Prussian War, in which the Prussian Guard suffered seven thousand casualties in twenty minutes attacking entrenched French infantry at St. Privat, as well as by the sanguinary battles of the Boer War and the Russo-Japanese war of 1904–05—the lesson taught by the heaps of bodies that repeating rifles, rapid-firing artillery, and above all machine guns spewing six hundred bullets a minute, "as much ammunition as had previously been fired by half a battalion of troops," had decisively advantaged the defense over the offense. The generals were not fools. Yet when recent history shouted defense, they insisted "Attack is the best defense."[3]

In part they were reverting to type. Militaries prefer offense because it makes soldiers "specialists in victory" whereas defense makes them "specialists in attrition." Attrition takes time, it means a long war, it asks too much of politicians and publics. "[Long] wars are impossible at a time when the existence of a nation is founded upon the uninterrupted progress of commerce and industry," the eponymous von Schlieffen, the chief of staff of the German army from 1891 to 1905, reasoned. "A strategy of attrition cannot be conducted when the maintenance of millions depends on the expenditure of billions."[4]

In Germany the "demi-god" status of the officer corps rested on

"Sturmangriff" (Assault) by Ernst Barlach

Bismarck's three short successful wars fought in six years. The General Staff was expected to match that legacy in 1914 in a strategic environment inimical to it. The generals had three alternatives to aggressive war. One was politically untenable, one psychologically inconceivable, one strategically impossible.

To solve the problem lit up by Bismarck's map of Africa—France on one side, Russia on the other, Germany in the middle—Germany could have transformed itself into Sparta. Liberal Germany could have been snuffed out under the spiked helmet, socialist workers conscripted, Prussian Junkers taxed. Preparing Germans for "a long war against superior enemies," the generals could have demanded the militarization of the state, economy, and society, something even Hitler didn't dare in peacetime.[5]

Or Germany could have achieved Peter Durnovo's dream—détente with Russia. A band of generals close to retirement could have told the kaiser: We do not know how to win a two-front war. Conceding that truth, however, would have "challenged the self-image of the general staff officers and questioned the entire position of the army in the structure of the Reich."[6]

If Germany could not escape a two-front war with diplomacy, the general who led Bismarck's wars, Helmuth von Moltke the elder, recommended standing on the defensive in the west while attacking Russia in the east. Despite its laureled source, considerations of national strategy militated against that idea. "Offense in the East and Defense in the West would have implied that we expected at best a draw," Bethmann Hollweg, Germany's wartime chancellor, wrote in his memoirs. "With such a slogan no army and no nation could be led into a struggle for its existence."[7]

Privately, the broodier sort of generals foresaw a long-lasting war, a "mutual tearing to pieces," in the words of Moltke the elder's nephew and Schlieffen's successor as chief of staff, Moltke the younger. To the War Ministry in 1912, the younger accurately described Germany's two-front challenge: "We will have to be ready to fight a lengthy campaign with numerous, hard, lengthy battles until we defeat *one* of our enemies." Evidence like that has changed the minds of historians, who no longer see Moltke as a votary of "the short-war illusion." Calculating that "specialists in victory" were likelier to gain bigger budgets than "specialists in attrition," Moltke and his generals gave "lip service to the short war panacea" when talking to officials like Bethmann, who promised Germans that the war would be a "brief storm." Deceived into believing that victory was assured, Germany's civilian leaders "never felt the need to rethink" whether war was an option for Germany. For confining their candid gloom to their diaries and letters—the war would be "a general European massacre," Moltke wrote his wife—Förster indicts the soldiers who launched the war for their "almost criminal lack of responsibility."[8]

Just as Stig Förster, using materials from the former East German military archive, has prompted a revision of the "short-war illusion," so Terence Zuber, a retired U.S. Army officer and German-trained historian, has challenged an even greater shibboleth, the Schlieffen plan.

Until Zuber unsettled the field it was universally accepted that Germany followed Schlieffen's short-war strategy in August 1914. The "Schlieffen Plan" envisioned a gray flood sweeping through Belgium into northern France and then arcing around Paris and smashing the French army up against its own fortifications on France's western border. On the basis of evidence he discovered in the East German archives, Zuber contends that the Schlieffen Plan was *not* Germany's strategy in 1914 and in a series of books and papers published since 1999 has defended his interpretation against all comers. "All the older literature needs to be revised in the light of Zuber," concluded Hew Strachan, a preeminent historian of World War I.[9]

The memorandum Schlieffen wrote upon retiring as chief of staff in the winter of 1905–06, in the words of a scholar refereeing the debate, "was not the blueprint for war in 1905 or 1914, or even a war plan at all, but rather an elaborate ploy to increase the size of the German army." Schlieffen fashioned a miracle strategy to defeat the French army and win the war in forty days. But the troops to execute it did not exist and the meticulous Schlieffen never tested it in a war game. The plan depended on "ghost divisions" that it was the government's urgent duty to animate by implementing "universal conscription," which, Schlieffen wrote, "we invented . . . and demonstrated to other nations the necessity to introduce" only to "relent in our own endeavors." If the War Ministry did not take this politically risky step (which would fill out the army with Social Democrats, precluding the kaiser from using it to "decapitate" the Social Democrats), Germany would lose the war. It didn't and Germany did. The Schlieffen ploy failed.[10]

As for the "Schlieffen Plan," the generals "invented" it after the war to rescue the mystique of Prussian militarism from the disgrace of defeat. The German army lost the battle of the Marne in September 1914 because Moltke failed to swing the German rightwing around Paris to envelop the French army from the west. This deviation from the master's blueprint cost Germany the war. That was the legend of the Schlieffen Plan spun by the General Staff and accepted in classic works like Barbara Tuchman's *The Guns of August* (1962). In truth, according to Zuber, "There never was a 'Schlieffen Plan.'"[11]

Moltke unleashed his offensive against France in August 1914 not from an expectation of victory in one battle (and certainly not by following the super-secret "Schlieffen Plan" then in the possession of Schlieffen's two elderly daughters!), but out of fear that Germany would

lose its power if it waited.* War was "now or never." "The prospect
of the future seriously worried him," the German Foreign Secretary
Gottlieb von Jagow wrote of a March 1914 meeting with Moltke.
"Russia will have completed her armaments in 2 to 3 years. The military superiority of our enemies would be so great then that he did
not know how he would cope with them." He asked Jagow "to gear
our policy to an early unleashing of war." The assassination of Franz
Ferdinand in June gave Moltke "his chance," Förster writes. "He would
not allow it to slip away."[12]

Geography lent the cult of the offensive a surface plausibility in Germany. To survive a two-front war, it *had* to subdue one of its enemies
before turning on the other; that, say Zuber's critics, was the strategic
dilemma to which the desperate ambition of Schlieffen's valedictory
answered. But in France the absurdity of the cult should have been
patent. Under the political necessity of respecting Belgium's neutrality (or else forfeit Britain's support) until the last minute, it needed to
adopt a "counteroffensive" strategy—defense followed by counterattack. The politics of the French army, however, vetoed defense.[13]

In the wake of the Dreyfus Affair, French politicians on the left had
sought to "republicanize" an army hierarchy that had covered up a
miscarriage of justice against a Jewish staff officer falsely accused of
spying for Germany: "Military values of unthinking obedience and
blind loyalty seemed irreconcilable with the democratic values of due
process, tolerance, equality, and the rule of reason."[14]

Socialists like Jean Jaurès wanted France to defend itself with an
army of citizen reservists. Reformers within the military wanted to
use reservists as front line troops to democratize the army and allow
France to compensate for its demographic inferiority vis-à-vis Germany. While traditional French strategy called for charging across
the Alsace-Lorraine frontier at the first shot, the reformers favored

---

*"In 1914 many of the German people, and in 1939 nearly all of the British, felt
justified in going to war, not over any specific issue that could have been settled by
negotiation, but *to maintain their power*; and to do so while it was still possible, before
they found themselves so isolated, so impotent, that they had no power left to maintain and had to accept a subordinate position within an international system dominated by their adversaries." Michael Howard quoted in Jack S. Levy, "Declining
Power and the Preventive Motivation for War," *World Politics* 40, no. 1 (1987): 95.

waiting until the Germans committed themselves before counterattacking.[15]

The unreconstructed officer corps seethed over these incursions on its institutional autonomy. It feared that reserves would weaken its control over the army, resented a reformed training regime to instill "discipline via respect" instead of via brutality, and watched with dismay as the number of applicants for St. Cyr, the prestigious military academy, declined from 3,400 in 1892 to 800 in 1912.[16]

The nationalist revival after Agadir gave the military establishment an opening to undo republicanization and trump citizen-based defense. Since 1904 French intelligence had known that to increase their offensive punch the Germans planned to use reserves as front line troops, but the French General Staff "manufactured fake German documents" showing the opposite. The enemy won't use reserves, they argued, and neither should we.[17]

To replace reservists, the generals successfully lobbied to expand the regular army by adding an extra year to the two-term of French conscripts. Plucked overnight from civilian life, reservists were suited to defense but only regulars were regarded as equal to the attack. Therefore, to keep the door shut against the reserves, the General scrapped the reformer's "counteroffensive" strategy in favor of the *offensive à outrance*—the offensive at all costs.

Vitalist cant about French élan and the bayonet charge prevailing against soulless German machine guns masked a bureaucratic coup. Staff officers suspected of defense were forced out or transferred to field commands. Even standing on the defensive long enough to read a German thrust and then counterattack was now deemed "unworthy of the French character."

The French army "no longer knows any other law than the offensive," General Joffre, the chief of staff appointed under Joseph Caillaux, avowed. In the first six weeks of the war, 329,000 Frenchman became casualties obeying a law decreed to defend the French army against the values of the French republic. When Clemenceau later remarked that war was too important to be left to the generals, he knew what he was talking about.[18]

Fighting from trenches, the Boers had raked attacking British regulars during the war of 1899–1902; yet British generals dismissed the unpleasantness on the South African veld as inapplicable to the European battlefield and insulting to the British fighting man. As General W. G. Knox, speaking for his kind, stipulated, "The defensive is never an acceptable role to the Briton, and he makes little or no study of it." For the aristocratic British officer corps, "The Boer fondness for trenches was in fact seen as evidence of their lack of breeding—real gentlemen would stand and fight."[19]

Russia had defeated Napoleon by drawing him into its depths, but it too succumbed to the cult, adopting "an impossibly offensive strategy" involving dual attacks on Germany and Austria. General V. A. Sukhomlinov, the minister of war, called on the army to emulate its enemies by "dealing rapid and decisive blows."[20]

The generals created the cult of offensive to win the inside game with their governments and then became its prisoners. In August 1914 the clashing armies followed the same playbook of self-slaughter. By mid-September 1914, a mere six weeks after the opening of hostilities, the attacks inspired by the cult—the German march on Paris, the French *offensive à outrance* into Lorraine, the Russian invasion of East Prussia, and the Austrian incursion into Serbia—had ended in slaughter and stalemate. Reflecting on the last offensive of the year, the German attempt to break the Allied lines in Belgium and seize the Channel ports, the *Times* of London observed on December 2 that "The Battle of Flanders died of the spade." So did the offensive.[21]

"We were all blind," General Erich von Falkenhayn, who succeeded von Moltke in September and who ordered the Flanders offensive, confided to a visiting military attaché. "The Russo-Japanese War represented an opportunity for us to learn about the tactical consequences of the new weapons and combat conditions. Instead we believed that the trench warfare that was characteristic of this war was due to logistical problems and the national traditions of the belligerents . . . The force of the defensive is unbelievable!"[22]

Alsatian soldiers of the Ninety-ninth Infantry Regiment who had endured the "Wackes" taunts of Lieutenant von Forstner in Zabern were used—and used up—in Falkenhayn's attacks around Ypres. Some tried to desert, but were shot running toward the French lines. Caught in no-man's-land, they stood for the 380,000 men from Alsace-Lorraine who fought in the German army. Treated as "the enemy in our ranks," eighty in ten thousand deserted compared to one in ten thousand among other German men. The wholesale transfer of units to the eastern front, where they could not desert, destroyed morale, and the last months of the war saw thousands of soldiers from Alsace-Lorraine mutiny at the Beverloo training camp in Belgium and only expedients like removing their rifles' springs kept other units from following suit.★[23]

Under Falkenhayn, the Germans were the first to wield the spade, digging in above the Ainse River to check the Allied counteroffensive that ended the Battle of the Marne. This shift to the defensive "must be considered the real turning point of the war." Near noon on September 3, just as the French were encountering the wire that the Germans had strung in front of their trenches, an aide to a French general opened his office door. "General," he inquired, "do you want lunch to be prepared?" "Lunch!" the general snorted. "We shall be sleeping twelve miles from here on the Suippe. I certainly hope we aren't staying more than an hour in this spot!" They stayed four years.[24]

In the east, the war of movement continued, but from the North Sea coast of Belgium to the Swiss border, the exhausted armies dug in, creating "a temporary crisis in the business of war," in the words of Marshal Ferdinand Foch. "Some way had to be found which would enable the offensive to surmount the obstacle and break through the shield which the ground everywhere afforded the soldier," Foch wrote in his *Memoirs*, stating the riddle of "the trenches," the defining battle-scape of World War I.[25]

★"Alsatians and Lorrainers did not fare much better in French hands. Soon after the war's outbreak, the French interned thousands [of them] living on French soil; they were joined by some eight thousand Alsatians deported from parts of southern Alsace 'liberated' during the first weeks of the conflict and by an unspecified number of Lorrainers taken hostage during the French army's initial advance." Paris maids and servants from the "lost provinces" were sent to "concentration camps." "The pervasive suspicion of Alsatians and Lorrainers, the lingering doubts about their patriotic trustworthiness," extended into the peace, when purge trials and persecutions of those deemed too German marred the restoration of the "lost sisters" to France. Laird Boswell, "From Liberation to Purge Trials in the 'Mythic Provinces': Recasting French Identities in Alsace and Lorraine, 1918–1920," *French Historical Studies* 23, no. 1 (2000): 4.

A man in a trench was almost invulnerable to rifle and machine-gun fire. To kill or wound him with a shell required a lucky shot; by one contemporary estimate, it took 329 shells to hit one German soldier. To clear the trench a hand grenade had to be thrown or shot into it. But to get within range—60 to 120 feet—required crossing no-man's-land alive, possible only for small groups mounting nocturnal trench raids, and not for masses of men advancing in daylight against a "storm of steel" from machine guns and artillery. Mobility and mass had ruled warfare since antiquity. Opponents were either flanked or crushed. Trench warfare mocked these principles. If, trying to defeat the Allies before the million-man American Army took the field, the Germans had not raised up out of their trenches and taken the offensive in the spring of 1918, the war would have lasted a year or more longer.[26]

Mud was the soldiers' shield. European man tried to cheat death by submerging himself in the "greasy tide" of rainy, thin-soiled Flanders and Picardy. Three French soldiers speak for millions.

"The front-line trench is a mud-colored stream, but an unmoving stream where the current clings to the banks," one wrote. "You go down into it, you slip in gently . . . At first the molecules of this substance part, then you can feel them return together and hold on with a tenacity against which nothing can prevail."

"Sometimes the two lips of the trench come together yearningly and meet in an appalling kiss, the wattle sides collapsing in the embrace," another observed. "Twenty times over you have patched up this mass with wattles, yet it slides and drops down. Stakes bend and break . . . Duckboards float, and then sink into the mire. Everything disappears into this ponderous liquid: men would disappear into it too if it were deeper."

To yet another, writing in a soldier-edited "trench paper," the mud seemed alive—and hungry: "At night, crouching in a shell-hole and filling it, the mud watches, like an enormous octopus. The victim arrives. It throws its poisonous slobber out at him, blinds him, closes round him, buries him . . . For men die of mud, as they die of bullets, but more horribly. Mud is where men sink and—what is worse—the soul sinks . . . Look, there, there are flecks of red on that pool of

"Debout Les Morts!" (1917) (The Dead Rise Up!) by Frans Masereel

mud—blood from a wounded man. Hell is not fire, that would not be the ultimate in suffering. Hell is mud!"[27]

On his first night in the trenches, Robert Graves "saw a man lying on his face in a machine-gun shelter."

I stopped and said: "Stand-to, there." I flashed my torch on him and saw his foot was bare. The machine-gunner beside him said:

"No good talking to him, sir." I asked: "What's wrong? What's he taken his boot and sock off for?" I was ready for anything wrong in the trenches. "Look for yourself, sir," he said. I shook the man by the arm and noticed suddenly that the back of his head was blown out. The first corpse I saw in France was this suicide. He had taken off his boot and sock to pull the trigger of his rifle with his toe; the muzzle was in his mouth.[28]

The mutual siege warfare of the trenches was a psychic Calvary. "All *poilus* have suffered from *le cafard*," a *poilu*, the French "grunt," testified, using an expression for overmastering misery "which has no precise linguistic equivalent in the English vocabulary of the Great War." To be alive was to be afraid—of snipers, shells, mines, and gas; of drowning in mud, burning in liquid fire, and freezing in snow; of the enemy in front of you and the firing squad behind; of lice and

"Toter Sapenpost" (1924) (Dead Sapenpost) by Otto Dix

rats, pneumonia, and typhus; of cowardice, hysteria, madness, and suicide.[29]

Graves's great fear was of being hit by "aimed fire" traceable to a marksman's malevolent intent. The least likely way to die in the war, the bayonet thrust in the gut, was the most terrifying. More rational was the terror instilled by "the monstrous anger of the guns," as the poet Wilfred Owen personified artillery. Unaimed shellfire was the major killer in the trenches. Under saturation bombardment, there was no escape. For nine straight hours, on February 21, 1916, at Verdun, eight hundred German artillery pieces fired forty shells a minute on the French positions. "I believe I have found a comparison that conveys what I, in common with all the rest who went through the war, experienced in situations like this," Ernst Jünger wrote. "It is as if one were tied to a post and threatened by a fellow swinging a sledgehammer. Now the hammer is swung back for the blow, now it whirls forward, just missing your skull, it sends the splinters flying from the post once more. That is exactly what it feels like to be exposed to heavy shelling without cover."[30]

Jünger's image captures the emotional trauma specific to trench warfare. In his 1918 book *War Neurosis* the psychiatrist John T. MacCurdy hypothesized that industrial warfare was uniquely stressful because soldiers were forced to "remain for days, weeks, even months, in a narrow trench or stuffy dugout, exposed to constant danger of the most fearful kind . . . which comes from some unseen force, and against which no personal agility or wit is of any avail." Nor, unless in hand-to-hand combat, could the men "retaliate in any personal way." Their memories were seared with inadmissible fear and inexpressible rage. The worst sufferers from war neurosis or "shell-shock," as a *Lancet* article labeled it in early 1915, were the defenseless artillery spotters who hung over the battlefield in balloons while the enemy fired shot after unanswered shot at them. "Medical officers at the front were forced to recognize that more men broke down in war because they were not allowed to kill than collapsed under the strain of killing," observes the historian Joanna Bourke. To spare himself, perhaps Graves's barefoot suicide needed to turn his death-will on a German.[31]

Soldiers could look away from terrible sights; there was no escape from the pounding nightmare of the guns. Of the firing of a giant

"The Grenade" (1915) by Max Beckmann

mortar, an American correspondent with the German army in
Lorraine reported: "There was a rush, a rumble, and a groaning—
and you were conscious of all three at once . . . The blue sky vanished in a crimson flash . . . and then there was a remote and not
unpleasant whistling in the air. The shell was on its way to the enemy." What did it sound like to *him*? "You hear a bang in the dis-
tance and then a hum coming nearer and nearer until it becomes a
whistle," a British soldier remembered. "Then you hear nothing for
fractions of a second until the explosion." "The lump of metal that will
crush you into a shapeless nothing may have started on its course,"
wrote Ernst Jünger, recalling the thought that filled his mind while
he "cower[ed] . . . alone in his hole" during a bombardment. "Your
discomfort is concentrated on your ear, that tries to distinguish amid
the uproar the swirl of your own death rushing near." Paradoxically,
the shells that couldn't be heard, those fired from trench mortars just

across no-man's-land, were the likeliest to kill. Terrifying as the din was, men had more to fear from the silence.[32]

Artillery broke men; it could not break the trench barrier. A rain of shells might bury a stretch, but not men guarding it. Carrying their machine guns and rifles, they could ride out the bombardment in deep dugouts built into the inner walls of the trench, then surface in time to decimate the attacking infantry. The machine gun, which had necessitated the trench, could not break it. The grenade was "an excellent weapon to clear out the trenches that assaulting columns are attacking," in the words of *Tactics and Duties for Trench Fighting*, a U.S. Army manual. Of flamethrowers, exploited by the Germans in their 1918 breakout attacks, *Tactics and Duties* bleakly concluded: "It is impossible to withstand a liquid fire attack if the operators succeed in coming within sixty yards" of the trench. "The only means of combating such an attack is to evacuate." Grenades and flamethrowers were tactical weapons. Gas was potentially strategic.[33]

In April 1915, the Germans released a 150-metric-ton cloud of chlorine along a seven-mile front near Ypres. The cloud slowly wafted across no-man's-land, turning from white to yellow-green as it crept closer to the two divisions of Franco-Algerian soldiers holding the line. Choking for life, they panicked and ran, German infantry in pur-

"Sturmtruppe geht unter Gas vor" (Shock Troops
Advance under Gas) by Otto Dix

suit. "We had seen everything—shells, tear-gas, woodland demolished, the black tearing mines falling in fours, the most terrible wounds and the most murderous avalanches of metal—but nothing can compare with this . . . death-cloud that enveloped us," one *poilu* wrote in a trench paper. The Germans captured two thousand prisoners and fifty-one guns but had not accumulated the reserves to convert this tactical success into a breakthrough, a failure that gave rise to the myth of the "missed opportunity." ("After the war, many of the experts felt that the Germans could have dealt a decisive blow on the western front if they had made the necessary deployments.") Far along in their preparations to deploy and defend against gas, the Allies rapidly adapted. Within months both sides were using it, especially to deny mobility to the other side. Thus "poison gas, which was supposed to bring an end to trench warfare, . . . became the strongest factor in promoting the stasis of the war," and intensifying its horror.[34]

What finally broke the barrier was the tank used in combination with artillery and infantry. "The turning point of the war," according to a postwar German government commission, was the emergence from out of an early morning mist of French tanks counterattacking the German lines at Soisson on July 18, 1918—tanks that rolled over obstacles vital to the defenders' sense of security.* "Tank fright" ramified. It colored what General Ludendorff called "the black day of the German army," the August 8 attack at Amiens of four hundred British tanks (and eight hundred planes) that punched an eight-mile bulge in the German lines. The British took eighteen thousand prisoners, batches at a time surrendering to single tanks. And whereas eight thousand Germans were killed on August 8, the tank-accompanied

---

* It wasn't tanks alone but tanks as the new element of a combined arms attack that tipped the balance toward the offense: "A German officer captured on 21 August said that a BEF attack with infantry, artillery and tanks would *always* get through; one with infantry and artillery alone would get through three times out of four; but one with infantry and tanks unsupported would get through only one time out of four." Tim Travers, *How the War Was Won: Factors That Led to Victory in World War One* (London: Pen & Sword Classics, 1992), 140. Also see Jonathan Boff, "Combined Arms During the Hundred Days Campaign, August–November 1918," *War in History* 17, no. 4 (2010): 459–78. Of 202 attacks mounted by Third Army in the hundred days, 50 were with combined arms, infantry, artillery, and tanks. The success rate of these attacks was 90 percent.

British troops, attacking in the open, recorded half that number of fatalities over *four* days. By neutralizing the machine gun, the armored tank lifted the "storm of steel" fatal to attacking infantry.[35]

Ten Australian and Canadian divisions crossed no-man's-land with those tanks at Amiens. Leaving the protection of the trenches, the men went "over the top." Henri Barbusse evoked that moment: "Each one knows that he will be presenting his head, his chest, his belly, the whole of his body, naked, to the rifles that are already fixed, the shells, the heaps of ready-prepared grenades and, above all, the methodical, almost infallible machine-gun—to everything that is waiting in silence out there—before he finds the other soldiers that he must kill."[36]

The Germans collapsed at Soissons and Amiens because they had lost one million irreplaceable men who had gone over the top in their last-ditch "peace offensives" between March and July. The nearly four years since the Battle of Flanders had proved the axiom that he who attacked lost heavily in men whatever few yards he gained in territory. On the relative safety of the trenches, consider the contrast between the casualties suffered by the German army in February 1918, when it stood on the defensive, and in March, when it attacked. Manning the trenches in February found 1,705 soldiers killed, 1,147 missing, and 30,381 wounded. Attacking in March the figures were 31,000 killed, 19,680 wounded, 180,898 missing.[37]

Amiens showed how far tanks could shift the odds to the attacker. However, while the tank could break into the German lines, with its vulnerability to shells, liability to breakdown, and short range it could not break *through* them. Of the 414 tanks in the August 8 attack at Amiens, just 38 were usable on the 11th and only 6 on the 12th. As the supple of tanks ran down in September and October the British high command reverted to the high-casualty infantry-artillery assault. Thus when the British "Tommy" took the offensive in the fall of 1918 he had grim occasion to look back on the "victory of the spade" as a victory for life over death.[38]

In licensing the spade, the generals licensed survival, a biological imperative that sapped the appetite for aggression. The trenches spawned a live-and-let-live solidarity between enemies sharing the same mud, enduring the same privations, and resenting in equal measure the same callousness toward their sufferings found at headquarters, in rear billets, on the home front, and in the patriotic press—a solidarity feared by the brass on both sides, who, sensing in it the makings of a politics of life stronger than nationalism, strove to break it.

On Christmas Eve 1914, Christmas, and New Year's Day, soldiers from the opposing armies fraternized in no-man's-land, primarily in the thirty-mile British sector but also in scattered places along the much longer length manned by the French. The Germans, sentimentalists over Christmas, took the initiative. CONCERT OVER HERE TONIGHT. ALL BRITISH TROOPS WELCOME, read a notice above a German trench. Football was played. Boxing matches proposed: He'll fight anybody but an Irishman, some Germans shouted about their champion. Gifts were exchanged, along with information about the war, not all of it welcome. Captain J. R. Somers-Smith, of the London Brigade, claimed that a German asked him "in all seriousness"—"By how many Germans was London taken?" The high command took a hard line against this "unauthorized intercourse with the enemy" and aside from scattered manifestations it was not repeated.[39]

YOU NO FIGHT, WE NO FIGHT. This German sign captured one aspect of the truce that outlasted Christmas, an example of the live-and-let-live system that evolved from the need to survive. The average width of no-man's-land was 250 to 300 yards, well within mortar range. But some stretches were much closer. In the section held by the Fourteenth British Division, the British and German trenches ran through the ruins of the same school. "In consequence, nobody thinks of throwing grenades about—a case of 'those who live in glass houses,'" a British officer wrote. At Blangy the trenches were six feet apart. Violence in such close quarters was suicidal. So violence was curbed. Neither side could eat if shelling went on at meal times. So shelling was curtailed then. Burial details were often spared. Patrols in no-man's-land stayed in their lanes, nodding as they passed.[40]

Live and let live lasted until late 1915, when Sir Douglas Haig replaced Sir John French as commander in chief of the BEF. Because live and let live cut against Haig's policy of "ceaseless attrition," he set out to destroy it with trench raids and mining. Introduced by an elite Canadian unit, the trench raid was a devilish innovation. A heavily

"Trench Fight" by Frederick Horsman Varley

armed party of raiders seized a section of German trench; then "re-treated quickly so that support troops on the German side were caught in artillery fire."[41]

The attrition was mutual, the Germans responding in kind. Exploiting the memory of the Christmas truce, in one instance they used music as a ruse. "At six minutes to midnight [the band] opened with 'Die Wacht Am Rhein,'" a German officer wrote home. "It continued with 'God Save the King' . . . Then as the last note sounded, every bomber in the battalion, having been previously positioned on the fire-step, and the grenade-firing rifles, trench mortars and bomb-throwing machine, all having registered during the day, let fly simultaneously into the trench; and as this happened the enemy, who had very readily swallowed the bait, were clapping hands and loudly shouting 'encore.'"

Doubtless that was not the end of it. Over three days one furious British brigade, enacting an epic "hate," as the men termed spasms of retributive violence, flung thirty-six thousand grenades at the German trenches opposite.[42]

Too much can be made of live and let live. For one thing, it coexisted with sniping; and, as soldiers' letters attest, with prisoner killing. And the attrition of everyday life in the trenches (an average of nine hundred Frenchmen and thirteen hundred Germans died every day of the war) generated an appetite for vengeance. "The Third Reich comes from the trenches," said Rudolph Hess, Hitler's deputy.[43]

"You seek to do justice to the Germans," Clemenceau told Woodrow Wilson during the Versailles Peace Conference. "Don't think they'll ever forgive us: all they will do is seek an opportunity to take revenge." For *their* part, Clemenceau, Wilson, and Lloyd George answered to publics that regarding Germany were not prepared to live and let live. Promised during the war that "Germany will pay!" they meant to collect in the peace.[44]

The infernal cycle of revenge. In the forest of Compiègne on November 11, 1918, Marshal Ferdinand Foch (second from right) and other Allied officers after receiving the German surrender inside the railway carriage; Hitler and generals waiting for the French generals to surrender at the same place in the same car on June 22, 1940.

H. G. Wells's 1917 novel *Mr. Britling Sees It Through* conveys the climate of hatred seeded by the slaughter of sons. "Some one must pay me," declares Letty Britling, pay for the death of her Teddy:

> I shall wait for six months after the war, dear, and then I shall go off to Germany . . . And I will murder some German . . . It ought to be easy to kill some of the children of the Crown Prince . . . I shall prefer German children. I shall sacrifice them to Teddy . . . Murder is such a little gentle punishment for the crime of war . . . It would be hardly more than a reproach for what has happened. Falling like snow. Death after death. Flake by flake. This prince. That statesman . . . That is what I am going to do.[45]

At a ceremony marking the sixty-fifth anniversary of the D–Day landings in Normandy, French president Nicolas Sarkozy spoke of "the infernal cycle of vengeance" that had doomed Europe to centuries of war. The journey of a railway car tracks the twentieth-century cycle. The 1918 Armistice was signed in a wagon-lit in a clearing in a forest at Rethondes. In June 1940, German engineers freed the wagon-lit from the museum to which it had been annexed and returned it to the clearing. When, on June 22, the French generals arrived to sign the armistice with Adolf Hitler that ended hostilities between France and Germany, they found it covered by a Nazi flag. "The cycle of revenge could not be more complete." But it had one more turn yet. Spirited to Berlin, the wagon-lit was "destroyed in an RAF raid."[46]

8

HOME FRONTS I

Finished at forty!

—Winston Churchill

NINETEEN FOURTEEN ended with the war not yet biting deep into British life. The mobilization of economic production, the draft, food queues three thousand people long, "Government Bread" admixed with potato flour, the woman fined for feeding beefsteak to her Pekingese, invitees to dinner parties bringing potatoes instead of flowers—these indices of "total war" lay in the future.[1]

The war was only days old when the chancellor of the exchequer, Lloyd George, reassured the "City," London's Wall Street, that "the Great War" would not interfere with "business as usual." Certainly that was the motto of professional football, which drew three million fans during the fall season. "This is no time for football," the Tory *Evening News* complained. "This nation, the Empire, has got to occupy itself with more serious business." While nearly half the men of working age would be in uniform by 1918, in 1914 women were just beginning to replace men in shops, banks, and factories. But rejection awaited both the woman who told a recruiter, "Take myself, an able-bodied woman, aged 27, sound in health, and fond of a scrap" and the pioneering Scottish doctor Elsie Inglis who, on petitioning the War Department to form "her own ambulance unit," was told, "My good lady, go home and sit still."[2]

Denied the chance to enlist, young women still wanted "their share" of the war, "and the easiest way to gain this was the ownership of a soldier-lover," the author of *Women's Wild Oats* noted. To prevent "khaki fever" from plunging girls into "grave moral danger," older middle-class women from the Women's Patrols and the Women Police Service kept nocturnal watch over couples in cinemas and public parks, especially in towns with large military camps.[3]

In the war's first months, khaki fever also took a surprisingly respectable form: "The Bishop of London went into khaki, and vicars went into khaki, and seemed to imagine puttees were episcopal gaiters," a journalist recalled. God was enlisted to do his bit for king and country, high churchmen stoking hatred for the hun. This would mount with the casualties and the years and the propaganda, but already in August–September 1914 the *Daily Mail* featured boxed messages like this: REFUSE TO BE SERVED BY AN AUSTRIAN OR GERMAN WAITER. IF YOUR WAITER SAYS HE IS SWISS, ASK TO SEE HIS PASSPORT. And it's doubtful if a notice a Kentish barber put in his window— THIS IS A INGELISCHE SCHOPP—protected the glass.[4]

The greatest story in history was unfolding in Flanders, but the *Times* still devoted its front-page to advertisements and announcements. At first glance these appear to be business as usual. As in March so in December lovers wooed and quarreled in the Personals column: "Please understand that were we the last two persons on earth, and I found myself on the same continent that contained you, I should— emigrate." To which, two days later, came the reply: "DWM—If you are the author of Tuesday's message and it is addressed to me, I do assure you most sincerely that the sentiment is cordially reciprocated— only more so. James J. A." But in March Wanted ads like this one were inconceivable: "Death's Head Hussar's helmet wanted by a lady." And the war dominates the entries under Marriage: "A marriage took place very quietly at St. Judes Church, S. W., between Captain Donald Knox Anderson and Miss Mary Annabella Sandiland. No invitations were issued owing to mourning in the bridegroom's family." Such notices, along with Tablets of Honor listing (but not numbering) the dead, wounded, and missing were the one wholly honest connection between the front and the home front to appear in print. Otherwise, censorship amounting to a press blackout kept the experience of those who served from those left behind.[5]

The "press lords" suppressed bad news without being asked. In

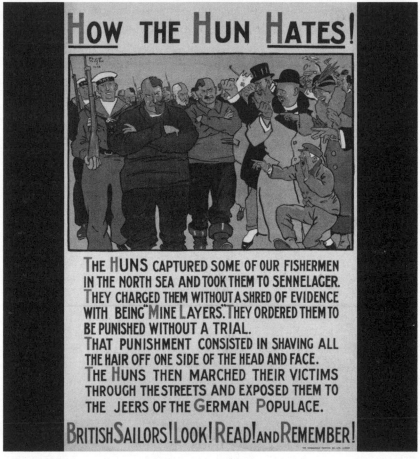

How to Hate the Hun

October 1915, for example, C. P. Scott, editor of the *Manchester Guardian*, received a letter from an "educated" corporal wounded at Loos that, as he wrote a friend, was "too damaging for publication," for "it appears that in that engagement we again shelled our own men and that we lost hill 70 after winning it in just that way . . . P.S. Just heard from Lloyd George. Shall be lunching with him tomorrow."

Such figures as Scott, Lord Northcliffe, proprietor of the *Times* and the *Daily Mirror* (known to the troops as the *Daily Prevaricator*), and Max Aitken, later Lord Beaverbrook, of the *Daily Express* could be counted on by their cabinet friends to sacrifice scoops to keep secrets. "Social ostracism apparently meant more to the newsmen than their professional duty to inform the public," one historian concludes. Then, too, discretion could yield honors. A commoner could rise to a baronet, a baron to a privy councilor, a privy to a viscount by telling the people only what the government wanted them to know. Thus Britons did not learn until after the war of Allied catastrophes like the loss of three hundred thousand French soldiers in August 1914 nor of the annihilation of three Russian army corps at Tannenberg in East Prussia in September, nor, in real time, of alternatives to endless war like Lord Landsdowne's peace plan, which was debated by the cabinet in late 1916 but not published until November 1917, when he surfaced it in a letter to the *Daily Telegraph*. The Defence of the Realm Act, which banned the publication of information useful to the enemy, including weather reports and chess problems, was superfluous. As Sir George Riddell, chairman of the Newspaper Proprietors' Association, testified after the war, "The secrecy imposed upon the press was in no case violated."[6]

Significantly, C. P. Scott's informant about the friendly fire at Loos was a soldier, not a war correspondent. The *Daily Chronicle*'s man at the front, Philip Gibbs, conceded in a postwar memoir that "There was no need of censorship of our dispatches. We were our own censors." Patriotism did not require "conscious falsehood," only selective truth, the leaving out of "horrors." Gibbs felt he "had to spare the feelings of the men and women who have sons and husbands still fighting in France." Gibbs and the five other correspondents from the major dailies embedded with the chateau soldiers of General Headquarters could anticipate knighthoods—if their copy pleased the generals. And what pleased the generals was work infused with "a certain jauntiness of tone . . . a brisk implication that the men enjoyed nothing better than 'going over the top,'" according to C. E. Montague, a *Manchester Guardian* editor turned soldier. The "cheerfulness in the face of vicarious torment and danger" that marked the war reporting the soldiers read on leave or wiped their arses on in the trenches "roused the fighting troops to fury."[7]

The correspondents had to conform to the war policy of their papers. At the *Times* that was "to increase the flow of recruits . . . , an aim that would get little help from accounts of what happened to recruits once they became soldiers," the paper wrote in its official his-

"The First Searchlights at Charing Cross" (1914) by C. R. W. Nevinson.
An American sailor recalled that as the Zeppelins approached bobbies bicycled
through London's streets shouting, "Tike cover! Tike cover!"

tory. The editors and war correspondents believed they served the
country, but their real master was the war.[8]

Gibbs had to be broken to the war's service. When he tried to expose the Loos scandal a military censor, acting "in defence of the
High Command and its tragic blundering," cut forty pages from his
report. Gibbs learned his lesson. Sixty thousand British soldiers were
killed or wounded on the first day of the Somme. Yet *Daily Chronicle*

readers gained no clue of this massacre from Gibbs's dispatch, which began, "It is, on balance, a good day for the British and French." July 1, 1916, was the worst day in the history of the British army.[9]

At a London dinner honoring him in December 1917, Gibbs spoke freely to a company that included the prime minister. It was "the most impressive and moving description" of the war that he had heard, Lloyd George wrote to his friend C. P. Scott. "Even an audience of hardened politicians and journalists was strongly affected," he noted. "The thing is horrible and beyond human nature to bear . . . If people really knew, the war would be stopped tomorrow. But of course they don't know and they can't know. The correspondents don't write and the censors would not print the truth." If people really knew—but the British, French and German people did not know, and the war did not stop.[10]*

The historian John Keegan ends his history of the First World War with this question: "Why, when the hope of bringing the conflict to a quick and decisive conclusion was everywhere dashed to the ground within months of its outbreak, did the combatants decide neverthe-less to persist in their military effort, to mobilize for total war and eventually to commit the totality of their young manhood to mutual

---

*On July 31, 1914, Germany promulgated a "State of Siege," suspending the "right to express opinion freely by word, print or picture." Press censorship "ranged from food shortages, casualty lists, notices of deaths, and mentions of peace demonstra-tions, to advertisements for quack venereal disease cures (since they might prevent sufferers from consulting a qualified physician.)" Alice Goldfarb Marquis, "Words as Weapons: Propaganda in Britain and Germany During the First World War," *Journal of Contemporary History* 13, no. 3 (July 1978): 472, 76. "Nothing was to chal-lenge the impression of German domestic unity and resolve, while in the official reading German troops remained in the field in order to defeat Russian despotism and British designs on world hegemony . . . The operational reports from the front never once mentioned a German defeat until the fall of 1918, when the whole pro-paganda campaign collapsed along with the army." Roger Chickering, *Imperial Ger-many and the Great War, 1914–1918* (Cambridge, UK: Cambridge University Press, 2004), 49, 48. As for France, "There is no doubt that by leaving it in ignorance of the gravity of certain military defeats, of diplomatic failures and of the horrors of war, censorship went a long way towards helping the French civilian front to stand firm." Like the British "Tommy," the French *poilu* "was filled with animosity, even contempt, for the journalists." Jean-Jacques Becker, *The Great War and the French People* (New York: St. Martin's Press, 1986), 63.

and essentially pointless slaughter?" Lloyd George's commentary answers for his war and the wars since.[11]

The public was not told about the war, and the public did not want to know. Many still clung to "the image of war as a fundamentally clean and decent, if rather hazardous, activity." Had soldiers, pressed for the truth, been willing to tell, words might have failed them. More profoundly than censorship, language kept the war's secrets. The era's "high diction" construed the facts of industrialized mass slaughter through the prism of war as a school of character. To dip into Paul Fussell's inspired list in *The Great War and Modern Memory*, in the Georgian English of 1914:

The enemy is	the foe
The front is	the field
Danger is	peril
To attack is	to assail
One's chest is one's	breast
To be stolidly brave is to be	staunch
To be cheerfully brave is to be	plucky
Bravery considered after the fact is	valor
The legs and arms of young men are	limbs
To die is	to perish
The dead are	the fallen[12]

Trench warfare was incommunicable in this language, still favored by press and pulpit, setters of cultural tone. Frederick Henry, an American volunteer ambulance driver serving with the Italian army during its death struggle with the Austrians in Ernest Hemingway's 1929 novel *A Farewell to Arms*, suggests how it sounded to soldiers. When an officer asserts of the men lost during the campaigning season, "What has been done this summer cannot have been in vain," Henry reflects: "I was always embarrassed by the words sacred, glorious, and sacrifice and the expression in vain . . . There were many words that you could not stand to hear and finally only the names of places had dignity . . . Abstract words such as glory, honor, courage or hallow were obscene beside the concrete names of villages, the numbers of regiments, and the dates." Using abstractions to wrest meaning from "sacrifices [that] were like the stockyards at Chicago if nothing was done with the meat," civilians spoke a different language from soldiers. If you knew what we suffered, soldiers thought, you would force the politicians to stop the war. But you don't know, and we can't tell you. Not in words you would understand. Civilian innocence kept the war going. Soldiers resented it, and wished the war would come home.[13]

"They hated the smiling women in the streets," Philip Gibbs wrote of soldiers on leave. "They loathed the old men . . . They prayed God to get the Germans to send Zeppelins to England—to make the people know what war meant."* God did not release the Zeppelins until January 1915. However, the German navy answered Gibbs's prayer on December 16, 1914, with the first foreign attack on the British Isles since John Paul Jones in 1778.[14]

Clausewitz's "fog of war" suggests a parallel concept, the fortuity of war, for the moments when events obey what Frederick the Great called "His Majesty, Chance." In late August 1914 in the Baltic Sea, chance handed the Allies their "principal war-winning weapon," according to Churchill. In thick fog, at night, with Russian warships nearby, the German cruiser *Magdeburg* ran aground on a Russian island in the Gulf of Bothnia. With his ship in shallow water—at daylight pebbles were visible on the Baltic bottom—the captain ordered the signalman to row the ship's dingy out to deeper water in order to throw overboard the *Magdeburg's* lead-lined signal book. But, before he could get away, shells tore into the *Magdeburg* and a few hours later, in Churchill's words, "The body of a drowned German under-officer was picked up by the Russians . . . and clasped in his bosom, by arms rigid in death, were the cipher and signal books of the German Navy." The Russians offered these to the Royal Navy and on an

---

*The animus felt by British soldiers toward civilians during World War I was not repeated in World War II, when soldiers' deaths in battle did not exceed civilian deaths from German bombing until September 1941. "Of course the [bombing] raids caused much suffering and hardship. In the long run they cemented national unity. They were a powerful solvent of class antagonism and ensured, too, that there was none of the hostility between fighting men and civilians which had characterized the first World War." A. J. P. Taylor, *English History, 1914–1945* (New York: Oxford University Press, 1965), 504–5; for civilian deaths, see 502.

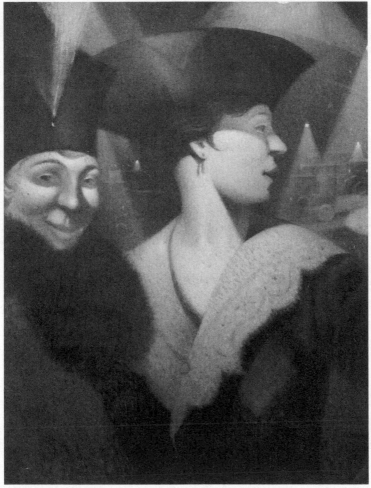

"War Profiteers" (1917) by C. R. W. Nevinson. Soldiers bitterly resented
"business as usual" at home. Newspapers, with their patriotic
falsification of the war, they hated.

October afternoon at the Admiralty in London, Churchill "received
from the hands of our loyal ally these sea-stained priceless documents." Priceless because they enabled the Admiralty to crack the
German naval and diplomatic code.[15]

To master the code took weeks of work by an ill-sorted band of
cryptanalysts, mathematicians, Egyptologists, and professors of German gathered in Room 40 of the Old Admiralty Building—and

even then, to fill a lacuna in the code, they needed a fisherman to turn up at the Admiralty with a parcel of German books netted in the North Sea. But, finally, on December 14, 1914, Room 40 achieved a breakthrough. It confidently reported that five German battle cruisers were leaving their protected base on Germany's North Sea coast on the fifteenth to raid the Yorkshire coast of England on the morning of the sixteenth. Here for the taking, in Churchill's still-excited postwar prose, was "this tremendous prize—the German battle cruiser squadron whose loss would fatally mutilate the whole German Navy." The navy mobilized four battle cruisers from Cromarty, a flotilla of cruisers and destroyers from Rosyth and Scapa, eight submarines, and a squadron of six super-dreadnought battleships to bar the exits from the minefields sown by both sides in those waters and sink the enemy battle cruisers. The trap was set, the weather was clear, the Germans were ignorant.[16]

The Admiralty made no effort to alert the people living along the coast, they were the British bait. The battle cruisers were the *German* bait. Their mission was to attract a sizeable portion of Britain's Grand Fleet and, exploiting their twenty-six-knot speed, lead their pursuers on a chase across the North Sea into the waiting guns and torpedoes of Germany's nearly entire High Sea Fleet. Room 40 had failed to detect this feature of the German plan.[17]

At dawn on December 16 on the eastern edge of the Dogger Bank, destroyers and cruisers from the High Sea Fleet collided with their opposite numbers from Britain's Battle Squadron. The Naval Staff Monograph sets the scene: "A few miles away on the port bow of the High Sea Fleet, isolated and several hours' steaming from home, was the most powerful homogenous squadron of [our] Grand Fleet, the destruction of which would at one blow have . . . placed the British and German fleets on a precisely even footing . . . a condition for which the Germans had been striving since the outbreak of the war." Six British dreadnoughts against twenty German—Room 40 had baited the wrong hook. In the first of a skein of reversals of fortune, however, the fog of war clouded the mind of the German admiral. Minutes from victory, thinking he had encountered the destroyer screen of the twenty-five dreadnought Grand Fleet itself, and mindful of the kaiser's warning that no harm must befall what Churchill derided as

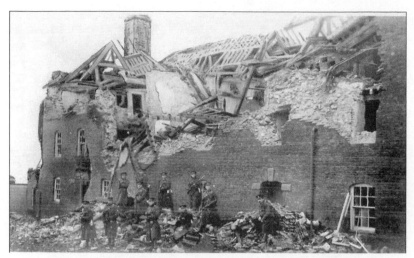

After the raid: the Scarborough Coastguard Station

Germany's "luxury fleet," he turned away and sailed for home, leaving the five German battle cruisers to shift for themselves.[18]

At around seven A.M., a few miles off the resort town of Scarborough, British fishermen were startled as, slicing past them at high speed, black warships made toward the coast. The battle cruisers divided: *Derfflinger* and *Von der Tann* to bombard Scarborough and Whitby while *Sedlitz*, *Blücher*, and *Moltke* would attack Hartlepool. Article 1 of the Hague Conference of 1907 prohibited "the bombardment by naval forces of undefended ports, towns, villages, dwellings or buildings." Scarborough and Whitby were such towns; Hartlepool was defended by a battery of three six-inch guns on the seafront.[19]

The war came home to Scarborough at about eight A.M. A postman was putting letters through the mail slot of a house a street or two back from the coast when he was decapitated by a high-explosive shell, which also killed the woman behind the door waiting for her mail to drop. A baby in its sleep, a maid mailing a letter, Mrs. Duffield on her walk, a wife in her kitchen, her husband at his shop—all were killed "when engaged in the ordinary activities of life," as the *Times*, with the anthropological clarity of first observation, prophetically described war's reach in the age of Guernica, Coventry, Hamburg, Hiroshima, Hanoi, and New York. With teutonic patience, the cruisers fired

More hate for the Hun. Churchill displeased the king by denouncing as
"baby killers" the German sailors who launched five hundred
shells at the undefended town.

broadsides from one side, then came about to exercise the guns facing
seaward on the first pass, firing from six hundred yards. The shelling
knocked down rows of houses, punched holes in the Grand Hotel above
Scarborough beach, gored roofs, tumbled chimneys, and smashed windows. "In one small shop," the *Times* reported, "the window of which
had been blow out, a placard bearing the words, 'Business as Usual,' was
displaced." Is that thunder? a woman near the Scarborough train station,

startled by the noise, asked a passing soldier. No, he replied, "being familiar with the sound."[20]

Casualties were about the equivalent of a day's "wastage" on Britain's 130-mile sector of the western front. No foreign enemy had killed Britons on British soil in over a century. The Royal Navy had prevented it.

At the Admiralty, confidence was high that the "baby killers" would be sunk by noon. The position and puissance of the several British squadrons marked on the map between the Germans and their base promised to distract the public from Scarborough and Hartlepool with victory. But it was not to be. Fog, luck, and insouciant signaling by the British admiral, Sir David Beatty, saved the raiders at four different moments, and by midafternoon they were gone. Speaking for the country, the coroner at the Scarborough inquest asked, "Where was the Navy?"[21]

"We had to bear in silence the censures of our countrymen," Churchill wrote in *The World Crisis* (1923). "We could never admit for fear of compromising our secret information where our squadrons were, nor how near the German raiding cruisers had been to their destruction." As cover for Room 40, the rumor that Britain ran a peerless spy system in Germany was officially encouraged.[22]

On November 30, 1914, the editor of the *Nation*, H. W. Massingham, registered a consensus view of Britain's wartime leader: "If you want a tonic . . . have a look at the Prime Minister. Unquestionably Mr. Asquith is carrying his burden with great courage; with a steady, massive, self-reliant and unswerving confidence which is in itself a moral asset of no slight value."[23]

War had rendered Herbert Asquith's British phlegm bracing. As early as August, *Punch* had spied out this paradox in a cartoon, "Cool Stuff," depicting Asquith keeping his wry countenance despite the kettles-full of hot criticism being poured over him. "His personality is worth to the Empire an army in the field, a squadron of *Queen Elizabeths* at sea," a Conservative politician wrote as late as March 1915. A postwar critic, with the full record of Asquith's two years as wartime prime minister available to him, questioned whether Asquith's personality was the right stuff for a country at war. After nearly a decade in office, Asquith, a bibulous social lion who did not start work until eleven thirty A.M., was calm because spent, "a cistern and not a fountain." Sir William Robertson, the chief of the Imperial General Staff in late 1916, when Lloyd George led a successful cabinet revolt that toppled Asquith from power, drew a similar distinction between Asquith and his successor: "Asquith was too judicious a temperament to run a war, whereas Lloyd George by contrast was the only civilian leader who could say 'Yes' or 'No' without hesitation." Yet, in the

British phlegm. It was reassuring in the first months of the war, but Asquith had to transcend it to save France.

supreme crisis of the early war, the cool leader caught fire, the cistern overflowed, H. H. Asquith said no.[24]

Crashing blindly into a German army of two hundred thousand on its march into Belgium, the seventy-five-thousand man British Expeditionary Force (BEF) suffered severe casualties and was retreating alongside its French ally when, in an August 30 telegram, Sir John French, the British commander, informed London that the BEF was "shattered" and insisted on withdrawing it from the battle line for at least eight days and marching it south, for refitting behind Paris.[25]

"Eight days! Eight days! Within eight days, will not the Germans be in Paris?" Raymond Poincaré desperately noted in his diary. The French president appealed to Asquith to overrule his general. Breaking from his bridge game, Asquith called an emergency postmidnight meeting of the cabinet. To the few ministers reachable at short notice he read out Poincaré's moving letter, then paused, as if waiting for a volunteer to speak his mind for him. "He never spoke a word in Council if he could get his way without it," Churchill observed of his taciturn chief. But now Asquith spoke: "If [the BEF quits the field] the French will be left uncovered, Paris will fall, the French Army will be cut off and we shall never be able to hold our heads up in the world again. Better that the British Army should perish than that this shame should fall on us."[26]

Sir Edward Grey, the foreign secretary, initially favored letting General French act as he thought right—but Asquith's words swayed him. Grey voted with a unanimous cabinet to dispatch that totem of British militarism, Lord Kitchener, Kitchener of Khartoum (K of K) newly (and eagerly) recruited by the Liberal government to serve as secretary of state for war, to France "to put the fear of God" into General French.★ Asquith's intervention saved the Anglo-French alliance, the French army, and in all probability, France.[27]

★ Here is Kitchener as seen by Vera Brittain in her diary: "Friday September 4th: Kitchener is said to be over at Ostend with an army of 500,000 composed of men of all nations. They are said to intend, after Germany has been gradually lured to Paris, to attack the back of the German Lines . . . The move is a grand one, while the very name of Kitchener, & his presence on the actual battlefield will fill the British with courage, & strike terror into German minds."

On a military decision with political implications, and stiffened by K of K, Asquith could wrest control of the war from his generals. But suppose the politics were opaque, and Kitchener obdurate. What would Asquith do *then*? Events set in motion at the turn of the year would soon answer.

Winston Churchill is "irredeemably associated with the operation at the Dardanelles," the debacle depicted in the 1981 film *Gallipoli*. But blaming Churchill for the Dardanelles is like blaming Donald Rumsfeld, secretary of defense in the George W. Bush administration, for the Iraq War. Like President Bush in 2003, Asquith in 1914 was the "decider," not Churchill. Asquith's responsibility for the Dardanelles can be traced through some unusual documents—his love letters.[28]

The war had transformed the prime minister's epistolary romance with Venetia Stanley, his twenty-seven-year-old confidante and his daughter Violet's closest friend, from an indiscretion into a crime. Specifically, what the smitten sixty-two-year-old was doing—sharing intelligence with Venetia that German spies would kill for—violated the Official Secrets Act enacted by his own government in 1911. At a time when the government was monitoring homing pigeons lest they be used to send messages to the enemy, its leader was tipping Venetia off about matters ranging from the sinking of the battleship *Audacious* by a mine to this revelation of December 21, 1914: "By the way, Winston revealed to me as a profound secret, wh. he is not going even to breathe to Grey, that to-morrow (Tues) the Germans are contemplating a new naval adventure against us. So keep your eyes open, as I shall. I shall say nothing to any other human being." That the Admiralty had advance knowledge of German naval movements was Britain's *top* secret. Asquith's indiscretion looks especially flagrant when set against this Admiralty directive issued by Churchill: "The less said to outsiders about naval matters, by speech or letter . . . the better. Many of the most harmful disclosures are made innocently and unwittingly . . . They are not in any circumstances to write letters which have the slightest reference to naval matters, without submitting them to the Censor beforehand."[29]

Venetia got the inner history of the Dardanelles livened by declarations like "I love you more than ever—more than life!" and "I can honestly say that not an hour passes without thought of you" (plausible

THE
DARDANELLES
1915

RUSSIAN
EMPIRE

Danube R.

ROMANIA

Bucharest •

Danube R.

0 Miles   50
0 Kilometers   50

BULGARIA

Black Sea

The Bosporus

Golden Horn

Constantinople

*Sea of
Marmara*

*Aegean
Sea*

TURKEY

Gallipoli

The Dardanelles

© 2012 Jeffrey L. Ward

considering that in August 1914, a consequential month in British history, he wrote her twenty-six letters, some upwards of three thousand words long).* Asquith played up the role of Churchill, who appears—her letters to Asquith have not survived—to have fascinated Venetia, rousing flashes of jealousy from the prime minister: "I did not know until your letter today that you liked Winston quite so much as all that." In early November, days after the British lost two ships in an action off the coast of Chile "far from glorious to the Navy," Asquith warned his first lord of the Admiralty that it was "time he bagged something & broke some crockery." His hold on office weakened by growing criticism of his conduct of it, Churchill did not need to be prodded twice. "His volatile mind is at present set on Turkey and Bulgaria . . . he wants to organize a heroic adventure against Gallipoli and the Dardanelles: to which I am altogether opposed," Asquith confided on December 3. On Christmas Eve, Churchill "[is] meditating fearsome plans of a highly aggressive kind to replace the present policy of masterly inactivity." Asquith shared his young minister's frustration with the siege warfare of the trenches, and he approvingly quoted to Venetia Churchill's question from a crucial December 30 memorandum: "Are there not other alternatives than sending our armies to chew barbed wire in Flanders?"[30]

Alternatives were explored, but when, on January 2, Grand Duke Nicholas, commander in chief of the Russian army, asked Kitchener

---

* "The publication of the Asquith letters [in 1982] . . . unleashed a rash of speculation on what A. J. P. Taylor called, in his own review of the book, 'the burning question: did they or didn't they?' " Perhaps the closest student of the matter, Naomi B. Levine, believes the answer is yes: "There is no clear-cut evidence to support a firm conclusion that Venetia was Asquith's mistress . . . But the nature of the Prime Minister, his reputation as an importunate lecher, his need to touch, to talk with and be with women, [his wife] Margot's illness and subsequent disinterest in sex, Venetia's totally unconventional and liberated views . . . , her lack of any sense of sin or morality, and some of the language used in the letters themselves strongly suggest that the affair had a strong sexual component, even if actual consummation may not have taken place." Naomi B. Levine, *Politics, Religion and Love: The Story of H. H. Asquith, Venetia Stanley and Edwin Montagu, Based on the Life and Letters of Edwin Samuel Montagu* (New York: NYU Press, 1991), 233, 235. "Winston Churchill's daughter, Mary, later wrote that her mother Clementine disliked 'Mr. Asquith's predilection for peering down "Pennsylvania Avenue" (the contemporary expression for a lady's cleavage) whenever he was seated next to a pretty woman.' " 112.

for "a demonstration of some kind against Turks elsewhere, either naval or military" to relieve Turkish pressure on the Russian army in the Caucasus, the War Council settled on the Dardanelles, the forty-mile strait between the Aegean and the Sea of Marmara flanked by the barren Gallipoli Peninsula and the Asian mainland. To Venetia, Asquith mocked the expertise on the Near East displayed by some makers of Near East policy, telling of finding Lloyd George "searching for Gallipoli on a map of Spain."*[31]

Ignorance stimulated grandiosity. The attack was to be no mere demonstration. Its objectives were to occupy Constantinople, open the Bosporus to Russian shipping (enabling the tsarist government to finance its loans from the Allies) and Western arms shipments to Russia, drive Turkey out of the war, and draw the neutral Balkan states into it on the winning side. Churchill went further, imagining British gunboats steaming up the Danube to attack Vienna.[32]

Seizing Constantinople would make tangible the British promise to Russia that as King George V assured the Russian ambassador in any postwar settling of accounts with the Turks, "this city must be yours." Grey had urged the Straits on Russia to steer its foreign minister, Serge Sazonov, away from the alarming war aims he unveiled in September, one of which—the dismemberment of Germany—would be realized by Soviet Russia only after the defeat of Nazi Germany in 1945. Grey, in 1914, wanted to preserve Germany and Austria-Hungary, whose breakup Russia also sought, as Great Powers to maintain a postwar balance of power in Europe against Russia. His conception was "to keep Russia out of Prague, Vienna, Budapest, Belgrade, Bucharest, and Sofia [and Berlin] by installing it in Constantinople." Russia must stay in the war, and if this required reversing fifty years of British policy on the Straits, or overriding French

---

*"To his credit Lloyd George did not fall into the trap of underrating Turkish soldiers as a fighting force. He noted their devoted resistance in the last phase of the Balkan war of 1912 when Constantinople was in danger . . . Yet Lloyd George's insight was only partial. He managed to subscribe to the view that a British fleet appearing off Constantinople would, by itself or with minimal military assistance, bring about the capitulation of the Turkish Empire." Trevor Wilson, *The Myriad Faces of War: Britain and the Great War, 1914–1918* (Cambridge, UK: Polity Press, 1986), 112, n. 8.

objections to awarding the Straits to Russia, or refusing Greek help in taking Constantinople, something anathema to Petrograd, so be it.[33]

After the war, the Bolsheviks published the text of the Anglo-Franco-Russian Straits Agreement of 1914–1915 to expose the territorial motives of the Allies in what Trotsky labeled "the great imperialist slaughter." From her cabinet seat ("What do you think, my darling?") Venetia Stanley witnessed imperialism's spoils being divvied up. Lapsing into the shorthand of empire used to check off exotic places and peoples on the map like the claret and sole on a gentleman's club menu, Asquith explained that Russia's claim to Constantinople and the Dardanelles was acceptable—provided "both we and France should get a substantial share of the carcase of the Turk."[34]

These maximalist war and postwar goals were to be achieved by minimal means: An all-naval attack on the Gallipoli forts by a fleet of obsolete battleships. The odd reference among the principals to the impressionable "Oriental mind" suggests the racial hauteur with which these Englishmen approached "the Turk," who, their war plan assumed, would surrender at the sight of a British tar. "If the fleet gets through the narrows," Kitchener assured one of his generals, "Constantinople will fall of itself." This of a city of about one million people that with its sheltering bay, the Golden Horn, forms what one historian calls "a natural fortress, difficult . . . to attack."[35]

It might have worked—at least the ships might have got through the Straits—if the naval attack had been combined with a landing of troops on the European side of the peninsula, the troops to attack the Turkish forts from the rear while the fleet engaged them from the front. But at a February 24, 1915, meeting of the council, Kitchener set his face against sending troops.

"We are all agreed (except K) that the naval adventure in the Dardanelles should be backed up by a strong military force," Asquith wrote Venetia later that day. "I say 'except K' but he quite agrees in principle. Only he is very sticky about sending out there the 29th Division, which is the best one we have left at home . . . He wants to have something in hand, in case the Germans are so far successful against the Russians . . . as to be able to dispatch Westwards a huge army . . . to try & force through Joffre and French's lines." Cool, skeptical

Asquith had fallen for the geostrategic romance of the attack: "One must take a lot of chances in war & I am strongly of the opinion that the chance of forcing the Dardanelles, & occupying Constantinople, & cutting Turkey in half, and rousing on our side the whole Balkan peninsula, presents such an opportunity that we ought to hazard a lot elsewhere rather than forgo it." But Asquith, who was only the elected leader of the British people, understood the risk of challenging K of K. "If he can be convinced, well & good: but to discard his advice and overrule his judgment on a military question is to take a grave responsibility. So I am rather anxious."[36]

Backed by Kitchener, Asquith had overruled Sir John French, but French was only a general. Kitchener was a symbol. His iron stare, militant mustache, and pointing finger on the famous recruiting poster above the legend YOUR COUNTRY NEEDS YOU helped motivate three million Britons to volunteer for service in the first two years of the war. "He is not a great man," Asquith's wife, Margot, reportedly said of him. "He is a great poster." And therefore a great political problem. With his ties to the Tory Party and press, and a hold over the British public such that "angry crowds" burned copies of the *Daily Mail* in the London Stock Exchange and circulation fell by a million after it blamed Kitchener for a dearth of shells at the front, K of K had the last word on all matters military.[37]

A 1906 Admiralty study put before Asquith of a "Joint Naval and Military Attack upon the Dardanelles" did not so much as consider a ships-alone attack, citing Admiral Nelson's dictum that "any sailor who attacked a fort was a fool" (he lost an arm attacking one). In 1911, Churchill himself had informed the cabinet that "it is no longer possible to force the Dardanelles and nobody should expose a modern fleet to such peril"—which by 1915 included 82 guns of large caliber housed in 35 forts and strongpoints that the Turks had been working on continuously for centuries, 230 mobile guns and howitzers, minefields protected by hidden batteries and swarms of floating mines. This history and those facts were why "every naval officer at the Admiralty . . . [has] come out strongly against unaided action by the fleet," Maurice Hankey, secretary of the War Council, informed Asquith.

Yet Asquith succumbed to Churchill's "rugged fluency" on behalf of an all-naval attack. "The idea caught on at once," Hankey recalled of this decisive January meeting of the War Council. "The whole atmosphere changed. Fatigue was forgotten." When Churchill had "a scheme agitating his powerful mind . . . he is indefatigable in pressing it upon the acceptance of everyone who matters in the decision," Lloyd George observed. At the War Council on January 13, 1915, Churchill was indefatigable. To prevail at such moments, he recommended "flair based on previous study."[38]

The first attack, on March 18, 1915, broke a good deal of Allied crockery: Out of the twelve battleships engaged, mines sunk three, one with the loss of nearly all hands. The Turks lost a handful of guns. Weeks earlier, in the Caucasus, the Russians had routed the Turkish army that Grand Duke Nicholas had asked the British to prevent being reinforced from the west with a "demonstration," voiding the rationale for Gallipoli even "before a gun had been fired" there.* Resisting pressure to mount another attack from Churchill, in possession of an intercept from the kaiser to the German admiral at Constantinople indicating, wrongly, that the Gallipoli forts were out of ammunition, the British admiral on the spot, John de Robeck, decided that ships could not "take" the Dardanelles alone. Soldiers were needed to silence the Turkish forts, naval gunfire at ranges as close as seven hundred yards having failed. Kitchener, fearing that "the effect

─────────────────

*This battle, at Sarikamish in Russian Armenia, began the Armenian genocide. "At least 150,000 Armenians who lived on the Russian side of the frontier were serving in the Tsar's army. [The Ottoman minister of war] Enver [Pasha] persuaded himself that his defeat . . . had been due to three units of Armenian volunteers, who included men who had deserted from the Ottoman side." As the Russians advanced into Anatolia, the Ottoman soldiers turned on Armenians on the Turkish side of the frontier. Ottoman officials ordered the execution of Armenian leaders suspected of fomenting rebellion in concert with their coreligionists, the Russians. As early as April 27, the Russians claimed that "the populations of over a hundred villages had been massacred." On May 25, 1915, the Ottoman minister of the interior "announced that Armenians living near the war zones would be deported to Syria and Mosul . . . The violence of war against the enemy without enabled, and was seen to justify, extreme measures against the enemy within." An estimated 1.2 to 2 million Armenians died in these massacres and deportations. Hew Strachan, *The First World War* (New York: Penguin, 2003), 109–15.

of a defeat in the Orient would be very serious," promptly overruled himself and dispatched the soldiers.[39]

The British had forfeited the only advantage possessed by attacking troops in the war—surprise. All the advantages now lay with the defending Turks, who had time to reinforce their defenses with thousands of men and hundreds of guns from Austria's Skoda works. The "British gave me four full weeks before their great landing," General Liman von Sanders, commanding the German Military Mission in Turkey, recalled in his memoirs; "the time was just sufficient to complete the essential arrangements." And with that landing on April 25 began one of the "the First World War's human catastrophes," an epic of fruitless sacrifice by the Australian, New Zealand, British, and French invaders and tenacious resistance by the Turkish defenders, "laying to rest the notion of the Turk as a worthless fighting man," and creating a foundation myth of modern Turkey and its mythic hero, Mustafa Kemal. On April 25, in the decisive action of the campaign, he rallied his troops to hold the heights of Sari Bair against attacking Anzac troops with the instantly legendary command, "I don't order you to attack. I order you to die."[40]

As for the fighting on Gallipoli: "We have been amusing ourselves by trying to discover the longest period of absolute quiet," an Australian colonel wrote home from the Anzac Cove beachhead. "We have been fighting now for 22 days, all day and all night, and most of us think that . . . the longest period during which there was absolutely no sound of gun or rifle fire throughout the whole of that time was 10 seconds. One man says he was able on one occasion to count fourteen but nobody believes him." That testimony supplies a mordant coda to Asquith's flippancy to Venetia Stanley about a division of troops departing from England for Gallipoli: "How lucky they are to escape Flanders & the trenches and be sent to the 'gorgeous East.'"[41]

Venetia competed with the war for his attention. He would divert himself from discussions on strategy to write her a few lines. For example, on January 13, 1915: "We are now (4 p.m.) in the midst of our War Council, wh. began at 12 . . . A most interesting discussion, but so confidential and secret that I won't put anything down on paper, but I will talk fully to you to-morrow (if we meet then) or if not in the course of our drive Friday." A letter from her had arrived at three,

FOR CONSTANTINOPLE

**THESE SEVEN-LEAGUE TRENCH BOOTS OUGHT TO
DO THE TRICK**

They didn't. This painting was made by an Anzac soldier serving on Gallipoli.
It expresses the strategic conception behind the attack and the imperial swagger
soon lost in dubious battle. The Anzacs "were in constant trouble with the
British authorities responsible for discipline." General Allenby would not have
them in his Egyptian theater. In France "they were the bane of authority,"
providing "the highest rates of desertion, insubordination and venereal disease."
See Douglas Gill and Gloden Dallas, "Mutiny at Etaples Base in 1917,"
Past & Present, no. 69 (November 1975): 100.

and he had stirred himself by "taking one or two furtive glances" at it
while his ministers debated the next act of the war and the afternoon
waned and "to-morrow" approached. He said nothing until the end,
"when I intervened with my conclusions." One of these was to attack
the Dardanelles.[42]

Blamed for what the *Morning Post* called THE DARDANELLES BLUNDER, which it defined as overriding the advice of "his naval colleagues" that "the Navy alone" could not carry the straits, Churchill was forced out of the Admiralty in May 1915 as the Tories' price for forming a coalition government with the panicky Liberals.* Churchill's official biographer, Sir Martin Gilbert, suggests that Asquith only agreed to pay it because his heart was broken.[43]

For Venetia Stanley, whose "guiding principle" was in her words to get "the maximum of fun" out of life, the secret sharer relationship with the prime minister had become a "crushing and frightening emotional burden," Asquith's biographer, Roy Jenkins conjectures. Asquith sensed something was wrong. "I thought once or twice yesterday, for the first time in our intercourse, that I rather bored you," he mildly complained after a weekend visit with her at the end of April. On May 12, "the soul of my life" shattered him with the news that she had decided to marry Edwin Montagu, Asquith's former parliamentary private secretary and current holder of the minor cabinet office of chancellor of the Duchy of Lancaster. Montagu had asked for Stanley's hand at least twice since 1912, pressing his suit ("O, how I pant for you") despite her declarations that she found him physically "repulsive." A more formidable barrier for a young woman raised in country-house luxury was the condition in Montagu's father's will that to inherit his fortune Edwin had to marry within the Jewish faith. When Venetia converted to meet that condition, she earned her family's censure for "turning Jewish for 8000 pounds a year."[44]

Venetia as a "Jewess" Asquith found "repugnant and repulsive." On May 14, he wrote her:

> Most Loved,
> As you know well this breaks my heart.

---

*From the official Australian history: "So through Churchill's excess of imagination, a layman's ignorance of artillery, and the fatal power of young enthusiasm to convince older and slower brains, the tragedy of Gallipoli was born." Churchill quotes this damning judgment on himself in *The World Crisis,* vol. 2, 1915 (London: Butterworth, 1923), 122.

I couldn't bear to come and see you.

I can only pray God to bless you—and help me. Yours[45]

Three days later, with Churchill girding to defend the government's handling of the Dardanelles before Parliament, Bonar Law, the Conservative leader, sought out Lloyd George at the Treasury to warn him to expect dirty weather from the opposition over Churchill, the Dardanelles, and the sensational charge printed in the *Times* on the fourteenth that the army was running out of shells. Lloyd George saw that the only way to forestall a damaging Conservative attack on the Liberals' conduct of the war was to invite the Tories into the government. He asked Law to wait and, taking the private passage running from the back of the Treasury, walked over to No. 10 Downing St. To Asquith he conveyed Law's threat and added his own—that he would resign unless Asquith removed the scandal-scarred production of munitions from Lord Kitchener's portfolio of responsibilities. With uncharacteristic precipitation Asquith said yes to both demands. "His torment had undermined his resolve," Gilbert concludes, echoing the opinion of Asquith's daughter-in-law, Cynthia, who confided to her diary: "Perhaps, if truth were known it is really the cause of the Coalition."[46]

Churchill's torment—"I am finished!"—will strike us as premature.[47]

9

HOME FRONTS II

We were hungry all the time; we had forgotten how it felt to have our stomachs full.

—A German man, recalling his wartime childhood

A S SNOW CRUSTED the Flanders mud in late November and early December 1914, Belgium nettled its British friends no less than its German conquerors. America had adopted "plucky little" Belgium, its travails publicized in full-page ads in major newspapers and on movie screens everywhere, and both sides were leery of offending opinion in the great neutral democracy.

To be sure, for Americans of articulate conscience (and British sympathies) it was already too late for Germany. By breaking its treaty commitments to honor Belgium's neutrality; by pulverizing Belgium's frontier fortresses with a terror weapon, the long-range 420 mm Big Bertha howitzer firing cement-crushing shells weighing over seventeen hundred pounds; by incinerating whole villages and towns and cultural monuments like the fifteenth-century library at the University of Louvain; by using Belgian civilians as human shields in firefights with Belgian and French troops and, from panic over phantom guerrillas, by executing at least six thousand other civilians—atrocities given early and sensational circulation in the United States by British propaganda—Germany had irretrievably alienated a formidable current of American opinion. "That an innocent nation in no way involved in the quarrel of these nations should thus be made the battlefield and offered as a sacrifice on the altar of

German militarism is the tragedy of the twentieth century," wrote
one American editor, speaking for many others. "History will look
long with angry countenance on this crime and follow it with its
nemesis."[1]

Belgium was devastated, Belgians hungry. How hungry the British
learned in late September when an emissary from Antwerp arrived in
London to purchase food and plea for help. An extraordinary American answered the call.

In a January letter to Woodrow Wilson the American ambassador
to Great Britain, Walter Hines Page, described meeting "a simple,
modest, energetic little man who began his career in California and
will end it in Heaven . . . But for him Belgium would have starved."
An American can't read about the relief of Belgium without wistful
pride in the can-do spirit of Herbert Hoover and his America.[2]

The forty-year-old Hoover was among the world's most successful
mining engineers, with interests in silver, lead, zinc, and copper pits
from Bolivia to Siberia. For years he had lived in London, the center
of international finance for the mining industry. England was not the
likeliest social fit for the blunt, square-jawed American described by
a French banker as "the type of American businessman" with "a face
somewhat brutal, *fruste* [rough, unpolished]." An orphan at nine, raised
by a succession of relatives, so poor that he lived in a shack off the
Stanford campus as a member of its first class, Hoover, every inch
the self-made man, felt the sting of British snobbery. On a transatlan-
tic trip to America, he related in his autobiography, he shared a table
with "an English lady of great cultivation" with whom he enjoyed
good talk at mealtimes. At the farewell breakfast, she asked, "'I hope
you will forgive my dreadful curiosity, but I should like awfully to
know—what is your profession?' I replied that I was an engineer. She
emitted an involuntary exclamation and [said], 'Why, I thought you
were a gentleman.'"[3]

Weeks before Europe fell into war, Hoover and his wife, Lou,
booked passage on the *Lusitania* to take their boys to school in America. On August 3, in a changed world, Hoover "inquired by telephone of the steamship office if the ship would be sailing as scheduled.
The young woman at the other end said, 'Sure, she will be sailing to

Herbert Hoover in 1917

Germany. Don't you know there's a war on?' I concluded that the *Lusitania* would not sail." He could not know it at the time, "but on Monday, August 3rd, my engineering career was over forever." Later that day a call from the American embassy in London put him on "the slippery road of public life."[4]

Partly on a reputation for inspired competence earned during the war, he commanded that road until he slipped on the Great Depression. Leave it to the "wonder boy," President Calvin Coolidge remarked about a problem he bequeathed to his successor. Coolidge spoke sardonically, but at both ends of the Great War, Europeans would have meant "wonder boy" sincerely. Recalling a time when people were eating coal dust, wood shavings, and sand, Peter Drucker, a pioneer of Hoover's discipline of management, testified, "Like practically every child in Vienna, I was saved by Herbert Hoover whose feeding organization provided school lunches. They left me with a lasting aversion to porridge and cocoa—but definitely saved my life and that of millions of children throughout Continental Europe."[5]

The caller from the American embassy asked Hoover to help a crowd of Americans milling outside the gates—the first contingent of tens of thousands of travelers, including thirty thousand teachers, fleeing the war zone. They were angry. Many had run out of money. All wanted to get home *now* but, having booked passage on ships not scheduled to leave for weeks and unable to cash American checks at British banks fearing war-driven runs, had no idea how or with what. Something must be done. Doing was Hoover's passion. He contacted his engineer friends in London and, shortly, "we were on top of our job"—raising and disbursing more than a million dollars and arranging passage to America for 120,000 people.[6]

That mass movement of humanity completed, Hoover was packing to return to America when a brother American engineer, just arrived from Brussels, visited him. Millard Shaler had slipped through the German lines with enough money to buy twenty-five hundred tons of food for the hungry citizens of Brussels. Refugees from other parts of Belgium reported hunger in their localities; the Germans were foraging all the food they could seize, leaving nothing to the natives. "It's better that the Belgians starve than that we do," the Prussian finance minister advised Bethmann Hollweg. Shaler was a member of the Committee for the Relief of Belgium (CRB) formed by a group of American expatriates to relieve the stricken country of nine million people. Hoover's prodigies on behalf of his stranded countrymen made him the man to lead it.[7]

"I was not bothered over administrative matters such as purchase and overseas shipment and internal transport of large quantities of material," Hoover wrote. "Any engineer could do that." In a letter to a Belgian priest Hoover expanded on "that":

To beg, borrow and steal nearly $1.8 million worth of food every week; to ship it overseas from America, Australia, the Argentine, and India; to transverse three belligerent lines; transport it through a country with a wholly demoralized transportation service; to see that it reaches civilians only, and that it is adapted to every condition from babyhood to old age and to do this with a machinery operated by the self-denial of volunteer effort, is a labor only rendered possible by the most steadfast teamwork on the part of all.

The team included a handful of American engineers, forty American Rhodes Scholars studying at Oxford and recruited by Hoover to monitor food deliveries in Belgium—these few Americans and forty thousand Belgian and French women responsible for feeding 12,500 communes.[8]

Such Herculean administrative challenges did not trouble Hoover and his engineers. What did was the politics of hunger. The Belgian people were caught between "a German army of occupation and a British naval blockade." Hoover worried that "the fixity of opinion on both sides as to the righteousness of their respective attitudes was such that the Belgians would starve before responsibilities could be settled." The blockade barred shipments of food to Belgium. Winston Churchill had convinced his Cabinet colleagues that by feeding the Belgians the Allies would be relieving the Germans of the burden of ruling a starving people. The first lord of the Admiralty hectored the Foreign Office to charge Hoover, under suspicion for visiting Belgium, with being a German spy and haul him before the King's Bench. "After tedious hearings," Hoover wrote, "we were exonerated and eulogized."[9]

Persuading the British not only to lift the blockade but also to pay for the food to feed their ally—private charity could not raise the needed sums—Hoover discovered his inner politician. In early December, Prime Minister Asquith agreed to see him. Hoover later told the American minister to Belgium, Brand Whitlock, his version of what transpired.

Beforehand, Hoover wrote out a letter to his fellow Stanford alumnus, Will Irwin, a well-connected journalist then in New York, instructing him to "hold this until I send a cablegram releasing it, then blow the gaff, and let the work of revictualing go up in a loud report that shall resound over the world to England's detriment." He brought

And the Greatest of These Is Charity

CALIFORNIA'S AID TO THE STARVING BELGIANS

The American farmer to the rescue. Persuading the British and
German governments to let neutral America open its cornucopia to
Belgium was not easy, but Hoover was up to the job.
There was nothing, it seemed, he couldn't do.

the letter with him to see Asquith, and made his pitch for the Allies
to feed Belgium. Asquith called that "a monstrous idea." Britain
would never allow food to be sent "simply to fill the vacuum created
by the German requisitions."[10]

Hoover played the American card, declaring that England "had
America's sympathy only because America feels pity for suffering Belgium." Then, handing Asquith a copy of his letter to Irwin, he threatened the PM: "I will send [this] telegram at once, and tomorrow

morning the last vestige of pity for England in America will disappear. Do you want me to do it?"

Asquith fleered. He was prime minister. They were sitting in No. 10 Downing Street. He was not "accustomed" to being spoken to in that way. This American engineer was no a gentleman. "On the ground that my emotion for the results which must ensue from a negative reply on his part, was sufficient to justify any tone which I used," Hoover apologized.

Asquith recovered his dignity sufficiently to say, "You told me you were no diplomat, but I think you are an excellent diplomat, only your methods are not diplomatic."

Appearing before the whole cabinet (including Churchill) on December 7, Hoover again wielded "the club of public opinion" and again prevailed. Sir Edward Grey, the foreign secretary, guided the cabinet in American matters, and it was his constant refrain that "the surest way to lose this war would be to antagonize Washington." Subject to the condition that the Germans agree not to steal it and that Hoover warrant they didn't, the British would sustain the Belgian people.[11]

In real time Hoover spoke no ill of the Germans. A week before Christmas, with the blockade lifted, he told the *Times* that of the ten million dollars' worth of food already provided "not one mouthful has gone down a German throat yet—we have had nothing but help." Truth waited for his *Memoirs*. Passing from Holland into Belgium for the first of forty visits, "I had an indescribable feeling of entering a land of imprisonment." In Berlin he found "something . . . automatic and inhuman" in the officials, civilian and military, all in uniform, with whom he discussed the British deal.[12]

Diplomatically, he allowed that while shooting Belgian civilians during the war's first days might be excused on grounds of military necessity—welcome words coming from a Quaker humanitarian—continued levies on Belgium's meager foodstocks, inviting mass starvation, would brand Germany with the "mark of Cain" before history and American public opinion. Conversely, "No German act would do more to win over the American people" than ceasing that practice. Wall Street money was flowing into England and the seaboard elite was strongly Anglophile, but Berlin had not given up on the American

Nothing that the American people have had the privilege of doing during the war has more deeply enlisted their interest and Sympathy than the relief of the Sufferings of the stricken population of Belgium

Woodrow Wilson

Note to Herbert Hoover from Woodrow Wilson (1917)

heartland. Hoover knew when he played it that the American card would win this hand. The Germans accepted his terms and granted him the freedom of Belgium.[13]

At a feeding center in Brussels, he and Brand Whitlock wept as adults and children, some in wooden shoes, filed past them for soup and bread and a special high-calorie cracker made of fats, cocoa, sugar, and "containing every chemical needed for children" cooked up by Hoover's can-do-anything engineers. The food came from America. Each of Iowa's ninety-nine counties contributed a carload of flour;

Salt Lake City, fifty cars; Alabama, a shipload from Mobile. Through contacts at the Chicago Mercantile Exchange, Hoover had worked the greater farm belt. The first shipments were gifts: thereafter, the British paid, but, with Old Glory stamped on every sack of flour or grain, the United States got the credit. A Belgian diplomat told Whitlock that no country in history had ever been so "kind" to another. In truth American farmers made money off Belgium relief. That hardly signified to the citizens of Brussels who, to celebrate Washington's birthday, marched through the streets of their German-occupied city waving homemade American flags.[14]

Writing to an English friend at year's end, the essayist M. Andre Chevrillon marveled at the transformation wrought by the declaration of war on August 4: "I thought I knew the French, but they astonish me. The change in less than a week from political agitation and the atmosphere of the Caillaux trial to discipline and silence and unanimous determination was marvelous. It shows how little one knows of the hidden depths that lie under the more or less tossy and frothy surface of the nation."[15]

Featured in twenty *New York Times* stories and editorials in July, Joseph Caillaux received only two mentions in August and one in September noting his appointment as paymaster with the rank of lieutenant to an Army Corps headquartered at Bethune. He disappeared from the French press, the government fearing that his name might raise hopes for an early peace (Woodrow Wilson fell under the same ban).

The German press operated under no such constraint. German newspapers had criticized the inferior quality of France's artillery powder, alleging that it often failed to ignite since profit-gouging arms makers made it from ground-up old vests rather than fine cotton. That is the background of the cartoon appearing in the satirical magazine *Kladderadatsch* on August 2, 1914, the day before Germany declared war on France, depicting two artillery officers consoling Madame Caillaux. "If Madame Caillaux had used a French cannon instead of a Browning," the caption reads, "Calmette would still be alive."[16]

In June, Caillaux and Jean Jaurès agreed to form a ministry of the Left and President Raymond Poincaré said he was resigned to naming Caillaux premier. In August, Jaurès was dead and Caillaux a pariah, a symbol of the French culture war inked over by the German invasion. Thus when Joseph and Henriette Caillaux sought diversion in Paris, the grand restaurants refused to serve them; their patrons, perhaps guilty over reveling in the tossy and frothy of the trial, demanded it. When Caillaux complained of this treatment to the military governor of Paris, he was given fifteen days of "rigorous military detention" for quitting his post in Bethune. After his release, the Caillaux were dining in a local café crowded with English officers when Joseph, believing the Englishmen were laughing at him, burst from his chair and threw a punch at one of them—unhappily for Caillaux, a boxer in civilian life. Sir John French demanded Caillaux's removal from proximity to his army. The French government obliged, sending Caillaux on a mission to South America. In mid-December he arrived in Buenos Aires, where, the New York Times reported, "The press comment on his presence is not at all cordial."[17]

From early 1915 Raymond Poincaré believed that Caillaux was at the center of a group of businessmen and journalists discussing a separate peace with German diplomats and accepting cash from the German government to influence French policy. Praise from across the Rhine by papers like the Kölnische Zeitung contrasting Caillaux the peacemaker of 1911 with Poincaré the war-plotting revanchist reinforced suspicions that Joseph Caillaux was Germany's man if not Germany's agent: "If Monsieur Caillaux had remained in office, if Madame Caillaux's gesture had not been made, the plot against the peace of Europe . . . would not have succeeded." Right-wing newspapers gave currency to conspiracy theories linking Caillaux to a "Jewish-German spy invasion." Volunteering as a military nurse at a Vichy hospital, Henriette was booed off the wards, while on the street Action Française thugs attacked the couple. They fled to Rome, where Caillaux was overheard boasting that war weariness would sweep him back to power and he would negotiate peace with Germany. When these heresies reached Paris, the press attacked him for "defeatism," coining a new word. "The chief of the pacifists . . . is extremely unpopular," Izvolski reported to St. Petersburg.[18]

Poincaré feared otherwise. No French leader could forget the precedent of 1871, when in the wake of France's defeat by Germany rebels seized Paris and proclaimed the revolutionary government of the Commune. In late July 1914, Poincaré addressed the danger of wartime dissension in his diary: "Although Austria has declared war on Russia, Count Szecsen still remains comfortably in the Rue de Varenne and tells his dentist: 'The Commune will save us.' But the Commune is the sequel of defeat, and, no thank you, my dear Mr. Ambassador, we are not there yet."[19]

Had they got *there* in 1917? After years of stalemate indistinguishable from defeat, would a new Commune save the enemy? Poincaré saw discouraging signs everywhere. Under the strain of war his union sacrée had broken up, the only Catholic minister and the only socialist minister resigning from the government in September 1917. A wave of strikes in the clothing industry spread to munitions factories. Defeatist propaganda, circulated in newspapers friendly to Caillaux, was blamed. In the spring of 1917, in despair at being thrown away in costly frontal assaults, whole regiments of soldiers mutinied; by August what one senior officer called "a general strike against the war" had destabilized 49 of the army's 113 infantry divisions. The bad war news would soon get worse. The United States was a year away from fielding an army in France. Revolutionary Russia was pulling out of the war, freeing up hundreds of thousands of German soldiers on the eastern front to swell an attack, expected in early 1918, on the western front. That replay of August 1914 nearly four years on would give the lie to Allied propaganda that Germany was finished. The moment would seek its man—Caillaux.[20]

In late 1917, Poincaré told an associate, "We must choose between Caillaux and Clemenceau. My choice is made." Prosecute Caillaux, he urged his choice for prime minister: "Fate has placed him at the crossroads of all the paths of treason." Clemenceau replied, "Caillaux is a bandit . . . justice will be done."[21]

Charged with high treason, Caillaux was jailed without trial. Writing to the former premier in prison, Anatole France addressed him as "the great citizen who vanquished Germany in 1911 without costing France one drop of blood." Poincaré was afraid that sentiment would take hold if the public mind began to associate Joseph Caillaux with peace, not treason. With Paris once more menaced by a rampant German army, the time was not right to try Caillaux.[22]

Georges Clemenceau (1841–1929) by Félix Vallotton

Not until February 1920, two years after his imprisonment and six years after his passionate defense of Henriette, did Caillaux once more mount the stage of a courtroom. Ripping holes in the government's case, casting himself as a man persecuted for his ideas, reprising his tears for Henriette, Caillaux "defiantly told a jury full of nationalists that time would prove the price of victory to have been exorbitant." Acquitted of treason, he was convicted of a trumped-up lesser charge—"having had relations with the subjects of an enemy power"—fined, stripped of his civil rights, and banished from all major cities. He was widely seen as a victim of the malevolence of Clemenceau, who conceded that he had "discover[ed] traitors because he needed them" in order to stamp out defeatism. That perception contributed to Caillaux's political comeback in the 1920s and 1930. By then, many sadly agreed with him that France would have gained a "moral hegemony of Europe" if it had made peace after its victory on the Marne, sparing millions of lives.[23]

That was the mood of the 1930s. At the turn of the year 1914, though sorrowed by the 581,167 casualties suffered between August and November, the French still responded to calls for war unremitting. In rhetoric that suggests the pen of Raymond Poincaré, Premier René Viviani voiced the will to hit back hard in a December speech. Before delivering it, Viviani remarked to his defense minister, Alexandre Millerand, that France might be satisfied if Germany returned Alsace without Lorraine. If Viviani ever said that again, Millerand replied, he would demand his resignation. Overcompensating for this lapse, before a Chamber of Deputies in which three seats bore wreaths of evergreen tied with the tricolor sashes worn into battle by the dead legislators who once occupied them—addressing this grave body Viviani breathed fire. The applause was almost continuous but reached its height when he declared:

> Against barbarity and despotism; against the system of provocations and methodical menaces which Germany called peace; against the system of murder and pillage which Germany called war; against the insolent hegemony of a military caste which loosed the scourge, France, the emancipator, France, the vengeful, at the side of her allies, arose and advanced to the fray . . . There is at this time only one single policy: a combat without mercy until such time as we can accomplish the definite liberation of Europe, won by a victory ensuring peace . . . France, acting in accord with her allies, will not sheathe her sword until after taking vengeance for outraged right; until she has united for all time to the French fatherland the provinces ravished from her by force . . . and until Prussian militarism has been crushed . . . and Europe finally regenerated.[24]

"Combat without mercy": In a September 1922 issue of *Foreign Affairs* the journalist and politician André Tardieu brought home to American readers what that had cost France:

> The war bled us terribly. Out of our population of less than 38,000,000 there were mobilized 8,500,000; 5,300,000 of them were killed or wounded . . . not counting 500,000 men who have

From *Croquis de Temps de Guerre* (1919) (Wartime Sketches)
by Théophile Alexandre Steinlen

come back to us from German prisons in very bad physical condition.

Almost 4,000,000 hectares of land were devastated, together
with 4,000 towns and villages, 600,000 buildings were destroyed,
among them 20,000 factories and workshops . . .

To measure what we have undergone, suppose that the war had
taken place in America, and that you had suffered proportionately.
You would have had 4,000,000 of your men killed and 10,000,000
wounded. All your industries from Washington to Pittsburgh
would have ceased to exist. All your coal mines would have been
ruined. That is what the war would have meant to you. That is
what it has meant to us.[25]

"They will not be able to make us do it another day; that would be
to misconstrue the price of our effort," a Verdun veteran wrote. The
French could not pay it twice in a generation. Verdun held out for

ten months in 1916; twenty-four years later German troops seized the forts, the citadel, and the city in twenty-four hours.[26]

Part of the price of victory in 1918 was defeat in 1940. They could not be made to do it again.

On December 2, 1914, the sixty-sixth anniversary of Francis Joseph's rule, the Austrian army marched into Belgrade. Its commander, General Oskar Potiorek, wired Vienna that he was laying "the town and fortress of Belgrade" at "His Majesty's feet." The grateful monarch named a street in Sarajevo after Potiorek, and Viennese marched in a torchlight parade to celebrate the one victory in an autumn of debacles in which the Serbs and Russians had mauled the Austro-Hungarian army. Twelve days later, suffering what Churchill called an "ignominious, rankling and derisory defeat" the Serbian army drove the Austrians out of Belgrade. "It took them over four months to obtain admission to Belgrade," the *New York Times* noted, "and it seems to have taken less than a day to turn them out." This "second signal defeat at the hands of little Serbia" was "a bitter blow . . . to the Austro-Hungarian monarchy."[27]

Francis Joseph was habituated to bitter blows. He had accommodated the war by sacrificing thirty minutes of sleep, rising from his iron cot at half past three A.M., instead of his prewar four. Increasingly, a United Press International (UPI) correspondent reported from Vienna, "In his court he is treated like a child," spending his days working at a desk with an oval portrait of his assassinated wife set on easel before his gaze at all times. His palpable decline renewed his subjects' pity. A popular "postal photo" showed him seated at a table, his bowed head in his hands. The photograph was taken after an incident at a military hospital. Stopping at the bedside of a heavily bandaged soldier, he had asked, "My good man can I do anything for you?" When the soldier said nothing, a nurse interjected, "His majesty is speaking to you." The emperor repeated the question. "Yes, you can put a bullet through my head," the soldier answered, nearly shrieking. "Both of his arms and legs have been shot away," the nurse explained. At this the old man slumped down in a chair and wept. Physically infirm, he was alive enough morally to feel his responsibility for that

A pathetic Francis Joseph. He had at least one moment of
moral clarity before the final fog.

soldier's suffering and perhaps, when routine failed him, for the
949,000 of his soldiers killed, wounded, missing, or taken prisoner in
1914. "He has not asked to visit the hospital since," UPI noted, ending
a dispatch entitled: AUSTRIAN RULER SAD AND BROKEN.[28]

"Austria-Hungary is not a Fatherland but rather a prison of numerous
nationalities all panting to escape," Serbia's foreign minister declared
before the war, raising the issue of whether the national minorities
would fight for Austria. The war opened an avenue of escape. A headline in a Swiss paper asked, AUSTRIA PERILED BY A REVOLUTION? The
Rumanians were reportedly refusing to serve in Hungarian regiments,
the Czechs deserting from the army, the Croats seditious. Fighting
Russia, Serbia, and soon Italy, the questions of where the Austro-
Hungarian army would get the men to contain nationalist revolts, and
whether if ordered they would shoot their brothers were up in the air.

Now, with the army reeling from defeats in Poland and Serbia, was the time for the nationalities to break out of the prison.[29]

Improbably, they stayed put. Clearly, the nationalities were not "panting to escape"—not yet. And, despite reports of a Christmas Day march of Viennese women shouting, "Give us back our husbands and sons!" and student demonstrators being shot in Budapest, Austria-Hungary's core was not "periled" by revolution. Remarkably, the belief that it was the emperor's duty, in Francis Joseph's words, to "act as a unifying force for the minorities of Central Europe which were too weak to remain independent if left to their own devices," still held firm, even among the minorities themselves.[30]

The mystique of the emperor as the empire's unifier and the nations' protector survived the emperor's death on November 20, 1916. Retiring for bed that night, "summoning up his life in his final words," Francis Joseph instructed his valet, "Tomorrow morning, at half-past three."[31]

To an American correspondent who observed him at a 1914 pre-Christmas service at his western operational headquarters in Belgium, Kaiser Wilhelm "looked his part in the present historical drama" displaying "the saddest face I have ever seen in my life." The kaiser's stricken visage reminded him "of the expression you catch on certain portraits of Lincoln—the reflective, far-off look."[32]

The comparison was inapt. Lincoln ran his war. The supreme warlord surrendered his to the generals. As early as November 1914 he confided to dinner-party guests that "the General Staff tells me nothing and never asks my advice. If people in Germany think I am the Supreme Commander, they are grossly mistaken. I drink tea, saw wood, and go for walks, which pleases the gentlemen." Occasionally, he broke from these pursuits to offer suggestions, often barbarous and mostly ignored. For example, he proposed that the ninety thousand Russian soldiers captured at the battle of Tannenberg in September 1914 be driven onto a bare waterless strip of land in the Baltic Sea and starved to death.[33]

An irritant to the generals at the start of the war, the kaiser ended it as the puppet of Hindenburg and Ludendorff, the generals who, in July 1917, ousted Chancellor Bethmann Hollweg. The political brake on Prussian militarism gone, the Second Reich, conceived in war in 1871, fulfilled its destiny. In 1917–18, the question italicized by the Zabern incident of 1913 was settled. No longer a state with an army, with fifty-year-olds conscripted and sixteen- to sixty-year-olds facing compulsory labor in armaments factories, Germany was at last an army with a state.[34]

On the home front, hunger was the war. Under Britain's "starvation blockade," the German people lost 525,000 tons of "human mass," according to a late-1918 report. Prewar Germany imported 45 percent of its calories and 44 percent of its animal protein and all of its nitrates for fertilizer. The blockade severed these lifelines.[35]

In 1917, Britain's War Food Committee calculated that while the blockade would impair the "health and efficiency of the German na-

Von Hindenburg.

Field Marshal Paul von Hindenburg (1847–1934) by Félix Vallotton. The very model of the Prussian general, Hindenburg and his middle-class brain, Erich Ludendorff, effectively ruled Germany after they ousted Chancellor Bethmann Hollweg, who foolishly had made Hindenburg chief of staff.

tion," there were enough calories to go around to prevent starvation. The committee did not figure on the German farmer, who, according to a 1920 Royal Statistical Society paper analyzing why the committee got it wrong, "not only did his best to maintain his stock alive, if necessary using for this purpose food which ought by law to have applied to man, but he also . . . insisted on eating as much as he did before the War." The farmer in addition struck deals with arms manufacturers to supply food to their workforces at inflated prices, diverting food from the cities. A run of bad harvests further cut supply. The army competed with the civilian population for food and with the rural economy for manpower—by 1917, women ran 80 percent of farms in Baden. The result: Blockade and war left "the great part of the civilian population during this time . . . in a state of chronic starvation."[36]

Children suffered worst. Their limbs swelled with hunger edema. Rickets softened their bones, their jaws broke, their teeth fell out. Among women, deaths from tuberculosis rose by two thirds. On a city streetcar, the "stench of wasting tissue" sickened an American journalist.[37]

The death reek of the trenches, where the ground bristled with feet, skeletons, skulls, had come home. (Of the mud caking the uniform of her lover, killed in Flanders, Vera Brittain recorded, "It was as though it were saturated with dead bodies . . . All the sepulchers and catacombs of Rome could not make me realize mortality and corruption as vividly as did the smell of those clothes.") The experience of mass death—its smell, look, nearness—joined civilian and soldier in Germany as it separated them in England. In December 1918, the German National Health Office blamed the blockade for 763,000 "excess civilian deaths," a figure cut in half a decade later. Many died; more never lived: Births fell by half between 1914 and 1918.[38]

Divided by politics, religion, region, caste, and class, Germans had experienced a rush of unity in August 1914. "Over all individual fates stands that which we feel as the highest reality: the experience of belonging together," a conservative minister declared. "The limitations of our egos broke down, our blood flowed to the blood of the other, we felt ourselves one body in a mystical unification," a feminist journalist recalled of the "spirit of 1914." Hunger, however, divided Germans anew, family against family.[39]

In his novel *Class of 1902*, Ernst Glaser conveys a picture of social decomposition. "It was a hard winter to the end," he wrote of the "turnip winter" of 1916–17:

> The war now got past the various fronts and pressed home upon the people. Hunger destroyed our solidarity: The children stole each other's rations . . . Soon the women who stood in pallid queues before shops spoke more about their children's hunger than about the death of their husbands . . . A new front was created. It was held by women against an entente of field gendarmes and controllers. Every smuggled pound of butter, every sack of potatoes successfully spirited in by night, was celebrated in their homes with the same enthusiasm as the victories of the armies two years before.
>
> Soon a looted ham thrilled us more than the fall of Bucharest.[40]

Soldiers returning from home with tales of privation undermined morale at the front. Confronted by their families' piteous struggle, more and more men overstayed their leaves or deserted outright, "and the front lines became thinner," General Ludendorff reported. Perhaps 10 percent of troops being transported from the eastern to the western front in late 1917 simply jumped off their trains. The army's medical service, overwhelmed, was widely exploited. "In one transport of the wounded," a 1918 army investigation found, "of 594 men only 217 could be described as ill." In the ultimate comment on conditions at home, some soldiers on leave or recovering from wounds found themselves "anxious to return to the battlefield."★[41]

"It will be long before this nation will be in any condition to be regarded again as a menace to the peace of Europe," ventured the au-

---

★ Contrast Germany in World War II: "How strong the identification with the oppressor remained despite all the hate and doubt which many Germans may have felt . . . can also be seen by the fact that, throughout the war, there occurred no noteworthy breakdown of morale among either the fighting forces or the German people as a whole . . . The Germans never ceased to obey." Norbert Elias, *The Germans: Power Struggles and the Development of Habitus in the Nineteenth and Twentieth Centuries* (New York: Columbia University Press, 1996), 387.

thor of the 1920 Royal Statistical Society paper on hungry Germany. The *Weekly Dispatch* for September 8, 1918, imagined "the Huns of 1940" as a "physically inferior race."[42]

Resentment over the "diktat" of the Versailles Treaty went far to confound that prediction. Even more embittering than the treaty, however, was the Allies' post-Armistice decision not only to continue the blockade but also to extend it to the Baltic. Intended to pressure the German delegates to the Peace Conference to sign the treaty no matter how punishing its terms, this ploy in the politics of starvation succeeded all too well.

The damnable part was that Germany possessed the gold reserves to buy food from abroad. But Premier Georges Clemenceau, who with the other members of the Big Three, Lloyd George and Woodrow Wilson, framed the treaty, would not hear of it. He claimed the gold for France as a down payment on German war reparations.

It was time for what John Maynard Keynes called "the only man who emerged from the ordeal of [Versailles] with an enhanced reputation . . . [a] complex personality with his habitual air of weary Titan (or, as others might put it, exhausted prizefighter)"—it was time for Herbert Hoover to act.

Bearing on his conscience reports of German children with "huge rickety foreheads, their small arms just skin and bones, and above the crooked legs with their dislocated joints, the swollen, pointed stomachs of hunger edema," Hoover intervened with Lloyd George. At a meeting of the Supreme Council the prime minister shamed the French into yielding on the gold by waving a possibly inspired telegram from a British general in Germany complaining that his men were growing mutinous from seeing starving children in the streets. But the damage was done and it was incalculable. Nothing so tore the mask of righteousness off the face of the Allies as the months of suffering inflicted on the German people between the Armistice on November 11, 1918, and the signing of the treaty on June 28, 1919, five years to the day after the assassination of Franz Ferdinand— "suffering . . . greater under the continued blockade than prior to the Armistice." And nothing so tainted German democracy in German

„Noch eine Waffenstillstandsverlängerung und sie wird reif sein für den Frieden!"

This 1919 cartoon from *Simplicissimus* is a comment on the
post-Armistice starvation blockade of Germany, a consequential
blunder on the part of the Allies. Clemenceau (hands in pocket)
is recognizable on the right.

hearts as their new government's unavailing protests to the victors
while hunger "intensified into famine."[43]

The Allies would not have won the war without starving the German people—so British statesmen and navalists believed. Historians
tend to agree. The metaphor adopted by one of them expresses a

scholarly consensus: Germany was crushed between the "hammer" of the Allied armies in France and the "anvil" of the blockade at home. But victory through hunger, followed by peace through vengeance, came at a terrible price. The children on the anvil constituted the core of the Nazi Party. In the crucial 1932 elections, in a multiparty field, Germans aged eighteen to thirty gave the NSDP 42 percent of their vote. "National Socialism is the organized will of youth," went a party slogan.[44]

Hunger drew the war generation to the Nazis rather than, say, to the Social Democrats, less than 8 percent of whose members were under twenty-five. In 1934, a Columbia University sociologist, Theodore Abel, offered cash prizes for "the best personal life history of an adherent of the Hitler movement." The NSDP publicized the project in its local headquarters. Abel received nearly six hundred essays. Peter Loewenberg summarized the findings in a 1971 paper, "The Psychohistorical Origins of the Nazi Youth Cohort": "The most striking emotional affect expressed in the Abel autobiographies are the adult memories of intense hunger and privation from childhood." As one man recalled, "We were hungry all the time; we had forgotten how it felt to have our stomachs full."

"Their earliest memories are of their mother crying a great deal and of all the people wearing black," Loewenberg writes of two sisters whose father was killed in 1915. People wore black for fathers killed at the front and children starved at home: Mortality among one- to five-year olds was 50 percent greater in 1917 than in 1913 and 75 percent greater for those five to fifteen. With fathers at the war, mothers in the field or factory, siblings dead or dying, "All family life was at an end," an essayist lamented.[45]

Hitler was for many an idealized father figure—after the sisters mentioned above saw him speak at a Kassel rally in 1931 they "were so exhilarated that neither of them could sleep all night . . . and prayed for the protection of the Führer." For others the Nazi Party was a substitute family. "It was wonderful to belong to the bond of comradeship of the SA," wrote a man who lost his father during the war. The Depression reactivated the ravening insecurity of childhood on the anvil and its legacy of unacceptable feeling—anger at missing

"Germany's Children Are Starving!" by Käthe Kollwitz

fathers, attraction to seductive mothers, shame over the antisocial makeshifts survival forced on families. Needing to project these emotions onto the "other," the children of hunger attached themselves to a movement that invited the violent acting out of forbidden impulses while promising to restore the security and warmth torn from them during the war. Seeking release from childhood, Loewenberg concludes, "What they recreated was a repetition of . . . [it]. They gave to their children and to Europe in greater measure precisely the traumas they had suffered as children and adolescents a quarter of a century earlier."[46]

AN INJURY TO CIVILIZATION

The war against armed imperialism is over.

—Woodrow Wilson, November 11, 1918

THE WAR HAD barely begun when Woodrow Wilson volunteered the good offices of the United States to end it.* Expecting France to lose the battle of the Marne, then raging, the American ambassador in Berlin, James W. Gerard, secretly proffered generous terms to the Germans: They could demand indemnities and colonies from France—so long as they agreed to restore the territorial status quo ante in Europe. Deputy Foreign Minister Zimmermann rejected the president's mediation: "A treaty on the pattern offered here" was not acceptable. Germany wanted more than money and Morocco, as a document drawn up for the German chancellor, Bethmann Hollweg, that same day, September 9, reveals.[1]

The so-called September Program, reflecting the appetites of the

---

* "If I had been President," Theodore Roosevelt wrote to the British ambassador to the United States, Cecil Spring-Rice, on October 3, 1914, "I should have acted on the thirtieth or thirty-first of July, as head of a signatory power of the Hague treaties, calling attention to the guaranty of Belgium's neutrality and saying that I accepted the treaties as imposing a serious obligation which I expected not only the United States but all other neutral nations to join in enforcing." Simeon Strunsky, "Theodore Roosevelt and the Prelude to 1914," *Foreign Affairs* 4, no. 1 (October 1925): 151. "Some support for Roosevelt's argument came from Russia, which replied to Wilson's August 4 offer of good services that the offer came 'too late' and 'should have been made earlier.'" Kendrick A. Clements, "Woodrow Wilson and World War I," *Presidential Studies Quarterly* 34, no. 1 (March 2004): 71, n 36.

industrial interests identified with the names Thyssen, Hugenberg, and
Krupp, laid down the war aims pursued by Germany until October
1918. "The general aim of the war [is] security for the German Reich
in west and east for all imaginable time," the document noted with the
same pre-Marne megalomania in which the army struck a medal commemorating the entry of German troops into Paris. Belgium "must be
reduced to a vassal state" and France's "revival as a great power made
impossible for all time." France must also give up its ore fields, and pay
an indemnity so crushing as to rule out an armaments buildup. Bethmann was being moderate, having rejected the kaiser's "bizarre idea"
to render areas of Belgium and France "free of human beings," or at
least Belgian and French ones; "deserving [German] NCO's and men"
would settle the vacated territory. A German-dictated peace would
see the creation of a "central European economic association . . . under
German leadership." "Mitteleuropa, politically and economically our
world-historical task," would encompass Europe "from the Pyrenees to
Memel, from the Black Sea to the North Sea, from the Mediterranean
to the Baltic . . . in a single customs unit [to match] the over-mighty
productive resources" of the United States. In the east, Bethmann
beat back Pan-German demands to annex St. Petersburg. It would be
enough for Russia to surrender Poland, Lithuania, Courland, Livonia,
Estonia, and the Ukraine.[2]

The prospect of victory on the Marne prompted Bethmann to formu-
late Germany's war aims. Their victory on the Marne stirred the Allies
to propound their own September Program. Meeting in Petersburg on
September 13–14, the French agreed to support Russia's annexation of
the Straits and a chunk of eastern Poland in return for Russia's support
not only for the return of Alsace-Lorraine but for France's annexation of
"as much of Rhenish Prussia and the Palatinate as she wished."[3]

"It is no lust of conquest that inspires us," the kaiser promised the
Reichstag on August 4 as the war began. Lust took a month. Death
excused it. Germany required a peace, Bethmann wrote to the kaiser, "which is felt by the German people to recompense it in full for
the enormous sacrifices which it has made." The deaths of thousands
justified the deaths of millions. The argument from "in vain" masked
Germany's designs on Lithuania, Russia's on Constantinople, Britain's on the Middle East, and France's on the Rhineland.[4]

By November 1914, General von Falkenhayn had seen enough of trench warfare to conclude that Germany could not win a two-front war. "So long as Russia, France and Britain held together, it would be impossible to defeat our enemies decisively enough to get a decent peace," he informed Bethmann. "Either Russia or France must be chiseled off." Falkenhayn urged Russia. The tsar's mother belonged to the Danish royal family, and in December, through Copenhagen, Bethmann sounded out the Russians. "The Tsar and Sazonov [are] confident of victory," Bethmann's Danish contacts reported.[5]

Still, Nicholas remained vulnerable to his manners: "He will not refuse to discuss a settlement through the king of Denmark." Further soundings convinced Bethmann that a separate peace was not in the cards. The Russians were too afraid of revolution to risk bringing the army home from the front, where relief was anticipated in a supply crisis (predicted by Peter Durnovo) that saw living soldiers taking their rifles off dead ones and units without rifles fighting with clubs. "Ruling circles in Petersburg hope that the Straits will soon be opened and that they will receive all necessary material by this route," he wrote to Falkenhayn. That deliverance depended on the British attack on the Dardanelles succeeding.[6]

Such illusory hopes sustained the war. Gas would bring victory. Submarines would. Tanks would. Nothing did. "Some way there must be out of this bloody entanglement that was yielding victory to neither side . . . Every day came the papers with the balanced story of battles, losses, destructions, ships sunk, towns smashed. And never a decision, never a sign of a decision," H. G. Well's Mr. Britling reflects. Writing on the war's ninetieth anniversary, a contemporary historian echoes Wells in 1917: "A war that was supposed to have a beginning, a middle, and an end, had a middle and a middle, and then another middle, and then another year and another battle and another last push, and a middle that went on and on."[7]

Duration mattered in this war, and not just because the longer it went on, the more men died. Consider if it had ended early in 1917. "There would have been no collapse in Russia followed by Communism, no breakdown in Italy followed by Fascism, and Germany would not have signed the Versailles Treaty, which has enthroned Nazism in Germany," Winston Churchill told an American journalist in 1936. But

"Europe 1916" by Boardman Robinson

U.S. entry into the war renewed the lust for conquest (and revenge) on the Allied side, while Russia's withdrawal from it after the Bolshevik revolution in October similarly inflamed the Germans.[8]

Nineteen seventeen brought the hard men to power—Lloyd George in Britain, Clemenceau in France, Hindenburg and Ludendorff in Germany, Alexander Kerenksy in Russia. The provisional government installed by the February revolution that toppled Nicholas II had since fallen under the sway of Kerensky, the charismatic war minister who imitated Napoleon to the point of tucking his right arm into his tunic; and in June, overruling his generals, Kerensky unleashed an abortive offensive against the German lines. Desertions exceed the nearly four hundred thousand casualties, "trench Bolshevism" spread among the soldiers who stayed with their units, and millions of square miles were lost to the counterattacking Germans.[9]

Before U.S. belligerency consigned peace to the lost history of 1917, there were two scenarios for ending the war. One was Lloyd George's "fight to the finish" won by "a knockout." In a January speech to Congress, Woodrow Wilson predicted that such a victor's peace "would leave a sting, a resentment, a bitter memory upon which terms of peace would rest, not permanently, but only as upon quicksand." Wilson's alternative was "peace without victory." Their armies deadlocked and their regimes shaking above the earthquake of war, the combatant nations, he believed, must soon turn to the still-neutral United States to broker a compromise peace.[10]

But peace without victory also would have rested upon quicksand—of power not resentment. With the German army unbroken and Germany still under authoritarian rule, the war's roots remained intact. After the United States joined the Allies, the president himself recognized this, blaming the conflict on "Prussian militarism" and embracing as one of its goals the liberation of the German people from the "military clique in Berlin." Under Wilson's peace, a war to realize the territorial ambitions of the September Program and end Germany's vulnerability to a starvation blockade might have broken out even sooner than in 1939. As it was, the armistice came before the war and the November 1918 revolution that brought the socialists briefly to power had completed the destruction of the old order in Germany. This was notably preserved in the civil service and the judiciary, which were not purged of personnel appointed under the monarchy; in the schools, which as before the war trained German youth to despise democracy; in the universities, where the professoriate remained "inveterate supporters of a dead past"; and, above all, in a Prussian officer corps that blamed the Diktat of Versailles on the civilian government, "barely tolerated" the republic, and hankered for a restoration of authoritarian rule.[11]

If in the fall of 1918 the Allies had spurned German peace overtures, continued their offensive, and occupied Germany, they might have achieved a victory on the 1945 model. But that would have taken harder men, a longer war, and many more casualties. The Allied publics would not have stood for a real "knockout" blow. So World War I ground on to its inconclusive end on November 11, 1918, in the railway carriage in the forest of Compiègne, having by then inflicted what Woodrow Wilson saw would be "an injury . . . to civilization . . . which can never be atoned for or repaired."[12]

ACKNOWLEDGMENTS

I have first to thank four fine writers and an outstanding editor for improving, aggregately, nearly every page of this book.

My friends William Craig, author of *Yankee Come Home: On the Road from San Juan Hill to Guantánamo*, to be published in 2012 by Bloomsbury; Douglas Bauer, an accomplished novelist and essayist, as well as a gifted editor; and Rachel Shteir, author most recently of *The Steal: A Cultural History of Shoplifting*, identified lapses of style, organization, and thinking in several chapters. My son, Aaron, film critic for the *Connecticut Valley Spectator* from 2004 to 2009, rewrote much of the Russia chapter, showing me by example that long sentences can be broken into shorter ones without slowing the pace of paragraphs.

George Gibson, the publisher of Walker & Company and editor of *The Lost History of 1914*, suggested many changes in wording and refinements in logic to which I could only respond, "Of course! Why didn't I think of that?" Further, George persuaded me to make the separate chapters speak to one another, stitching up the book from the inside, to paraphrase E. M. Forster, with recurring images and parallel dilemmas and cameo appearances of characters met earlier. Thanks to my longtime and much-respected agent Rafe Sagalyn for putting my work in George's hands. George's assistant, Lea Beresford, not only secured permission for the illustrations (a time-consuming job), but suggested replacements when the ones desired were not available. I am very grateful to her. Also to Laura Phillips, the production editor who saw the manuscript into print with great care and much-appreciated tolerance for my incessant changes.

Two distinguished historians generously vetted the Russia and Germany chapters. Patricia Herlihy, author of a fascinating work of social history, *The Alcoholic Empire: Vodka and Politics in Late Imperial Russia*, that I relied on in chapter 2, offered informed criticism mixed with selective but welcome endorsement of my general picture of Russia on the eve of war. James Sheehan, a professor of German history at Stanford, took the risk of saying just what he thought of the school of history that I had uncritically regurgitated in an early draft of chapter 1. Though it sacrificed months of work, I cut the discussion he prompted me to think through. The Dartmouth political scientist Richard Ned Lebow, a prodigious scholar in the field of security studies, shared his wisdom with me in conversation and in books and papers that I drew on throughout.

Led by senior producer Karen Shiffman and host Tom Ashbrook, my colleagues on the staff of *On Point*, which in 2011 celebrated its tenth anniversary on National Public Radio, buoyed me to do my best work by daily displaying theirs.

My wife, Lois, edited the manuscript with an artist's eye for clarity, style, grammar, and structure; a skeptic's habit of challenging windy assertions; and a highly literate reader's sense of when enough—evidence, explanation, detail—is enough. I'm grateful to her for all that, and much more.

IMAGE CREDITS

p. i Constant, "8 × La Guerre 8," 1951, lithography, 40.1 × 27.8 cm © 2011 Artists Rights Society (ARS), New York c/o Pictoright Amsterdam

p. v Courtesy of the Naval Historical Foundation

p. 28 *Simplicissimus*

p. 45 *Der Wahre Jacob*

p. 48 *London Illustrated Weekly*

p. 50 *Der Wahre Jacob*, May 1905

p. 104 Courtesy of the Linen Hall Library (Belfast)

p. 123 © 2011 Artists Rights Society (ARS), New York/VG Bild-Kunst, Bonn

p. 125 Courtesy of the National Library of Ireland

p. 126 Courtesy of the National Library of Ireland

p. 135 © 2011 Artists Rights Society (ARS), New York/SOMAAP, Mexico City

p. 143 © 2011 Artists Rights Society (ARS), New York/SOMAAP, Mexico City

p. 147 *Puck*, March 5, 1913

p. 160 © 2011 Artists Rights Society (ARS), New York/SOMAAP, Mexico City

p. 164 *Punch*

p. 206 *Simplicissimus*, July 8, 1912

p. 216 "Éducation," *L'Assiette au beurre*, March 11, 1905: 206. Special Collections, University of Delaware Library, Newark, Delaware

p. 220 *Punch*, 5 April 1905

p. 221 *Der Wahre Jacob*, March 1906

p. 241 Courtesy of the Mary Evans Picture Library

p. 258 "Debout Les Morts!" (1917) (The Dead Rise Up!) by Frans Masereel © 2011 Artists Rights Society (ARS), New York/VG Bild-Kunst, Bonn

p. 259 "Toter Sapenpost" (1924) (Dead Sapenpost) by Otto Dix © 2011 Artists Rights Society (ARS), New York/VG Bild-Kunst, Bonn

p. 261 "The Grenade" (1915) by Max Beckmann © 2011 Artists Rights Society (ARS), New York/VG Bild-Kunst, Bonn

p. 262 "Sturmtruppe geht unter Gas vor" (Shock Troops Advance Under Gas) by

NOTES

NOTES FOR THE INTRODUCTION

1 Annika Mombauer, "Contingent and Eminently Avoidable Mistakes" is from Holger Afflerbach and David Stevenson's introduction to *An Improbable War? The Outbreak of World War I and European Political Culture before 1914* (New York: Berghahn Books, 2007), 2. Here is an example supporting Mombauer's contention that "certain key individuals" desired war: "When Germany delivered its July 31 ultimatum to Russia to cease its mobilization by noon the next day or face German mobilization, Bethmann Hollweg [the German chancellor] deliberately omitted a sentence (which was included in telegrams to other embassies) warning that mobilization would for Germany mean war. German leaders went out of their way to soften their warning to Russia so that the Russians would not actually capitulate and possible rob Germany of the opportunity to fight its war against France and Russia." Kier A. Lieber, "The New History of World War I and What It Means for International Security Theory," *International Security* 32, no. 2 (Fall 2007): 186–87.

2 Stefan Zweig, *The World of Yesterday* (Lincoln: University of Nebraska Press, 1964), 27, 1, 60. For strikes, see CBS News DVD *World War I: The Complete Story*, ep. 3, "Doomed Dynasties," narrated by Robert Ryan. For "escaping forward," see Arno J. Mayer, *The Persistence of the Old Regime: Europe to the Great War* (New York: Pantheon, 1981), 319. "The inner spring of Europe's general crisis was the overreaction of old elites to overperceived dangers to their overprivileged positions," 304.

3 For attitudes of European powers toward the Mexican Revolution, see Friedrich Katz, *The Secret War in Mexico: Europe, the United States, and the Mexican Revolution* (Chicago: University of Chicago Press, 1981), 550–78. For Britain's need for Mexican oil, see Arthur S. Link, *Wilson: The New Freedom* (Princeton: Princeton University Press, 1956), 370.

4 George F. Kennan, *The Decline of Bismarck's European Order: Franco-Russian Relations, 1875–1890* (Princeton: Princeton University Press, 1979), 3.

5 Ibid.

NOTES FOR CHAPTER 1

1 August Heckscher, *Woodrow Wilson* (New York: Scribner's, 1991), 440. On the two Germanys metaphor in France, see Michael E. Nolan, *The Inverted Mirror: Mythologizing the Enemy in France and Germany, 1898–1914* (New York: Berghahn, 2005), 5. On Prussian militarism, see especially Karl Liebknecht, *Militarism* (New York: B. W. Huebch, 1917) and Nicholas Stargardt, *The German Idea of Militarism: Radical and Socialist Critics 1866–1914* (Cambridge, UK: Cambridge University Press, 1994). For general treatments, see Alfred Vagts, *A History of Militarism* (New York: Norton, 1938), V. R. Berghahn, *Militarism: The History of an International Debate 1861–1979* (New York: Cambridge University Press, 1981), and John R. Gillis, ed., *The Militarization of the Western World* (New Brunswick: Rutgers University Press, 1989). For a vivid fictional portrait of militarism's reach into the German soul, see Heinrich Mann, *Man of Straw* (New York: Penguin Books, 1979).

2 John C. G. Röhl, *Wilhelm II: The Kaiser's Personal Monarchy, 1888–1900* (New York: Cambridge University Press, 2004), 1. For von Moltke, see Dennis E. Showalter, "The Political Soldiers of Bismarck's Germany: Myths and Realities," *German Studies Review* 17, no. 1 (February 1994): 64.

3 Seen in Eda Sagarra, *A Social History of Germany, 1648–1914* (New York: Holmes & Meir, 1977), 242.

4 For "militarism" and "militarization," see Gillis, *Militarization*, 1. For United States spending more than the world, see Andrew J. Bacevich, *The New American Militarism: How Americans Are Seduced by War* (New York: Oxford University Press, 2005), 17.

5 For "in all but name," see Hans-Ulrich Wehler, *The German Empire 1871–1918* (New York: Berg, 1985), 56. Also see Michael Stürmer, *The German Empire, 1870–1918* (New York: Modern Library, 2000), 33. For "map of Africa," see 83. For comparative figures, see Niall Ferguson, *The Pity of War* (New York: Basic Books, 1998), tables 10 and 13, 92 and 110. George F. Kennan, *The Fateful Alliance: France, Russia, and the Coming of the First World War* (New York: Pantheon, 1984).

6 Von Moltke seen in Ferguson, *The Pity of War*, 137.

7 John C. G. Röhl, "The Emperor's New Clothes: A Character Sketch of Kaiser Wilhelm II," in John C. G. Röhl and Nicholas Sombert, eds., *Kaiser Wilhelm II: New Interpretations, The Corfu Papers* (New York: Cambridge University Press, 1982), 40. For uniforms, see Holger H. Herwig, *"Luxury" Fleet: The Imperial German Navy, 1888–1918* (London: The Ashfield Press, 1980), 18–19. For visits to the Zoo-Aquarium, see CBS News DVD *World War I: The Complete Story*, ep. 3, "The Doomed Dynasties," narrated by Robert Ryan.

8 For "Bebel," see William H. Maehl, "Bebel's Fight against the Schlachtflotte, Nemesis to the Primacy of Foreign Policy," *Proceedings of the American Philosophical Society* 121, no. 3 (June 1977): 213ff. Tirpitz sidelined prophets of submarine warfare. See the account by the editor of the *Berliner Tageblatt*, Theodor Wolff, who invited the submariners to write anonymous articles for the paper, in *The Eve of 1914* (London: Gollancz, 1935), 73–74. Falkenhayn to Tirpitz, see Alfred Vagts, "Land and Sea Power in the Second German Reich," *Journal of the Ameri-*

can Military Institute 3, no. 4 (Winter 1939), 220. For the navy, see Herwig, *"Luxury" Fleet: The Imperial German Navy, 1888–1918*, 20, 23; for number of marks, see 256.

9 For wariness about drafting soldiers from cities, see David M. Rowe, "The Tragedy of Liberalism: How Globalization Caused the First World War," *Security Studies* 14, no. 3 (July–September 2005): 425.

10 For Reichstag resistance to expanding the army, see Dennis Showalter, "From Deterrence to Doomsday Machine: The German Way of War, 1890–1914," *Journal of Military History* 64, no. 3 (July 2000): 687–94. For the kaiser, see Ferguson, *The Pity of War*, 137.

11 For War Ministry official, see Ferguson, *The Pity of War*, 137. For taxes, see Showalter, "From Deterrence to Doomsday Machine," 687. For beer and tobacco, see Maehl, "Bebel's Fight," 213. Germany had immense power *potential*, but failed to mobilize it. In their paper, "Comparing the Strength of Nations," *Comparative Political Studies* 19 (April 1986): 39–70, Jacek Kugler and William Domke "construct an overall index of actualized power that takes into account not only a nation's economic resource base (as measured by GNP) but also its political capacity to mobilize this resource base." Their metrics show "Germany in 1914 to be almost equal in actualized military power to Britain, France, and Russia combined." Seen in Dale C. Copeland, *The Origins of Major War* (Ithaca: Cornell University Press, 2000), 271, n. 68.

12 For "media monarch," see Christopher Clark, *Iron Kingdom: The Rise and Downfall of Prussia, 1600–1947* (Cambridge: Harvard University Press, 2006), 589. "Hun's speech" cartoon seen in Röhl, *The Kaiser's Personal Monarchy*, 1042–44.

13 For "prig," see Gordon A. Craig, *Germany, 1866–1945* (New York: Oxford University Press, 1978), 238. For Fontane and background, see Volker Durr, "The Image of the Prussian Officer in Literature and History," in Volker Durr, Kathy Harms, Peter Hayes, eds., *Imperial Germany* (Madison: University of Wisconsin Press, 1985), 75–89. For "Karl Kraus," see Edward Timms, *Karl Kraus: Apocalyptic Satirist: Culture and Catastrophe in Habsburg Vienna* (New Haven: Yale University Press, 1989), 316. Hermann Broch, *The Sleepwalkers: A Trilogy* (Boston: Little, Brown, 1932), 158.

14 Michael Howard seen in Geoffrey Best, "The Militarization of European Society, 1870–1914," in John R. Gillis, ed., *The Militarization of the Western World* (New Brunswick: Rutgers University Press, 1989), 21.

15 For "second Jena," see Clark, *Iron Kingdom*, 599.

16 See the account in Clark, *Iron Kingdom*, 596–99; also see the coverage in the London *Times* beginning on October 18, 1906, and continuing to November 12, 1906. For a dramatic treatment, see Carl Zuckmayer, *The Captain of* Köpenick: *A Modern Fairy Tale in Three Acts* (London: Geoffrey Bles, 1932). For Voigt's accomplice, the kaiser's amusement, and the two bags of cash, see Benjamin Carter Hett, "The 'Captain of Köpenick' and the Transformation of German Criminal Justice, 1891–1914," *Central European History* 36, no. 1 (2003): 23–30. Noting the mitigating circumstances that surround his armed robbery conviction, the court gave Voigt a reduced sentence. His case "demonstrates the remarkable transformation in the German criminal justice system in the last years before the First World War."

17 For "Burckhardt," see Hans-Ulrich Wehler, *The German Empire, 1871–1918* (New York: Berg, 1985), 27.

18 For Bismarck and monarchy, see the review by Geoffrey Wawro, "The Shrewdest of the Shrewd," *Wall Street Journal*, April 9, 2011: "What made Bismarck stand out in a liberalizing era was his . . . insolent confidence in absolute monarchy and his acute insight into how to save and prolong it." "Forces of order" and "Holstein," seen in Michael R. Gordon, "Domestic Conflict and the Origins of the First World War: The British and German Cases," *Journal of Modern History* 46, no. 2 (June 1974): 204, 212. For war scares, see A. J. P. Taylor, *The Course of German History* (New York: Routledge, 1968), 157. "The government's area of greatest constitutional freedom was in foreign and military affairs. Exploiting its free hand, it repeatedly trumped up foreign policy challenges on the eve of elections to boost vote totals for the ruling coalition." Jack Snyder, *From Voting to Violence: Democratization and Nationalist Conflict* (New York: Norton, 2000), 107.

19 Quotation from Wehler, *The German Empire*, 30.

20 For "escape forwards," see Wehler, *The German Empire*, 198. For "Gerard," see James Watson Gerard, *My Four Years in Germany* (New York: Doran, 1917), 318. "To my mind, the course which really determined the Emperor and the ruling class for war was the attitude of the whole people in the Zabern Affair and their evident growing dislike of militarism." This view seemed to take hold among American publicists: "The Zabern Affair showed the Pan-Germans that they had to make war before 'liberal Germany' rebelled. It must be recognized as one of the immediate causes of the war." Seen in Barry Cerf, *Alsace-Lorraine Since 1870* (New York: Macmillan, 1919), 89. Writing a year after the war, Cerf cites a publication of the Committee of Public Information in Washington, the wartime propaganda agency, titled "German Militarism and Its German Critics" as the source of that judgment about the significance of Zabern.

21 J. Ellis Barker, "Autocratic and Democratic Germany: The Lessons of Zabern," *The Nineteenth Century and After* (February 1914). For the Duke of Ratibor, see Wehler, *The German Empire*, 199. For Bethmann Hollweg in the July Crisis, see Roger Chickering, *Imperial Germany and a World Without War, The Peace Movement and German Society, 1892–1914* (Princeton: Princeton University Press, 1975), 414. The biographer quoted is Konrad Jarausch from *The Enigmatic Chancellor: Bethmann Hollweg and the Hubris of Imperial Germany* (New Haven: Yale University Press, 1973), 158. The school of historians is that identified with the work of Fritz Fischer (1908–99).

22 For "skirted decision" see W. J. Mommsen, "The German Empire as a System of Skirted Decisions," in *Imperial Germany, 1867–1918* (New York: Arnold, 1995). Germany as an "army with a state" is a formulation credited to a "contemporary of Frederick the Great" and originally applying to Prussia. See Leonard Smith, *From Mutiny to Obedience: The Case of the French Fifth Infantry Division during World War I* (Princeton: Princeton University Press, 1994), 250. Also see Emilio Willems, *A Way of Life and Death: Three Centuries of German Militarism* (Nashville:

Vanderbilt University Press, 1986), 32; and F. G. Stapleton, "An Army with a State, Not a State with an Army," *Historical Review* (September 2003): 38–43. The classic history of Prussian militarism is Gordon A. Craig, *The Politics of the Prussian Army* (New York: Oxford University Press, 1955).

23 For "Bülow," see Mark Hewitson, "Germany and France before the First World War: A Reassessment of Wilhelmine Foreign Policy," *English Historical Review* 15, no. 462 (June 2000): 578. C. P. Gooch, *Franco-German Relations 1871–1914* (London: Longman's, 1923), 6.

24 For shifting French opinion on the "lost provinces," see E. Malcolm Carroll, *French Public Opinion and Foreign Affairs, 1870–1914* (New York: Century, 1931); Gooch, *Franco-German Relations*, 9. For recruits, see Graham Robb, *The Discovery of France: A Historical Geography from the Revolution to the First World War* (New York: Norton, 2007), 324. For "Raymond Poincaré," see the London *Times*, January 21, 1914. Also see John Keiger, "Jules Cambon and the Franco-German Détente, 1907–1914," *Historical Journal* 26, no. 3 (September 1983): 656.

25 Bismarck quotation taken from Gerhard Ritter, *The Sword and the Scepter: The Problem of Militarism in Germany,* vol. 1, *The Prussian Tradition* (New Haven: Yale University Press, 1964), 257. For "glacis," see Craig, *Germany,* 29–30. "The ambivalence on which the German effort to assimilate Alsace-Lorraine was to founder" was evident from the start. "The inhabitants were informed . . . that they were wanted not for their own sake, but for the terrain on which they lived." At the same time, "they were assured" that the Germans had come to liberate what Bismarck called "the German hearts of the Alsatians . . . from the bondage of French culture." See Otto Pflanze, *Bismarck and the Development of Germany,* vol. 2 (Princeton: Princeton University Press, 1990), 119.

26 Napoleon quotation seen in George Wharton Edwards, *Alsace-Lorraine* (Philadelphia: Penn Publishing, 1918), 39. For "French Revolution," see Alan Kramer, "*Wackes* at War: Alsace-Lorraine and the Failure of German National Mobilization, 1914–1918," in John Horne, ed., *State, Society and Mobilization during the First World War* (New York: Cambridge University Press, 1997), 107. For "Teutonic patience," see E. A. Vizetelly, *The True Story of Alsace-Lorraine* (New York: Stokes, 1918), 267. For Germanizing of names, see Barry Cerf, *Alsace-Lorraine Since 1870* (New York: Macmillan, 1919), 55–56. On the schools, see Stephen Harp, "War's Eclipse of Primary Education in Alsace-Lorraine, 1914–1918," *Historian* 57, no. 3 (Spring 1995): 1–8.

27 Treatment of recruits from Nicholas Stargardt, *The German Idea of Militarism: Radical and Socialist Critics 1866–1914* (Cambridge, UK: Cambridge University Press, 1994), 40. Suicides were actually higher among drill instructors than recruits. See Dennis E. Showalter, "Army and Society in Germany: The Pains of Modernization," *Journal of Contemporary History* 18, no. 4 (October 1983): 601–4.

28 For Burckhardt on Alsace-Lorraine, see Wehler, *The German Empire*, 93.

29 The following account closely follows David Schoenbaum, *Zabern, 1913,* and the reporting in the *New York Times*. See the dispatches for October 19, 1913; November 4, 1913; November 21–23, 30, 1913; December 1–8, 20, 21, 24, 25,

28, 1913; January 6–8, 11, 12, 14, 16, 31, 1914; February 2, 1914. Also see the London *Times* and the *Chicago Tribune* for many of the same days.

30 For Wedel and the kaiser's youthful indiscretion, see John C. G. Röhl, "The Emperor's New Clothes: A Character Sketch of Kaiser Wilhelm II," 43–51. For kaiser's paean to the "Army," see Röhl, *The Kaiser's Personal Monarchy*, 2. For "more than a thousand Alsatians" in the paragraph above, see Cerf, *Alsace-Lorraine Since 1870*, 96. This 1919 book smacks of wartime propaganda, casting doubt on the veracity of that number.

31 Gooch, *Franco-German Relations*, 6.

32 David Schoenbaum, *Zabern 1913: Consensus Politics in Imperial Germany* (London: Allen & Unwin, 1982), 112.

33 Alex Hall, *Scandal, Sensation, and Social Democracy: The SPD Press and Wilhelmine Democracy 1890–1914* (New York: Cambridge University Press, 1977), 140.

34 *New York Times*, December 20–21, 1913, editorial.

35 Kevin McAleer, *Dueling: The Cult of Honor in Fin-de-Siècle Germany* (Princeton: Princeton University Press, 1994), 41, 114–17. For "specially ground" sword, see the London *Times*, January 12, 1914.

36 McAleer, *Dueling*, 25. Also see "Dueling and Maltreatment in the German Army," the London *Times*, March 21, 1906.

37 For SPD, see McAleer, *Dueling*, 33; Eckart Kehr, *Economic Interest, Militarism, and Foreign Policy: Essays on German History* (Berkeley: University of California Press, 1977). For "Liebknecht," see Liebknecht, *Militarism*, 91, For Marx, see David Blackbourn, *Class, Religion and Local Politics in Wilhelmine Germany: The Centre Party in Wurttemberg before 1914* (New Haven: Yale University Press, 1980), 3. For "middle-class parties," see Craig, *Germany*, 338.

38 *New York Times,* December 4, 1913.

39 For Bethmann's uniform, see Alex Hall, *Scandal, Sensation, and Social Democracy: The SPD Press and Wilhelmine Germany 1890–1914* (New York: Cambridge University Press, 1977), 117. For royal banquets, see Wehler, *The German Empire*, 156. For "transgressed its authority" and "Austrian ambassador," see Konrad H. Jarausch, *The Enigmatic Chancellor: Bethmann Hollweg and the Hubris of Imperial Germany* (Princeton: Princeton University Press, 1973), 451, n. 37, 102.

40 *New York Times*, December 4, 1913. For Bethmann as "leafless trunk," see Theodor Wolff, *The Eve of 1914* (London: Gollancz, 1935), 342. For stenographic transcript, see *German History in Documents and Images,* vol. 5 of *Wilhelmine Germany and the First World War, 1890–1918, Parliament Debates in the Zabern Affair* (1913). Available online at www.ghi-dc.org.

41 Schoenbaum, *Zabern, 1913*, 125, 140.

42 London *Times*, December 7, 1913, February 13, 1914.

43 Schoenbaum, *Zabern, 1913*, 125; *New York Times*, December 7, 1913.

44 For SPD support for a parliamentary system of government, see Richard Breitman, "Negative Integration and Parliamentary Politics: Literature on German Social Democracy, 1890–1933," *Central European History* 13, no. 2 (1980): 183–84. For insignificant, see Schoenbaum, *Zabern, 1913*, 156. For Saxon, see Jarausch, *The Enigmatic Chancellor*, 103.

45 For "Chancellor crisis," see the London *Times*, December 6, 1913. For SPD hesitations, see Craig, *Germany*, 300. Quotation from *Düsseldorf Volkzeitung* from Mary Nolan, *Social Democracy and Society: Working-Class Radicalism in Düsseldorf, 1890–1920* (New York: Cambridge University Press, 1981), 235.

46 Schoenbaum, *Zabern, 1913*, 131.

47 See the London *Times*, December 20, 1913, and the *New York Times*, December 20, 1913.

48 For spiked helmets, see the London *Times*, January 6, 1914; *New York Times*, January 7, 1914.

49 Quotations from press opinion in the London *Times*, January 11, 1914. For the kaiser's 1912 threat to smash the constitution of Alsace-Lorraine, see Barry Cerf, *Alsace-Lorraine Since 1870* (New York: Macmillan, 1919), 88.

50 See Schoenbaum, *Zabern, 1913*, 154–55, 158–59. For "middle-class parties," see Craig, *Germany*, 300; Bethmann quotation from Schoenbaum, 157.

51 For "permanent threat of *Staatsstreich*," see Wehler, *The German Empire*, 200; phrase seen in David Blackbourn, *Class, Religion and Local Politics in Wilhelmine Germany: The Centre Party in Wurttemberg before 1914* (New Haven: Yale University Press, 1980), 4.

52 Craig, *Germany*, 174–78.

53 For Bismarck's resignation, see Pflanze, *Bismarck and the Development of Germany*, 358–73. For Bülow, see Brett Fairbairn, *Democracy in the Undemocratic State: The German Reichstag Elections of 1898 and 1903* (Toronto: University of Toronto Pres, 1997), 235.

54 For Waldersee, fighting in insurgent towns, and the enemy within, see Wehler, *The German Empire*, 158.

55 On broadening of SPD appeal, see Matthew Jeffries, *Contesting the German Empire, 1871–1918* (Malden, MA: Blackwell, 2008), 115.

56 Figures on voting in Prussia seen in Hett, "The Captain of Köpenick," 30. For 1912 elections, see Carl E. Schorske, *German Social Democracy, 1905–1917: The Development of the Great Schism* (Cambridge: Harvard University Press, 1955), 226–41, and franchise issues, 150.

57 Nolan, *Social Democracy and Society*, 233 chart, 236.

58 Schorske, *German Social Democracy*, 168.

59 For Crown Prince, see the London *Times*, January 23, 1914. Details on the memo are from Schoenbaum, *Zabern, 1913*, 11–13 and V. R. Berghahn, *Germany and the Approach of War in 1914* (New York: St. Martin's Press, 1973), 163. Meinecke seen in Wehler, *The German Empire*, 218. For Hitler and Pan-Germans, see Fritz Fischer, "Twenty-Five Years Later: Looking Back on the 'Fischer Controversy' and Its Consequences," *Central European History* 21, no. 3 (September 1988): 219

60 London *Times*, January 23, 1914. For ass, see Wolff, *The Eve of 1914*, 320. On the SPD and the general strike: "If the idea of answering a general mobilization order with a call for a general strike ever formed part of accepted social-democratic thinking, it did so for a very short time only, and even this may be an exaggeration." Typical of SPD rhetoric in this respect was the 1913 Reichstag declaration of Hugo Hasse that "we have always emphasized the impossibility,

once war has broken out, of organizing a mass strike." Dieter Groh, "The 'Unpatriotic Socialists' and the State," *Journal of Contemporary History* 1, no. 4 (October 1966): 159, 163.

61 London *Times*, January 23, 1914.

62 The kaiser's 1905 quotation is from Fritz Fischer, *From Kaiserreich to Third Reich: Elements of Continuity in German History* (London: Allen & Unwin, 1986), 46.

63 See Craig, *Germany*, 300–301. For suspending civil rights for Jews, see Roger Chickering, *We Men Who Feel Most German: A Cultural Study of the Pan-German League, 1886–1914* (Boston: Allen & Unwin, 1984), 287. For the kaiser's anti-Semitism and 1919 letter, see John C. G. Röhl, *The Kaiser and His Court: Wilhelm II and the Government of Germany* (Cambridge, UK: Cambridge University Press, 1994), 348.

64 For lecture, see the London *Times*, January 6, 1914.

65 For von Papen's coup and Hindenburg's ear, see Anthony Grenville, "Authoritarianism Subverting Democracy: The Politics of Carl Zuckmayer's 'Der Hauptmann von *Köpenick*,'" *Modern Language Review* 91, no. 3 (July 1996): 643–44. Also see Craig, *Germany*, 417, 561–62. For "pretext," see Richard Breitman, "On German Social Democracy and General Schleicher 1932–33," *Central European History* 9, no. 4 (December 1976): 354.

NOTES FOR CHAPTER 2

1 Leon Trotsky, *1905* (New York: Random House, 1971), v. For Nicholas's letters, see Orlando Figes, *A People's Tragedy: The Russian Revolution, 1891–1924* (New York: Penguin, 1996), 24. Also, Mark D. Steinberg, *The Fall of the Romanovs: Political Dreams and Personal Struggles in a Time of Revolution* (New Haven: Yale University Press, 1995), 6.

2 For the Durnovo Memorandum, see Frank Alfred Golder, ed., *Documents of Russian History 1914–1917* (New York: Century, 1927), 3–28. For supply crisis in 1915, see V. I. Gurko, *Features and Figures of the Past: Government and Opinion in the Reign of Nicholas II* (Palo Alto: Stanford, 1939), 549–50. Also see Dominic Lieven, "Bureaucratic Authoritarianism in Late Imperial Russia: The Personality, Career, and Opinions of P. N. Durnovo," *Historical Journal* 26, no. 2 (June 1983): 391–402.

3 David MacLaren McDonald, *United Government and Foreign Policy in Russia 1900–1914* (Cambridge: Harvard University Press, 1992), 199, 203, 202.

4 For *Novoe vremia*, see I. V. Bestuzhev, "Russian Foreign Policy February–June 1914," *Journal of Contemporary History* 1, no. 3, (July 1966): 100–01.

5 For warming trend, see Serge Sazonov, *Fateful Years, 1909–1916* (London: Cape, 1928), 117. For Chandler, see Thomas K. McCraw, ed., *The Essential Alfred Chandler: Essays Toward a Historical Theory of Big Business* (Cambridge: Harvard Business School Press, 1988), 48.

6 For Korean venture, see Gurko, *Features and Figures of the Past*, 295. Also David Schimmelpennick van der Oye, "The Immediate Origin of the War," and V. I. Lukoianov, "The Bezobrazotsky," in John W. Steinberg et al., eds., *The Russo-Japanese War in Global Perspective: World War Zero* (Leiden, Boston: Brill, 2005–

2007). For Nicholas to Stolypin, see Maurice Paléologue, *An Ambassador's Memoirs* (New York: Doran, 1923), 98. For "being," see *The Memoirs of Count Witte* (Armonk, NY: M. E. Sharpe, 1990), 190. For more on the war see Dietrich Geyer, *Russian Imperialism: The Interaction of Domestic and Foreign Policy 1860–1914* (New Haven: Yale University Press, 1987), 230.

7 For "young physician," see Barry Scherr, "The War in the Russian Literary Imagination," in Steinberg et al., *The Russo-Japanese War*, 155–56.

8 On effects of war on revolution, see John Bushnell, "The Specter of Mutinous Reserves: How the War Produced the October Manifesto," in Steinberg, *The Russo-Japanese War*, 333–348.

9 Figes, *A People's Tragedy*, 191. For explained to mother, see Dominic Lieven, *Nicholas II: Emperor of All the Russias* (London: Murray, 1993), 149.

10 "No war . . . no revolution," is Bushnell's formulation, "The Specter of Mutinous Reserves," 348.

11 McDonald, *United Government and Foreign Policy*, 110. The theme of avoiding war to avoid revolution follows McDonald, *United Government and Foreign Policy in Russia* and David M. McDonald, "A Lever Without a Fulcrum: Domestic Factors and Russian Foreign Policy, 1905–1914," in Hugh Ragsdale, ed., *Imperial Russian Foreign Policy* (New York: Cambridge University Press, 1993). For Stolypin's reforms, see Figes, *A People's Tragedy*, 224. For full pacification, see McDonald, *United Government and Foreign Policy in Russia*, 117. For "twenty years," see Norman Stone, *Europe Transformed* (Cambridge: Harvard University Press, 1984), 197. For more on Stolypin's program, see Peter Waldron, *Governing Tsarist Russia* (London: Palgrave, 2007), 93–94, repression on 92.

12 McDonald, *United Government and Foreign Policy in Russia*, 103–11.

13 Ibid., 114–17, also McDonald, "Fulcrum Without a Lever," 288–90. For proposed Anglo-Russian attack on the Straits, see M. S. Anderson, *The Eastern Question, 1774–1923* (New York: Macmillan, 1966), 280. For border dispute with Persia and background on the Straits, see William L. Langer, "Russia, the Straits Question and the European Powers, 1904–1908," *English Historical Review* 44, no. 3 (January 1929): 59–85.

14 For Austrian records, see Steve Beller, *Francis Joseph* (New York: Longman, 1996), 196. Aehrenthal's "readiness to cheat" and "rascally glee" as well as "Serbian historian" seen in Luigi Albertini, *The Origins of the War of 1914*, vol. 1 (New York: Oxford University Press, 1952), 191, 210, 300. For background, see Geoffrey A. Hosking, *The Russian Constitutional Experiment: Government and Duma, 1907–1914* (Cambridge: Cambridge University Press, 1973), 228–33. Also, McDonald, *United Government and Foreign Policy*, chap. 6, 127–51.

15 For Nicholas to his mother, see Dominic Lieven, *Nicholas II*, 249.

16 For German ultimatum, see Bernadotte E. Schmitt, *The Annexation of Bosnia 1908–1909* (Cambridge: Cambridge University Press, 1937), 194ff. For "diplomatic Tsushima," see Robert D. Warth, *Nicholas II: The Life and Reign of Russia's Last Monarch* (Westport, CT: Praeger, 1997), 183.

17 For shift in terms of alliance, see Bernadotte E. Schmitt, *The Annexation of*

Bosnia 1908–1909 (Cambridge: Harvard University Press, 1937), esp. 201–07 and 249–53. For Bismarck's disavowal of designs on the Balkans, see Michael Stürmer, *The German Empire* (New York: Modern Library, 2000), 35.

18 For Stolypin's assassination, see Figes, *A People's Tragedy*, 230, and Kokovtsov, 271–72.

19 Characterization of Kokovtsov from Nicholas de Basily, *The Abdication of Emperor Nicholas II of Russia* (Princeton: Kingston Press, 1984), 68.

20 For "Black Hundreds," see Figes, *A People's Tragedy*, 197. For Durnovo, see Sarah Abrevaya Stein, "Faces of Protest: Yiddish Cartoons of the 1905 Revolution," *Slavic Review* 61, no. 4 (Winter 2004): 732–61. For pogroms, see Stone, *Europe Transformed,* 200. For number of pogroms, the tsar's portrait, and Nicholas to his mother see Sergei Podbolotov, ". . . and the entire mass of Loyal People Leapt Up": The Attitude of Nicholas II Towards the Pogroms," *Cahiers du Monde russe* 45, no. 1–2 (January–June 2004): 195, 96, 99. The author exonerates Durnovo of any knowledge of the anti-Semitic pamphlets printed by his ministry and quotes his orders to regional governors to suppress pogroms.

21 For Kiev pogrom (1905), see William C. Fuller, *The Foe Within: Fantasies of Treason and the End of Imperial Russia* (Ithaca: Cornell University Press, 2006), 44. For Mendel Beilis, see Figes, *A People's Tragedy*, 241–44. For "Bogrov," see Abraham Ascher, *P. A. Stolypin: The Search for Stability in Late Imperial Russia* (Stanford: Stanford University Press, 2001): 380–89. For "Even as they waited," see Robert K. Massie, *Nicholas and Alexandra* (New York: Atheneum, 1967), 216–17. For Kokovtsov's comments, see H. H. Fisher, ed., *Out of My Past: The Memoirs of Count Kokovtsov* (Stanford: Stanford University Press, 1935), 272–74.

22 Kokovtsov, *Out of My Past*, 274–75. For Nicholas on "Englishman," see Witte, *Memoirs*, 189. For "nightmare" and "guiltless mass," see Podlbolotov, 200. For Nicholas's role in the notorious 1913 trial for "ritual murder" of Mendel Beilis, see Hans Rogger, "The Beilis Case: Anti-Semitism and Politics in the Reign of Nicholas II," *Slavic Review* 25, no. 4 (December 1966): 615–29. Nicholas knew Beilis was innocent before he came to trial "but carried on with the prosecution in the belief that his conviction would be justified in order to prove that the Jewish cult of ritual murder was a fact," Figes, *A People's Tragedy*, 243.

23 Kokovtsov, *Out of My Past*, 349.

24 L. C. F. Turner, *Origins of the First World War* (New York: Norton, 1970), 34. "Joffre" is from *The Memoirs of Count Kokovtsov*, 371. For "reforms," see George Edward Snow, "The Kokovtsov Commission: An Abortive Attempt at Labor Reform in Russia in 1905," *Slavic Review* 34, no. 4 (December 1972): 780–96.

25 Sazonov, *Fateful Years*, 288.

26 The description of Sukhomlinov is from Massie, *Nicholas and Alexandra*, 271. Sukhomlinov's career and marriage is the subject of William C. Fuller Jr., *The Foe Within: Fantasies of Treason and the End of Imperial Russia* (Ithaca: Cornell University Press, 2006), which is also the source of "lasted for a couple of hours" in the paragraph above, 80. For number of machine guns, see Alan K. Wildman, *The End of the Russian Imperial Army: The Old Army and the Soldiers' Revolt* (Princeton: Princeton University Press, 1980), 74.

27 For "banquets," see Kokovtsov, *Out of My Past*, 340. For Nicholas on "public opinion," see Witte, *Memoirs*, 190.

28 Bestuzhev, "Russian Foreign Policy February–June 1914," 103.

29 Sidney Bradshaw Fay, *The Origins of the World War*, vol. 11 (New York: Macmillan, 1928), 298. These are 1914 figures. For a comparison of this crisis with that of July 1914, see David Stevenson, "Militarization and Diplomacy in Europe before 1914," *International Security* 22, no. 1 (Summer 1997): 140–60. Unless otherwise indicated, all subsequent quotations from the meeting with Nicholas are from *The Memoirs of Count Kokovtsov*, 340–49, hereafter cited as *Kokovtsov*.

30 *Kokovtsov*. For Alexander, see Fay, *Origins of the World War*, 480.

31 *Kokovtsov*, continued. L. C. F. Turner, "The Russian Mobilization in 1914," *Journal of Contemporary History* 3, no. 1 (January 1968): 66–67. Fay, *Origins of the World War*, 67; George F. Kennan, *The Fateful Alliance: France, Russia, and the Coming of the First World War* (New York: Pantheon, 1984). For Alexander listening to the Marseillaise, see David M. McDonald, "The Durnovo Memorandum in Context: Official Conservatism and the Crisis of Autocracy," *Jahrbücher für Geschichte Osteuropas*, 1, no. 4 (1996): 488.

32 Luigi Albertini, *The Origins of the War of 1914*, vol. 1 (London: Oxford University Press, 1952), 401. For Francis Ferdinand, see E. C. Helmreich, "An Unpublished Report on Austro-German Military Conversations of November, 1912," *Journal of Modern History* 5, no. 2 (June, 1933): 200.

33 For the shift in the French commitment, see the discussion in Albertini, *The Origins of the War of 1914*, 402–26, quotations are from 424, 407. Also see Gordon Wright, *Raymond Poincaré and the French Presidency* (Stanford: Stanford University Press, 1942), 29. "Poincaré presented the idea that Russia might drag France into a war originating in the Balkans, but by ceasing to restrain his ally this one time he showed that the French government would accept such a war if necessary." For Poincaré's denial see Bernadotte Schmitt, *Foreign Affairs* 5, no. 1 (October 1926): 132–47. "When Izvolski telegraphed St. Petersburg in November 1912 that Poincaré had said that 'it was for Russia to take the initiative . . . the role of France to lend her the most active assistance'—[Poincaré] protested this interpretation of his language" by an ambassador who "was not ashamed to substitute his own ideas for those of his government" or to misrepresent the views of the French government. For "Russia will not fight," see William C. Wohlforth, "The Perception of Power: Russia in the Pre-1914 Balance," *World Politics* 39, no. 3 (April 1987): 359; for British cable, see Fay, *Origins of the World War*, 328. For "Foch" and "Wilson," see John C. Cairns, "International Politics and the Military Mind: The Case of the French Republic, 1911–1914," *Journal of Modern History* 25, no. 3 (September 1953): 275.

34 *Kokovtsov*. For Sukhomlinov, see Fuller, *The Foe Within*, 242–50.

35 Wohlforth, "The Perception of Power," 362. "In no other country (with the possible exception of Germany) was the assessment of Russian lower than in Russia herself." Wohlforth, 365. For Bethmann Hollweg, see Dale Copeland, *The Origins of Major War* (Ithaca: Cornell University Press, 2000), 64. "Bismarck was not an exponent of preventive war. It was, he once remarked, equivalent to shooting yourself in the head because you are afraid to die." Christopher Clark, *Iron Kingdom: The Rise and Downfall of Prussia, 1600–1945* (Cambridge: Harvard University Press, 2007), 549.

36 For "the last crisis," see Fritz Fischer, *War of Illusions: German Policies from 1911 to 1914* (New York: Norton, 1975), 332. A. J. P. Taylor, *The Struggle for Mastery in Europe 1848–1918* (New York: Oxford University Press, 1971), 507.

37 For Russia's trade, see Fischer, "War of Illusions," 330–31. For "Sazonov," see Albertini, *The Origins of the War of 1914*, 416.

38 For "Nicholas," see McDonald, *United Government and Foreign Policy*, 202. On Russia's source in Vienna, see Alex Marshall, "Russian Military Intelligence 1905–1917: The Untold Story Behind Tsarist Russia in the First World War," *War in History* 4, no. 4 (2004): 393–423.

39 The discussion of the von Sanders mission draws heavily on Robert L. Kerner, "The Mission of Liman von Sanders. I. Its Origin," *Slavonic Review* 6, no. 16 (June 1927): 12–27; also "The Mission of Liman von Sanders. II. The Crisis," *Slavonic Review* 6, no. 17 (December 1927): 344–62; also "The Mission of Liman von Sanders. III." *Slavonic Review* 6, no. 18 (March 1928): 533–60; and "The Mission of Liman von Sanders. IV. The Aftermath," *Slavonic Review* 7, no. 19 (June 1928): 90–112. For other views of Liman's mission, see Ulrich Trumpener, "Liman von Sanders and the German-Ottoman Alliance," *Journal of Contemporary History* 1, no. 4 (October 1966): 179–92, and H. S. W. Corrigan, "German-Turkish Relations and the Outbreak of World War in 1914: A Reassessment," *Past and Present* no. 36 (April 1967): 144–52. For background on the Balkan Wars, see Syed Tanvir Wasti, "The 1912–1913 Balkan Wars and the Siege of Edirne," *Middle Eastern Studies* 40, no. 4 (July 2004): 59–78. For Sazonov's prewar diplomay, see Ronald Bobroff, "Behind the Balkan Wars: Russian Policy toward Bulgaria and the Turkish Straits, 1912–13," *Russian Review* 59, no. 1 (January 2000): 76–95.

40 Kaiser's gloss on the cable is from Fay, *Origins of the World War*, 506.

41 For Liman, see Kerner, "The Mission of Liman von Sanders. IV. The Aftermath," 111. Summary of consequences of closing the Straits is from Henry Morgenthau, *Ambassador Morgenthau's Story* (Garden City, NY: Doubleday, Page, 1918), 7. For Turkey's entrance into the war, Robert J. Kerner, "Russia, the Straits, and Constantinople, 1914–1915," *Journal of Modern History* 1, no. 3 (September 1929): 400–15. For "Liman Pasha," see *The Memoirs of Raymond Poincaré 1914* (London: Heinemann, 1929), 26. Quotation about Bolshevism is from A. J. P. Taylor. Seen in Peter Vansittart, *Voices from the Great War* (New York: Franklin Watt, 1984), 45.

42 Scenes with Bethmann and the kaiser are from *Kokovtsov*, 384–94.

43 For Bethmann's being out of the loop on the von Sanders decision, see Gordon A. Craig, *Germany 1866–1945* (New York: Oxford University Press, 1978), 337, n. 106. For "I sensed," see Copeland, *The Origins of Major War*, 83. For "private joke," see Rodrick R. McLean, *Royalty and Diplomacy in Europe, 1890–1914* (Cambridge: Cambridge University Press, 2001), 37.

44 For the kaiser on the "racial struggle," see Keith Wilson, "Hamlet—With and Without the Prince: Terrorism at the Outbreak of the First World War," *Journal of Conflict Studies* 27, no. 2 (2007): 5 (electronic form). For "mad," see McClean,

Royalty and Diplomacy in Europe, 1890–1914, 44. Wilhelm's effect on Nicholas is the subject of Lamar Cecil, "William II and His Russian 'Colleagues,'" in Carol Fink, Isabel V. Hull, and MacGregor Knox, eds., *German Nationalism and the European Response, 1890–1945* (Norman: University of Oklahoma Press, 1985), 106–33. For British reaction to Liman, see the London *Times*, November 29, 1913.

45 For Russia's growth, see Hew Strachan, *The First World War* (New York: Penguin, 2003), 14.

46 For arrival in Constantinople, see Liman von Sanders, *Five Years in Turkey* (Annapolis: U.S. Naval Institute Press, 1927), 3.

47 "Von Strempel" is from Kerner, "The Mission of Liman von Sanders. II. The Crisis," 348; "sop" is from Kerner, "The Mission of Liman von Sanders. III," 556.

48 *Novoe vremia* and the Russian military attaché are from Fischer, "War of Illusions," 348, 338.

49 For Britain's adviser to the Turkish navy, see Samuel R. Williamson Jr., "German Perceptions of the Triple Entente after 1911: Their Mounting Apprehensions Reconsidered," *Foreign Policy Analysis* 7 (2011): 210. "Zabern" is from Kerner, "The Mission of Liman von Sanders. III," 556.

50 McDonald, *United Government and Foreign Policy in Russia*, 190: Raymond Cohen, "Threat Perception in International Crisis," *Political Science Quarterly* 93, no. 1 (Spring 1978): 93–107.

51 Bismarck spoke to Russia's dilemma in a parable about two travelers in a carriage. One reaches for his pistol, and the other must respond. See James J. Sheehan, *Where Have All the Soldiers Gone? The Transformation of Modern Europe* (Boston: Houghton Mifflin, 2008), xviii–xix.

52 This account follows Albertini, *The Origins of the War of 1914*, 541–50. Kokovtsov gave a version of the January 13 meeting more favorable to Sazonov to a writer in *Foreign Affairs* in 1929: "[Sazonov's] report was in the nature of an academic discussion of future preparations, and was absolutely remote from the idea of directing Russia along the path of immediate and aggressive policy in the Turkish question." See Michael T. Florinsky, "Russia and Constantinople: Count Kokovtsov's Evidence," *Foreign Affairs* (October 1929): 139. During the July Crisis, German chancellor Bethmann Hollweg made a similar argument to Sazonov's above. Whereas Sazonov posited the worst-case scenario of France, persuaded that Russia would not fight, jumping its Dual Alliance traces and allying with Germany, the Riezler diaries quote Bethmann maintaining that if Germany failed to support Austria in its confrontation with Serbia over Sarajevo, Austria would seek "a rapprochement with the Western powers whose arms are wide open, and we shall lose our last military ally." See V. R. Berghahn, *Germany and the Approach of War in 1914* (New York: St. Martin's Press, 1973), 192.

53 For Tsaritsyn, see Gregory L. Freeze, "Subversive Piety: Religion and the Political Crisis in Late Imperial Russia," *Journal of Modern History* 68, no. 2 (June 1996): 340, n. 130. Rasputin's misdeeds are from Edward Radzinski, *The Rasputin File* (New York: Doubleday, 2000) and Richard Pipes, *The Russian Revolution* (New York: Alfred A. Knopf), 199.

54 *Kokovtsov*, 293. Incident combines Massie, *Nicholas and Alexandra*, 200; Alex De

Jong, *The Life and Times of Grigori Rasputin* (New York: Carroll & Graf, 1982), 190; Bernard Pares, *The Fall of the Russian Monarchy* (London: Cape, 1939), 148–49.

55 For "Moscow journal," see Massie, *Nicholas and Alexandra*, 216; "Rasputin-schina," see Freeze, *Subversive Piety*, 339.

56 Radzinski, *The Rasputin File*, 265.

57 Scene follows *Kokovtsov*, 295–300.

58 For Kokovtsov's testimony, see Radzinski, *The Rasputin File*, 205.

59 For snub, see Pares, *The Fall of the Russian Monarchy*, 149. *Kokovtsov*, 220. For Alexandra's antagonism toward Stolypin, see Greg King, *The Man Who Killed Rasputin: Prince Felix Youssouprov and the Murder That Helped Bring Down the Russian Empire* (Secaucus: Citadel Press, 1995), 40.

60 For Nicholas's trip, see Figes, *A People's Tragedy*, 5. For "financial aversion," see M. Loukianov, "Conservatives and 'Renewed Russia,' 1907–1914" *Slavic Review* 61, 4 (Winter 2002): 775.

61 Patricia Herlihy, " 'Joy of the Rus': Rites and Rituals of Russian Drinking," *Russian Review* 50, no. 2 (April 1991): 131–47.

62 Patricia Herlihy, *The Alcoholic Empire: Vodka and Politics in Late Imperial Russia* (New York: Oxford University Press, 2002), 138ff.; Joan Neuberger, *Hooliganism: Crime, Culture, and Power in St. Petersburg, 1900–1914* (Berkeley: University of California Press, 1993), 35–43, 124–25, 220–21, 226–27, 285–89.

63 Herlihy, *The Alcoholic Empire*, 159–60; David R. Costello, "*Novoe vremia* and the Conservative Dilemma, 1911–1914," *Russian Review* 37, no. 1 (January 1978): 46–48.

63 Herlihy, *The Alcoholic Empire*, 138–45. For bread riot, see Wildman, *The End of the Russian Imperial Army*, 130. For concoction, see Figes, *A People's Tragedy*, 298. History repeated itself in 1985, when Mikhail S. Gorbachev "restricted vodka sales to get Russians back to the assembly line." Vodka taxes provided 25 percent of the entire Soviet budget. "The Kremlin tried to patch the budget hole by printing more money, which worsened the hyper-inflation that hastened the downfall of the communist state." See Mark Lawrence Schrad, "Moscow's Drinking Problem," *New York Times,* April 17, 2011.

64 This discussion of Kokovtsov's firing follows Fay, *Origins of the World War*, 512–31, and *Kokovtsov*, 407–31. For "greasy pole," see Figes, *A People's Tragedy*, 278.

65 Dominic Lieven, *Nicholas II: Emperor of All the Russias*, 178.

66 For anti-German party, see Albertini, *The Origins of the War of 1914*, vol. 11, 182. For Bethmann, see Fritz Fischer, "Twenty-Five Years Later: Looking Back on the 'Fischer Controversy' and Its Consequences," *Central European History* 21, no. 3 (September 1988): 215. For Baron Taube on removal of the restraining brake, see David M. McDonald, "The Durnovo Memorandum in Context: Official Conservatism and the Crisis of Autocracy," 494. Fay, *Origins of the World War*, 536–38. For Sazonov, see Robert J. Kerner, "Russia, the Straits, and Constantinople, 1914–1915," *Journal of Modern History* 1, no. 3 (September 1929): 402. For Taube, see Albertini, 550, n. 2. Abraham Ascher ventures that had *he* lived, Stolypin, "given his previous insistence that Russia must avoid war," would "have tried to keep Russia at peace" in 1914. From the State Council, "Durnovo might have sided with Stolypin in pressing for the avoidance of war, and they, supported by other rightists fearful of war, might have made an impact at the court. This is all speculation, to be sure." Ascher, *P. A. Stolypin*, 392–94. Kokovtsov "had neither the force of personality nor the political skills" to have performed that role.

67 Albertini, *The Origins of the War of 1914*, vol. 11, 294. For Sazonov and partial mobilization, see Jack S. Levy, "Preferences, Constraints, and Choices in July 1914," *International Security* 15, no. 3 (Winter 1990–1991): 180, n. 101. For "all-or-nothing choice," see Stephen Van Evera, "Why Cooperation Failed in 1914," *World Politics* 38, no. 1 (October 1985): 104. David Stevenson argues that the "Period Preparatory for War" measures, "applied in the military districts opposite Germany as well as opposite Austria-Hungary"—purchasing "horses, food, and fodder," clearing the "frontier railways of rolling stock," and "under the guise of maneuvers mov[ing] up extra forces to the border"—"to some extent *were* mobilization," were seen as such by the Germans, and if continued would have "obliged Germany to mobilize" even if Russia had not openly proclaimed mobilization. See Stevenson, "Militarization and Diplomacy in Europe before 1914," 152–53. For scene with Alexandra, see Theodor Wolff, *The Eve of 1914* (London: Gollancz, 1935), 553.

68 For "criminologists," see David R. Costello, "*Novoe vremia* and the Conservative Dilemma," *Russian Review* 37, no. 1 (January 1978): 47.

69 For strike, see the accounts in Leopold Haimson, "The Problem of Social Stability in Russia, 1905–1917" (Part One), *Slavic Review* 23, no. 4 (December 1964): 619–642, esp. 635–42; Robert B. McKean, *St. Petersburg Between the Revolutions: Workers and Revolutionaries, June 1907–February 1917* (New Haven: Yale University Press, 1990), 308–14; Hans Rogger, "Russia in 1914," *Journal of Contemporary History* 1, no. 4 (October 1966): 98–101.

70 For Potemkin crowds, see Rogger, "Russia in 1914," 107. For Pourtalés, see Fay, *The Origins of the World War*, vol. II, 306; details also taken from the London *Times*, July 20–26, 1914.

71 Richard Ned Lebow, "The Deterrence Deadlock: Is There a Way Out?" *Political Psychology* 4, no. 2 (June 1983): 336. For declining numbers of executions, see S. S. Oldenburg, *Last Tsar: Nicholas II, His Reign and His Russia* (Gulf Breeze, FL: Academic International Press, 1975), 75.

72 For strikes after August 1, see Rogger, "Russia in 1914," 108. For Cambon, see Fay, *Origins of the World War*, vol. II, 305. For "drown in blood," see Wohlforth, "The Perception of Power," 360.

73 Follows D. W. Spring, "Russia and the Coming of War," in R. J. W. Evans and Harmut Pogge von Strandmann, eds., *The Coming of the First World War* (New York: Oxford University Press, 1988), esp. distinction of "publics" on 58, also 80–86. For "according to a colleague," see Rogger, "Russia in 1914," 109. For trade figures, see Geyer, *Russian Imperialism*, 308. For "literate," see Fay, *The Origins of the World War*, 265. For newspaper circulations, see Thomas Riha, "Riech: A Portrait of a Russian Newspaper," *Slavic Review* 22, no. 4 (December 1963): 663–82.

74 For "liberal review," see Rogger, "Russia in 1914," p. 109; also on liberal views, Leopold Haimson, "The Problem of Social Stability in Urban Russia, 1905–1917 (Part Two)," *Slavic Review* 24, no. 1 (March 1965): 1–22. For centrist member, see

Geoffrey A. Hosking, *The Russian Constitutional Experiment: Government and Duma, 1907–1914* (Cambridge: Cambridge University Press, 1973), 240–41.

75 For "Kurchernigo," see Josh Sanborn, "The Mobilization of 1914 and the Question of the Russian Nation: A Reexamination," *Slavic Review* 59, no. 2 (Summer 2000): 272–73. For Russian casualties, see Melissa K. Stockdale, "My Death for the Motherland Is Happiness," *American Historical Review* 109, no. 1 (February 2004), 89, n. 32, total deaths, and Figes, *A People's Tragedy*, 773.

76 Nicolas de Basily, *The Abdication of Emperor Nicholas II of Russia* (Princeton: Kingston Press, 1984), 95–96. I elided a word in the final quotation—"not"— between "Germany" and "allowed," for ease of reading.

NOTES FOR CHAPTER 3

1 The Asquith quotation above seen in David French, "The Edwardian Crisis and the Origins of the First World War," *International Review of History* 4, no. 2 (May 1982): 218. For the *Times* quotation, see David Powell, *The Edwardian Crisis: Britain, 1901–1914* (New York: Palgrave, 1996), 162. On the danger of civil war, Powell writes, "There can be little doubt that if the Liberals had gone ahead with their Home Rule Bill without securing agreement on [excluding Ulster from it] a violent rebellion in Ulster would have resulted, with every likelihood of national para-militaries becoming involved in a virtual civil war," 161.

2 For spy, see Samuel R. Williamson Jr., "German Perceptions of the Triple Entente after 1911: Their Mounting Apprehensions Reconsidered," *Foreign Policy Analysis* 7 (2011): 205–14.

3 For hostility to Germany, see Michael Ekstein, "Sir Edward Grey and Imperial Germany in 1914," *Journal of Contemporary History* 6, no. 3 (1971): 9. Hobhouse, see Keith M. Wilson, *The Policy of the Entente: Essays on the Determinants of British Foreign Policy 1904–1914* (London: Cambridge University Press, 1985), 145. For "economy of truth," see Cameron Hazlehurst, "Asquith as Prime Minister, 1908–1916," *English Historical Review* 85, no. 336 (July 1970): 519. For balance, see John W. Coogan and Peter F. Coogan, "The British Cabinet and the Anglo-French Staff Talks, 1905–1914: Who Knew What and When Did He Know It?" *Journal of British Studies* 24, no. 1 (January 1985): 110–31.

4 For Churchill, see Randolph S. Churchill, *Winston S. Churchill: Young Statesman, 1901–1914, Volume 2* (Boston: Houghton Mifflin, 1967), 578–79.

5 For Hötzendorf, see Solomon Wank, "Some Reflections on Conrad von Hötzendorf and His Memoirs Based on Old and New Sources," in *Austrian History Yearbook*, vol. 1 (1965): 82.

6 On July 4 is from French, "The Edwardian Crisis and the Origins of the First World War," 218. Niall Ferguson, "The Kaiser's European Union," in Niall Ferguson, ed., *Virtual History: Alternatives and Counterfactuals* (New York: Basic Books, 1997), 276.

7 See Ian F. W. Beckett, *The Great War, 1914–1918* (New York: Pearson, 2001), 386.

8 Alvin Jackson, *Home Rule: An Irish History, 1800–2000* (New York: Oxford University Press, 2003), 9, 23. For "English bayonets," see Elizabeth A. Muenger, *The British Military Dilemma in Ireland: Occupation Politics, 1886–1914* (Lawrence:

University of Kansas Press, 1991), 3. Parnell quotation is taken from a John Redmond speech seen in the *Times*, April 9, 1914. For seven centuries, see David Gardner, "Royal Visit Will Dispel Ghosts of Once-Troubled Irish Relationship," *Financial Times*, May 16, 1911.

9 For Parnell's deal, see Patrick Buckland, *Ulster Unionism and the Origins of Northern Ireland 1886–1922* (New York: Barnes & Noble Books), 7. For more see F. S. L. Lyons, *Charles Stewart Parnell* (New York: Oxford University Press, 1977), and for Parnell on "march of a nation," see 351.

10 For background on the budget and elections, see R. J. Q. Adams, *Bonar Law* (London: John Murray, 1999), 38–9. For election and the Liberals' bargain, see Keith Jeffrey, *Field Marshal Sir Henry Wilson: A Political Soldier* (New York: Oxford University Press, 2006), 113. For Redmond, see George Dangerfield, *The Damnable Question: A History of Anglo-Irish Relations* (Boston: Little, Brown, 1977), 55. For Redmond in Limerick, see Pembroke Wicks, *The Truth about Home Rule* (Boston: Small, Maynard, 1913), 5.

11 Joseph P. Finnan, *John Redmond and Irish Unity, 1912–1918* (Syracuse: Syracuse University Press, 2004), 44.

12 For "ordinary people," see A. T. Q. Stewart, *The Ulster Crisis: Resistance to Home Rule, 1912–1914* (London: Faber & Faber, 1967), 27. For Kipling, see Finnan, *John Redmond and Irish Unity*, 59.

13 For mixed marriages, see Buckland, *Ulster Unionism and the Origins of Northern Ireland*, xxxvi. Devlin quoted in letter to the editor of the *Times,* March 20, 1914. For close to Catholic hierarchy, see Thomas C. Kennedy, "War, Patriotism, and the Ulster Unionist Council," *Éire-Ireland* 30, 3 and 4 (Fall/Winter, 2005): 190.

14 For Lady Londonderry, see Thomas C. Kennedy, "Troubled Tories: Dissent and Confusion Concerning the Party's Ulster Policy, 1910–1914," *Journal of British Studies* 46 (July 2007): 574. For Carson, see Geoffrey Lewis, *Carson: The Man Who Divided Ireland* (New York: Humbledon, 2005), 42–45.

15 For the trial, see Richard Ellmann, *Oscar Wilde* (New York: Knopf, 1988), 447–62. For classmate, see Hesketh Pearson, *The Life of Oscar Wilde* (London: Metheun, 1946), 26.

16 For "morning Home Rule passes," see Lewis, *Carson: The Man Who Divided Ireland*, 80 and "a foreign, probably hostile," xii. The words are Lewis's. For "savage," see Kennedy, "Troubled Tories," 574.

17 For "rodomontade," see Dangerfield, *The Strange Death of Liberal England* (Stanford: Stanford University Press, 1997), 97. For Law's speech, see Buckland, *Ulster Unionism and the Origins of Northern Ireland*, 85.

18 For Churchill in Belfast, see Lewis, *Carson: The Man Who Divided Ireland*, 88–90. For "confetti" see Buckland, *Ulster Unionism and the Origins of Northern Ireland*, 56.

19 Roy Jenkins, *Churchill: A Biography* (New York: Farrar, Straus and Giroux, 2001), 234–36.

20 For "Orange card," see ibid., 13, 100–03. For the Siege of Derry, see Thomas Babington Macaulay, *History of England*, vol. 5 (Boston: Houghton Mifflin, 1899), 140ff.

21 See Churchill's speech in the *Times,* March 16, 1914.

22 Winston S. Churchill, *The World Crisis* (London: Macmillan, 1923).

23 For "green glasses" and "very much the same," see Patricia Jalland, "A Liberal Chief Secretary and the Irish Question: Augustine Birrell, 1907–1914," *Historical Journal* 19, no. 2 (June 1976): 423, 428, n. 30. For "holding girls' hands," see Williamson, *The Politics of Grand Strategy: Britain and France Prepare for War, 1904–1914* (Cambridge: Harvard University Press, 1969), 311.

24 For "Covenant," see Robert Rhodes James, ed., *Winston S. Churchill: His Complete Speeches 1897–1963,* vol. 3, 1914–1922 (New York: Chelsea House, 1974), 2228. Also see Jackson, *Home Rule,* 131. Quotation from pledge seen in Thomas C. Kennedy, "War, Patriotism, and the Ulster Unionist Council," 193.

25 For letter, see Muenger, *The British Military Dilemma in Ireland,* 177. Census figures from Iain McLean and Tom Lubbock, "The Curious Incident of the Guns in the Night Time: Curragh, Larne and the U.K. Constitution," 28. Paper presented at the Political Studies Association of the UK Annual Conference, Bath, April 2007.

26 For "working of the Irish executive," see A. P. Ryan, *Mutiny at the Curragh* (London: Macmillan, 1956), 115. For "Irish-American low class politicians," see Ian Beckett, ed., *The Army and the Curragh Incident, 1914* (London: Bodley Head, 1986), 36. For "extremist limit," see Dangerfield, *The Strange Death of Liberal England,* 275. Carson quotation from Lewis, *Carson: The Man Who Divided Ireland,* 135.

27 Patricia Jalland, *The Liberals and Ireland: The Ulster Question in British Politics to 1914* (New York: St. Martin's Press, 1976), 220.

28 For "The Coup," see Charles Townshend, *Political Violence in Ireland: Government and Resistance Since 1844* (London: Oxford University Press, 1983), 251–52. For "Carson," see Nicholas Mosley, *Julian Grenfell, His Life and the Times of His Death, 1888–1915* (London: Persephone Books, 1999), 324.

29 Jalland, *The Liberals and Ireland,* 223.

30 Churchill, *Winston S. Churchill,* vol. 2, 484. For "hellish insinuation," see John Charmley, *Churchill: The End of Glory* (New York: Harcourt, 1993), 94. For details see "The Plot That Failed: A Chapter of History," the London *Times,* April 27, 1914.

31 Jalland, *The Liberals and Ireland,* 222.

32 For "war man," see Arthur J. Marder, ed., *Fear God and Dread Nought: The Correspondence of Admiral of the Fleet Lord Fisher of Kilverstone,* vol. 2, *Years of Power 1904–1914* (London: Cape, 1954), 363. For Clementine's note to Asquith, see Jenkins, *Churchill,* 275.

33 For "battleships," see Churchill, *Winston S. Churchill,* vol. 2, 482. For "proximity to the coasts," see Rhodes James, *Winston S. Churchill: His Complete Speeches,* 2273. For "by every means," see Dangerfield, *The Strange Death,* 274–75. For "shot and shell," see Beckett, *The Army and the Curragh Incident,* 236, and K. M. Wilson, "Sir John French's Resignation over the Curragh Affair: The Role of the Editor of the 'Morning Post,'" *English Historical Review* 99, no. 393 (October 1984): 809.

34 For Riddell, see Churchill, *Winston S. Churchill,* vol. 2, 471.

35 Jenkins, *Churchill*, 238.
36 London *Times*, March 16, 1914.
37 *The Earl of Oxford and Asquith, Fifty Years of Parliament*, vol. 1 (London: Cassell, 1926), 239. For "olive branch," see Jalland, *The Liberals and Ireland*, 219.
38 For "Army Annual Act," see Thomas C. Kennedy, "Troubled Tories: Dissent and Confusion Concerning the Party's Ulster Policy, 1910–1914," *Journal of British Studies* 46 (July 2007): 587. For "Wilson," see the Marquess of Anglesey, *A History of the British Cavalry 1816 to 1919*, vol. 7 (London: Leo Cooper, 1996), 10. For the debate, see the transcript in the London *Times*, March 20, 1914. For Carson's brogue, see Roy Foster and Alvin Jackson, "Men for All Seasons? Carson, Parnell, and the Limits of Heroism in Modern Ireland," *European History Quarterly* 39, no. 3 (July 2009): 423. For Carson striking the brass bound books, see A. P. Ryan, *Mutiny at the Curragh* (New York: Macmillan, 1956), 123.
39 For the *Times* obituary, see Anglesey, *A History of the British Cavalry*, 10. For two battalions, see Rhodes James, *Winston S. Churchill: His Complete Speeches*, 2279. For meeting, see A. P. Ryan, *Mutiny at the Curragh* (New York: Macmillan, 1956), 120–21. For "bloody fool," see Jalland, *The Liberals and Ireland*, 225.
40 For "grave emergencies," see Churchill, *Winston S. Churchill*, vol. 2, 477, also Jalland, *The Liberals and Ireland*, 229. For the "whole place," see Beckett, *The Army and the Curragh Incident*, 285.
41 For "two camps," see Beckett, *The Army and the Curragh Incident*, 287. For "mutinous disaffection," see Jeffrey, *Field Marshal Sir Henry Wilson*, 121. "It was not, in fact, a 'mutiny,' since no one actually disobeyed orders." For telegram, see Ryan, *Mutiny at the Curragh*, 127. For navy, see Ian F. W. Beckett and Keith Jeffrey, "The Royal Navy and the Curragh Incident," *Historical Research* 62, no. 147 (February 1989): 54–69. For "general mutiny," see Charles Townshend, "Military Force and Civil Authority in the United Kingdom," *Journal of British Studies* 28, no. 3 (July 1989): 271.
42 For Venetia Stanley, see Cameron Hazlehurst, *Politicians at War, July 1914 to May 1915* (New York: Knopf, 1971), 169. For "Lloyd George," see Jalland, *The Liberals and Ireland*, 227.
43 For Seely, see Anglesey, *A History of the British Cavalry*, 7. For Wilson on both sides, see McLean and Lubbock, "The Curious Incident of the Guns in the Night Time," 10, 11. For "I dictated the terms," see Stephen Mark Duffy, "'No Question of Fighting': The Army, The Government and the Curragh Incident, 1914," diss., Texas A&M, 1993, 166. Seely added two one-sentence paragraphs. The last read: "But [the Government] have no intention whatever of taking advantage of this right [to maintain law and order in support of the civil power] to crush political opposition to the policy or principles of the Home Rule Bill." General Gough asked his superior, General French, "whether he might interpret the last two paragraphs . . . to mean that the Army would not be used to coerce Ulster. Sir J. F. added to the paper over his initials, 'This is how I read it.'" From a memorandum written by H. A. Gwynne, on April 2, 1914, after speaking with his friend, Sir John French. See Wilson, "Sir John French's Resignation over the Curragh Affair," 809.

44 London *Times*, March 21, 1914.

45 See letter to the editor, the London *Times*, March 30, 1914.

46 Seen in "The Curragh 'Mutiny' 1914," Curragh Historical Articles, at http://www.curragh.info/articles/mutiny.htm.

47 See Beckett, *The Army and the Curragh Incident*, 281.

48 For regular law and houghing above, see Townshend, *Political Violence*, 51, 7. See F. S. L. Lyons, *Ireland Since the Famine* (London: Fontana, 1973), 320, 336, 387.

49 For mood in the North and Roscommon Herald, see London *Times*, May 19, 1914. For "blind eye," see Beckett and Jeffrey, "The Royal Navy and the Curragh Incident," 68.

50 For Churchill, see Rhodes James, *Winston S. Churchill: His Complete Speeches*, 2285. For "seventy-five thousand," see Lyons, 323.

51 For Nationalist MP above, see Stephen Gwynn, *John Redmond's Last Years* (London: Arnold, 1919), 61. For Asquith to the king, see Iain McLean, "The Constitutional Position of the Sovereign: Letters Between King George V and Prime Minister H. H. Asquith, Autumn 1913," Nuffield College, University of Oxford Working Paper, No. 3, 2008, 11. A Project Gutenberg eBook. For Churchill, see Rhodes James, *Winston S. Churchill: His Complete Speeches*, 2285.

52 For the failure of government, see Townshend, *Political Violence*, 276. Churchill, from *The World Crisis*, 181.

53 Churchill, *The World Crisis*, p. 181. For "complete disaster," see the London *Times*, June 29, 1914. For the kaiser's summer cruise and Bethmann Hollweg, see John C. G. Röhl, "Wilhelm II in July 1914," in Afflerbach and Stevenson, *An Improbable War*, 81. For "deliberately deceived," see David Stevenson, "The European Land Arms Race," in same volume, 140. For Lloyd George at Guildhall, see the London *Times*, July 9, 1914; for "none of the snarling," see London *Times*, July 23, 1914. Also see Cameron Hazlehurst, *Politicians at War, July 1915 to May 1915* (New York: Knopf, 1971), 61. For headlines, see London *Times*, July 6, 10, 11, 1914.

54 For "my house," see Kennedy, "War, Patriotism, and the Ulster Unionist Council," 196. For Redmond, see Gwynn, *John Redmond's Last Years*, 65.

55 London *Times*, July 25, 1914.

56 Seen in Churchill, *Winston S. Churchill*, vol. 2, 488–89.

57 London *Times*, July 28, 1914.

58 For Mausers, see Townshend, *Political Violence*, 260.

59 For montage of Irish reaction, see D. George Boyce and Alan O'Day, eds., *The Ulster Crisis 1885–1921* (New York: Palgrave, 2005), 200–01.

60 London *Times*, July 28, 1914.

61 London *Times*, July 30, 1914.

62 For Asquith and Redmond after the failure of the Buckingham Palace Conference, see Donald Lammers, "Arno Mayer and the British Decision for War: 1914," *Journal of British Studies* 12, no. 2 (May 1973): 145–46, n. 30.

63 For Sava River, see Samuel R. Williamson, Jr., "Aggressive and Defensive

Aims of Political Elites? Austro-Hungarian Policy in 1914," in Afflerbach and Stevenson, *An Improbable War*, 72. For Asquith's speech, see Gwynn, *John Redmond's Last Years*, 67.

64 London *Times*, August 2, 1914. For Asquith and Churchill, see Dominic D. P. Johnson and Dominic Tierney, "The Rubicon Theory of War: How the Conflict Reaches the Point of No Return," *International Security* 36, no. 1 (Summer 2011): 35.

65 See Keith M. Wilson, *The Policy of the Entente: Essays on the Determinants of British Foreign Policy 1904–1914* (New York: Cambridge University Press, 1985), 141–47.

66 For note to Lloyd George, see Hazlehurst, *Politicians at War*, 294–95.

67 London *Times*, August 5, 1914.

68 For Craig, see A. T. Q. Stewart, *The Ulster Crisis, Resistance to Home Rule, 1912–1914* (London: Faber & Faber, 1967), 238; for Milner, 232. For Asquith, see Roy Jenkins, *Asquith* (London: Collins, 1964), 322–23.

69 For "grave miscalculation," see Röhl, "Wilhelm II in 1914," 79.

70 For "I am going," see Dangerfield, *The Strange Death of Liberal England*, 339. For Redmond's speech, see Gywnn, *John Redmond's Last Years*, 69–71. For Redmond's son, see Joseph P. Finnan, *John Redmond and Irish Unity, 1912–1918* (Syracuse: Syracuse University Press, 2004), 212.

71 For speech, see Gwynn, *John Redmond's Last Years*, 81–82. For Wicklow comment, see Lyons, *Ireland Since the Famine*, 328; for "Dev," 383; for "Proclamation," 369; for "green-liveried servants," 249. Also see James McConnel, "Recruiting Sergeants for John Bull? Irish Nationalist MPs and Enlistment During the Early Months of the Great War," *War in History* 14, no. 4 (2007): 406–28.

72 Finnan, *John Redmond and Irish Unity*, 2.

73 Lyons, *Ireland Since the Famine*, 386.

74 For conscription, see Trevor Wilson, *The Myriad Faces of War, Britain and the Great War, 1914–1918* (Cambridge, UK: Polity Press, 1986), 566, 645. For toast, see Finnan, *John Redmond and Irish Unity*, 4.

NOTES FOR CHAPTER 4

1 Epigraphs are from Mark Cronland Anderson, *Pancho Villa's Revolution by Headlines* (Norman: University of Oklahoma Press, 2000), 171, and Arthur S. Link, *Woodrow Wilson: Confusions and Crises 1915–1916* (Princeton: Princeton University Press, 1964), 292. For Norris, see Arthur S. Link, *Wilson: The New Freedom* (Princeton: Princeton University Press, 1956), 336.

2 For great and crying wrongs, see Link, *Confusions and Crises*, 394.

3 Friedrich Katz, *The Life & Times of Pancho Villa* (Stanford: Stanford University Press, 1998), 311–12. For "greatest Mexican," see Arthur S. Link, *Wilson: The Struggle for Neutrality 1914–1915* (Princeton: Princeton University Press, 1960), 239. For Wilson on "the man on the make," see John Morton Blum, *Woodrow Wilson and the Politics of Morality* (Boston: Little, Brown, 1956), p. 62. London *Times*, February 4, 1914.

4 For smuggling, see Andrés Reséndez Fuentes, "Battleground Women: *Solda-deras* and Female Soldiers in the Mexican Revolution," *Americas* 51, no. 4 (April 1995): 543.

5 Katz, *Pancho Villa*, 337.

6 For *La Nación*, Arthur S. Link, *Wilson: The New Freedom* (Princeton: Princeton University Press, 1956), 405, for "Remember that God," 5. "President Wilson," see Arthur S. Link, ed., *The Papers of Woodrow Wilson*, vol. 29, *Dec. 2, 1913–May 5, 1914* (Princeton: Princeton University Press, 1979), 94. For American diplomat's wife, see Lloyd C. Gardner, "Woodrow Wilson and the Mexican Revolution," in Arthur S. Link, ed., *Woodrow Wilson and a Revolutionary World, 1913–1921* (Chapel Hill: University of North Carolina Press, 1982), 6. For "You cannot," see Link, *The New Freedom*, 321. For Fourth of July speech, see Thomas A. Knock, *To End All Wars: Woodrow Wilson and the Quest for a New World Order* (New York: Oxford University Press, 1992), 28.

7 Friedrich Katz, "Rural Uprisings in Preconquest and Colonial Mexico," in Friedrich Katz, ed., *Riot, Rebellion, and Revolution: Rural Social Conflict in Mexico* (Princeton: Princeton University Press, 1986), 65–95.

8 Adolfo Gilly, *The Mexican Revolution* (London: Verso, 1983), 22–23, 368, n. 16. For branding of Indians, see John Gibler, *Mexico Unconquered: Chronicles of Power and Revolt* (San Francisco: City Light Books, 2009), 27.

9 Gilly, *The Mexican Revolution*, 23; Friedrich Katz, "Rural Rebellions after 1810," in Katz, ed., *Riot, Rebellion, and Revolution*, 521–61. "Something is scaring politicians here," reports Nicholas Casey in the January 15, 2010, edition of the *Wall Street Journal*. "It's the number 10." He quotes a historian who says that "[Revolution] is like a tradition that happens every hundred years." A leading Mexico City newspaper ran three columns on one day headlined THE FEAR OF 2010, THE IMPENDING REVOLUTION, and 2010: THIRD REVOLUTION.

10 Gilly, *The Mexican Revolution*, 23–25.

11 Carlos Fuentes, *The Old Gringo* (New York: Farrar, Straus and Giroux, 1985), 61–62.

12 Gilly, *The Mexican Revolution*, 25.

13 "Over half the nation's territory" seen in Gilbert G. González and Raúl Fernandez, "Empire and the Origins of Twentieth-Century Migration from Mexico to the United States," *Pacific Historical Review* 71, no. 1 (February 2002): 38; "fifty thousand villages," see Gilly, *The Mexican Revolution*, 46, 373.

14 For details on diet, see González and Fernandez, "Empire and the Origins," 31–38. Katz, "Rural Rebellions after 1810," 533. "When [the revolution] is over," see Gilly, *The Mexican Revolution*, 46.

15 Details on the Díaz system of social containment are taken from Frank McLynn, *Villa and Zapata: A Biography of the Mexican Revolution* (London: Jonathan Cape, 2000), 53–4, 7, and Katz, *Pancho Villa*, 123.

16 For Madero, see John Womack Jr., *Zapata and the Mexican Revolution* (New York: Vintage, 1970), 55. McLynn, *Villa and Zapata*, 25–32. Gilly, *The Mexican Revolution*, 59–63.

17 For the text of the plan, see Nora E. Jaffary, Edward W. Osowski, and Susie S.

Porter, *Mexican History: A Primary Source Reader* (Boulder: Westview, 2009), 298–300. Also see Womack, *Zapata and the Mexican Revolution*, 70. Katz, *Pancho Villa*, 54. Eric R. Wolf, *Peasant Wars of the Twentieth Century* (New York: Harper & Row, 1969), 16.
18 Katz, *Pancho Villa*, 63.
19 For "school," see McLynn, *Villa and Zapata*, 58. For "A rifle sight" see Anderson, *Pancho Villa's Revolution by Headlines*, 7. Martín Luis Guzmán, *Memoirs of Pancho Villa* (Austin: University of Texas Press, 1976), 3.
20 For Reed, see Katz, *Pancho Villa*, 7. For "Robin Hood," see Link, *The Papers of Woodrow Wilson*, vol. 29, 229.
21 For Villa's early life, see Katz, *Pancho Villa*, 67–77. Eric Hobsbawm, *Bandits* (New York: Pantheon, 1981), 17, 33.
22 Katz, *Pancho Villa*, 72.
23 McLynn, *Villa and Zapata*, 68–69. For Villa's descent into barbarism, see Thomas H. Naylor, "Massacre at San Pedro de la Cueva: The Significance of Pancho Villa's Disastrous Sonora Campaign," *Western Historical Quarterly* 8, no. 2 (April 1977): 125–150. "In Sonora, Villa lost his capacity for responsible leadership. He became instead a callous, vindictive demon," 150.
24 For American doctor, see Katz, *Pancho Villa*, 75. For reporter, see Arthur S. Link, *Wilson: The Struggle for Neutrality* (Princeton: Princeton University Press, 1960), 234. For Villa's fear of poisoning, see Katz, *Pancho Villa*, 242; for "scores of promises," see 148.
25 For "Johnny," see Gilly, *The Mexican Revolution*, 393.
26 Katz, *Pancho Villa*, 77.
27 For "barely able to," see Gilly, *The Mexican Revolution*, 75. Zapata's threat to Madero from Womack, *Zapata and the Mexican Revolution*, 127.
28 For "anarchy," see Katz, *Pancho Villa*, 115. "Durnovo," see Frank Alfred Golder, *Documents of Russian History 1914–1917* (New York: The Century Co., 1927), 19–21.
29 For "Attila of the South," see Samuel Brunk, "The Sad Situation of Civilians and Soldiers: The Banditry of Zapatismo in the Mexican Revolution," *American Historical Review* 101, no. 2 (April 1996): 331–53. For "energetic purification," see Gilly, *The Mexican Revolution*, 88–89. "English estate owner," see Katz, *Pancho Villa*, 121; "There is no respect," 132; "Suppose a wealthy white man," 121.
30 For the forerunner of coups to come, see Katz, *Pancho Villa*, 193–95.
31 For man "of unstable temper" and details of Villa's return to Mexico, see Katz, *Pancho Villa*, 205–06.
32 For "nine rifles," see Guzmán, *Memoirs of Pancho Villa*, 95.
33 For "The time for leaving," see Link, ed., *The Papers of Woodrow Wilson*, vol. 29, 353, 55. "In fact" and "He once said," see Link, *The New Freedom*, 67–68.
34 For "Taft wanted," see Blum, *Woodrow Wilson and the Politics of Morality*, 88.
35 For "the mere existence" and "to inquire," see Peter V. N. Henderson, "Victoriano Huerta and the Recognition Issue in Mexico," in *Americas* 41, no. 2 (October 1984): 151–76.
36 For "Huerta," see Michael C. Meyer, *Huerta: A Political Portrait* (Lincoln: University of Nebraska Press, 1972), 138.

37 For assassinated deputy, see Charles G. Cumberland, *The Mexican Revolution*: *The Constitutionalist Years* (Austin: University of Texas Press, 1972), 67. "The force of America," Blum, *Woodrow Wilson and the Politics of Morality*, 84.

38 For "the only satisfactory," see Cumberland, *The Mexican Revolution*, 105. ASARCO, see Katz, *Pancho Villa*, 313. For Wilson at Mobile, see Mark T. Gilderhus, "Revolution, War, and Expansion: Woodrow Wilson in Latin America," in John Milton Cooper Jr., ed., *Reconsidering Woodrow Wilson* (Baltimore: Johns Hopkins University Press, 2008), 171.

39 Friedrich Katz, *The Secret War in Mexico: Europe, the United States, and the Mexican Revolution* (Chicago: University of Chicago Press, 1981), 149. For U.S. racial attitudes toward Mexicans, see Mark C. Anderson, "What's to Be Done with 'Em? Images of Mexican Cultural Backwardness, Racial Limitations, and Moral Decrepitude in the United States Press, 1913–1915," *Mexican Studies* 14, no. 1 (Winter 1998): 23–70.

40 Anderson, *Pancho Villa's Revolution by Headlines*, 45–48.

41 For "bribe," see Meyer, *Huerta*, 119; "settling a revolution" is from Kendrick A. Clements, "Emissary from a Revolution: Luis Cabrera and Woodrow Wilson," *Americas* 35, no. 3 (January 1979): 358.

42 "So long as," see Link, *The Papers of Woodrow Wilson*, vol. 29, 229; "My ideal," 516, and "for the land," 519. For "John Reed," see the *New York Times*, April 27, 1913.

43 For "Mr. Bryan considered" and Hohler, see Link, *The Papers of Woodrow Wilson*, 255–61. For "messenger," the London *Times*, February 4, 1914. "Supposing a man," Katz, *Secret War*, 257. "A patriot and," Anderson, *Pancho Villa's Revolution by Headlines*, 25.

44 For "bloodbath," see Clements, "Emissary from a Revolution," 364.

45 Katz, *Pancho Villa*, 326–30.

46 For "undertaken the obligation" and "Mexico is on," see the London *Times*, February 23, 1914.

47 For "You have the" see Anderson, *Pancho Villa's Revolution by Headlines*, 24. For Fierro, see Katz, *Pancho Villa*, 329. "An examination would," the London *Times*, February 24, 1914.

48 For "He seems, so," see Link, *The Papers of Woodrow Wilson*, vol. 29, 293.

49 For "stealing pretty women," see Katz, *Pancho Villa*, 289; for Juárez, see 224.

50 For "intellectual," see Katz, *Pancho Villa*, 179. For the limits of Villa's radicalism, see Alan Knight, "Peasant and Caudillo in Revolutionary Mexico 1910–1917," in D. A. Brading, ed., *Caudillo and Peasant in the Mexican Revolution* (New York: Cambridge University Press, 1980), 33–34.

51 For "press gang," see Andrés Reséndez Fuentes, "Battleground Women," 532–33. For paragraph, Katz, *Pancho Villa*, 229–52.

52 For "What is your role," see Katz, *Pancho Villa*, 296.

53 For "I formed the," see Guzmán, *Memoirs*, 96–97.

54 For "Some of them," see Link, *The Papers of Woodrow Wilson*, vol. 29, 123. For all other references, see Andrés Reséndez Fuentes, "Battleground Women," 533, 543, 544.

55 Katz, *Pancho Villa*, 544.

56 For Jaurès quotation, see Brynjolf J. Hovde, "French Socialism and Franco-German Relations, 1893–1914," *Journal of Political Economy* 35, no. 2 (April 1927): 268. For fear of revolution, see Arno J. Mayer, *The Persistence of the Old Regime: Europe to the Great War* (New York: Pantheon, 1981), 304. For war and counterrevolution, see Arno J. Mayer, *Dynamics of Counterrevolution in Europe, 1870–1956: An Analytical Framework* (New York: Harper Torchbooks, 1971), 134–49. For attitudes of European powers toward the Mexican Revolution, see Katz, *Secret War*, 550–78. For *Morning Post*, see Dennis R. Hidalgo, "The Evolution of History and the Informal Empire: *La Decena Trágica* and the British Press," *Mexican Studies* 23, no. 2 (Summer 2007): 347–49. Quotation on the international significance of the Mexican Revolution is from Lloyd C. Gardner, "Woodrow Wilson and the Mexican Revolution," in Arthur S. Link, ed., *Woodrow Wilson and a Revolutionary World, 1913–1921* (Chapel Hill: University of North Carolina Press, 1982), 4.

57 For massacre, see Joshua Charles Walker, "Immigrants at Home: Revolution, Nationalism, and Anti-Chinese Sentiment in Mexico, 1910–1935," senior honor thesis, presented by Ohio State University, 2008, Walker quotes from a U.S. consul on the scene. *Washington Post*, April 24, 1914. "Their soldiers numbered," Guzmán, *Memoirs*, p. 153.

58 For movie men, see John Womack Jr., "Pancho Villa: A Revolutionary Life," *Journal of the Historical Society* 11, no. 1 (Winter 2002): 27–29. "So that it seemed," Andrés Reséndez Fuentes, "Battleground Women," 541, n. 77.

59 For "They are able," see the London *Times*, January 6, 1914. "What are you," Katz, *Pancho Villa*, 293.

60 For "Villa led charges," see Guzmán, *Memoirs*, 150; for "[The federals] were dying," see 159. Details of battle taken from the *Washington Post*, March 24–29, 1914. For casualties, see the London *Times*, April 3, 1914. For the seven rings of dead, and French and German gunners, see the *New York Times*, April 4, 1914. For retreat of federals, see the *New York Times*, April 5, 1914.

61 Katz, *Pancho Villa*, 304. Description of Villa holding court at the hotel is from the *New York Times*, April 4, 1914.

62 For "Huerta had roughly," see Katz, *Secret War*, 248. For "the utter demoralization," see Alan Knight, *The Mexican Revolution*, vol. 2 (New York: Cambridge University Press, 1986), 163. Huerta's farewell, the *New York Times*, July 16, 1914.

63 For officers pocketing pay of dead soldiers, see Meyer, *Huerta*, 101.

64 Lind-Wilson follows the discussion in Knight, *The Mexican Revolution* (New York: Cambridge University Press, 1986), 150–55. Also see Lind's March 12 letter to Bryan, in Link, *The Papers of Woodrow Wilson*, vol. 29, 338. Also Blum, *Woodrow Wilson and the Politics of Morality*, 11. For Lind's "very violent language," see Larry D. Hill, *Emissaries to a Revolution: Woodrow Wilson's Executive Agents in Mexico* (Baton Rouge: LSU Press, 1973), 175.

65 Knight, *The Mexican Revolution*, 151; "gun by gun" from the London *Times*, April 19, 1914.

66 For speech, see Link, *The Papers of Woodrow Wilson*, vol. 29, 471–74.

67 For "President Wilson did," see Link, *The Papers of Woodrow Wilson*, vol. 30, 235, 223.

68 For battleships, see the *New York Times*, April 15, 1914. For Mexican Navy, see Holger H. Herwig and Christon I. Archer, "Global Gambit: A German General Staff Assessment of Mexican Affairs, November 1913," *Mexican Studies* 1, no. 2 (Summer 1985): 311, n. 20.

69 See the colorful account in Michael C. Meyer, "The Arms of the Ypiranga," *Hispanic American Historical Review* 50, no. 3 (August 1970): 543–56. For a slightly different telling, see Thomas Baecker, "The Arms of the Ypiranga: The German Side," *Americas* 30, no. 1 (July 1973): 1–17.

70 For Tumulty, and for a vivid rendering of the Veracruz fighting, see Jack Sweetman, *The Landing at Veracruz* (Annapolis: United States Naval Academy Press, 1968), 48. For "Wilson may also," see Lloyd C. Gardner, "Woodrow Wilson and the Mexican Revolution," in Arthur S. Link, ed., *Woodrow Wilson and a Revolutionary World* (Chapel Hill: University of North Carolina Press, 1982), 23–24.

71 For "levas and taxes," see Hill, *Emissaries to a Revolution*, 175. For "unnerved," see Link, *The New Freedom*, 402. For speeches, see Michael C. Meyer, *Huerta*, 199ff.

72 "Huertista press," Knight, *The Mexican Revolution*, 58. "Zapata," see Womack, *Zapata and the Mexican Revolution*, p. 186. For "Villa," the *New York Times*, April 21, 1914.

73 For "*Dresden*," see the *New York Times*, April 27, 1914. For demonstrations in Mexico, Meyer, *Huerta*, 200–01.

74 For *Paris Journal*, *The New Freedom*, 402, and the *New York Times*, April 25–26, 1914.

75 For "Hart," see John Mason Hart, *Revolutionary Mexico: The Coming and Process of the Mexican Revolution* (Berkeley: University of California Press, 1987), 312. For more on Hart's work, see John Foran, "Reinventing the Mexican Revolution: The Competing Paradigms of Alan Knight and John Mason Hart," *Latin American Perspectives* 23, no. 4 (Autumn 1996): 115–31. "Had either work [Hart's book and Knight's *The Mexican Revolution*] appeared in the absence of the other, it would likely have been hailed as *the* definitive English-language study of the revolutionary years," 116.

76 For House, see Link, *The Papers of Woodrow Wilson*, vol. 29, 135. "Little evidence" follows Knight, *The Mexican Revolution*, 157.

77 "German General Staff," see Herwig and Archer, "Global Gambit," 324–25. "War plans," Blum, *Woodrow Wilson and the Politics of Morality*, 90. For "Tasker Bliss," see Linda B. Hall and Don E. Coerver, *Revolution on the Border: The United States and Mexico, 1910–1920* (Albuquerque: University of New Mexico Press, 1990), 50. For harsh assessment of U.S. "offensive" military capacity, see the military correspondent of the London *Times*, April 24, 1914.

78 For European reaction, see Link, *The New Freedom*, 402, and the *New York Times*, April 25–26, 1914.

79 For "editor of the Nation," see Link, *The Papers of Woodrow Wilson*, vol. 29, 496; for Wilson's speech, 110–12.

80 For reaction in United States, the *New York Times*, April 21–23, 1914, and (for Theodore Roosevelt) April 29, 1914.

81 Details from Knight, *The Mexican Revolution*, 156, and the *New York Times*, April 21–22, 1914. For Borah, see Hall and Coerver, *Revolution on the Border*, 55.

82 For "war enthusiasm," see the *Washington Post*, April 21, 1914. For "events must take," see Link, *The Papers of Woodrow Wilson*, vol. 30, 360, 362; for Argentina, Chile, and Brazil meditation, 524. Also the *New York Times*, April 26, 1914.

83 For Villa, see the *New York Times*, May 1, 1914. For emerging tension, see Link, *Wilson: The Struggle for Neutrality*, 237.

84 For "Daniels," see Meyer, "The Arms of the Ypiranga," 555. For "The Americans' transfer," see Hart, *Revolutionary Mexico*, 312.

85 Gilly, *The Mexican Revolution*, 326, 334. "If history were just a matter of economic statistics, it would not be far from the truth to say that virtually nothing changed in the course of the Mexican Revolution, and that all things considered there was no revolution." For "the power and," see Alan Knight, "The Mexican Revolution: Bourgeois? Nationalist? Or just a 'Great Rebellion'?" *Bulletin of Latin American Research* 4, no. 2 (1985): 18. For "status legitimized," see John Gibler, *Mexico Unconquered*, 38.

86 For Pershing, see Link, *Confusions and Crises*, 280–318; for skirmish, see 305. For "plea for help," see Katz, *Pancho Villa*, 612.

87 For Columbus State Bank, see James A. Sando, "German Involvement in Northern Mexico, 1915–1916: A New Look at the Columbus Raid," *Hispanic American Review* 50, no. 1 (February 1970): 70–88.

88 For answer to plea for help, see Katz, *Pancho Villa*, 612. For Baker, see Barbara W. Tuchman, *The Zimmermann Telegram* (New York: Ballantine Books, 1994), 198–99. For Carranza and Germany, see Mark T. Gilderhus, "The United States and Carranza, 1917: The Question of De Jure Recognition," *Americas* 29, no. 2 (October 1972): 219–22.

89 Tuchman, *The Zimmerman Telegram*, 184–200.

90 Katz, *Pancho Villa*, 612. For Britain's submission within six months, see Dirk Steffen, "The Holtzendorff Memorandum of 22 December 1916 and Germany's Declaration of Unrestricted U-boat Warfare," *Journal of Military History* 68 (January 2004): 216–17. For von Hindenburg, see the essay by Ernst Fraenkel in *Wilson's Diplomacy*, 74. For cartoonists, see Eberhard Demm, "Propaganda and Caricature in the First World War," *Journal of Contemporary History* 28, no. 1 (January 1993): 185. For Bethmann, see Konrad H. Jarausch, *The Enigmatic Chancellor: Bethmann Hollweg and the Hubris of Imperial Germany* (New Haven: Yale University Press, 1973), 295–305. "Having sacrificed his own better judgment and used his integrity to defend a step about which he had the gravest reservations, Bethmann became the scapegoat for the failure of the ultimate weapon to perform the expected miracle."

91 For "bushwacker," see Knight, "Peasant and Caudillo," 33.

92 Katz, *Pancho Villa*, 732ff.

93 Ibid., 628.

94 Ibid., 764–805; quotation from the intelligence agents is on 781. Katz's discussion of the assassination is exhaustive.

95 Ibid., 740, 745. For "mule," see John Womack Jr., "Pancho Villa: A Revolutionary Life," *Journal of the Historical Society* 11, no. 1 (Winter 2002): 41.

NOTES FOR CHAPTER 5

1 For the epigraph, see Robert A. Kann, "Archduke Franz Ferdinand and Count Berchtold," in Robert A. Kann, *Dynasty, Politics and Culture: Selected Essays*, ed. Stanley B. Winters (Boulder, CO: Social Science Monographs, 1991), 295. For collar, see Alan Palmer, *Twilight of the Habsburgs: The Life and Times of Emperor Francis Joseph* (New York: Atlantic Monthly Press, 1994), 66. For "Bosnian station," see 308. For walks in Ischl, see Frederic Morton, *Thunder at Twilight, Vienna 1913/1914* (New York: Da Capo, 2001), 86–88. For "all are dying," see Joachim Remak, *Sarajevo: The Story of a Political Murder* (New York: Criterion, 1959), 167.

2 Annika Mombauer, "The First World War: Inevitable, Avoidable, Improbable or Desirable? Recent Interpretations on War Guilt and the War's Origins," *German History* 25, no. 1 (2007): 82–85. The last clause is from a historian, Graydon A. Tunstall, quoted by Mombauer. Also see Samuel R. Williamson Jr. and Ernest R. May, "An Identity of Opinion: Historians and July 1914," *Journal of Modern History* 79 (June 2007): 359.

3 For question, see Lieutenant General Baron von Margutti, *The Emperor Francis Joseph and His Times* (New York: Doran, 1924), 302.

4 For three times as much, see Alan Sked, *The Decline and Fall of the Habsburg Empire 1815–1918* (New York: Longman, 1989), 262. For Napoleon, see Andrew Wheatcroft, *Habsburgs, Ottomans and the Battle for Europe* (New York: Perseus Books, 2008), 254.

5 For Treitschke, the Francis Joseph quotation, and honor, see Avner Offer, "Going to War in 1914: A Matter of Honor?" *Politics & Society* 23, no. 2 (June 1995): 213–41. For manifesto, see Robert A. Kann, "Dynastic Relations and Power Politics 1848–1918," *Journal of Modern History* 45, no. 3 (September 1973): 409.

6 For meetings, see Palmer, *Twilight of the Habsburgs*, 312. For details on Francis Joseph, see Jean-Paul Bled, *Franz Joseph* (Cambridge, UK: Blackwell, 1992), 49, 206; for "crushed" private self, 209.

7 Daniel Unowsky, *The Pomp and Circumstance of Patriotism: Imperial Celebrations in Habsburg Austria, 1848–1916* (West Lafayette, IN: Purdue University Press, 2005), 29.

8 For mobilization orders, see Norman Stone, "Army and Society in the Habsburg Monarchy, 1900–1914," *Past and Present*, no. 33 (April 1966): 100. Description taken from Joseph Roth's novel, *The Radetsky March* (Woodstock: Overlook Press, 1995), 192–93.

9 For old man, see Brigitte Hamann, *Hitler's Vienna: A Portrait of the Tyrant as a Young Man* (New York: Taurus Parke, 2010), 90. London *Times*, April 19, 1902.

10 First quotation is from Joseph Redlich, *Emperor Francis Joseph of Austria: A Biography* (New York: Macmillan, 1929), 475. For comment of fifteen-year-old Sisi, see Bled, *Franz Joseph*, 87.

11 For Francis Joseph's affair with Anna see Palmer, *Twilight of the Habsburgs*, 219–20.

12 For Katharina, see ibid., 237, 243–44.

13 Joseph Baernreither, *Fragments of a Political Diary* (London: Macmillan, 1936), 176, 231. For 1881, see Steven Beller, *Francis Joseph* (New York: Longman, 1996), 136.

14 For Serbian overture, see Theodor Wolff, *The Eve of War* (London: Victor Gollancz, 1935), 207–08. For false report, see Margutti, *The Emperor Francis Joseph and His Times*, 332.

15 Rural folk is from Peter Urbanitsch, "Pluralist Myth and National Realities: The Dynastic Myth of the Habsburg Monarchy—A Futile Exercise in the Creation of Identities," *Austrian History Yearbook* 35 (2004): 124.

16 Baernreither, *Fragments of a Political Diary*, 176. For lights, see Allan Janik and Stephen Toulmin, *Wittgenstein's Vienna* (Chicago: Ivan Dee, 1996), 41–42. For chamber pot, see Bled, *Franz Joseph*, 199. For tank, see William M. Johnston, *The Austrian Mind: An Intellectual and Social History, 1848–1938* (Berkeley: University of California Press, 1977), 55.

17 For children, see Maureen Healy, *Vienna and the Fall of the Habsburg Empire: Total War and Everyday Life in World War I* (New York: Cambridge University Press, 2004), 218. For Austrian idea, see George V. Strong, "The Austrian Idea: An Idea of Nationhood in the Kingdom and Realms of the Emperor Franz Joseph," *History of European Ideas* 5, no. 3 (1984): 293–305. For soldiers, see Mark Cornwall, ed., *The Last Years of Austria-Hungary: Essays in Political and Military History, 1908–1918* (Exeter, UK: University of Exeter Press, 1990), 103.

18 For kitsch, see Urbanitsch, "Pluralist Myth and National Realities," 101–41. Mrs. Stukla is from a Polish novel quoted in Unowsky, "The Pomp and Circumstance of Patriotism," 125–26.

19 London *Times*, August 19, 1902.

20 Source for the emperor's reaction is Margutti, *The Emperor Francis Joseph and His Times*, 131. For suicide threat, see Rudolph Binion, "From Mayerling to Sarajevo," *Journal of Modern History* 47, no. 2 (June 1975): 312, n. 209. For Francis Joseph's statement on the renunciation, see the London *Times*, June 29, 1900. Baron Margutti was with the emperor in Bad Ischl on June 28, 1914. Remak says the "almost blasphemous allusion" to Franz Ferdinand that Margutti attributes to the emperor is a thirdhand account that is "dubious at best." Remak, *Sarajevo*, 160.

21 For handwritten note, see Margutti, *The Emperor Francis Joseph and His Times*, 303.

22 For daughter, see Palmer, *Twilight of the Habsburgs*, 324.

23 For medieval rite, see the London *Times*, January 31, 1889. Third-class funeral seen in Immanuel Geiss, ed., *July 1914: The Outbreak of the First World War, Selected Documents* (New York: Scribner, 1967), 56, n. 4. For indifference, see

Palmer, *Twilight of the Habsburgs*, 326. For courage above survival, see Richard Ned Lebow, *A Cultural Theory of International Relations* (New York: Cambridge University Press, 2008), 357. The death grip of the ancien régime follows the analysis of Arno J. Mayer, *The Persistence of the Old Regime, Europe to the Great War* (New York: Pantheon, 1981). "'Premodern' elements" is on 5–6. For Czernin, see Margaret Macmillan, *Paris 1919* (New York: Random House, 2001), 244.

24 Hugh Seton-Watson, *German, Slav, and Magyar* (London: Williams and Morgan, 1911), 32. Redlich, *Emperor Francis Joseph of Austria*, 503. Baernreither, *Fragments of a Political Diary*, 303.

25 Robert Musil, *The Man Without Qualities* (New York: Vintage, 1996), 180.

26 For hyphens, see Norman Stone, "Hungary and the Crisis of July 1914," *Journal of Contemporary History* 1, no. 3 (July 1966): 157. For funeral, see Beller, *Francis Joseph*, 165.

27 See Palmer, *Twilight of the Habsburgs*, 293–95. For deputies, see Luigi Albertini, *The Origins of the War of 1914*, vol. 2 (New York: Enigma Books, 2005), 13. For Tisza, see Stone, "Hungary and the Crisis of July 1914," 157.

28 Beller, *Francis Joseph*, 190–92. For three hundred Rumanians, see Peter F. Sugar, "The Nature of Non-Germanic Societies under Habsburg Rule," *Slavic Review* 22, no. 1 (March 1963): 27.

29 For Franz Ferdinand, see Robert A. Kann, "William II and the Archduke Francis Ferdinand in Their Correspondence," *American Historical Review* 57, no. 2 (January 1952): 323–51. For German nationalism, see Janik and Toulmin, *Wittgenstein's Vienna*, 39. Also see "Germans or Czechs: Which Shall Dominate the Rule of Austria and Hungary?" the *New York Times*, December 5, 1897. For the language issue as a whole, see R. J. W. Evans, "Language and State Building: The Case of the Habsburg Monarchy," *Austrian History Yearbook* 35 (2004): 1–24. In complaining about the Magyars to the kaiser, the archduke employed the "all" of conversation: German linguistic nationalism, from which the Czechs and Slovenes suffered, ran the Magyar variety a close second as a source of ethnic tension in the monarchy.

30 For mule, see Robert A. Kann, *Dynasty, Politics and Culture: Selected Essays*, ed. Stanley B. Winters (Boulder, CO: Social Science Monographs, 1991), 167. For language restrictions on the Romanians, see Sugar, "The Nature of Non-Germanic Societies under Habsburg Rule," 25. For Magyar conquest, see Solomon Wank, "Pessimism in the Austrian Establishment at the Turn of the Century," in Solomon Wank et al., eds., *The Mirror of History: Essays in Honor of Fritz Fellner* (Santa Barbara: ABC-CLIO, 1988), 298. For letter to Berchtold, see Kann, *Dynasty, Politics, and Culture*, 129. For wreaths, see Arthur J. May, *The Passing of the Habsburg Monarchy*, vol. 1 (Philadelphia: University of Pennsylvania Press, 1966), 39.

31 Stefan Zweig, *The World of Yesterday* (Lincoln: University of Nebraska Press, 1964), 216. For red tape, see Johnston, *The Austrian Mind*, 48. For temper, see Luigi Albertini, *The Origins of the War of 1914*, vol. 2 (New York: Enigma Books, 2005), 4.

32 For slattern, see Morton, *Thunder at Twilight: Vienna*, 33. For the chamberlain, see Rebecca West, *Black Lamb and Grey Falcon* (New York: Penguin, 2007), 339, 346.

33 For the game, see West, *Black Lamb and Grey Falcon*, 334.

34 For the archduke's assassination as a major cause of the war, see Joachim Remak, "1914—The Third Balkan War Reconsidered," *Journal of Modern History* 43, no. 3 (September 1971): 353–66.

35 Seton-Watson, *German, Slav, and Magyar*, 109–11. For United States of Greater Austria, see Bled, *Franz Joseph*, 300.

36 May, *The Passing of the Habsburg Monarchy*, 192–96; for world war, see 190. Serbia was not alone in fanning Pan-Slav feeling in Bosnia. Here, speaking in December 1913, is the Russian ambassador to Belgrade, M. Hartwig: "After the question of Turkey, it is now the turn of Austria. Serbia will be our best instrument. The day draws near when . . . Serbia will take back *her* Bosnia and *her* Herzegovina." Seen in Albertini, *The Origins of the War of 1914*, 190.

37 Margutti, *The Emperor Francis Joseph and His Times*, 125.

38 Seen in May, *The Passing of the Habsburg Monarchy*, 28.

39 London *Times*, April 10, 1909.

40 Kann, "Correspondence," 347.

41 For Austrian historian, see Solomon Wank, "The Archduke and Aehrenthal: The Origins of a Hatred," *Austrian History Yearbook* 33 (January 2002): 77–104.

42 Albertini, *The Origins of the War of 1914*, 49, 50, 87. For the Black Hand, see Jan G. Beaver, *Collision Course: Franz Conrad von Hötzendorf, Serbia, and the Politics of Preventive War* (Jan Beaver, 2009), 141–42. For Egypt, see Morton, *Thunder at Twilight*, 190. For Yugoslav state, see David MacKenzie, "Serbian Nationalist and Military Organizations and the Piedmont Idea, 1844–1914," *East European Quarterly* 16, no. 3 (September 1982): 335–40. For a fictional portrayal of "Apis," Princip, and Franz Ferdinand as the latter two converge on Sarajevo, see Bruno Behm, *They Call It Patriotism* (Boston: Little, Brown, 1932).

43 Wank, "The Archduke and Aehrenthal," 19–20. For insane, see A. J. P. Taylor, *The Habsburg Monarchy, 1809–1918* (Chicago: 1976), 225. Palmer, *Twilight of the Habsburgs*, 296.

44 Hinsley seen in Richard Ned Lebow, "Franz Ferdinand Found Alive: World War I Unnecessary," in Philip Tetlock et al., eds., *Unmaking the West: Counterfactual Thought Experiments in History* (Ann Arbor: University of Michigan Press, 2006).

45 See Kann, "Correspondence," 347. For Franz Ferdinand's wavering, see Samuel R. Williamson Jr., *Austria-Hungary and the Origins of the First World War* (New York: St. Martin's Press, 1991), 129–31.

46 For Potiorek scenario, see Samuel R. Williamson Jr., "Influence, Power, and the Policy Process: The Case of Franz Ferdinand, 1906–1914," *Historical Journal* 17, no. 2 (June 1974): 434.

47 For twenty-five times, see Alan Kramer, *Dynamic of Destruction: Culture and Mass Killing in the First World War* (New Haven: Yale University Press, 2007), 84. For Conrad, see Samuel R. Williamson Jr., "Review: The Habsburg Monarchy after Ausgleich," *Historical Journal* 21, no. 2 (January 1978): 434. For background on Conrad, see Gunther Rothenberg, *The Army of Francis Joseph* (West Lafayette, IN: Purdue University Press, 1998).

48 For letter to Berchtold, see Kann, *Dynasty, Politics and Culture*, 122. The translation used is from Graydon A. Tunstall, Jr., "Austria-Hungary," in Richard F. Hamilton and Holger H. Herwig, eds., *The Origins of World War I* (New York: Cambridge University Press, 2008), 124. For sheep, see Bled, *Franz Joseph*, 302. Quotation about prewar plans from Stone, "Hungary and the Crisis of July 1914," 170.

49 For disparity in divisions, see Rothenberg, *The Army of Francis Joseph*, 173. For comparative spending, see Taylor, *The Habsburg Monarchy*, 229. For July 7 meeting, see Tunstall, "Austria-Hungary," 146.

50 For Conrad on "two principles," see Richard Ned Lebow, *Between Peace and War: The Nature of International Crisis* (Baltimore: Johns Hopkins University Press, 1981), 26.

51 Conrad to von Moltke is from Tunstall, "Austria-Hungary," 170; to mistress on 177.

52 Richard Ned Lebow, "Franz Ferdinand Found Alive." Also see Richard Ned Lebow, "Counterfactual Thought Experiments: A Necessary Teaching Tool," *History Teacher* 40, no. 2 (2007): 1–17. For a robust theoretical defense of counterfactual history, see Niall Ferguson, "Virtual History: Towards a 'Chaotic' Theory of the Past," in Niall Ferguson, ed., *Virtual History: Alternatives and Counterfactuals* (New York: Basic Books, 1999), 1–90. For Kann, see "Emperor Franz Joseph and the Outbreak of World War I: A Reflection on Dr. Heinrich Kanner's Notes as a Source," in Kann, *Dynasty, Politics, and Culture*, 306. For Berchtold and Franz Ferdinand, see Williamson, *Austria-Hungary and the Origins of the First World War*, 37. For Berchtold and the Great Power argument, see Lebow, *A Cultural Theory of International Relations*, 352.

53 For Serbian flags above, see the London *Times*, June 29, 1914. For Conrad and Gina, see Williamson, *Austria-Hungary and the Origins of the First World War*, 49–50. Also see Frederic Morton, *Thunder at Twilight*, 43–45, 68, 121. Also Rothenberg, *The Army of Francis Joseph*, 164. For Conrad on Ulster, see Jerome de Wiel, "Austria-Hungary, France, Germany and the Irish Crisis from 1899 to the Outbreak of the First World War," *Intelligence & National Security* 21, no. 2 (April 2006): 253. See also F. W. Bridge, "The British Declaration of War on Austria-Hungary in 1914," *Slavonic and East European Review* 47, no. 109 (July 1969): 401–22.

54 For Franz Ferdinand's warning to Berchtold against Conrad, see Williamson, *Austria-Hungary and the Origins of the First World War*, 146.

55 Holger Afflerbach and David Stevenson, introduction to a volume they edited, *An Improbable War? The Outbreak of World War I and European Political Culture before 1914* (New York: Berghahn Books, 2007), 4.

56 Follows Lebow, "Franz Ferdinand Found Alive."

57 Bethmann to Riezler, seen in David M. Rowe, "The Tragedy of Liberalism: How Globalization Caused the First World War," *Security Studies* 14, no. 3 (July–

September 2005), 445. For Great Program, see Allan K. Wildman, *The End of the Russian Imperial Army: The Old Army and the Soldiers' Revolt, March–April 1917* vol. 1 (Princeton: Princeton University Press, 1980), 72.

58 For lung, see Redlich, *Emperor Francis Joseph of Austria*, 523. For Francis Joseph's illness and Franz Ferdinand's train, see Palmer, *Twilight of the Habsburgs*, 322. For what Francis Joseph said to his nephew at their last meeting, see Binion, "From Mayerling to Sarajevo," 315.

NOTES FOR CHAPTER 6

1 For praise of Caillaux above, see *Kölnische Zeitung*, April 14, 1915. For quotation, the epigraph, see Roger Martin du Gard, *Summer 1914* (New York: Viking, 1941), 480–81. For Gerard, see A. T. Q. Stewart, *The Ulster Crisis: Resistance to Home Rule, 1912–1914* (London: Faber & Faber, 1967), 271, n. 13. For von Moltke, see Mark Hewitson, "Images of the Enemy: German Depictions of the French Military, 1890–1914," *War in History* 11, no. 1 (January 2004): 24 and 8–9.
2 For General Staff, see Hewitson, "Images of the Enemy"; for *Kladderadatsch*, 26. On France's relative depopulation, see Karen Offen, "Depopulation, Nationalism, and Feminism in Fin-de-Siècle France," *American Historical Review* 89, no. 3 (June 1984): 648–76. For German views of France, see Mark Hewitson, "Germany and France before the First World War: A Reassessment of Wilhelmine Foreign Policy," *English Historical Review* 115, no. 462 (June 2000): 570–606, esp. 577.
3 For number of governments, see Robert Tombs, *France 1814–1914* (New York: Longman, 1996), 472. For Bülow, see Hewitson, "Germany and France before the First World War," 577.
4 For German critic, see Koenraad W. Swart, *The Sense of Decadence in Nineteenth-Century France* (The Hague: Martinus Nijhoff, 1964), 237–38.
5 For details of mobilization and illustrative anecdotes, see Tombs, *France 1814–1914*, 481. For statistics on conscripts, see John F. V. Keiger, *Raymond Poincaré* (New York: Cambridge University Press, 1997), 189.
6 Jean-Jacques Becker, *The Great War and the French People* (New York: St. Martin's Press, 1986), 5.
7 André Maurois, *A History of France* (New York: Farrar, Straus and Giroux, 1956), 495. "I went to put on my uniform which my father wanted to see," Maurois writes. "My father looked me over with the severity of an old soldier. 'You must polish up your buttons.' He was sad at my leaving but full of hope for France and happy to see a son of his taking part in the war of revenge of which he had dreamed ever since 1871." Seen in Peter Vansittart, *Voices from the Great War* (New York: Franklin Watts, 1984), 35.
8 For the brutish boche, see Ruth Harris, "The 'Child of the Barbarian': Rape, Race and Nationalism in France during the First World War," *Past & Present*, no. 141 (November 1993): 170–206; for illustration of ape-like Germans closing in on a terrified French girl, see after 188. For spirit of "they shall not pass," see Stéphane Audoin-Rouzeau, *Men at War 1914–1918: National Sentiment and Trench Journalism in France During the First World War* (Providence: Berg, 1992), 182. "More or less consciously the soldiers appear forced into national feeling; this

feeling obtrudes on them at the death of their comrades, the acclaim of local people, at a front-line advance or retreat . . . It is in this sense that the concept of duty must be understood."

9 For ban on Caillaux's name, see Becker, *The Great War and the French People*, 59.

10 For the Caillaux affair, see Benjamin F. Martin, *The Hypocrisy of Justice in the Belle Époque* (Baton Rouge: LSU Press, 1984), 151–224; Peter Shankland, *Death of an Editor: The Caillaux Drama* (London: William Kimber, 1981); Edward Berenson, *The Trial of Madame Caillaux* (Berkeley: University of California Press, 1992). London *Times*, March 17, 1914. For Germans, see Berenson, 4.

11 For number of articles, see Martin, *The Hypocrisy of Justice*, 180. For benefiting friends, see Berenson, *The Trial of Madame Caillaux*, 74, 79. For private conversations, see Gordon Wright, *Raymond Poincaré and the French Presidency* (Stanford: Stanford University Press, 1943), 108, n. 10. For Caillaux and arms race, see Martin, *The Hypocrisy of Justice*, 151. For French defense spending, see Geoffrey Barraclough, *From Agadir to Armageddon: Anatomy of a Crisis* (New York: Holmes and Mier, 1982), 159.

12 The quotation from the Belgian ambassador seen in E. D. Morel, *Diplomacy Revealed* (Manchester: National Labour Press, 1923), 281, 247.

13 Details and quotation taken from Rudolph Binion, *Defeated Leaders: The Political Fate of Caillaux, Jouvenal, and Tardieu* (New York: Columbia University Press, 1960), 18.

14 Berenson, *The Trial of Madame Caillaux*, 49–51.

15 Ibid., 51.

16 For confusion with Caillaux's father, see Berenson, ibid., 20; also see 47–48.

17 Ibid., 83. Also see Martin, *The Hypocrisy of Justice*, 170.

18 Berenson, *The Trial of Madame Caillaux*, 49, 65.

19 Gambetta quotation is from Peter Shankland, *Death of an Editor*, 16. For Caillaux on Clemenceau, see 209. For Clemenceau on Caillaux, see Gregor Dallas, *The Heart of a Tiger: Clemenceau and His World* (New York: Graf, 1993), 406, 506.

20 Berenson, *The Trial of Madame Caillaux*, 142.

21 Ibid., 142–43. The quotation from Berthe Gueydan taken from a front-page story in the *New York Times*, July 25, 1914. For three letters, see the *New York Times*, March 24, 1914.

22 Berenson, *The Trial of Madame Caillaux*, 148–49, 189.

23 The quotation from Charles de Gaulle seen in Louis Begley, *Why the Dreyfus Affair Matters* (New Haven: Yale University Press, 2007), 48.

24 The examples are all from Tombs, *France 1814–1914*, 46–60. For swag of mourning cloth, see Laird Boswell, "From Liberation to Purge Trials in the 'Mythic Provinces': Recasting French Identities in Alsace and Lorraine, 1918–1920," *French Historical Studies* 23, no. 1 (2000): 2.

25 The dimensions of the great imperialist carve-up of the globe are taken from Eric Hobsbawm, *The Age of Empire* (New York: Pantheon, 1987), 59. For deaths, see J. Thomson, "The Results of European Intercourse with the Africans," *Contemporary Review* 57 (January 1890): 339–52. Worse was to come. "There was only one man who could be accused of the outrages which reduced the native population [of the Congo] from between 20 to 40 million in 1890 to 8,500,000 in 1911—Leopold II." Selwyn James, *South of the Congo* (New York: Random House, 1943), 305. Seen in Hannah Arendt, *The Origins of Totalitarianism* (New York: Meridian, 1964), 185, n. 2.

26 For the French, see Tombs, *France 1814–1914*, 200–211. For Ferry, see C. P. Gooch, *Franco-German Relations, 1870–1914* (London: Longman's, 1923), 21. The quotation from Ferry is from Tombs, 207. For French newspaper readers and General Lyautey, see Eugen Weber, *The Nationalist Revival in France, 1905–1914* (Berkeley: University of California Press, 1968), 93–94.

27 For battle, see Ross E. Dunn, *Resistance in the Desert: Moroccan Resistance to French Imperialism 1881–1912* (Madison: University of Wisconsin Press, 1977), 234–36. Douglas Porch, *The Conquest of Morocco* (New York: Knopf, 1983), 199.

28 For the Mahdi and France's problems, see Porch, *The Conquest of Morocco*, 231, 11.

29 See Pierre Guillen, "The *Entente* of 1904 as a Colonial Settlement," in Prosser Gifford and Wm. Roger Louis, eds., *France and Britain in Africa: Imperial Rivalry and Colonial Rule* (New Haven: Yale University Press, 1971), 333–38. For British India and quotation, see Tombs, *France, 1814–1914*, 201. For red-brick plains, see Roger Martin du Gard, *Lieutenant-Colonel de Maumort* (New York: Knopf, 1999), 524–25. For "puppet state," see A. J. P. Taylor, *The Struggle for Mastery in Europe, 1848–1918* (New York: Oxford University Press, 1971), 414. For English influence in Morocco, see Christopher Andrew, "German World Policy and the Reshaping of the Dual Alliance," *Journal of Contemporary History* 1, no. 3 (July 1966): 140.

30 For "arrive first," see Christopher M. Andrew and A. S. Kanya-Forstner, *The Climax of French Imperial Expansion 1914–1924* (Stanford: Stanford University Press, 1981), 11. For French anger, see Tombs, *France, 1814–1914*, 206.

31 For Fashoda and Omdurman, see Porch, *The Conquest of Morocco*, 140–42.

32 For *Daily Telegraph* and Catholic paper, see E. Malcolm Carroll, *French Public Opinion and Foreign Affairs, 1870–1914* (New York: Century, 1931), 175, 176. For the *Times* on Fashoda, see Richard Ned Lebow, *Between Peace and War: The Nature of International Crisis* (Baltimore: Johns Hopkins University Press, 1981), 322.

33 For at the turn of the century, see Guillen, "The Entente of 1904," 334. Also see Robert A. Doughty, *Pyrrhic Victory: French Strategy and Operations in the Great War* (Cambridge: Harvard University Press, 2005), 38. For Paris crowd, see Samuel L. Williamson, Jr., *The Politics of Grand Strategy: Britain and France Prepare for War, 1904–1914* (Cambridge: Harvard University Press, 1969), 5. For Bois de Boulogne, see Luigi Albertini, *The Origins of the War of 1914*, vol. 1 (New York: Enigma Books, 2005), 146. For Ireland, see Jerome De Wiel, "Austria-Hungary, France, Germany and the Irish Crisis from 1899 to the Outbreak of the First World War," *Intelligence & National Security* 21, no. 2 (April 2006): 242–43.

34 For Britain's courtship of Germany, see Bernadotte E. Schmitt, "Triple Alliance and Triple *Entente*, 1902–1914," *American Historical Review* 29, no. 3 (April 1924): 454. For another view of British courtship, see Paul W. Schroeder, "World War I as Galloping Gertie: A Reply to Joachim Remak," *Journal of Modern History*

44, no. 3 (September 1972): 326. "Britain never really tried or wanted" an Anglo-German alliance.

35 Guillen, "The Entente of 1914," 364.

36 For Bismarck, see Gooch, *Franco-German Relations*, 16. Quotation from Tombs, *France 1814–1914*, 206.

37 For horse, see Albertini, *The Origins of the War of 1914*, 161. Account of the Kaiser's visit follows Porch, 137–39.

38 Helmuth Stoecker, *German Imperialism in Africa* (London: C. Hurst, 1986), 237.

39 Bülow seen in Stocker, 237. For the "paltry" fruits of expansion under the Kaiser, see Holger H. Herwig, *"Luxury" Fleet: The Imperial German Navy, 1888–1918* (London: The Ashfield Press, 1987), 102.

40 Lenin quoted in Annika Mombauer, *The Origins of the First World War: Controversies and Consensus* (New York: Longman, 2002), 108.

41 For Bülow, Pan-Germans, and Krupp, see Stoecker, *German Imperialism*, 233, 236, 237, 240. For the "French press," see Gooch, *Franco-German Relations*, 43.

42 For Bülow's memoirs, see Albertini, *The Origins of the War of 1914*, 153–54. For conference, see 173–74. For France's claims, see Stoecker, *German Imperialism*, 241. For Churchill, see Schmitt, "Triple Alliance and Triple *Entente*," 451.

43 For roars of laughter, see Barraclough, *From Agadir to Armageddon*, 2–3. For wry comment, see A. J. P. Taylor, *The Struggle for Mastery in Europe, 1848–1918*, 467, n. 2.

44 For place in the sun, see Hewitson, "Germany and France before the First World War," 570.

45 For Kiderlen and Russia, see Bernadotte E. Schmitt, *The Annexation of Bosnia 1908–1909* (Cambridge: Cambridge University Press, 1937), 194–95. For Kiderlen to kaiser, see Stoecker, *German Imperialism*, 246. For Cambon, see Binion, *Defeated Leaders*, 37. For fuller account, see C. P. Gooch, "Kiderlen-Wächter," *Cambridge Historical Journal* 5, no. 2 (1936): 178–92. Agadir was a closed port, Mogador an open one; the chances of "complications"—meeting a foreign warship—were higher there; and so the Mogador option was dropped. See James L. Richardson, *Crisis Diplomacy: The Great Powers Since the Mid-Nineteenth Century* (New York: Cambridge University Press, 1994), 174.

46 Baron Greindl seen in E. D. Morel, *Diplomacy Revealed* (Manchester, UK: National Labour Press 1923), 177.

47 For loans, see E. D. Morel, *Morocco: Ten Years of Secret Diplomacy* (Manchester: National Labour Press, 1920), 37–39. For throne, see Roger Martin du Gard, *Lieutenant-Colonel de Maumont*, 530. For the lion, see Porch, *The Conquest of Morocco*, 211.

48 For "pictures were painted," see Theodore Wolff, *The Eve of 1914* (London: Gollancz, 1935), 38. For colonial pressure on the government, see C. M. Andrew and A. S. Kanya, "The French 'Colonial Party': Its Composition and Influence, 1885–1914," in *Historical Journal* 14, no. 1 (1971): 123. "The height of the Moroccan rebellion in the spring of 1911 coincided with the establishment in France of the weakest Government for more than twenty years, and one particularly vulnerable to colonialist pressure." For three cabinet members see Andrew and Kanya-Forstner, *The Climax of French Imperial Expansion*, 12.

49 For Caillaux, see Porch, *The Conquest of Morocco*, 221.

50 For the Belgian consul, see Morel, *Morocco*, 199.

51 For Mangin, the French officer, and the backdated request, see Porch, *The Conquest of Morocco*, 218, 222.

52 Binion, *Defeated Leaders*, 41.

53 For de Selves, see Barraclough, *From Agadir to Armageddon*, 44, 134. For Germanophobia, see Berenson, *The Trial of Madame Caillaux*, 76.

54 Binion, *Defeated Leaders*, 40.

55 For Izvolski, see Binion, *Defeated Leaders*, 50.

56 For Lloyd George, Grey, and the escalation in crisis dynamics, see David Stevenson, "Militarization and Diplomacy in Europe before 1914," *International Security* 22, no. 1 (Summer 1997): 136–38. For Caillaux and Churchill, see Keith Wilson, "The Agadir Crisis, the Mansion House Speech, and the Double-Edgedness of Agreements," *Historical Journal* 15, no. 3 (September 1972): 518, n. 32, 521. A. J. P. Taylor argued that the Mansion House speech "was directed against Caillaux, not Kiderlen." Keith Wilson disputes this interpretation while respecting its logic—that London wanted to restrain Paris as much as it wanted to deter Berlin. See Taylor, *The Struggle for Mastery in Europe*, 469–71.

57 "Prestige," see Barraclough, *From Agadir to Armageddon*, 132–33. For Germany and Churchill, see David Stevenson, "The European Land Armaments Race," in Holger Afflerbach and David Stevenson, eds., *An Improbable War? The Outbreak of World War I and European Political Culture before 1914* (New York: Berghahn Books, 2007), 136.

58 Binion, *Defeated Leaders*, 39.

59 Ibid.

60 Gooch, "Kiderlen-Wachter," 189.

61 For Fondere, see Binion, *Defeated Leaders*, 43, 44. For kaiser's wrath, see Theodor Wolff, *The Eve of 1914*, 58–59.

62 For Baroness, see Binion, *Defeated Leaders*, 43, 44. For "Jena without war" and the Pan-German attack on Bethmann Hollweg, see Roger Chickering, *We Men Who Feel Most German: A Cultural Study of the Pan-German League, 1886–1914* (Boston: Allen & Unwin, 1984), 265.

63 For Asquith, see Shankland, *Death of an Editor*, 25. For hating Germans, see Binion, *Defeated Leaders*, 46, 49.

64 See the London *Times*, January 9–11, 1912.

65 For giggling, see Donald G. Wileman, "Caillaux and the Alliance, 1901–1912: The Evolution of a Disillusioned Conservative," *Canadian Journal of History* (December 1988): 368. For squeaky voice, see Theodore Zeldin, *France 1848–1945*, vol. 1 (New York: Oxford University Press, 1973), 703. For Caillaux's interjection, see David Watson, *Clemenceau: A Political Biography* (New York: McKay, 1974), 241. For attack on progressive reform, see Keith Hamilton, "The 'Wild Talk' of Joseph Caillaux: A Sequel to the Agadir Crisis," *International History Review* 9, no. 2 (May 1987): 196.

66 The discussion of Caillaux's political evolution closely follows Wileman, "Caillaux and the Alliance," 355–73. For number of strikes, see Barraclough, *From Agadir to Armageddon*, 30. Definition of nationalism is from Eugen Weber, *The National Revival in France, 1905–1914* (Berkeley: University of California Press, 1968), 7.

67 See David E. Sumler, "Domestic Influences on the Nationalist Revival in France, 1909–1914," *French Historical Studies* 6, no. 4 (Autumn 1970): 522.

68 Wileman, "Caillaux and the Alliance," 371–72.

69 For swing to the left, see Barraclough, *From Agadir to Armageddon*, 31. For all the countries, 15.

70 Quotation is from Wileman, "Caillaux and the Alliance," 373.

71 Weber, *The Nationalist Revival in France*, 95–96; minority, 3; Deschanel, 98; the senator, 99. For the provincial newspaper, see Carroll, *French Public Opinion*, 251. The estimate of the size of the political class is from Charles Maurass, the right-wing nationalist. Cited in Zeldin, *France 1848–1945*, 387–88. For the "sociology of nationalism," a quotation from Jean-Jacques Becker, see Paul B. Miller, *From Revolutionaries to Citizens: Antimilitarism in France, 1870–1914* (Durham, NC: Duke University Press, 2002), 180.

72 For Poincaré anecdote, see Keiger, *Raymond Poincaré*, 15. For 1920 article, see Wright, *Raymond Poincaré and the French Presidency*, 129, n. 99. Wright reports that the article "cannot be found at the Biblioteque Nationale or at the Sorbonne Library." Poincaré long sought to combat the image of *"Poincaré le guerre"*—the revanchist eager for war—and this article, with its revanchist recollection, would furnish the wrong sort of evidence. For long defile, see Raymond Poincaré, *The Memoirs of Raymond Poincaré* (London: Heinemann, 1928), 1.

73 For interview, see Poincaré, *The Memoirs of Raymond Poincaré*, 31. For French people not fearing war, see Carroll, *French Public Opinion and Foreign Affairs*, 260.

74 For higher standard, see Sumler, "Domestic Influences," 523, 528. For Joan of Arc and marches, see Miller, *From Revolutionaries to Citizens*, 181. For diary, see Keiger, *Raymond Poincaré*, 161.

75 For election, see Sumler, "Domestic Influences," 532–34. For Calmette's fog, see Wright, *Raymond Poincaré and the French Presidency*, 38.

76 For details on reptile fund, see Sidney B. Fay, *The Origins of the War*, vol. 1 (New York: Macmillan, 1927), 270, n. 79. Also James William Long, "Russian Manipulation of the French Press, 1904–1906," *Slavic Review* 31, no. 2 (June 1972): 343–54. Berenson, *The Trial of Madame Caillaux*, 235–36.

77 For Cossack, see Carroll, *French Public Opinion and Foreign Affairs*, 279. For Poincaré's implicit promise, see Glenn H. Snyder, "The Security Dilemma in Alliance Politics," *World Politics* 36, no. 4 (July 1984): 479. For Jaurès, see Brynjolf J. Hovde, "French Socialism and the Triple *Entente*, 1893–1914," *Journal of Political Economy* 34, no. 4 (August 1926): 471.

78 For Izvolski and Kokovtsov, see Carroll, *French Public Opinion and Foreign Affairs*, 204ff. For return letter, see Wright, *Raymond Poincaré and the French Presidency*, 53–55. For Izvolski on Poincaré's victory, see Shankland, *Death of an Editor*, 47.

79 Berenson, *The Trial of Madame Caillaux*, 225.

80 For quotations, see ibid., 225, 26, 27.

81 Ibid., 225.

82 For right-wing journalist, see ibid., 149. For nation as family, see 159. For 1895, see Offen, "Depopulation, Nationalism, and Feminism," 658.

83 For feminism, sterility, and abortion, see Offen, "Depopulation, Nationalism, and Feminism," For economist, Michael F. Nolan, *The Inverted Mirror: Mythologizing the Enemy in France and Germany, 1898–1914* (New York: Berghahn, 2005), 58. For divorce, see Berenson, *The Trial of Madame Caillaux*, 159, and for marital reform, 154.

84 For instigation and duel, see London *Times*, April 28, 1914. The contrast between electoral politics and cultural politics follows Berenson, *The Trial of Madame Caillaux*, esp. 168.

85 Caillaux on the elections seen in Wolff, *The Eve of 1914*, 285–86. For meeting in Chamber, see Harvey Goldberg, *The Life of Jean Jaurès* (Madison: University of Wisconsin Press, 1962), 455. For settee, see Shankland, *Death of an Editor*, 47–48.

86 Breathtaking, from Goldberg, *The Life of Jean Jaurès*, 455. For Jaurès on Russia, see Hovde, "French Socialism and the Triple *Entente*," 470, 72.

87 For comment to German socialist, see Shankland, *Death of an Editor*, 48.

88 For Sazonov on Poincaré, see Albertini, *The Origins of the War of 1914*, vol. 2, 194. For Poincaré's pledge of July 27, see Gerd Krumeich, *Armaments and Politics in France on the Eve of the First World War* (Dover, NY: Berg, 1984), 220.

89 For Paris juries, see Berenson, *The Trial of Madame Caillaux*, 82.

90 For Labori, see ibid., 241. For "On to Berlin!" see the *New York Times*, July 26, 1914. Poincaré, *The Memoirs of Raymond Poincaré*, 310.

91 For Churchill, see Shankland, *Death of an Editor*, 73. For Caillaux on Calmette's assault on Henriette's soul, see the *New York Times*, July 22, 1914. For details of Henriette's appearance, see Shankland, 52–53. The best source is the London *Times*, which ran long stories every day of the trial.

92 For the broken seals and the judge, see Martin, *The Hypocrisy of Justice*, 178–79.

93 For Figaro, see Shankland, *Death of an Editor*, 164. For toughs, see Berenson, *The Trial of Madame Caillaux*, 242.

94 Berenson, *The Trial of Madame Caillaux*, 243.

95 Details on Jaurès from Goldberg, *The Life of Jean Jaurès*, 470–72. For Villain, see Eugen Weber, *Action Française: Royalism and Reaction in Twentieth-Century France* (Stanford: Stanford University Press, 1962), 91. For Agadir, see Holger Afflerbach, "The Topos of Improbable War in Europe before 1914," in Afflerbach and Stevenson, *An Improbable War*, 162. Also Brynjolf J. Hovde, "French Socialism and the Franco-German Relations, 1893–1914," *Journal of Political Economy* 35, no. 2 (April 1927): 266. Anatole France seen in Shankland, *Death of an Editor*, 175.

96 For revolvers, see Berenson, *The Trial of Madame Caillaux*, 242.

97 For Agadir quotation from Caillaux, see Martin, *The Hypocrisy of Justice*, 183.

98 For Poincaré in the Assembly, see Sumler, "Domestic Influences," 537.

99 J. M. G. Le Clézio, *Desert* (Boston: David Godine, 2009), 343, 348.

100 Ibid., 349–51.

101 For Mangin on West African troops, see Joe Lunn, "'Les Races Guerrieres': Racial Preconceptions in the French Military about West African Soldiers during the First World War," *Journal of Contemporary History* 34, no. 4 (October 1999): 517–536. For tribes and recruitment methods, see Myron J. Echenberg, "Paying the Blood Tax: Military Conscription in French West Africa, 1914–1919," *Canadian Journal of African Studies* 9, no. 2 (1975): 176. For British observer, see John Terraine, "The Aftermath of Nivelle," *History Today* 27, issue 7 (July 1977): 428.
102 Morel seen in Barraclough, *From Agadir to Armageddon*, 155. For Churchill, see Bernadotte E. Schmitt, "Triple Alliance and Triple *Entente*, 1902–1914," *American Historical Review* 29, no. 3 (April 1924): 451. Blind quotations are from Paul W. Schroeder, "Stealing Horses to Great Applause: Austria-Hungary's Decision in 1914," in Afflerbach and Stevenson, *An Improbable War*, 29, 26.

Notes for Chapter 7

1 For German patrols, see Margaret H. Darrow, *French Women and the First World War: War Stories of the Home Front* (Oxford, NY: Berg, 2000), 99. For Belgian poet, Emile Verhaeren, see Barbara W. Tuchman, *The Proud Tower: A Portrait of the World before the War, 1890–1914* (New York: Knopf, 1966), 463. The bestselling book was *The Great Illusion: A Study of the Relation of Military Power to National Advantage* (1910) by Norman Angell, a British journalist. See Howard Weinroth, "Norman Angell and the Great Illusion: An Episode in Pre-1914 Pacifism," *Historical Journal* 17, no. 3 (1974): 551–74.
2 Stephen Van Evera, "The Cult of the Offensive and the Origins of the First World War," *International Security* 9, no. 1 (Summer 1984): 58–107.
3 "All in all, it can safely be said that the Schlieffen Plan made no sense," Stig Förster, "Dreams and Nightmares: German Military Leadership and the Images of Future Warfare, 1871–1914," in Manfred F. Boemke, Roger Chickering, and Stig Förster, eds. (New York: Cambridge University Press, 1999), 361. For St. Privat, see Michael Howard, The Franco-Prussian War (London; Hart-Davis War, 1962), 119. For machine guns, see Martin Van Creveld, "World War I and the Revolution in Logistics," in Roger Chickering and Stig Förster, eds., *Great War, Total War: Combat and Mobilization on the Western Front, 1914–1918* (New York: Cambrudge University Press, 2000), 65. "Attack is the best defense" is Schlieffen, seen in Van Evra, "The Cult of the Offensive," 59.
4 "Specialists in victory" is from Barry Posen quoted in Jack Snyder, "Civil Military Relations and the Cult of the Offensive, 1914 and 1984," *International Security* 9, no. 1 (Summer 1984): 122. For Schlieffen's fear of long wars rousing the "red ghost" of revolution, see Stig Förster, "Dreams and Nightmares," 360.
5 Follows Förster, "Dreams and Nightmares," 368.
6 See Gerhard P. Gross, "There Was a Schlieffen Plan: New Sources on the History of German Military Planning," *War in History* 15, no. 4 (2008): 431.
7 For von Moltke, the elder, see Jack Snyder, *The Ideology of the Offensive: Military Decision-Making and the Disasters of 1914* (Ithaca: Cornell University Press, 1984), 25. For Bethmann, see Snyder, "Civil-Military Relations," 126.
8 For brooding Moltke, see Förster, "Dreams and Nightmares," 363, 365, 373. For

Bethmann, see Van Evra, "The Cult of the Offensive," 58. For "lip service," see Holger H. Herwig, "Germany and the 'Short-War' Illusion: Toward a New Imterpretation?" *Journal of Military History* 66, no. 3 (July 2002): 693. Förster's indictment is on the same page. Also see Annika Mombauer, *Helmuth Von Moltke and the Origins of the First World War* (New York: Cambridge University Press, 2001), esp. 287–89.

9 For the new view of Schlieffen, see Terence Zuber, "The Schlieffen Plan Reconsidered," *War in History* 6, no. 3 (1999): 262–305. For the new view debated, see Terence M. Holmes, "The Reluctant March on Paris: A Reply to Terence Zuber's 'The Schlieffen Plan Reconsidered'" War in History 8, no. 2 (2001): 208–32 and Terence Zuber, "Terence Holmes Reinvents the Schlieffen Plan—Again," *War in History* 10, no. 1 (2003): 92–101. For a qualified synthesis, see Terence Zuber, "The Schlieffen Plan's 'Ghost Divisions' March Again: A Reply to Terence Holmes," *War in History* 17, no. 4 (2010): 512–25. For an objective assessment, see Keir A. Leiber, "The New History of World War I and What it Means for International Relations Theory," *International Security* 32, no. 2 (Fall 2007): 167–77; for Hew Strachan, see 30n.72.

10 For "ploy," see Lieber, "The New History of World War I," 9. Quotation from Schlieffen is from Förster, 368n.91. For risk of extending draft, see Gross, "There Was a Schlieffen Plan," 414.

11 For "invented," see Lieber (quoting Zuber), "The New History of World War I," 13. For "There never was," see Zuber, "The Schlieffen Plan Reconsidered," 305. On the other hand: "A recent bold claim by Terence Zuber, 'There never was a "Schlieffen plan," is interesting but utterly misleading. Not only Schlieffen's contemporaries, but also the men who implemented the plan in August 1914, had no doubt about the existence and authenticity of a Schlieffen plan." See Herwig, "Germany and the 'Short-War' Illusion," 683.

12 For Schlieffen's daughters, see Terence Zuber, "There Never Was a 'Schlieffen Plan': A Reply to Gerhard Gross," *War in History* 17, no. 2 (2010): 249.

13 The discussion of France follows, Jack Snyder, *The Ideology of the Offensive*, 44–106. Also Snyder, "Civil-Military Relations," 129–37, quotation is from 130.

14 Snyder, *The Ideology of the Offensive*, 52.

15 For French military reformers, see Samuel R. Williamson Jr., *The Politics of Grand Strategy: Britain and France Prepare for War, 1904–1914* (Cambridge: Harvard University Press, 1969), 114–17, 126.

16 Snyder, *The Ideology of the Offensive*, 74.

17 For fraudulent document, see Snyder, *The Ideology of the Offensive*, 53; for 1904, 81.

18 "Joffre" is from van Evra, "The Cult of the Offensive," 60. For French casualties, see Niall Ferguson, *The Pity of War* (New York: Basic Books, 199), 340.

19 For Knox, see Van Evera, "The Cult of the Offensive," 60. "Real gentlemen," see Gerard J. De Groot, *Blighty: British Society in the Era of the Great War* (New York: Longman, 1996), 23. For South African experience as inapplicable to Europe, see T. H. E. Travers, "Technology, Tactics, and Morale: Jean de Bloch, the Boer War, and British Military Theory, 1900–1914," *Journal of Modern History* 51, no. 2 (June, 1979): 269

20 See Stephen Van Evera, "Why Cooperation Failed in 1914," *World Politics* 38, no. 1 (October 1985): 84.

21 London *Times*, December 2, 1914.

22 For "Falkenhayn," see Holger Afflerbach, "Planning Total War? Falkenhayn and the Battle of Verdun, 1916," in Chickering and Forster, *Great War, Total War*, 118. For an astringent appraisal of Falkenhayn's generalship, see B. H. Liddell Hart, *Reputations: Ten Years After* (Boston: Little, Brown, 1928), 51–69.

23 For Ninety-ninth Regiment, see Barry Cerf, *Alsace-Lorraine Since 1870* (New York: Macmillan, 1919), 101–02. Details on the 380,000 soldiers are from Alan Kramer, "*Wackes* at War: Alsace-Lorraine and the Failure of German National Mobilization, 1914–1918," in John Horne, ed., *State, Society, and Mobilization in Europe during the First World War* (New York: Cambridge University Press, 1997), 105–21.

24 For "turning point," see Gordon A. Craig, *The Politics of the Prussian Army* (New York: Oxford University Press, 1955), 300. Henri Isselin, *The Battle of the Marne* (New York: Doubleday, 1966); *The Memoirs of Marshal Foch* (New York: Doubleday, 1931), 178–79.

25 *The Memoirs of Marshal Foch*, 178–79.

26 For "contemporary" estimate of number of shells to kill one German in the section above, see Alex Watson, "Self-Deception and Survival: Coping Strategies on the Western Front, 1914–1918," *Journal of Contemporary History* 41, no. 2 (2006): 264, n. 112.

27 Stéphane Audoin-Rouzeau, *Men at War 1914–1918: National Sentiment and Trench Journalism in France During the First World War* (Providence: Berg, 1992), 37–40.

28 Robert Graves, *Goodbye to All That* (New York: Doubleday, 1957), 101.

29 For "*le cafard*," see Audoin-Rouzeau, *Men at War*, viii. For "freezing," see Paul Fussell, *The Great War and Modern Memory* (New York: Oxford University Press, 2000), 88.

30 Ernst Jünger, *The Storm of Steel: From the Diary of a German Storm-Troop Officer on the Western Front* (New York: Fertig, 1996), 81.

31 For background, see the articles collected in the *Journal of Contemporary History* 35, no. 1 (January 2000): 7–108; Jay Winter, "Shell Shock and the Cultural History of the Great War"; Paul Lerner, "Psychiatry and Casualties of War in Germany, 1914–18"; Marc Roudebush, "A Patient Fights Back: Neurology in the Court of Public Opinion in France during the First World War"; Catherine Merridale, "The Collective Mind: Trauma and Shell-shock in Twentieth-century Russia"; Joanna Bourke, "Effeminacy, Ethnicity and the End of Trauma: The Sufferings of 'Shell-shocked' Men in Great Britain and Ireland, 1914–39"; Annette Becker, "The Avant-garde, Madness, and the Great War"; Eric Leed, "Fateful Memories: Industrialized War and Traumatic Neuroses"; George L. Mosse, "Shell-shock as a Social Disease."

32 For American correspondent (James Gordon Bennett), see the *New York Times*, December 16, 1914. For "British soldier," letter excerpted in the London *Times*, December 12, 1914. Jünger is from Joe Lunn, "Male Identity and Martial

Codes of Honor: A Comparison of the War Memoirs of Robert Graves, Ernst Jünger, and Kande Kamara," *Journal of Military History* 69, no. 3 (July 2005): 723.

33 George Bertrand and Oscar N. Solbert, *Tactics and Duties for Trench Fighting* (New York: Knickerbocker Press, 1918), 6, 228.

34 Ulrich Trumpener, "The Road to Ypres: The Beginnings of Gas Warfare in World War I," *Journal of Modern History* 47, no. 3 (September 1975): 460–80. For "strongest factor promoting stasis," see 102. Also see Ludwig F. Haber, *The Poisonous Cloud: Chemical Warfare in the First World War* (New York: Oxford University Press, 1986), esp. 98, 103, 109, 258.

35 "Turning point" and "tank fright" seen in Patrick Wright, *Tank: The Progress of a Monstrous War Machine* (New York: Viking, 2002), 109. For Amiens, see Tim Travers, *How the War Was Won: Factors That Led to Victory in World War One* (Barnsley, UK: Pen & Sword, 2005), 118–19.

36 Henri Barbusse, *Under Fire* (New York: Penguin Books, 2003), 223. For German casualties, see Travers, *How the War Was Won*, 108.

37 For comparison of German casualties in February and March 1918, see Richard Bessel, *Germany After the Great War* (New York: Oxford University Press, 1993), 6, n. 24.

38 Tank details seen in Ian F. Beckett, *The Great War 1914–1918* (New York: Pearson, 2001), 178. Also the point about tanks not being able to break through the German lines.

39 See Stanley Weintraub, *Silent Night: The Story of the World War I Christmas Truce* (New York: Plume Books, 2002). See also Alan Cleaver and Lesley Park, eds., *Not a Shot Was Fired: Letters from the Christmas Truce of 1914* (London: Operation Plum Puddings, 2006).

40 YOU NO FIGHT, Weintraub, *Silent Night*, 25. Tony Ashworth, *Trench Warfare 1914–1918: The Live and Let Live System* (New York: Holmes & Meier, 1980), esp. 118, 141, 186, 199, 209, 69. For "Blangy," see Denis Winter, *Death's Men: Soldiers of the Great War* (New York: Penguin, 1985), 213.

41 See Alexander H. Montgomery, "Cooperation Under Fire: Institutional and Cultural Dynamics During War," paper presented at the Forty-second Annual Convention of the International Studies Association, New Orleans, March 24–27, 2002. Available at ahm@stanford.edu.

42 See Ashworth, *Trench Warfare*, 210; for grenades, 69.

43 For "prisoner killing," see Brian Dollery and Craig R. Parsons, "Prisoner Killing: A Comment on Ferguson's Political Economy Approach," *War in History* 14, no. 4 (2007): 499–512. The practice was widespread. A French soldier at the Dardanelles testified: "Our men respect neither white flags, nor raised hands, nor surrender; they take no prisoners but kill them out of hand, they finish off the wounded, in short they do what the Turks will not do to us." Seen in Jean-Jacques Becker, *The Great War and the French People* (New York: St. Martin's Press, 1986), 46. A German officer wrote home: "We reserve our greatest hatred, just like you at home, for the lying English . . . As an officer I protect every prisoner. But woe to any Englishman who falls into the hands of the men." Seen in Alan Kramer, *Dynamic of Destruction: Culture and Mass Killing in the First World War* (New Haven:

Yale University Press, 2007), 64. For average deaths per day, see Stéphane Audoin-Rouzeau and Annette Becker, *14–18: Understanding the Great War* (New York: Hill and Wang, 2002), 22. For Hess, see David Stevenson, *Cataclysm: The First World War as Political Tragedy* (New York: Basic Books, 2004), 464.

44 For Clemenceau, see Audoin-Rouzeau and Becker, *14–18*, 228. Also Stéphane Audoin-Rouzeau, *Men at War*, 172.

45 H. G. Wells, *Mr Britling Sees It Through* (New York: Macmillan, 1917), 386.

46 See Alistair Horne, *To Lose a Battle: France 1940* (New York: Penguin, 1979), 647–48.

Notes for Chapter 8

1 Details from Trevor Wilson, *The Myriad Faces of War: Britain and the Great War, 1914–1918* (New York: Polity Press, 1988), 514–15.

2 For "business as usual," see Gerard J. De Groot, *Blighty: British Society in the Era of the Great War* (New York: Longman, 1996), 54. The *Evening News* quote seen in the London *Times*, September 3, 1914. For women who tried to volunteer, see De Groot, 67–69.

3 For "khaki fever" and vicars in puttees, see Angela Woollacott, " 'Khaki Fever' and Its Control: Gender, Class, Age and Sexual Morality on the British Homefront in the First World War," *Journal of Contemporary History* 29, no. 2 (April 1994), 325–47.

4 See Arthur Marwick, *The Deluge: British Society and the First World War* (London: Bodley Head, 1965), 89.

5 London *Times*, December 8, 10, 5, 1, 1914. For "Tablets of Honor," see Alice Goldfarb Marquis, "Words as Weapons: Propaganda in Britain and Germany during the First World War," *Journal of Contemporary History* 13, no. 3 (July 1978): 477.

6 Marquis, "Words as Weapons," 477–78. For "*Daily Prevaricator*," see Paul Fussell, *The Great War and Modern Memory* (New York: Oxford, 2000), 65.

7 For "leaving out the horrors," see De Groot, *Blighty*, 186. For "Montague," see Phillip Knightley, *The First Casualty: The War Correspondent as Hero, Propagandist, and Myth Maker from the Crimea to Vietnam* (New York: Harcourt, 1975), 99. Writing in the 1920s, the Viennese satirist Karl Kraus regretted that "My proposal to round up the war writers once peace was declared and have them flogged in front of the war invalids has not been realized." See Hans-Ulrich Wehler, *The German Empire 1871–1918* (New York: Berg, 1985), 215.

8 Knightley, *The First Casualty*, 110.

9 Ibid., 98, 100.

10 Marquis, "Words as Weapons," 488. De Groot, *Blighty*, 186.

11 For "Keegan," see Fussell, *The Great War*, 339. "There is no more discreditable period in the history of journalism than the four years of the Great War," a postwar commentator maintained. Conscious of the media's role in abetting the 2003 invasion of Iraq, many Americans might disagree. Censorship today masquerades as good taste. In 2009 the Pentagon required photojournalists to obtain the permission of the family before printing a photograph of a dead soldier or marine. Philip Gibbs wrote under the same inhibition in 1915. Suppressing the "horrors . . . inevitable in such fighting," Gibbs recognized, encourages a "moral cowardice which makes many people shut their eyes to the shambles, comforting their soul with fine phrases about the beauty of sacrifice." For the Pentagon policy, see Katherine Q. Seeyle, "Gates Assails News Agency for Publishing Photo of Marine Killed in Afghanistan," the *New York Times*, September 5, 2009.

12 For "the image of war," see John Turner, ed., *Britain and the First World War* (London: Unwin, 1988), Intro., 4. Fussell, *The Great War*, 21–22.

13 Ernest Hemingway, *A Farewell to Arms* (New York: Scribner, 1957), 191.

14 Fussell, *The Great War*, 86.

15 For "Frederick," see Alistair Horne, *To Lose a Battle: France 1940* (New York: Penguin, 1979), 172. For *Magdeburg*, see R. V. Jones, "Alfred Ewing and 'Room 40,'" *Notes and Records of the Royal Society of London* 34, no. 1 (July 1979): 65–90.

16 For Churchill, see Arthur J. Marder, *From the Dreadnought to Scapa Flow: The Royal Navy in the Fisher Era, 1904–1919*, vol. 11 (New York: Oxford University Press, 1965), 138.

17 Marder, *From the Dreadnought to Scapa Flow*, 135–42.

18 Ibid.

19 Ibid., 135, 137.

20 See the London *Times*, December 17–21, 1914.

21 Marder, *From the Dreadnought to Scapa Flow*, 147.

22 Seen in Jones, "Alfred Ewing and 'Room 40,'" 74.

23 For "Massingham," see George H. Cassar, *Asquith as War Leader* (London: Hambledon Press, 1994), 31.

24 For "British phlegm," see Fussell, *The Great War*, 181. For postwar critic, see Cameron Hazlehurst, "Asquith as Prime Minister, 1908–1916," *English Historical Review* 85, no. 336 (July 1970), 516. For Asquith's "day," see Wilson, *The Myriad Faces of War*, 411. For "cistern," see J. M. McEwen, "The Press and the Fall of Asquith," *Historical Journal* 21, no. 4 (December 1978): 871.

25 Martin Gilbert, ed., *Winston S. Churchill, Companion Volume III, part 1, July 1914–April 1915* (Boston: Houghton Mifflin, 1973), 76, n. 3.

26 For Diary, see Raymond Poincaré, *The Memoirs of Raymond Poincaré, 1914* (New York: Heinemann, 1928), 122. For "bridge game," George H. Cassar, *The Tragedy of Sir John French* (Newark: University of Delaware Press, 1985), 134. For "postmidnight," see Gilbert, *Companion Volume III*, 76. For "Churchill," see Hazlehurst, "Asquith as Prime Minister," 508. For Asquith's speech, see Cassar, *Asquith as War Leader*, 48.

27 Cassar, *Asquith as War Leader*.

28 For "irredeemably associated," see Wilson, *The Myriad Faces of War*, 200. For Asquith's responsibility, see Cassar, *Asquith as War Leader*, 62.

29 For Violet Asquith's friend, Colin Clifford, *The Asquiths* (London: John Murray, 2002), 133. For Official Secrets Act, see Cassar, *Asquith as War Leader*, 35. For "homing pigeons," see Wilson, *The Myriad Faces of War*, 153. For *Audacious*, see Gilbert, *Companion Volume III*, 222, 297. For "top secret," see Gilbert, 332. Churchill's Admiralty memorandum of February 3, 1915, seen in Gilbert, 481–82.

30 For "I love you," see Clifford, *The Asquiths*, 266. For numbers of letters written in August 1914, see Roy Jenkins, *Asquith* (London: Collins, 1964), 346. For "jealousy," see Gilbert, *Companion Volume III*, 494. For "crockery," see Wilson, *The Myriad Faces of War*, 110; for "Christmas Eve," see Wilson, 110. For "barbed wire," see Gilbert, 345.

31 For "Grand Duke," see Winston S. Churchill, *The World Crisis, 1915* (London: Butterworth, 1923), 93. For "searching for Gallipoli," see Gilbert, *Companion Volume III*, 558.

32 For "Danube," see Gilbert, *Companion Volume III*, 558.

33 For "this city must be yours," ibid., 622, n. 1. For Grey-Sazonov, see C. Jay Smith, "Great Britain and the 1914–1915 Straits Agreement with Russia: The British Promise of November 1914," *American Historical Review* 70, no. 4 (July 1965), 1021–22, also 1033–34. For "refusing Greek help," see David Fromkin, *A Peace to End All Peace* (New York: Holt, 2009), 128.

34 For "what do you think," see Gilbert, *Companion Volume III*, 251. For "carcase of the Turk," see Wilson, *The Myriad Faces of War*, 119.

35 For Kitchener, see Wilson, *The Myriad Faces of War*, 108. For "historian," see Fromkin, *A Peace to End All Peace*, 37.

36 Gilbert, *Companion Volume III*, 554–55.

37 For "three million," see De Groot, *Blighty*, 43. For *Daily Mail*, see De Groot, 186, 78. For "stock exchange," see Marquis, *Words as Weapons*, 493.

38 For "Admiralty study," see Cassar, *Asquith as War Leader*, 62. For Nelson, see Richard Hough, *The Great War at Sea, 1914–1918* (New York: Oxford University Press, 1983), 149. For "Churchill," see Hew Strachan, *The First World War* (New York: Penguin, 2005), 116–17. For "35 forts," see document in Gilbert, *Companion Volume III*, 511. For number of guns, see Edward J. Erickson, "Strength Against Weakness: Ottoman Military Effectiveness at Gallipoli, 1915," *Journal of Military History* 65, no. 4 (October 2001): 992. For "the idea caught on," see Martin Gilbert, *The Challenge of War: Winston S. Churchill, 1914–1916* (London: Minerva, 1990), 252. For flair, see Winston S. Churchill, *Great Contemporaries* (New York: Putnam's, 1937), 65.

39 For details of battle and "before a gun had been fired," see Hough, *The Great War at Sea*, 159; for De Robeck, see Gilbert, *The Challenge of War*, 375. For Kitchener, see Wilson, *The Myriad Faces of War*, 113–15. While Kitchener's quotation is from a War Council meeting of February 24, before the failure of the battleship attack of March 18, it gives his rationale for sending troops at the March 23 meeting of the council.

40 For "Austria's Skoda works," see Hough, *The Great War at Sea*, 161. For "Liman von Sanders," see Wilson, *The Myriad Faces of War*, 132, n. 1. For "the First World War's," see Roy Jenkins, *Churchill: A Biography* (New York: Farrar, Straus, 2001), 261. For "worthless fighting man" and "foundation myth," see Wilson, 135. For Kemal and legend, see Sean McMeekin, *The Berlin-Baghdad Express: The Ottoman Empire and Germany's Bid for World Power* (Cambridge: Harvard University Press, 2010), 187.

41 For "Australian colonel," see Wilson, *The Myriad Faces of War*, 138. For "How lucky," see ibid., 130.

42 For "We are now," see Gilbert, *Companion Volume III*, 412.

43 For the *Morning Post*, see Gilbert, *Companion Volume III*, 809.

44 For "maximum of fun," see Naomi B. Levine, *Politics, Religion and Love: The Story of H. H. Asquith, Venetia Stanley and Edwin Montagu* (New York: NYU Press, 1991), 201. For "crushing and frightening," see Jenkins, *Asquith*, 366. For "I thought once or twice," see Jenkins, 363. For "soul of my life," see Gilbert, *The Challenge of War*, 447. For "O, how I pant," see Levine, *Politics, Religion and Love*, 198, "8000 pounds," 315.

45 For "repugnant and repulsive," see Levine, *Politics, Religion and Love*, 306. "Most Loved," 295.

46 For Lloyd George, see Gilbert, *The Challenge of War*, 446, and Peter Fraser, "Lord Beaverbrook's Fabrications in Politicians and the War, 1914–1916," *Historical Journal* 25, no. 1 (March 1982): 156.

47 For Churchill on being "finished," see Jenkins, *Churchill*. For his "torment," see Gilbert, *The Challenge of War*, 447. In Winston Churchill, *The Second World War*, vol. 2 (Boston: Houghton Mifflin, 1949), Churchill wrote, "I was ruined for the time being in 1915 over the Dardanelles and a supreme enterprise cast away, through my trying to carry out a major and cardinal operation of war from a subordinate position. Men are ill advised to try such ventures." Seen in Raymond Callahan, "What About the Dardanelles?" *American Historical Review* 78, no. 3 (June 1973): 647.

NOTES FOR CHAPTER 9

1 For Belgium's ordeal, see John Horne and Alan Kramer, *German Atrocities: A History of Denial* (New Haven: Yale University Press, 2001). For American reaction, see Arthur S. Link, *Wilson: The Struggle for Neutrality* (Princeton: Princeton University Press, 1960), 14–15.

2 George H. Nash, *The Life of Herbert Hoover: The Humanitarian 1914–1917* (New York: Norton, 1988), 96.

3 Ibid., 140, 148.

4 For "slippery road," see ibid., 14.

5 For eating sand, see Margaret Macmillan, *Paris 1919* (New York: Random House, 2003), 60. Jack Beatty, *The World According to Peter Drucker* (New York: Free Press, 1998), 5.

6 *The Memoirs of Herbert Hoover* (New York: Macmillan, 1951–52), 144.

7 For Bethmann and Belgium, see Alan Kramer, *Dynamic of Destruction: Culture and Mass Killing in the First World War* (New Haven: Yale University Press, 2007), 42. For Shaler, see Eugene Lyons, *Will Irwin's Story* (New York: Human Events), 142–53.

8 For "beg, borrow," see Nash, *The Life of Herbert Hoover*, 83.

9 For "trouble," see *The Memoirs of Herbert Hoover*, 154; for "fixity of opinion," see 164; for Churchill, see 162.

10 Asquith, see Nash, *The Life of Herbert Hoover*, 70–71.

11 Ibid. For "surest way," see G. Paul Vincent, *The Politics of Hunger: The Allied Blockade of Germany, 1915–1919* (Athens: University of Ohio Press, 1985), 38. This incident is not mentioned by Will Irwin in his *Herbert Hoover: A Reminiscent Biography* (New York: Century, 1928), perhaps because he feared it might harm Hoover during that year's presidential campaign. Alternatively, Brand Whitlock, a novelist before turning diplomat, may have elaborated the scene beyond what Hoover would recognize as the truth.

12 London *Times*, December 19, 1914. *The Memoirs of Herbert Hoover*, 159.

13 For "mark of Cain," see Nash, *The Life of Herbert Hoover*, 77.

14 For "wept," see ibid., 62. For "cracker," see *The Memoirs of Herbert Hoover*, 176. For American food, "kind," and "parade," see ibid., 94–96

15 For Chevrillion, see the London *Times*, December 4, 1914.

16 For German artillery joke above, see Mark Hewitson, "Images of the Enemy: German Depictions of the French Military, 1890–1914," *War in History* 11, no. 1 (2004), 18.

17 *New York Times*, December 17, 1914.

18 For Poincaré, see John F. V. Keiger, "Poincaré, Clemenceau, and Total Victory," in Roger Chickering and Stig Forster, eds., *Great War, Total War: Combat and Mobilization on the Western Front, 1914–1918* (New York: Cambridge University Press, 2000), 255–58. *Kölnische Zeitung*, April 16, 1915. For Henriette, Izvolski, Rome, and Paris, see Rudolph Binion, *Defeated Leaders: The Political Fate of Caillaux, Jouvenal, and Tardieu* (New York: Columbia University Press, 1960), 77–79.

19 For Poincaré, see *The Memoirs of Raymond Poincaré* (London: Heineman, 1929), 17. Binion, *Defeated Leaders*, 80–81.

20 Binion, *Defeated Leaders*, 81–89. Details on 1917 developments taken from D. L. L. Parry, "Clemenceau, Caillaux and the Political Uses of Intelligence," *Intelligence and National Security* 9, no. 3 (July 1994), 473–93. For background of the mutinies, see Leonard V. Smith, "The Disciplinary Dilemma of French Military Justice, September 1914–April 1917: The Case of the 5e Division d'Infantrie," *Journal of Military History* 55, no. 1 (January 1991): 47–68.

21 Parry, "Clemenceau, Caillaux and the Political Uses of Intelligence."

22 Ibid.

23 Binion, *Defeated Leaders*, 81–89.

24 *Chicago Tribune*, December 23, 1914. For casualties see Jean-Jacques Becker, *The Great War and the French People* (New York: St. Martin's Press, 1986), 47. Millerand, see John F. V. Keiger, *Raymond Poincaré* (New York: Cambridge University Press, 1997), 212.

25 Seen in Robert A. Doughty, *Pyrrhic Victory: French Strategy and Operations in the Great War* (Cambridge: Harvard University Press, 2005), 1–2.

26 For veteran, Second-Lieutenant Raymond Jubert, see Alistair Horne, *The Price of Glory: Verdun 1916* (New York: Penguin Press, 1962), 326. For Verdun in 1940, see 344. For 1918 and 1940, see Becker, *The Great War and the French People*, 327: "The unbowed France of 1918 heralded the humbled France of 1940." Also: "Verdun . . . broke the French army, or at any rate strained it to such a degree that the country never recovered: France's last moment as a Great Power. When she did fall in 1940, this was partly because her people did not want to go through

Verdun again." Norman Stone, *World War One: A Short History* (New York: Basic Books, 2009), 96–97.

27 For "His Majesty's feet," see the *New York Times*, December 3, 1914. For Churchill and "casualties," see Holger H. Herwig, *The First World War: Germany and Austria-Hungary* (London: Arnold, 1997), 111–12, 120.

28 For anecdote, see the *Chicago Tribune*, January 2, 1915. The 1914 casualties are taken from Mark Cornwall, ed., *The Last Years of Austria-Hungary: Essays in Political and Military History, 1908–1918* (Exeter, UK: University of Exeter Press, 1990), 109.

29 For Serb foreign minister, see John Garland, "The Strength of the Austro-Hungarian Monarchy in 1914," part 1, *New Perspective* 3, no. 1 (September 1997): 1.

30 Francis Joseph quotation from George V. Strong, "The Austrian Idea: An Idea of Nationhood in the Kingdom and Realms of the Emperor Franz Joseph," *History of European Ideas* 5, no. 3 (1984): 301.

31 For half past three, see Jean-Paul Bled, *Franz Joseph* (Cambridge, UK: Blackwell, 1992), 322. Hundreds of thousands lined the Ringstrasse to view the funeral procession, but according to Joseph Redlich, a witness and Franz Joseph biographer, "genuine popular sorrow was not called out in Vienna by the death of Francis Joseph: Frightful losses in the war, which still raged, suffering and the permanent underfeeding of millions in the capital had produced a sort of apathy there." Seen in Maureen Healy, *Vienna and the Fall of the Habsburg Empire: Total War and Everyday Life in World War I* (Cambridge, UK: Cambridge University Press, 2004), 295.

32 *New York Times*, December 18, 1914.

33 Lincoln, see James M. McPherson, *Tried by War: Abraham Lincoln as Commander in Chief* (New York: Penguin, 2008). For the kaiser's 1914 dinner, see Gordon A. Craig, *Germany 1866–1914* (New York: Oxford University Press, 1978), 367. For "spit of land," see John C. G. Röhl, *The Kaiser and His Court: Wilhelm II and the Government of Germany* (Cambridge: Cambridge University Press, 1994), 14. Röhl writes: "That Wilhelm II was little more than a 'shadow Kaiser' during the First World War is not in dispute."

34 A formulation credited to a "contemporary of Frederick the Great" and originally applying to Prussia. See Leonard V. Smith, *From Mutiny to Obedience: The Case of the French Fifth Infantry Division During World War I* (Princeton: Princeton University Press, 1994), 250. For the program of the High Command, which aimed at "a complete militarization of society," see Hans-Ulrich Wehler, *The German Empire 1871–1918* (New York: Berg, 1985), 206–07.

35 For "50,000 tons," see Peter Loewenberg, "The Psychohistorical Origins of the Nazi Youth Cohort," *American Historical Review* 76, no. 5 (December 1971): 1468. For figures on imports, see William Van der Kloot, "Ernest Starling's Analysis of the Energy Balance of the German People During the Blockade, 1914–1919," *Notes and Records of the Royal Society of London* 57, no. 2 (May 2003): 187.

36 Van der Kloot, "Ernest Starling's Analysis," 187, 88. For "farms in Baden," see Richard Bessel, *Germany After the Great War* (New York: Oxford University

Press, 1993), 15. For "chronic starvation," the words of the Royal Statistical Society report, see Van der Kloot, "Ernest Starling's Analysis," 188.

37 For "rickets" and "wasting tissue," see Vincent, *The Politics of Hunger*, 139, 143. For "tuberculosis," see Bessel, *Germany After the Great War*, 39.

38 For "Vera Brittain," see Alan Bishop and Mark Bostridge, eds., *Letters from a Lost Generation: The First World War Letters of Vera Brittain* (Boston: Northeastern University Press, 1998), 211–12. For "excess deaths," see Christopher Birrer, "A Critical Analysis of the Allied Blockade of Germany, 1914–1918," *Journal of the Centre for First World War Studies* (2004): 49. For "births fell by half," see Elizabeth H. Tobin, "War and the Working Class: The Case of Düsseldorf 1914–1918," *Central European History* 28, no. 3–4 (1985).

39 For quotations illustrating the "spirit of 1914," see Jeffrey Verhey, *The Spirit of 1914: Militarism, Myth and Mobilization in Germany* (New York: Cambridge University Press, 2000), 5.

40 Excerpt from Glasser's novel, seen in Vincent, *The Politics of Hunger*, 21–22.

41 For "Ludendorff," desertions, and the army's medical service, see Richard Bessel, "The Great War in German Memory: The Soldiers of the First World War, Demobilization, and Weimar Political Culture," *German History* 6, no. 1 (April 1988): 24–55. For "anxious to return," see Belinda J. Davis, *Home Fires Burning: Food, Politics, and Everyday Life in World War I Berlin* (Chapel Hill: University of North Carolina Press, 2000), 221.

42 For "Statistical Society," see Van Der Kloot, "Ernest Starling's Analysis," 119. For "Huns of 1940," see Vincent, *The Politics of Hunger*, 67.

43 For Keynes on Hoover, John Maynard Keynes, *The Economic Consequences of the Peace* (London: Macmillan, 1919), 174. For "huge rickety heads," see Vincent, *The Politics of Hunger*, 81. For scene with Lloyd George, see John Maynard Keynes, *Essays in Biography* (New York: Palgrave Macmillan, 2010), 419–22. Also see Margaret Macmillan, *Paris 1919* (New York: Random House, 2003), 160. For post-Armistice blockade, see Peter Loewenberg, "The Psychohistorical Origins of the Nazi Youth Cohort," *American Historical Review* 76, no. 5 (December 1971): 1473–74.

44 For "hammer," see Tobin, "War and the Working Class," 72. For elections, see Loewenberg, "Psychohistorical Origins," 1470.

45 Loewenberg, "Psychohistorical Origins," 1498–99, 1477.

46 Ibid., 1457–1502, last quotation is from 1502.

Notes for An Injury to Civilization

1 Fritz Fischer, *Germany's Aims in the First World War* (New York: Norton, 1967), 118–19. For "secretly," see David F. Trask, "Military Imagination in the United States, 1815–1917," in Manfred F. Boemeke, Roger Chickering, and Stig Förster, eds., *Anticipating Total War: The German and American Experiences, 1871–1914* (New York: Cambridge University Press, 1999), 360. For the background to the mediation offer, see Arthur S. Link, *Wilson: The Struggle for Neutrality* (Princeton: Princeton University Press, 1960), 196–200.

2 Fischer, *Germany's Aims*, 103–05, 108. For "Mitteleuropa," see Konrad H.

Jarausch, *The Enigmatic Chancellor: Bethmann Hollweg and the Hubris of Imperial Germany* (New Haven: Yale University Press, 1973), 209. For premature medal, see Annika Mombauer, "The Battle of the Marne: Myths and Reality of Germany's 'Fateful Battle,'" *Historian* 68, no. 4 (Winter 2006): 750. For the debate over the significance of the "September Program," see Gordon A. Craig, *Germany 1866–1945* (New York: Oxford University Press, 1978), 365, n. 69.

3 See Roy A. Prete, "French Military War Aims, 1914–1916," *Historical Journal* 4, no. 28 (December 1985): 888–89.

4 Fischer, *Germany's Aims*, 108.

5 For Falkenhayn, see Fischer, *Germany's Aims*, 184. L. L. Farrar, "Carrot and Stick: German Efforts to Conclude a Separate Peace With Russia, November, 1914–December, 1915," *East European Quarterly* 10, no. 2 (Summer 1976): 162.

6 For Danish contacts, see Jarausch, *The Enigmatic Chancellor*, 238; for Bethmann to Falkenhayn, see 243.

7 H. G. Wells, *Mr Britling Sees It Through* (New York: Macmillan, 1917), 351, 288. Jay Winter, ed., *The Legacy of the Great War: Ninety Years On* (Columbia: University of Missouri Press, 2009), 111.

8 For Churchill, see J. F. C. Fuller, *A Military History of the Western World*, vol. 3 (New York: Da Capo, 1957), 271. From an interview given to the *New York Inquirer* in August 1936.

9 For Russia, see Orlando Figes, *A People's Tragedy: The Russian Revolution, 1891–1924* (New York: Penguin, 1996), 408–19.

10 For Wilson, see Thomas J. Knock, *To End All Wars: Woodrow Wilson and the Quest for a New World Order* (New York: Oxford University Press, 1992), 105–12.

11 For the survival of the old order, see the incisive analysis in Craig, *Germany*, 396–433, "dead past" is on 422. For "barely tolerated," see Eric D. Weitz, *Weimar Germany: Promise and Tragedy* (Princeton: Princeton University Press, 2007), 115–21.

12 For Wilson, see Knock, *To End All Wars*, 108–09.

INDEX

Note: *Italic* page numbers indicate illustrations.